ITALO BALBO

ITALO BALBO

A Fascist Life

CLAUDIO G. SEGRÈ

UNIVERSITY OF CALIFORNIA PRESS
BERKELEY   LOS ANGELES   LONDON

University of California Press
Berkeley and Los Angeles, California

University of California Press, Ltd.
London, England

© 1987 by
The Regents of the University of California

Library of Congress Cataloging-in-Publication Data

Segrè, Claudio G.
    Italo Balbo : a Fascist life.

    Bibliography: p.
    Includes index.
    1. Balbo, Italo, 1896–1940. 2. Fascism—Italy—
History—20th century. 3. Italy—Politics and
government—1914–1945. 4. Fascists—Italy—Biography.
5. Cabinet officers—Italy—Biography. 6. Air pilots—
Italy—Biography. I. Title.
DG575.B3S44 1987   945.091'092'4 [B]   86–16108
ISBN 0-520-05866-6 (alk. paper)

Printed in the United States of America
1 2 3 4 5 6 7 8 9

For Zaza and the kids, Gino, Francesca, Yuli

Contents

List of Illustrations   ix

Preface   xi

Acknowledgments   xv

Part One: The Blackshirt (1896–1926)   1

  1. Journalist: The Young Mazzinian   3

  2. Soldier: Hero of the *Alpini*   22

  3. *Squadrista:* Campaigns 1921   48

  4. *Squadrista:* Campaigns 1922   74

  5. *Quadrumvir:* The March on Rome   91

  6. *Ras* of Ferrara: The Intransigent   114

Part Two: The Aviator (1926–1934)   143

  7. Undersecretary: Douhet's "Disciple"   145

  8. Minister: Father of the *Aeronautica*   174

  9. Aviator: The Mediterranean Cruises   191

 10. Aviator: The First Atlantic Cruise   215

 11. Aviator: The Second Atlantic Cruise   230

 12. Air Marshal: The Road to Exile   266

Part Three: The Colonizer (1934–1940)   289

13.   Governor General of Libya: Builder and Colonizer   291

14.   Governor General of Libya: Creator of the Fourth Shore   311

15.   *Frondeur:* The Germanophobe   334

16.   Fascist: The Model Fascist's Fascism   363

17.   Soldier: North African Commander   375

18.   Soldier: Death of a Hero   392

Abbreviations   408

Notes   409

Bibliographical Note   450

Index   455

Illustrations

Maps

1. Aerial cruise to the Western Mediterranean   196
2. Aerial cruise to the Eastern Mediterranean   205
3. First Atlantic cruise, Italy-Brazil   221
4. Second Atlantic cruise, Italy–United States   232

Figures

1. Balbo and his mother   7
2. Balbo's father   8
3. Balbo the interventionist in 1915   20
4. Balbo and *squadristi* in Venice   55
5. Balbo breaks an agricultural strike   58
6. Balbo during the March on Ravenna   63
7. Balbo and Dino Grandi march on Ravenna   64
8. Balbo *quadrumvir* during the March on Rome   112
9. Balbo as militia commander   119
10. Balbo as pilot   195
11. Balbo and Henry Ford   203
12. SM.55X cockpit and instrument panel   219
13. SM.55X at anchor   238
14. Aerial armada soars over the Alps (July 1933)   239
15. Cartoon: "They gave us everything but rest and sleep"   240

16. Balbo as "Chief Flying Eagle"   245
17. New York paper heralds arrival of Balbo's armada   246
18. Cartoon: Balbo as "sportsman of the air"   251
19. Balbo advertises aviation gasoline   252
20. Mussolini greets Balbo after second Atlantic cruise   256
21. "Roman" triumph for Balbo and his aviators   258
22. Balbo greets colonists arriving in Libya   317
23. Balbo presents Libyan with citizenship certificate   330
24. Balbo reviews Nazi troops   356
25. Hitler hosts Balbo   357
26. Balbo and Goering   359
27. Balbo and family   365
28. Balbo as supreme commander in North Africa   389
29. Balbo and captured British armored car   390
30. News headline of Balbo's "heroic" death   393

Preface

What is fascism? What does it mean to be a good fascist? In the aftermath of World War I an entire generation wrestled with these questions—and then fought World War II over them. From a contemporary perspective, what they were fighting about is not easy to understand. *Fascist* these days applies to anything from right-wing terrorist groups in Italy to Third World military dictatorships, from ordinary policemen to motorcycle gangs. Nor is the past a clear guide. *Fascism* usually conjures up images of sadistic, jack-booted automatons in steel helmets and of Hitler marching past tens of thousands of followers drawn up in orderly rows at Nuremberg.

Hitler's Germany, however, wasn't typical of fascism. The term *fascism* derives from the Italian, from *fascio*, a perfectly ordinary word with no more sinister meaning than a bundle, a weight, a group or grouping. (When used in a political context, the English equivalent would be *league, alliance,* or *union;* the German would be *Bund*.) Fascism originated in Italy toward the end of World War I and scored its first great success with Mussolini's March on Rome in 1922. Mussolini's Italy, Franco's Spain, Peron's Argentina, Codreanu's Romania, and Mosley's gangs in England all claimed to find inspiration in "fascism." Cynics observed that what they had in common was a taste for Boy Scout style uniforms, colored shirts, and street brawling—and the cynics have a point. When two of the most prominent fascist powers, Italy and Germany, formed a partnership, the union proved to be a notoriously unhappy one.

The confusion over the nature of fascism, then, is not surprising. Even contemporaries could not agree. "Fascism is a dictatorship; such is the starting point of all definitions that have so far been attempted. Beyond that there is no agreement," concluded Angelo Tasca, the Italian socialist historian and anti-fascist militant in 1938. After nearly half a century, the comment still rings true. Tasca, however, did not despair of pinning down what fascism meant. One of the best ways to define fascism, he argued, was to tell its story.

The life of Italo Balbo is one good place to begin. During his lifetime, Italian fascist publicists often touted him as the model of the fascist generation, Mussolini's "new man." For once the publicists were right. Of all the major Italian fascist leaders, Balbo was virtually the only one to live the ideal fascist life—heroic, adventurous, self-sacrificing, patriotic. His reputation extended far beyond Italy. Thanks to his feats as an aviator, he enjoyed international renown. His circle of friends and acquaintances was a cosmopolitan one. He met personalities as diverse as Lindbergh and Goering, Hitler and Roosevelt. Everywhere he flew, from Latin America to the Soviet Union, from Chicago to Berlin, he presented himself as an emissary of Mussolini's Italy, of the new fascist generation.

As an emissary, he was a good choice. If one of Madison Avenue's advertising firms had taken on the task of planning a campaign to promote fascism, Balbo's broad smiling face, ornamented by the chestnut-colored goatee that was his trademark, would have made an ideal model for them. Reflecting the three main phases of his career, he might have been pictured first scowling fiercely and looking a bit like a musketeer or a pirate in the makeshift uniform of a Blackshirt and *quadrumvir* of the March on Rome. A second sequence might have shown him in his flying togs, grinning rakishly, cigarette dangling from the corner of his mouth, as the minister of aviation (1926–1933) and leader of two pioneering transatlantic flights. Finally, as governor of Libya (1934–1940), he might have been snapped in khaki shorts and sun helmet, inspecting road construction, or in a tuxedo as the gracious dinner-party host, welcoming international celebrities to the governor's palace in Tripoli.

Balbo enjoyed a good press. "Bluff yet suave, fearless and supple, he was not the type to pass unnoticed anywhere," the

New York Times remarked. Journalists of the day compared him to a Renaissance *condottiero*. "He was the only one among the Blackshirts who knew how to smile," wrote the wife of an Italian diplomat. So distinctive was he that some dissociated him from fascism and linked him with the tradition of the *Garibaldini*.

Balbo had far more to offer than an attractive presence and an engaging personality. He was intelligent and capable, and his abilities as an organizer were incomparable. He figured prominently in the lists of Mussolini's possible successors. "The fact is that if Mussolini were to disappear, Balbo is the only authentic fascist capable of governing and of being obeyed," his friend Ugo Ojetti, the writer and art critic, remarked. Together with Farinacci, Balbo was the only one of the *gerarchi* whom Mussolini feared as a potential rival.

Ironically, despite Balbo's role as a hero and emissary of the regime, what he meant by *fascism* is not easy to define. He was not a fascist of the "first hour" in 1919. He began as a radical republican and never gave up what he described as his "republican tendencies." He joined the fascist movement in 1921 as much for career motives as for ideology. The institutions and ideologies that we commonly associate with fascism—the totalitarian state, corporativism, racism—were all alien to him. When Mussolini sought rapprochement with the Nazis, Balbo bitterly opposed him. Ideology, however, may not be the best way to approach an understanding of what Balbo meant by *fascism*. He was a man of action more than a thinker. He exemplified perfectly the ideal of Mussolini's Italy: deeds over words. To understand Balbo's fascism—the model fascist's fascism—we must turn to his life.

A final word about my attitudes toward Balbo and fascism: like any biographer, I have tried to bring my subject to life and to do him justice. As his contemporaries found, and as my sources, written and oral, testified, he was a likeable man, blessed with intelligence, charm, courage, enthusiasm, and humanity. He was also a pillar of a corrupt and cynical regime, the friend and collaborator of a demagogue who led his nation to catastrophe. In these pages, the reader may at times succumb to Balbo's charm and fascination as I did. Nevertheless, I have not forgotten the real nature of the regime that Balbo promoted and served so well—and I hope the reader does not either.

Acknowledgments

Without the patience and generosity of Balbo's family and many friends in sharing materials and memories with me, this book would not have been possible. Nor could I have completed it without the support of numerous libraries, archives, foundations, and other institutions which I have listed below. If there are omissions, they are due to oversight, not ingratitude.

Paolo Balbo took time out from his busy schedule as a lawyer in Rome to put his father's archives—still in the possession of the family—at my disposal. He helped me to arrange many valuable interviews with Balbo's old friends and former collaborators. He shared with me his enthusiasm for flying, especially its pioneering phase. He did more than talk—he showed me. On a glorious April afternoon we donned flying suits, helmets, and goggles, and he took me up in his vintage red-and-white-striped De Havilland Tiger biplane for an unforgettable panorama of the Roman *campagna*—and of what flying meant in his father's day. In Rome, too, the late Donna Emanuella Balbo mastered her quiet, retiring nature to share her memories of her husband with me. In Ferrara, Egle Balbo Orsi recalled many of her childhood experiences with her brother. The Balbo family helped generously and unconditionally. They did not see the manuscript before its publication. I alone am responsible for its contents.

In Rome, especially for material on Balbo's career as an aviator, I benefited enormously from the wisdom and support of Maria Fede Caproni and the collections in the Museo Aeronautico Caproni di Taliedo. Others who generously assisted me with materials and interviews are: in Rome, Umberto Albini, Elena Argentieri, Giorgio Bassani, Bruno Bottai, Giuseppe Bucciante, Ranieri Cupini, Giorgio Pillon, Felice Porro, Folco Quilici, Mimì Buzzacchi-Quilici, Giuseppe Santoro; in Bologna, Don Lorenzo Bedeschi, Paolo Fortunati, Dino Grandi; in Ferrara, Raul Beretta, Annio Bignardi, Alberto Boari, Francesco De Rubeis, Gualtiero Finzi, Augusto Maran, Paolo Ravenna; in Prato, Guido Angelo Facchini; in Udine, the late Pietro Tassotti; in Milan, Ardito Desio; in Florence, Edda Ronchi Suckert.

Librarians and archivists on both sides of the Atlantic helped in countless ways to facilitate my research. I want to thank the following staffs: in Rome, of the Archivio Centrale dello Stato and of the Ufficio Storico dell'Aeronautica Militare; in Torino, of the Fondazione Einaudi and of the Centro Storico Fiat; in Ferrara, of the Biblioteca Comunale Ariostea. I am also grateful to the staff of the United States National Archives, Washington, D.C., and to Peter Duignan and Agnes F. Peterson and the staff of the Hoover Institution, Stanford, California.

Colleagues and friends—American, English, Italian, Israeli— shared works in progress with me, contributed material, answered questions, read the manuscript at various stages, and generally urged me onward. I profited immensely from the patience and support of William Braisted, Paul Corner, Renzo De Felice, Alexander J. De Grand, Lewis Gould, James Kunetka, Meir Michaelis, Alessandro Roveri, and especially from Gwyn Morgan's ruthless and enthusiastic marginalia. Cleo B. Weiser, while working on his M.A. paper under my direction, collected material from American aeronautical journals that proved invaluable to me. Wendy Bracewell and Ines Monti provided able research assistance.

For financial assistance, I am grateful to the National Endowment for the Humanities for a fellowship that helped me launch this project. I also received generous support at various stages from the American Council for Learned Societies, the American Philosophical Society, the Air Force Historical Foundation, the University of Texas at Austin Research Institute, and the Dora Bonham Fund of the Department of History, University of Texas at Austin.

All translations are mine unless otherwise noted. Since this book presents Libya as the Italians saw it, I have not hesitated to use Italian spellings of place names.

Part One

The Blackshirt (1896–1926)

Chapter One

Journalist: The Young Mazzinian

On June 28, 1940, about 5:30 in the afternoon, two aircraft approached the heavily fortified Italian military base at Tobruk in eastern Libya, not far from the Egyptian border. The sun was still high. The crews manning the anti-aircraft batteries around the harbor watched the intruders apprehensively. World War II was barely three weeks old and most of the gunners were inexperienced. A few minutes earlier, nine British bombers, in waves of three, had roared in from Egypt, attacked a local airfield, and disappeared again in the direction of the sun. The anti-aircraft crews could hear sirens; they saw and smelled the smoke from burning aircraft and from an exploding fuel dump. For all the gunners knew, the two aircraft, now approaching from the direction of the sun, were the enemy returning for another pass. The lead aircraft, flying low, provided a tempting target. In the confusion, few noted that it was a trimotor—not like the British twin-engine bombers. An edgy gunner fired a few rounds. Others followed. The lead aircraft was now in trouble. The pilot approached the runway as if to land. The target was too easy, even for the excited gunners. A shell hit the big bomber squarely. Pouring smoke and flames, the aircraft veered to its left, crashed onto a bank above the harbor, and exploded. A cheer went up from the anti-aircraft crews—they'd bagged one! A few moments later they learned the identity of their quarry: air marshal Italo Balbo, their commander in chief and a national hero. He was barely forty-four.

3

The official announcement of the incident consisted of two sentences. The communiqué stressed that "during an enemy bombing action" the aircraft piloted by Italo Balbo crashed in flames. To go down in a blaze of glory, fighting for his country, seemed an appropriate end for a soldier, aviator, patriot. For nearly two decades he had personified the fascist hero, the man of action who believed in always leading from the front. As details became available on the grapevine, however, those who knew Balbo well became more and more skeptical about the official story. "To get himself killed in that way on a sort of family outing," mused a friend, referring to the entourage of Balbo's family and friends who perished with him in the crash, "and the English say that he was killed by the Italians, not in combat. Why?"[1] Was he—surrounded by relatives and friends—on that last flight fleeing to Egypt to set up a government in exile? How could the Italian batteries have failed to recognize a trimotor? Had Mussolini set up the whole affair to eliminate a rival? Even those who rejected the more fanciful interpretations of the incident wondered. Balbo was an experienced pilot and war veteran. How had he gotten himself into such a dangerous and foolish situation? With all its ironies and tragicomic aspects, Balbo's flaming death over Tobruk was very much in tune with his life—his "fascist" life.

Balbo was from Ferrara, and proud of it. In the shadow of this splendid but faded Renaissance town, in the suburb of Quartesana, he was born on June 5, 1896.[2] Ferrara lies at the southeastern edge of the lush, monotonous Emilian plain of Northern Italy. The lagoons of Venice are located a little more than 100 kilometers to the northeast; the red-tiled roofs and towers of Bologna lie 50 kilometers to the southwest. The countryside is flat, marshy, and fertile, the fruit of a century of reclamation efforts. As the Po reaches the area around Ferrara, it opens into a delta before spilling into the Adriatic. Poplars, aspens, and willows mark the course of irrigation ditches, canals, and shipping channels. South of the city, toward the Adriatic, lie the *valli* of the Comacchio, great lagoons where armies of fishermen catch eels during their spring and autumn migrations.

Like so many other cities of the Emilia, Ferrara reached its greatest glory during the Renaissance, when the city numbered 100,000 and ranked with Florence, Milan, and Venice. Under the patronage of the Estes, Ferrara boasted one of the most brilliant courts of the era. Here Lodovico Ariosto composed his knightly epic *Orlando Furioso,* and Torquato Tasso his *Gerusalemme Liberata.* Borso d'Este built his Palazzo Schifanoia, ornamented with the allegorical frescoes of Francesco Cossa. Isabella d'Este commissioned leading painters to decorate her celebrated grotto. Lucrezia Borgia took as her third husband Alfonso I, son of Ercole I d'Este; Girolamo Savonarola, although he achieved his notoriety in Florence, was one of Ferrara's native sons.

Once the Renaissance faded, Ferrara went into decline and never regained its brilliance. Little wonder, then, that throughout his lifetime many viewed Balbo as a reincarnation of the city's past glories. His "court" of devoted friends, his patronage of the arts, his daring feats as a soldier and aviator, his marriage to a titled woman, his natural dignity and charm, all gave him the aura of a Renaissance prince or *condottiero.* "Dress Balbo in sixteenth-century armor, put him at the head of a band of daredevil horsemen, and he would look as if he had been taken live from Del Cossa's paintings in the Schifanoia Palace," rhapsodized a local admirer.[3] "A reincarnation of the militant and magnificent Italian princes of medieval days," concluded an English journalist in 1937.[4]

Princes were not the rule in Balbo's immediate family, however; schoolteachers were. Both his parents taught school and his birthplace was literally the schoolhouse of Quartesana. Thus, like many of the fascist *gerarchi,* Balbo was petty bourgeois. His parents' background indicates that their families had once occupied a higher position on the social scale. Through a series of misfortunes, especially to Balbo's father, the family had fallen on hard times. Much of Balbo's career was devoted to regaining that lost social status.

Balbo's father, Camillo (1855–1931), came from a Piedmontese family with a long military tradition. He liked to entertain his children with stories of his maternal grandfather, who had fought with Murat and the Italian army in Russia and had participated in Napoleon's retreat across the Beresina in 1812; another ancestor had served as a general in the Piedmontese army. Camillo himself had aspired to a military career, but when his father, a physician in a small community of the Monferrato area east of Turin, suffered a fatal fall from a horse, the son was forced to support the family. Instead of a soldier, Camillo became a schoolmaster.

"Bony and wiry, all nerves and imperious will, tenacious, unswerving in his attitudes and ideas, in the faithfulness of his friendships," so a friend remembered Camillo.[5] "It's necessary to do, to act, to move," Camillo often exclaimed.[6] Much of this nervous energy he channelled into politics. In harmony with his monarchist and liberal convictions, he founded the Circolo Monarchico "Umberto I"; he contributed anti-socialist and anti-clerical articles to local newspapers; he earned a reputation for fiery political oratory. Into his home he brought a strong sense of order, discipline, duty, and patriotism. His love of country was such that he planned to name his first daughter Trieste after one of Italy's unredeemed territories. Only at the moment of baptism did he give in to his wife's pleadings; the baby was called Maria Trieste. Camillo's severe and inflexible temperament led to frequent clashes with his sons. Nevertheless, in his restlessness, his patriotism, his devotion to friendship, his authoritarianism, Italo came to resemble his father.

As the youngest son, Balbo was particularly close to his mother and sisters. They shielded him from the severity of his father, and they lavished affection and admiration on him. That circle of admiring and supporting women later enlarged to include his wife and daughters. His mother, Malvina Zuffi, was a religious woman with family ties to the provincial nobility of Ravenna. Her mother was a Contessa Biancoli, a cousin of the Baraccas of Lugo. A photograph of Balbo in his uniform as general of the fascist militia shows him smiling warmly and tenderly, with a protective arm around this small, white-haired woman who barely comes up to his shoulder. Throughout his life he was sensitive to the anxiety that his adventurous life and political activities caused his mother. "The anguish that I read in my mother's face makes me tremble," he wrote during the hectic days before the March on Rome.[7] His rest and recreation during that period "consists in seeing myself reflected in my mother's shining face."[8] Balbo's sister Egle, two years his junior, was his favorite playmate. When Italo got into mischief, she sometimes feigned crying fits to distract the father from imposing a harsh punishment.[9]

Fig. 1. Balbo and his mother, Malvina Zuffi (G. Bucciante, ed., *Vita di Balbo*)

When Italo was two the family moved from Quartesana to Ferrara proper, to Via Mortara 49, a few houses away from the main street of Corso Giovecca and within easy walking distance of the center of town. As might be expected in a family of school-

Fig. 2. Balbo's father, Camillo Balbo (G. Bucciante, ed., *Vita di Balbo*)

teachers, the house was well provisioned with books. Maps studded the walls of the hallway, the living room, and the children's bedrooms. In this house Italo began his formal education. Like the rest of the Balbo children, he was taught by his parents throughout the primary grades. At five he knew how to read and write. At six or seven he sang patriotic songs that he learned from his father, and he recited verses his mother taught him about the glories of military life: "Ah, General! What a marvel!/All silver and tassels! . . ." and concluded with: "Brave and bold on the battlefield I'll be/There to win death or victory."[10]

Balbo learned natural science by studying collections of minerals and plants that his father had assembled. Geography and patriotic history got special emphasis. Camillo Balbo often referred to the maps on the walls of the house during his history lessons, and entertained and fascinated his children with stories of the deeds of great patriots and national heroes. Italo and his sisters took pride in knowing the maps so well that they could point out even minor rivers and cities at a glance. Later, as an aviator, Balbo delighted in identifying these sites from the air.

Ironically, for one who grew up surrounded by schoolteachers and schoolteachers-to-be—his sisters Egle and Maria and his brother Fausto all became teachers—Balbo remained an indifferent student. He was much too restless and undisciplined for systematic study. Yet in the humanistic and journalistic way typical of many of the *gerarchi*, Balbo was an educated man. He was "Dottore" Italo Balbo, a university graduate. He edited his own newspaper, the *Corriere Padano*. He published a stream of books, articles, and memoirs on subjects ranging from literary criticism to aerial warfare. Some of these works he produced in collaboration with others, and some pieces were undoubtedly ghostwritten for him, but when he had the time and inclination Balbo was perfectly capable of writing them himself. Among his closest friends were the literary critic Luigi Federzoni and Giuseppe Bottai, who had begun his career as an aspiring Futurist poet. Journalists, artists, and literary critics, as well as politicians and military men, belonged to Balbo's entourage.

At the house on Via Mortara, in addition to formal lessons Balbo first absorbed those fundamental values that shaped the rest of his life: a strong sense of patriotism, and a paternalistic concern for the less fortunate. There, too, Balbo first developed those temperamental qualities so typical of him: love of adventure, a natural sense of leadership, a passion for politics.

As a boy Balbo displayed a lively imagination and a taste for outdoor adventure. Playing with his sister Egle, Italo, in his imagination, discovered desert islands, mysterious continents, strange and savage peoples. Jules Verne's science fiction, Emilio Salgari's pirate romances, stories of Robinson Crusoe and Buffalo Bill stimulated the boy's dreams of adventure. During family vacations on the Adriatic at Cesenatico and Fano, Italo listened to the fishermen's stories of adventure and studied their maps and boats. He became a good storyteller and often entertained his friends with stirring tales of heroism. In the garden at Via Mortara he first developed his eye as a marksman. Shooting and hunting became his major forms of recreation throughout his life. As a world-renowned aviator and a colonial governor, he was to realize many of his childhood fantasies.

As a youth Balbo already displayed his gregariousness and his talents as a leader. To all his playmates, whether they were middle class or from humbler backgrounds, he was known simply as Italo. At a time when it was the custom for children to greet their teachers and elders with a polite *"riverisco* (my respects)," he asked why the beggars in the street should not be treated with the same courtesy. He showed his sense of paternalistic generosity: for the poorest of his playmates he always had some small gift, and he often declared, "When I'm grown up, I'll support you all."[11] As an adult he retained these charitable habits. On visits home from transatlantic flights or from the governorship in Libya, he supplied his mother, his sisters, and his nephew and niece with ten-lire notes to distribute to the poor. If they objected that such charity was futile, even counterproductive, he replied, "They'll change their ways; we should meet their needs. You'll see that they'll work. Anyway, what does it matter? We don't do good deeds for the sake of recognition." To a contemporary ear such sentimental stories sound suspiciously hagiographic, as if to compensate for Balbo's violence and brutality as a Blackshirt. Yet these values of paternalism and charity were typical of the middle class during Balbo's youth, and he remained true to them throughout his life. In 1938, as governor of Libya he organized the emigration of 1,800 impoverished families to the colony. At that time, in place of ten-lire notes, he distributed whole farms.

Balbo's "natural profession" was that of political activist and journalist.[12] When he was still in short pants, barely a teenager, he showed his bent for these activities. His fascination with politics derived in part from growing up in the Emilia-Romagna, which had a long tradition of political radicalism. His home was often the scene of passionate political arguments; father and sons were deeply divided. Camillo, good monarchist and patriot, considered himself a staunch Liberal. His traditional attitudes and programs did not appeal in the least to his older sons. In part out of ideological motives, in part out of rebellion against the father's authority, they espoused vastly different causes. Edmondo was a revolutionary syndicalist; Fausto a Mazzinian, a republican. Election time in the Balbo household meant a flurry of political activity and heated arguments. The administrative elections of August, 1907, when Italo was eleven, were typical.[13] Camillo wrote furious newspaper articles in the *Gazzetta* against the republicans and socialists. Edmondo contributed to the revolutionary syndicalist paper *Scintilla*. Fausto, determined to prove that the republicans of Ferrara were not the usual ridiculous handful, founded an electoral bulletin. It lasted for three issues and he wrote almost all of it himself—articles, manifestos, and poems. Egle recalled the political arguments at home with trepidation. There was only one prohibition: no banging of fists on the dinner table.

Balbo's fascination with and involvement in politics are easy enough to understand from his family background. But why he chose republicanism over his father's monarchism or his brother Edmondo's revolutionary syndicalism is less clear. In part the origins of his lifelong republican faith are generic. He described himself as "a child of the century which had made us all democratic anticlericals and republican sympathizers; anti-Austrians and irredentists who hated the bigoted and reactionary Hapsburg tyrant."[14]

The influence of his eldest brother, Fausto, was also fundamental. In personality and character the two brothers were diametrically opposed. Italo was exuberant, outgoing, adventurous, a natural leader; Fausto was a gentle, introspective poet, a teacher, literary scholar, and librarian. "He believed in the beauty of life and the goodness of mankind," a fellow student remarked of Fausto in his student days at the University of Bologna.[15] Fausto's published verses reflect his idealism and his gentle, affectionate temperament. His first book of poems, which won the praise of his teacher at Bologna, Giovanni Pascoli, celebrated such themes as the comfort of the family drawn around the hearth, anxieties over his father's illness, the warmth of his mother's embrace.[16] Fausto had just launched his career as a librarian and teacher when he died of tuberculosis on April 17, 1912; barely twenty-seven, he left a wife and two children.

The death affected Italo deeply. His school notebook from that period contains elegiac Carduccian verses, and he sought the comfort of his sister Egle. Throughout his life Italo remained devoted to Fausto's daughter, Fiorenza, and to his son, Lino, who died with his uncle in the crash at Tobruk. The manner of Fausto's death also haunted Italo. In later years he too feared that he had contracted the then-fatal disease.

In his politics, Fausto was an ardent Mazzinian. As in his personality, however, in his interpretation of the Master Fausto differed from his younger brother. Fausto believed in Mazzini the prophet and moralist, the great apostle of Nationalism. Young Italo, on the other hand, was attracted to Mazzini the conspirator and revolutionary, the organizer of adventurous expeditions to free oppressed peoples. He found kindred spirits in Ferrara's cafés, which were centers of political activity. Italo's favorite, frequented by the most radical and revolutionary elements, the republicans, socialists, and syndicalists, was the Caffè Milano, then located at the far corner of the Palazzo della Ragione, at the entrance to Via Porta Reno.[17] The Milano was always a center for political ferment. In the dark little room with the low ceiling and cheap furniture, the patrons, fueled by glasses of wine and cups of espresso, argued, harangued—and occasionally brawled.

The republicans who gathered at the Caffè Milano included General Ricciotti Garibaldi, son of the national hero, and Felice Albani and Antonio Giusquiano of the Partito Mazziniano, who represented the intransigent wing of republicanism—those who refused to compromise with the monarchy or with parliament. Felice Albani, with whom Balbo maintained a lifelong friendship even after he had formally severed all ties with republicanism, was the guiding spirit of the Partito Mazziniano.[18] What Albani stood for was less clear than what he stood against. He quarrelled both with his fellow republicans and with the socialists. He founded an ill-fated party, the Partito Repubblicano Socialista, which tried to combine the best of both worlds. Finally, he founded the Partito Mazziniano, whose minuscule strength was centered in the Romagna under the leadership of Giusquiano. Garibaldi represented the tradition of volunteerism and idealism of his father's Risorgimento expeditions. In Ricciotti Garibaldi's day, the primary goal was to free the Balkan nationalities. Thus, in 1897, with Felice Albani as a member of his staff, Garibaldi led a corps of red-shirted volunteers to support a Greek uprising against the Ottomans; in 1910, he planned an aborted expedition to free Albania; in 1912, he fought in the first Balkan war that pitted Greece, Serbia, and Bulgaria against the Turks. In 1914, before Italy joined the war, Ricciotti's sons led an expeditionary force to support the French in the Argonne. The Romagna, in particular, with its Garibaldian associations, was a focus for Redshirt activity. As a boy in Ferrara, Balbo encountered a survivor of the original Risorgimento expeditions, Stefano Gatti Casazza, and listened to his stories.[19] Young Italo was also familiar with a more recent example: the martyrdom in 1897 at Domokos, Greece, of the Forlì journalist Antonio Fratti.

With these models and influences as his guides, in 1910, at the age of fourteen, Balbo launched his career as a journalist and politician. General Garibaldi encouraged one of his earliest efforts: "Dear Balbo, I read your very skillful article with pleasure. It is necessary to write them frequently to educate the public."[20] The following year, at the age of fifteen, Balbo formally joined Albani's Partito Mazziniano. To the teenaged Balbo, republicanism had little to do with great political principles or concrete issues. Working men's salaries, peasants' wages, strikes, leagues, and cooperative movements did not interest him. He thought in terms of expeditions, crusades, risks, gambles, adventures, all in the name of patriotism. For Balbo, Mazzinianism was a state of mind, "a sense of total revolt against reality, a permanent protest against the actual state of things."[21] As a result, the future governor of Libya staunchly opposed the Italian colonial expedition there in 1911. "Why? To go against the grain, against reality, against the government," explained the syndicalist Sergio Panunzio, who knew the young Balbo well.[22]

The ideological content of Balbo's Mazzinianism at this time was thus not very clear and perhaps not very important. Far more significant was the way his republicanism acted as an insulator. While many of his generation swore allegiance to some form of socialism, Marxist or syndicalist, young Italo remained apart in an antithetical tradition. Balbo was not unique among the *gerarchi* in his republican background. His friends Bottai and Grandi, for instance, also went through republican phases. What made Balbo distinctive was the persistence of his faith. Although he formally severed ties with the republicans when he joined the fascists in 1921, Balbo never renounced what he called his "republican tendencies."

To embrace Mazzinianism fully meant to participate in a volunteer expedition. In 1910, Italo tried to join Ricciotti Garibaldi's expedition to Albania. The boy, still in short pants, wrote to Garibaldi, lying about his age. He equipped himself with the blanket from his bed and gathered his savings to buy long pants so that the other volunteers would not laugh at him. Then, without telling even his sisters, he tried to join the volunteers who were assembling near Ancona. The following day, Malvina Balbo received a letter from her son, explaining the reasons for his flight and asking forgiveness. A few days later, Italo returned, mortified: the expedition had been dissolved.

With all these political distractions, Camillo Balbo worried that his son would never complete his schooling. The final straw came when Italo organized a student strike at the Ginnasio Ariosto, where he was enrolled. The goal was a holiday on the Feast of San Giuseppe.[23] That incident decided Camillo to send his restless son away from Ferrara's temptations for a while.

For the academic year 1911–12, beginning in the autumn, Italo joined his brother Edmondo, seven years his senior, in Milan. Under Edmondo's direction Italo studied mathematics and science in preparation for his grammar school examinations at the end of the year. A family friend and Ferrarese, Professor Artioli, gave Italo lessons in Latin and Italian. Seventeen years later, high in the skies over Greece and Asia Minor on his flight to Odessa, Balbo excitedly traced the sites of Vergil's *Aeneid,* paying tribute to the memorable lessons of his old classics tutor.

Milan, however, provided no respite for Italo from politics. The city was undergoing even more political ferment than Ferrara, and Edmondo was as deeply involved as at home. He had shifted from revolutionary syndicalism to the Fasci d'Avanguardia, whose program was more nationalist and expansionist. The group lasted only about a year, during which time Italo accompanied his brothers to the meetings in Via Torino. He also contributed a few paragraphs to the organization's weekly newspaper, *La Giovine Italia*, which was aimed at university students. Academically, Italo's Milanese year ended successfully. During the summer of 1912 Italo passed his grammar school examinations. To complete his schooling he needed only to pass the high school examinations. Once again, his father sent him away from Ferrara, this time to study privately in San Marino. The results resembled those in Milan. Although Italo passed his examinations in the summer of 1914, he showed little interest in his studies. He much preferred radical politics and journalism.

Irredentist causes appealed to his deeply rooted patriotism, and so did syndicalism. For the irredentists he gave a fiery speech at the Teatro Comunale Rossini in Lugo on March 21, 1913, defending the Triestino Mario Sterle, whom the Austrian authorities had sentenced to five years at hard labor for his irredentist activities. A month later, Balbo published an article in the syndicalist paper *La Raffica*. This time the cause was the jailing of the editor, Romualdo Rossi, sentenced to nine months' confinement for—as Balbo put it sarcastically—"defamation of our beloved Savoyard monarchy." The article also attacked "the bourgeoisie that bleeds the proletariat" and vowed that in the "holy cause" of the proletariat, "we will fight as long as a breath of life remains in us."[24]

The syndicalist struggle during this period introduced Balbo to Michele Bianchi, his future fellow *quadrumvir* of the March on Rome. Bianchi, seven years older than Balbo, was at this time a leading revolutionary syndicalist labor organizer in Ferrara. When he ran unsuccessfully for a seat in the Chamber of Deputies in 1913, among his most enthusiastic supporters was seventeen-year-old Italo Balbo. With typical bravado, during the campaign Balbo debated an opponent who was fifteen years his senior and destined for political prominence; he was the socialist Bruno Buozzi, later a leader of the General Confederation of Labor.

Balbo's journalistic activities during this period did not focus exclusively on politics. In the spring of 1913, with Giuseppe Ra-

vegnani he founded a literary review, *Vere Novo*, which put out
only two issues. The publication was interesting for what it revealed about Balbo's literary tastes. D'Annunzio, later to be a
friend and flying comrade, he found decadent; Pascoli, his brother
Fausto's old professor, Italo considered mawkish and maudlin, almost effeminate. He preferred Carducci and the classics.[25]

Flying, too, occupied Balbo during the summer of 1913. For
the first time he wrote at length about his fascination with aircraft
and his longing to perform great deeds in the sky. Balbo was
seven when the Wright brothers made their historic flight at Kitty
Hawk in 1903; he was thirteen when Blériot made the first Chan-
nel crossing in 1909. Thus, his youth coincided with flying in its
infancy. Like many young men of his generation, Balbo eagerly
followed the air races and rallies promoted by newspapers and
other businesses. In September, 1911, for instance, Italo, then
fifteen, helped tend a signal fire for the Bologna-Venezia-Rimini-
Bologna rally sponsored by the *Resto del Carlino*.[26] Balbo also
followed the meteoric careers of the flying heroes of the day, and
mourned their deaths. Balbo was one of the thousands who in
September, 1910, mourned the young Peruvian Geo Chavez, the
first man to fly across the Alps—only to crash fatally as he prepared for his triumphant landing in Milan.

Three years after Chavez's death, a similar incident inspired
Balbo to commemorate another fallen aviator who had been his
friend. In July of 1913, Roberto Fabbri, a young Ferrarese of
Balbo's age, died in a crash at Malpensa airport in Milan. Balbo
paid tribute to his friend in a thirty-page pamphlet, "Roberto
Fabbri, the Youngest Aviator in the World: Memories and Notes
Compiled by His Friend Italo Balbo."[27] The work, dated Fano,
August, 1913, reflected the two sides of Balbo's personality: half
romantic fantasy, hero worship, and youthful projection; half dis-
passionate investigative reporting. The first half of the text is
reflected in the book's cover—a fanciful *art nouveau* design that
pictures a winged human figure seeking to embrace some long-
haired spirits of the winds. In this section, Balbo pays poetic
tribute to Fabbri, "who had looked death in the face contemptuously and had known how to die as a hero in a titanic struggle
against the elements." He had died "for the shining ideal of the
greatest of human conquests."

As a loyal son of Ferrara, Fabbri's greatest dream, according to Balbo, was "to salute from on high his beautiful sleeping city and awaken it with the thunder of his powerful motor, making his white aircraft soar around the manly towers of the Castello Estense." In pursuit of his dream, the daredevil Fabbri left for flying school in Milan with "a last handshake" before the train "disappeared into the dense fog." Perhaps reflecting his anxieties over his own mother, Balbo described how Fabbri's mother worried over her son. Rosa Fabbri was a "true martyr" and Balbo dedicated the work to her. Finally, Balbo made it clear that for all his dreams and plans, his friend was not merely a foolish and reckless adventurer: "Let us honor in him not the useless victim of a folly, but a hero who died gloriously on the battleground of science."

In the second half, the tone of the work changes abruptly. Here Balbo investigates the circumstances of the crash. Fabbri had his pilot's license and was soloing for the first time in an eighty-horsepower machine after training on a thirty-five-horsepower one. Balbo quoted excerpts from newspaper accounts of the accident that hinted that responsibility lay with the aircraft manufacturer, Caproni. In a long letter, also included, the company denied any responsibility and blamed the incident on Fabbri for doing stunts in the aircraft. In his conclusion Balbo sided with the newspapers and with his friend. He had had occasion, Balbo wrote, to admire Fabbri's "daring and not his rashness" and he did not believe in an accident caused by "any carelessness."

Nearly a year after he wrote this article, in the summer of 1914—just as the European powers blundered into war—Balbo successfully passed the examinations for his lyceum diploma in San Marino. Free, at least temporarily, from his academic bonds, he plunged enthusiastically into Italy's "intervention crisis." Between the outbreak of the war, in August of 1914, and the following May, Italy, though nominally a member of the Triple Alliance with Austria and Germany, remained neutral. The overwhelming majority of Italians favored this position. Italy's relations with Austria had soured long before the outbreak of the war; moreover, Austria had technically violated the Triple Alliance by declaring war against Serbia without consulting Italy. Balbo, however, supported the interventionist minority that eventually triumphed. Of course he had nothing to do with the anti-Giolittian cabal at the top—the king, prime minister Antonio Salandra, and foreign minister Sidney Sonnino—who saw in the war a chance to rally the country around the monarchy and to isolate Giovanni Giolitti and the Liberals. Nor was Balbo in contact with the industrialists who saw the war both as a source of new markets and new profits and as a way to weaken working-class organizations. Balbo joined the unruly interventionist mobs who took to the streets in cities like Milan and Rome. The leaders of these demonstrations ranged from *poseurs* such as Gabriele D'Annunzio to assorted revolutionary syndicalists such as A. O. Olivetti, Filippo Corridoni, and Michele Bianchi, to ex-anarchists such as Massimo Rocca. The ex-socialist newspaper editor Benito Mussolini emerged as a major figure at this time. Such a mixed crew agreed only that the war provided opportunities for new political alignments and perhaps even for the revolution that so far had eluded them. As Mussolini's *Popolo d'Italia* concluded, the revolutionary interventionists had got into the same train by accident and were bound for different directions.[28]

Balbo at eighteen, tall and thin, still clean-shaven, leaped onto the revolutionary interventionist train in the fall of 1914. For the first months he seems to have based himself in Milan, perhaps living with Mario Sterle and the Triestini irredentists. In the mornings he attended classes; in the evenings he frequented the *Popolo d'Italia*. Here he first met Mussolini, thirteen years older than he, a seasoned revolutionary and radical journalist. Balbo left no record of this first pre-war meeting. The long and often tormented relationship between the two men began in earnest during the spring of 1921, when Balbo assumed the direction of the Ferrarese *fascio*. During the interventionist crisis, Sandro Giuliani, the *Popolo d'Italia*'s editor, may have asked Balbo to contribute a commemorative article on Guglielmo Oberdan (1858–1882), the irredentist hanged by the Austrians for plotting to assassinate the emperor.[29]

Balbo also participated in the major pro-war rallies and in street scuffles against the neutralists. At demonstrations at Porta Romana, Piazza del Duomo, and Porta Venezia, Balbo appeared sometimes as featured speaker, sometimes as part of an informal band that beat off hecklers. One evening rally he recalled with particular relish. The fiery syndicalist Filippo Corridoni and the Belgian deputy Jules Destrée were haranguing the crowds assembled in a schoolyard near Porta Romana. A group of anti-war "socialists" heckled the orators, then approached the speakers' platform with "big cudgels." Balbo and his friends met the invaders head on and routed them.[30]

In addition to his activities in Milan, Balbo organized interventionist movements in Ferrara. In October, 1914, the revolutionary interventionists had formed the Fascio Rivoluzionario d'Azione Internazionalista, with Michele Bianchi as its head. By December the single *fascio* had become a network of local interventionist cells.

Balbo led a group of high school and technical school students who confronted the police with the ultimatum, "Either you declare war or we'll run you out of office." When the police tried to break up the rally, Balbo's friends encircled him protectively. In classic *Garibaldino* fashion, he proudly waved a tricolor borrowed from the local technical school. A battle for the flag broke out, and the students triumphed. In the evening they gathered at the Caffè Milano and at the editorial offices of the *Gazzettino Rosa*, boasting of their victory over the authorities. During this period Balbo once again sought to join an expedition of *Garibaldini*. This time the goal was to fight with the French at the Argonne. Again the expedition aborted. At the border, Balbo and his friends were sent home.

In a final frenzied gesture, Balbo, with twelve other anarchists, syndicalists, and ex-socialists from the Fascio Rivoluzionario, authored an interventionist manifesto. The authorities forbade him to distribute it on May 17. The manifesto was, however, published in the *Gazzetta Ferrarese* the following day. Moreover, a week later, May 24, Italy was formally at war with Austria-Hungary. Events moved so rapidly that later the prefect had difficulty explaining to his superiors why he had attempted to suppress such a manifesto.[31]

Why did Balbo want the war? Why was he determined to subject his unwilling countrymen to such carnage? Balbo, of course, had no more idea than anyone else how the war would turn out. He did not anticipate that it would last three and a half years; that it would claim 600,000 Italian casualties, mostly from

Fig. 3. Balbo the interventionist (left) in 1915 (G. Bucciante, ed., *Vita di Balbo*)

his own generation; that Italy would nearly collapse at Caporetto in October of 1917; that she would emerge "victorious" a year later, but so transformed that she tottered on the brink of revolution. Sergio Panunzio, a comrade of Balbo's interventionist struggles, concluded, "Do not ask why Italo Balbo wanted, willed the war. Like so many others, he did not know himself. What he knew was that intervention was necessary and that it was necessary to struggle and agitate for intervention."[32] A photograph of Balbo in 1915 suggests that his interventionism, like his republicanism, contained a stiff dose of romantic self-indulgence. For him, the war apparently suggested patriotic crusades and heroic adventures. In the photograph the radical republican, the agitator and firebrand, appears as the model of the middle-class dandy. He wears a dark overcoat and sports an umbrella as if it were a cane. His gloved hand clasps a small cigar. A wide-brimmed hat gives him an air between gaucho and conspirator. His dreamy eyes stare off into the distance. Next to Balbo, his hands thrust deep in his pockets, stands the anarchist Mario Poledrelli. He wears a three-piece suit and four-in-hand tie—reminders of his bourgeois background—and stares defiantly at the camera. Little wonder that the peasants, who made up half the army, and the neutralists protested the "war of the *signori*."[33]

At the end of the war, despite the horrors of the combat experience, Balbo's patriotism and his belief in the justice of Italy's cause remained unshaken. The war, he wrote, echoing sentiments and arguments of the revolutionary interventionists, had been necessary to defeat Prussian militarism, to battle for justice, to fulfill national demands that could no longer be put off.[34]

The interventionist experience prefigured a new set of political alliances and relationships that were to have momentous consequences after the war. In Ferrara, the radical Left linked with the conservative Right in the name of national unity and Italy and against the common enemy, socialism.[35] That alliance contained the nucleus of the post-war fascist triumph. Many names later to become prominent in fascist Ferrara first appeared as interventionist militants. For them, as for Balbo, war was to be a continuation of revolution by other means.

Chapter Two

Soldier: Hero of the *Alpini*

Ironically, for one so eager for battle, adventure, glory, Balbo had to wait nearly two years before he reached the front lines. It was not for lack of trying. Five days before war was officially declared, on May 24, 1915, Balbo volunteered for duty, and one hagiographical story has him marching resolutely to the front in defiance of orders.[1] His military record shows that he was assigned as a courier in the third military zone.[2] On July 4, 1915, he was accepted as a volunteer for the duration of the war; then abruptly, on November 8, he was released and sent home. Most likely Balbo was discharged because the military high command was prejudiced against volunteers and volunteer units and took every opportunity to eliminate them.[3] For nearly ten months, apparently, Balbo stayed in Ferrara. At last, at the end of September, 1916, he was drafted with the class of 1896. Six weeks later, on November 15, he was accepted as a reserve officer candidate. He trained for five months at Modena, and on April 28, 1917, he was posted to the 8th Alpine Regiment. On May 1, he joined the Val Fella battalion and at last reached the front.

The battalion was stationed in Val Raccolana in Carnia, a relatively quiet sector. Here Balbo was promoted to reserve second lieutenant. His memories of this period, written after the war, tended to be highly romantic, even nostalgic for the danger and for the comradeship with his fellow *Alpini*.[4] He recalled how during the long hours of watch "the wind howled in the gorges like the howls of a thousand hungry wolves"; how he and his comrades "crouched fearfully" in the trenches, straining to "steal from the night and the storm the slightest noise that was not that of the elements"; how the corporal called for the changing of the guard, and what it was like to leave a warm sleeping bag and pull on the "heavy goatskin trousers." He also recalled the "long unnerving patrols with their eternal waiting" while the enemy lay in ambush in the woods and every rock slide "made our hearts jump into our mouths."

Although he had done nothing special to distinguish himself, his superiors gave Balbo positive evaluations. He was described as "robust, with an attractive manner," and "a good element for alpine troops."

He has a good general education, speaks well and possesses good common sense. He knows the military rules and regulations adequately and also shows much good will and diligence and has much influence over his subordinates. He is disciplined, eager, and displays excellent moral and social values. In his private life he behaves well.[5]

In these circumstances, it was difficult to emerge as a hero. His earliest journalistic biographers, writing shortly after his death, when Italy was again at war and needed heroes, embellish his soldier's image with colorful incidents. Trapped in a crevasse where he had accidentally fallen, so they said, Balbo saved himself by grabbing a rock outcropping. When his strength began to fail, he nicked his wrists from time to time with his pocket knife to keep from fainting. Another time, an inner voice warned him to move away from a rock pile where he was reading and smoking; no sooner had he climbed down than the rock pile collapsed and tumbled into an abyss.[6]

Perhaps bored with the routine of patrols and trench life and seeing an opportunity to resume his love affair with flying, in mid-October of 1916 Balbo requested a transfer to the Aeronautica. He left the Val Fella battalion to begin pilot training at Turin. The official transfer is listed as October 22, 1917, two days before the Austro-German forces launched their devastating offensive that led to Caporetto. Whether Balbo ever began his training is unclear. His experiences must have been limited, for he did not receive his pilot's license for another decade.

When he heard the news of the Caporetto breakthrough, Balbo went to rejoin his old unit, stopping in Ferrara to visit his family.

The enemy, however, had surrounded and captured the Val Fella battalion. The combination of circumstances—losing his unit, and visiting his family—may have fostered the rumor, spread by his enemies in later years, that he, like hundreds of other soldiers, deserted after Caporetto. Such a story has no confirmation in his military record, nor does it seem characteristic of him. If he had deserted, moreover, it appears highly improbable, given his father's sense of patriotism and military duty, that Balbo would have sought refuge at home.[7]

By November 10, Balbo was back at the front with the 8th Alpine Regiment. He fought briefly on the Tagliamento as part of the rear-guard action after Caporetto, and on November 16 he joined the Monte Antelao battalion of the 7th Alpine Regiment. Throughout the winter and early spring of 1918, the unit was stationed in the Dossi subsector of Monte Altissimo on the right bank of the Adige River—another quiet zone. In five months, only one man died and five were injured. His superiors during this period found him physically fit, though "not very strong," and his conduct acceptable. He was "direct, sometimes a bit thoughtless and impulsive" but "at the slightest warning [he] falls into line."[8]

At the beginning of April, 1918, the Monte Antelao battalion left the trenches for duty behind the lines, and Balbo, as of May 11, transferred to the Pieve di Cadore battalion. His solid but undistinguished military career reached a turning point: he was put in charge of the battalion's assault platoon. Strictly speaking, this was not a unit of the famous *arditi*, the elite and privileged shock troops constituted in the summer of 1917. However, the platoon's missions were often as difficult and dangerous as those of the *arditi* and after the war, the term *arditi* was used for both kinds of units.[9]

The unit's orders were to carry out "a very active night patrol."[10] From their position on the slopes of Monte Altissimo, at an altitude of about 600 meters, Balbo and his men left the safety of their trenches and barbed wire—usually at night—to survey the enemy lines at the foot of the mountain. According to his commander, Major Luigi Sibille, who took a liking to Balbo, the young lieutenant distinguished himself immediately "for the enthusiasm and high spirits" with which he trained and prepared his men for their missions. Then, almost nightly in July and August, 1918, he carried out his patrols "at a time and over terrain that was unusually dangerous" and against an enemy "particularly active and emboldened by a recent success." He even committed his unit against superior enemy forces, "attacking them with such impetus" as to render necessary the intervention of his own machine guns and artillery to disengage him. These actions were not particularly bloody, at least on the Italian side; the battalion suffered only one casualty during the summer. Also, generally speaking, the top brass disliked expending artillery and precious shells to settle what were supposed to be minor skirmishes. Nevertheless, Balbo's actions on August 14 were judged worthy of mention in the Supreme Command's *Daily War Bulletin* for August 15 and he was awarded a silver medal for valor. According to his commander, Balbo led his unit "with such daring and spirit of self-sacrifice as to earn him the best sort of authority over his subordinates, who followed him later in truly tragic circumstances which brought honor not only to him but to the battalion."[11]

The tragic circumstances to which Major Sibille alluded occurred a little more than two months later. During the last week of October, 1918, on the anniversary of the Caporetto defeat, the Italians took their revenge. They launched a final great offensive that culminated in the victory of Vittorio Veneto. The goal of the operation was to cut off the Austrian armies in the mountains from those in the plain. Balbo's Pieve di Cadore battalion was one of the units assigned to capture the Monte Grappa. The operation was a subsidiary one, but it proved to be the bloodiest of all. Although the Hapsburg empire was on the verge of collapse, the Austrian armies fought fiercely. Of the 39,000 Italians dead and wounded at Vittorio Veneto, two-thirds met their fate on the Grappa.

The Grappa, like much of the Italian front, was a limestone plateau, ranging in altitude from 1,200 to 1,700 meters. Water and vegetation were scarce and the population made a meager living from pasturing livestock. Under wartime conditions the area became a desert, without water, without vegetation, without dwellings, without firewood. The troops huddled in caves, trenches, or dugouts, trying to shield themselves from howling winds, fog, or snow. As on the Western Front, the men endured

days and nights of artillery barrages, then attacked and counter-
attacked highly fortified positions at a huge cost in casualties.
Continuous shelling reduced the mountainous terrain to a lunar
landscape. This was the "glorious Calvary of the Alpini," as Balbo
described it afterwards.[12]

For the first two days of the offensive, the Pieve di Cadore
battalion was held in reserve. Meanwhile, from the peaks of
Monte Solarolo, Valderoa, Spinoncia Asolone, and Pertica, Austrian guns decimated the other units. Battalions were virtually
destroyed within a few hours.[13] Shortly after midnight on October
27, Balbo's unit reached its position on a little saddle between
Solarolo and Valderoa, but only after suffering heavy losses. That
afternoon Balbo's advance platoon was ordered to lead two companies against the well-entrenched Austrians. "We had to make
the final effort" with a "mutilated" battalion—one which had lost
a company and had been decimated from attacks on the three
previous days, Balbo recalled.[14] But what did numbers matter? he
asked rhetorically; the order to advance had been given. "We had
to win or die." At 3 P.M., Balbo and his men reached the advance
Italian trenches at Malga Solarolo and then pushed on to a cavern
scarcely two hundred meters from the enemy trenches. At 4 P.M.,
with units from the Val Toce battalion, the final assault began. In
well-ordered lines, "as if on a parade ground," they charged forward "to meet a glorious destiny." The battlefield was a scene of
carnage. To advance meant "to hurdle . . . over little piles of
bodies" while enemy machine guns "mowed down the ranks,"
Balbo recalled a decade later at a commemorative ceremony.[15]
After a few meters forward, the men flung themselves to the
ground to catch their breaths. Then, with cries of "Savoia" and
"Cadore" and "the name of their beloved land on their lips and in
their hearts," they hurled themselves into a hail of machine-gun
fire and exploding grenades. Not a "bit of earth" escaped the
"rain of lead and steel"; the Italian attack wavered, then dissolved. Balbo was among the fortunate few who were not hit. He
rolled into a shell crater and pretended to be dead, "so as not to
be made prisoner" and "so as not to flee in humiliation before the
enemy." Only seventeen of his comrades survived the assault.
For several hours he remained in the crater "among the dismal
moans of the dying"; by nightfall many of them moaned no

longer. Under cover of darkness, Balbo tended the wounded and with them made his way back to Italian lines. For this episode he was awarded a second silver medal.

Three days later, on October 30, Balbo distinguished himself again. This time he lead a probing attack against the Austrian positions on Monte Valderoa. The costs of these operations were enormous. In two days a battalion like Pieve di Cadore would lose nearly five hundred men, or nearly half its strength. Despite these sacrifices, the Italians reached few of their objectives on Monte Grappa. The Austrians, however, had been forced to commit their reserves and feared the Italian advance in the valley. On the night of October 30/31, the Austrians began to retreat. On October 31, Balbo commanded the first wave that broke enemy resistance on Monte Valderoa. His platoon led the Pieve di Cadore's pursuit over Monte Fontana Secca, down the Val Stizzon, and onto Feltre. At Rasai, three kilometers from Feltre, on Balbo's own initiative his platoon broke up the enemy rear guard's resistance. In house-to-house fighting, Balbo and his men cleared the way for the main force to descend on Feltre. Together with a platoon from the Exilles battalion, Balbo and his men entered the town at 5:30 that evening. The attack on October 30 and the pursuit of the enemy troops into Feltre earned him a bronze medal.

With a bronze and two silver medals, Balbo had a good war record. True, as his critics point out, his outstanding deeds were confined primarily to the last two weeks of the war.[16] True also that toward the end of the war, medals were easier to win. Nor can there be any doubt that fascist hagiography exaggerated his deeds: the image of Balbo entering Feltre first and alone, to the cheers of the villagers, stands as a good story for children.[17] Nor at this stage of his career does Balbo deserve to rank with World War I heroes such as D'Annunzio or Battisti, Cantore or Locatelli.[18] Among Balbo's peers, Bottai saw more action and earned more medals; others, like Grandi, who made captain, concluded their World War I military careers at a higher rank. Nevertheless, Balbo did see combat—which Mussolini, for instance, did not—proved himself several times under fire, and demonstrated his talents as a leader.

Experiencing the horror of the trenches at Dosso Casina, at

Malga Solarolo, and at Monte Grappa did nothing to alter Balbo's
political views. Wilsonian idealism, the ideology of the Russian
revolution, Futurism, and the myriads of other utopias failed to
tempt him. If anything, his patriotic Mazzinian convictions became more fixed. Ten years after the war, in 1928, in trying to
explain the tenacity and self-sacrifice of veterans like himself,
Balbo spoke of "the moral climate on the Grappa." There "every
act" that was not one of "complete dedication to the religion of
the Patria" appeared to be "naturally banished."[19]

Balbo remained officially in uniform until May, 1920. However,
his military assignments during the eighteen-month period between the Armistice and his discharge left him plenty of time to
pursue other activities: he completed his university studies; he
met and courted his future wife; he resumed his political and
journalistic activities. Balbo's freedom to pursue his own interests
while he was still in uniform was not unusual in the immediate
post-war period. With three million men under arms in 1918, the
job of demobilization was mammoth. Both the government and
the soldiers had reasons for delaying the process. The government wanted to control the rate at which soldiers were absorbed
into the economy. Officers like Balbo preferred to enjoy the prestige and benefits of their rank as long as possible. Among these
benefits was the opportunity to attend university classes while
retaining military privileges and salaries.

A few days after the Armistice Balbo was officially admitted to
the University of Florence, but he did not attend classes. Instead,
he was assigned, as many veterans were, to a reconstruction program in a war-damaged area. For about five months he served in
the Friuli, as prefectoral commissioner of the little community of
Pinzano al Tagliamento, not far from Udine. Balbo acted as an
interim administrator until local government, interrupted by the
war, could be reestablished. He revived government services,
stabilized the community's finances, directed the repair of a
bridge and a river embankment along the Piave. The future governor of Libya carried out these administrative tasks "with real
expertise and obtained the same proficiency from his men," according to his commanding officer.[20]

In March, 1919, Balbo left his battalion to pursue his studies at the prestigious Istituto Superiore di Scienze Sociali "Cesare Alfi-eri" (today the faculty of political science at the University of Florence). Founded in 1874, the institution was the oldest of its kind in Italy, in Europe second only to the Ecole Libre des Sciences Politiques in Paris. Traditionally, the "Cesare Alfieri" had been a training ground for Italy's high-ranking diplomats, politicians, and civil servants.[21] Yet diplomacy or civil service, in the conventional sense, was just the opposite of what Balbo had in mind: he wanted to become a respectable revolutionary. Unless he had completed his studies, he "considered it impossible and unworthy for a young man to confront the problems of conquering the state."[22] Balbo also enrolled in the "Cesare Alfieri" for a prac-tical motive: the school was one of the few institutions which then would admit students without a diploma from a high school. Al-though nominally Balbo had a diploma, he needed to make up examinations in Latin, mathematics, physics, natural history, and philosophy.[23]

Balbo's academic record at the "Cesare Alfieri" was on a par with his earlier studies: he applied himself sporadically and the results were mediocre. His best subject, perhaps as a reflection of his childhood, was geography, and his favorite professor was the geographer Olinto Marinelli. In colonial legislation, statistics, and finance—all of which might have proved useful to a future colo-nial governor—he did not do well. Worst of all for him were subjects related to law. After four tries, he finally passed the examinations for administrative law and for Italian law. In what is probably an apocryphal story, promoted by anti-fascists, Balbo bullied his way through the examination in international law. En-raged at his apparent failure, Balbo confronted his examiner, Pro-fessor Breschi:

"Either you give me an 18 (a passing grade) or you'll be in trouble."
"I can't. You don't know anything. You have no right to be pro-moted."
"Either you give me an 18 or you'll be in trouble."

In the end, Balbo got his eighteen.[24]

The final requirements for his degree consisted of a *tesina orale*, an oral discussion or debate before a panel of professors on a selected theme, and a written thesis. In the *tesina orale* Balbo argued that the newly constituted League of Nations would not prove to be an instrument of peace and justice; on the contrary, it would become a source of new oppression and new injustices that would provoke new conflicts. No record remains of Balbo's arguments, but one of his examiners found his manner memorable. The face still showed signs of adolescence; the beginnings of the musketeer's goatee stuck out with a certain petulant defiance. With an "imperturbability that appeared to be impudence, that audacious young man, bold and at the same time modest, continued to speak his mind" before the committee of "solemn internationalist jurists, believers in that Genevan Olympus." He reminded the examiner of "one of those street urchins who throw stones at the mighty" and "thus make history."[25]

Balbo's written thesis, "The Economic and Social Thought of Giuseppe Mazzini," once again reflected how central Mazzini was to his intellectual and spiritual formation. Like his director, Balbo may well have sought in the topic some answers to Italy's post-Armistice dilemmas, some solution to the conflict between "the material interests of class and the spiritual ones of the nation."[26] In six chapters, totaling 111 pages—with exceptionally generous margins—he tried to draw Mazzini's often fragmented social and economic thought into a coherent whole.

The thesis read less like a scholarly investigation than an anti-socialist political tract. First, Balbo attacked Mazzini's contemporary opponents—social thinkers from Blanc to Proudhon. He berated them for their materialism in contrast to Mazzini's idealism and his doctrine of "love and brotherhood." Mazzini, too, Balbo admitted, was anti-capitalist and favored working-class associations, but that was only because in his day capitalists exploited the workers. If capitalism were administered for the benefit of all, without egoism, everyone would benefit, Balbo wrote. Capitalists must "open their hearts" to the needs of the working class. Through Mazzini's doctrine of association and through cooperatives, private property should become accessible to all. This was a curious affirmation, for in his thesis Balbo attacked the "red leagues"—the socialist labor unions and cooperatives—that were springing up throughout Italy. These were not free associations, Balbo objected. The members were forced to join by the threat of boycott. "Is this the principle of liberty that should rest in the sovereign people? To me it seems a return to tyranny, perhaps an even more refined tyranny," he wrote. Through class conflict and violence, the working classes were gaining everything they wanted, Balbo harangued. Within a month and a half of completing his thesis, Balbo, the good Mazzinian, would be translating thought into action by leading Blackshirt assaults against the socialist organizations. Balbo concluded with a typically Mazzinian plea for a democratic republic. The "privilege" of the monarchy must be abolished, he declared. He also recalled his readers to the Mazzinian doctrine of idealism and of duty: "The purpose of life is not that of being more or less happy, but to make oneself and others better, and to combat injustice and error is not a right but a duty."

In its evaluation, dated November 30, 1920, the examining committee concluded that the work was "an adequate if not complete" study of Mazzini's economic thought and also showed "a sincere veneration for the great thinker." Only two out of eight members of the examining committee gave Balbo less than the maximum grade of ten; Balbo was awarded "distinction," with 78 out of a possible 80.

Pinzano al Tagliamento, where Balbo was stationed, was not far from San Daniele del Friuli. During the winter of 1919, a mutual friend introduced Balbo to Emanuella Florio, a shy, retiring girl of eighteen, who was to become his wife.[27] At first glance, Balbo and "Donna Manù," as she came to be known, appeared to be a mismatch of social backgrounds and personalities. The Florios were a noble family originally from Spalato (Dalmatia). Manù had been brought up as a lady: sheltered, protected, tutored privately. Her quiet, refined manner seemed incompatible with Balbo's restlessness, his exuberance, his self-confidence and gregariousness. From her family's point of view, in social terms Balbo was a "complete unknown"; he was not even from the Friuli. Moreover, his career prospects appeared cloudy. Although he vaguely mentioned banking, he spoke mostly of journalism. Count Florio objected strenuously to his daughter's relationship with the thin young man who had recently acquired a scraggly goatee, but not, as yet, a university degree. Nevertheless, Balbo and Donna Manù were very sure of each other. She was attracted by his cheerfulness and self-confidence and was quite certain that he would amount to something. While she worked to win over her family's objections, the two carried on a highly romantic courtship. Two and three times a week, furtive express letters went back and forth between her home and the Pensione Gonnelli in Florence where Balbo was staying. In the spring of 1924, Count Florio died. The engagement, which had lasted nearly five years, ended in marriage in the chapel of the Florio country home on September 29, 1924. For a honeymoon, the couple went to Constantinople.

Despite the contrasts in their backgrounds and temperaments, and the demands that Balbo's career made on family life, the marriage was a happy one. The Balbos had two daughters and a son: Giuliana (b. 1926), Valeria (b. 1928), and Paolo (b. 1930). Balbo's ambitious and adventurous temperament meant that he was gone for long periods of time and was often involved in hazardous enterprises. Inevitably, Donna Manù worried about whether he would return and often feared airplane crashes. His prestige and sociability also led Balbo to become involved with other women. Nevertheless, toward his wife and family he always remained affectionate and protective, zealously guarding them from any hint of scandal. He carried pictures of the women in his family—his wife, his mother, his daughters—in the cockpit with him on transatlantic flights. And he paid tribute to his wife in another way: the Savoia Marchetti 79 trimotor that he flew while governor of Libya bore the civil registration marking "I-MANU."

At the end of the academic year of 1919, Balbo returned to his old regiment at Udine. Formally, he was still in uniform, still subject to military discipline. Nevertheless, with the blessings of his superiors, he once again plunged into the political and journalistic battles that the war had interrupted. As a student in Florence, he joined the Associazione Arditi. Together with Francesco Giunta, president of the Associazione Nazionale dei Combattenti, he probably took part in anti-socialist demonstrations, street brawls and shootings "against the savage and bestial persecutors of officers and those who denigrated the war."[28] He also resumed his journalism. For six months he edited a weekly military newspaper, *L'Alpino*. As a military publication, *L'Alpino* was nonpolitical—or at least nonpartisan. It was dedicated, Balbo wrote in his first, programmatic editorial, to promoting and strengthening "the marvelous brotherhood of the family of *Alpini*" and to recapturing "a nostalgic echo of our lives lived in the gray-green uniform."[29] On political matters, at least nominally, the paper did no more than urge its readers to participate in the political process; beyond that, "we do not advise anything, for in these columns we exalt only faith in the Fatherland," he wrote at the time of the November, 1919, elections.[30]

L'Alpino's nonpolitical stance, however, was only a pose. In the first place, nonpolitical military newspapers had gone out with Caporetto. The Italian military command concluded that one reason for the disaster was a lack of communication between officers and enlisted men. Officers were therefore instructed to discuss current affairs with their men and to promote trench newspapers that explained the government's policies.

Moreover, "faith in the Fatherland" was not an innocuous patriotic slogan. Like so many other returning veterans, Balbo felt that the victory Italy had won on the battlefields, the faith in the nation for which he and his comrades had sacrificed at the front, was being dissipated by the politicians at home. The politicians settled for a shameful peace in Paris; they failed adequately to honor the returning veterans and to protect them from the insults of the socialists and other anti-war demonstrators; they granted an amnesty to deserters from the army; they investigated Caporetto when—according to Balbo—only those who had fought the war had a right to judge.[31]

Thus, when Balbo urged his readers to "defend the war, 'your war,' because you fought it," when he urged his readers not to allow the war "to be denigrated or nullified," he was clearly pressing the attack against the government. He was doing the same in his enthusiastic support for D'Annunzio's Fiume expedition. "The soul exults and trembling erupts in a single cry: 'Viva Fiume Italiana,'" proclaimed *L'Alpino*. About the seditious aspects of the enterprise, about D'Annunzio's incitement to break military discipline by calling on the garrisons to follow him, Balbo, of course, wrote nothing. In addition to lending editorial support for the Fiume expedition, Balbo raised money. *L'Alpino*,

Balbo later proclaimed proudly, was "the first that dared to speak out among the military of a revolt against Nitti's timid regime and for this had the honor of being censored."[32]

Balbo's patriotism, his frantic desire to save Italy's victory and her good name from the sinister forces that he perceived as threatening her, fairly screams from the pages of *L'Alpino*. Nowhere, however, did he offer a program, a specific ideology or set of principles. There was no reference to Mussolini nor to the first meetings of the fascist movement, which had begun during the spring. Nor is there any reference to Mazzini or to republicanism. What Balbo preached, very simply, was a patriotic faith in "the PATRIA" and a violent opposition to socialism. "Socialism doesn't create poets," Balbo wrote; in socialism "everything is founded in materialism, in hate, in spitefulness."[33] By contrast, he praised the sacrifices of his comrades in the trenches. In typically D'Annunzian language that broke down the line between sacred and secular, in imagery that elevated the cause of the nation to a religion, as Mazzini had preached, Balbo evoked the memory of a fallen comrade, martyred for Italy: "First the water, then the fire, then the two together tortured our arduous path, all bristling with thorns. Monte Valderoa, Monte Solarolo, in those days your fateful peaks worthily represented the bloody altar of the Fatherland!"[34] For a romantic and exasperated young patriot of twenty-three, there could be no higher tribute than to be linked with the martyrs of the Risorgimento and to "die like a poet."

In mid-December of 1919, Balbo produced his last issue as editor of *L'Alpino*. "Leaving the paper is painful," he wrote, but the war was over and "we are all returning to a civilian life of study and work." However, he vowed to maintain the program of "purest patriotic faith" and to "battle against the traitors and the denigrators of the Victory."

Of his homecoming, Balbo tells us, "I was nothing more, in essence, . . . than one of the many, one of the four million veterans of the trenches."[35] Like so many of his comrades-in-arms, he was appalled and disgusted at what he found. "To fight, to struggle, to come home to the land of Giolitti, who transformed every ideal into a business proposition? No. Better to deny everything, to destroy everything, in order to renew from the ground up," he declared in his diary.

His own Ferrara in 1919–1920 provided a shocking example of everything that—to his mind—had gone wrong with post-war Italy.[36] Unlike other major northern cities such as Milan and Turin, which had boomed with war-related industries, Ferrara and its surroundings had outwardly changed very little. The Castello, the Renaissance palaces, the Duomo still dominated the city's skyline. The city remained very much a provincial center of petty tradesmen, minor bureaucrats, artisans, and craftsmen. Industry in Ferrara still meant the six refineries that had been producing sugar and alcohol from sugar beets in 1914. The small businesses ranged from food processing to manufacturing gloves and small electrical and household appliances, soap making, and salt processing.

The countryside, too, appeared unchanged. In the spring and summer of 1919, a view from the top of one of the province's hundred *campanili* would have revealed a familiar scene: a yellow sea of grain mottled with deep green splotches of hemp. Wheat, planted over 60,000 hectares—a quarter of the province's surface—reigned unchallenged as the king of crops. Tall, slim hemp plants covered 30,000 hectares. Smaller plantings of corn, sugar beets, rice, tobacco, fodder, and vineyards rounded out the province's agricultural produce.

Yet behind the tranquil facade, Ferrara seethed, for 1919–1920 were the years of the *biennio rosso,* the "red biennium." Suddenly, and with shocking speed, the "socialist revolution" appeared to have triumphed. Following a sweeping socialist victory in the local elections of 1919, the red flag flew from the *Castello* and from the churches.[37] Monday replaced Sunday as a day of rest. Many churches were closed because so few went to pray. Children were no longer named after Christian saints: Ateo, Spartaco, Lenin, even Ribellione came into fashion. In the "red baronies," the bosses of the socialist labor organizations wielded enormous power. Ferrara was experiencing nothing less than "a dictatorship of the proletariat, a soviet," the prefect reported in January, 1920.[38]

The "socialist revolution" during the *biennio rosso* was neither as sudden nor as unprecedented as it appeared. It was the culmination of a long and bitter economic and social struggle in the Ferrarese. For nearly two generations, the *agrari*—the grain, hemp,

and sugar kings who ruled the province in alliance with the urban
middle classes—had battled successive waves of socialist and revolutionary syndicalist labor organizers. At stake was control over the
unruly army of poverty-stricken agricultural laborers.

The post-war socialist electoral victory was a continuation of the
earlier struggle. Now, however, socialist power appeared to be
crushing and irreversible. In the autumn of 1920, Gaetano Zirardini, secretary of the Chamber of Labor, boasted without much
exaggeration "of my 100,000 members."[39] Even more telling was
the calculation that a pro-fascist historian made at this time. The
population of the province was around 300,000, of whom about
half were working adults. If the sympathizers were added to Zirardini's 100,000, "it is easy to understand what a tiny minority
remained to represent the bourgeoisie."[40]

In reality, the socialists had erected a colossus with feet of clay.
Thousands of agricultural workers in the countryside enrolled in
the socialist leagues during the *biennio rosso*, but often under
duress. Pro-fascist accounts liked to dwell especially on the boycott—the exclusion of the victim from organized society—as an
example of socialist inhumanity and barbarism.[41] Cut off from public services, from the freedom to frequent public places, from the
comfort of his friends, the victim was persecuted like a "mad dog"
and in the end was forced to "plead for mercy."

The socialists also resorted to violence. A prefect's report of
July, 1920, claimed that "columns of hundreds of armed league
members have committed and are committing serious crimes
against persons and property."[42] In 1920 throughout the province
there were 192 incidents of arson, in addition to destruction of
crops and mutilation or destruction of livestock.[43] Thus, the
socialists—as the fascists did later—relied on a healthy dose of
coercion and violence, as well as persuasion and consensus, to
build their organizations. It is difficult to imagine them doing
otherwise. Among the impoverished masses of the Po Valley—the
small landowners, sharecroppers, day laborers—liberty and the
rule of law were of considerably less interest than where the next
meal was coming from. The experiences of the war veterans and
the example of the Russian revolution gave additional sanction to
violence. On the other hand, violence and coercion assured
neither commitment nor loyalty among the rank and file. Even at

the height of socialist power, astute observers doubted how long socialist rule would last. "We know perfectly well how many people, forced to adhere to the Leagues, silently and longingly await the day of liberation," remarked a Ferrara newspaper in July of 1920.[44]

In the meantime, the apparent socialist triumph frightened and outraged those groups that had been accustomed to wielding power in the province—the *agrari* and the urban middle classes. They resented the challenge to their authority. In addition, their fury contained a powerful moral element. The socialists appeared to violate every standard of what the middle class considered "proper" conduct and patriotism. In February, 1917, Balbo wrote of the socialist demonstrators: "As far as those scoundrels of local neutralism are concerned, besmirchers of the good name of our town, give them a good whipping—with the pen, and if necessary in some more convincing way."[45] He promised to take care of those "other Austrians" (meaning the socialists) when the time came.

But when the time came in 1919–1920, the middle classes in Ferrara at first had no place to turn. They had lost at the ballot box in November, 1919, and the government refused to intervene. When Balbo, on returning to civilian life, resumed his battle against the "traitors and denigrators of victory," as he put it, he did so as a republican. Like the rest of the middle classes, he knew virtually nothing about fascism. As he tells us himself, there was not much to know. Until the end of 1920, the movement was the work of an elite, of those who had the "good fortune to find themselves materially as well as spiritually close to Mussolini," he explained charitably.[46]

Three-quarters of those who attended the meeting at San Sepolcro in March, 1919, the traditional date for the founding of Italian fascism, were Milanese. The rest, scattered throughout Italy, were "spirited patrols, but few in number and without much influence." About the elections of 1919, in which the movement made a wretched showing, he said nothing. He was equally silent about early fascism's utopian program, which advocated radical measures such as universal suffrage, a progressive income tax, social security, and easy divorce.

Just eighteen months later in Emilia, Romagna, and Ferrara, a new "fascism" emerged. This "agrarian fascism," violent, militant, dedicated to the repression of the socialist political and labor organizations, was a far cry from the idealism of "urban fascism." This was the fascism that Balbo ultimately embraced and led to victory. Like the socialist movement, "agrarian fascism" in Ferrara at the end of 1920 developed with remarkable speed and power. Throughout 1919, groups of war veterans and middle-class patriots, inspired by ideals like those of the San Sepolcro program, attempted repeatedly to found a *fascio* in Ferrara. They failed miserably.[47] Their movement appeared to serve no function. War veterans who might have filled fascism's ranks joined either the socialists or the right-wing veterans' organizations. Petty bourgeois patriots favored existing parties to fight off the socialists. Fascism's self-description as an "anti-party" only served to confuse matters.

A year later, in a vastly different political climate, the political "space" that fascism could not find throughout 1919 appeared at last. Italy's post-war political crises did not seem any closer to solution. Everywhere the "bolshevik avalanche" appeared to be triumphing; traditional parties and institutions seemed powerless to stop it. In this climate, in October, 1920, the first *fascio* in Ferrara was constituted.[48] At the end of the month the *fascio* had about two hundred members. By December 13, the prefect reported that the organization was "rapidly increasing its strength" and could count nearly a thousand members.

The nature of the *fasci* in these early stages was very different from the disciplined, quasi-military organization that Balbo developed some months later. The *fasci* resembled brotherhoods or goliardic clubs. The members prided themselves on their favorite haunts, their rituals, their eccentricities. Such, for example, were the *Celibanisti*.[49] Originally, they numbered twenty. Olao Gaggioli, a printer, was honored with the first membership card in the *Celibanisti*. During the war he had served as a lieutenant in the *bersaglieri* and had been wounded and decorated several times. Disappointed at how quickly his fellow citizens forgot about his military exploits, he became active in the "fascism of the first hour" at San Sepolcro and founded the first *fascio* in Ferrara. Arturo Breviglieri, who was given the second membership card in the *Celibanisti*, had before the war been a metal worker on construction projects in Paris. During the war, he had served as a machine gunner with an assault division. At the time of the formation of the *Celibanisti*, he was unemployed. "Modest, good, generous, with the sensitivity of a woman and a courageous heart," according to a fascist chronicle, Breviglieri had only three loves, "Italy, his mother, his comrades in the *fascio*."[50] This "ever calm" and smiling ex–machine gunner became one of the *fascio*'s earliest martyrs, in a gunfight with the socialists at Pontelagoscuro in April of 1921. Balbo later named one of the colonial villages in Libya after him. Other prominent members of the *Celibanisti* included Alberto Montanari, another war veteran whose two chief occupations were playing cards and going to meetings of the *Celibanisti;* Giulio Divisi, who later became one of Balbo's right-hand men in Ferrara; Francesco Brombin, a patriotic professor of Italian language and literature who taught at the Vincenzo Monti technical institute; and "Finestra Chiusa," a semi-literate local character who had earned his nickname because he had lost one eye. The most famous member of the group was the Duce himself. When Mussolini, on a visit to Ferrara, heard of the *Celibanisti*, he asked to be included.

The group gathered at the Caffè Mozzi behind the Piazza del Duomo daily, after the midday meal and after supper. They developed the custom of drinking cherry brandy before going home: despite its apparently foreign origins, the *Celibanisti* claimed that the drink came from Zara and was "italianissimo." One day Breviglieri said without thinking, "Give me a *celibano*." The expression caught on. The group devised a membership card made of leather, with the symbols of the city of Ferrara, birds, a man's head, and various hieroglyphics. They held their political reunions in members' homes.

This odd assortment of ex-soldiers, idealists, students, frustrated patriots, and hangers-on busied themselves with activities that ranged from goliardic stunts to authentic political violence. Flag-snatching incidents were common. Twice, Gaggioli wrote, the red flag waving over the Castello disappeared, "to the most joyful comments of the citizens and the most hydrophobic threats of the enemy."[51] If there was a socialist meeting or demonstration, the fascists organized a counterdemonstration and challenged the socialists with fists and clubs; if there was a public concert in the piazza or in a theater, the fascists demanded to hear patriotic hymns, and whistled and stamped until they got their way. Fascist squads successfully protected the livestock and feed belonging to boycotted families. After dark, the fascists delighted in marching through the streets of Ferrara in a show of strength. Because they were so few, they resorted to various tricks to give the illusion of large numbers. They marched up and down the same street two or three times, to give the impression of two or three squads marching by. At other times, they would mark time beneath a window while simultaneously slapping their thighs. To the sleepy audience, half-listening behind shuttered windows, the stamping and muffled clapping sounded like a group three or four times its actual size.

Even the most outspoken anti-fascists such as Gaetano Salvemini remembered these early fascists with a certain indulgence. Two years of virtually unbroken triumphs had destroyed the agricultural workers' sense of proportion and had made them "like spoiled children," Salvemini wrote.[52] Moreover, their leadership often could no longer control them. To be a fascist at this time, during November and December of 1920, took considerable moral and physical courage.

Picturesque and romantic, courageous and committed as they were, no one took these first fascists seriously. They suffered from unsavory backgrounds and reputations. They were not the stuff out of which to create a mass movement. Then the fascists enjoyed a stroke of good fortune. Two well-publicized and bloody clashes with the socialists, one in Bologna and one a month later in Ferrara, played into their hands. For the fascists and their frightened middle-class sympathizers, the encounters at the Palazzo d'Accursio (Bologna) in November and at the Castello Estense (Ferrara) on December 20 provided an excuse to strike out at the socialists. In Ferrara, more than 14,000 attended the funeral of the three "martyred" fascists killed in an apparent socialist ambush in the city's main piazza. As Balbo wrote in his diary, those two episodes marked the beginning of "the definitive march of fascism toward the revolutionary conquest of the country."[53]

The new and widespread interest in the *fascio* brought it serious problems.[54] The sudden influx of members changed the nature and the goals of the organization so rapidly that it came close to splitting. The *fascio* was no longer taking a purely anti-socialist position but instead was favoring "conservative interests" such as those of the *agraria,* complained Olao Gaggioli's younger brother, and he added, "The *fascio* has become nothing more nor less than the bodyguard of the sharks." The central committee in Milan took the threat of schism seriously enough to dispatch an emissary with the mission of disciplining and purifying the movement in Ferrara. Just at this time, in the aftermath of the Castello Estense events of December 20 and with the Ferrarese *fascio* in crisis, Italo Balbo, decorated war hero and university graduate, returned home for the Christmas holidays.

Until the holidays, Balbo had been campaigning in the Ferrara countryside for his party—the republican party.[55] Basing himself in Lugo, he went forth daily, by car, by bicycle, by cart, to spread the Mazzinian creed among the people. He campaigned in places so remote that not even his comrades were sure where he was. When his worried mother telegraphed the republicans in Lugo, they told her only that he was out in the country. Two and three times a day, small groups of peasants, bundled up against the cold, gathered to hear the valorous war veteran and university graduate, Dottore Italo Balbo, expound on the virtues of republicanism and denounce the defeatist and subversive socialists. Thin and nervous, with a scraggly beard and a wild mop of hair, he looked more like a consumptive poet or Mazzinian conspirator than a war hero. The audience probably did not mind. What they enjoyed most were his furious harangues when socialists tried to shout him down. From time to time, as he spoke, he paused as if he were short of breath. Although he said nothing of his health, his friends knew that he worried about sharing his older brother Fausto's fate. In Ferrara, his mother despaired; until he came home, she would fear that he was one of the victims of the Castello Estense.

Balbo's first encounter with the fascists of Ferrara indicates how little he knew of them. According to one account—admittedly a hostile one—he was "fighting bolshevism by playing poker" at the Caffè Estense when a group of fascists marched by. "Who pays them?" he wanted to know.[56] A few days later, he watched a group of fascists preparing for an expedition. So caustic and provocative was his attitude that the fascists threatened to make him their first

victim. Yet, in a little over a month, Balbo had not only joined the
fascio, he had become its political secretary.

The story of Balbo's "conversion" is difficult to piece together.
His sudden change of heart and his meteoric rise to power naturally alienated many of the pioneers of the *fascio*. Their testimony
in the matter is often the most detailed. On the other hand,
Balbo's relations with his "employers" and supporters, the big
landowners, remain obscure. His enemies claimed that Balbo's
transition to fascism was a mercenary affair, pure and simple.[57]
The *agraria* hired him. They wanted him to build the local *fascio*
from an uncertain and unsavory gang of idealists and malcontents
into a reliable instrument with which to destroy the socialist labor
organizations. They needed a bright young man, preferably a
respectable sort—but one who would not be afraid to break a few
heads—to lead their forces. What more ideal candidate than
twenty-four-year-old Italo Balbo? He came from a good middle-
class family; he had earned enough medals to qualify as a war
hero; he was even "Dottore" Italo Balbo, a university graduate.
Balbo's friends naturally told another story. Although he was not a
founder of the local *fascio*, he had always sympathized with its
ideals and his conversion contained a strong element of idealism,
they explained.[58]

Both sides can claim a bit of the truth. Certainly there were
career aspects to Balbo's conversion. In January, 1920, he was a
young and ambitious war veteran, engaged to be married, yet
without career prospects other than the uncertainties of his pre-
war radical journalism and politics. To portray him purely as an
opportunist who sold himself to the highest bidder, however, is
misleading. For anyone seeking a political career in January of
1921, fascism was still a leap in the dark. If Balbo had been interested only in security, he might have chosen far more judiciously.

Three men from the *fascio*, Barbato Gattelli, Olao Gaggioli,
and Guido Torti, carried out the negotiations.[59] Gaggioli was a
much-decorated war veteran; Gattelli, the son of a petty industrialist; Torti, a postal employee. All three had been among the
pioneers of the *fascio* and figured in the dissident movement that
gave Balbo many headaches in later years. Friends and foes agree
that Balbo insisted on three conditions before he would join the
local fascists: a monthly salary; immediate nomination to party

secretary; and guarantee of a position in a bank once the fascists had triumphed. Balbo's enemies, especially Torti, made much of the career aspects in the deal. But as Balbo's supporters pointed out, in effect he was taking on a full-time political position which precluded his working elsewhere. Furthermore, as any politician would, Balbo wanted to secure himself in case his party did not emerge victorious. There is disagreement about his salary. Some claim that it was fabulous for a young university graduate of twenty-four; others argue that it was not in the least excessive. The figure usually given is 1,500 lire a month, but others claim only 800 lire. The latter figure does not seem excessive; the central committee in Milan was paying its operative in Ferrara about the same amount to reorganize the *fascio*.[60]

Balbo's friends naturally stressed the ideological side of his conversion. They pictured him as one who had always sympathized with fascism's ideals, beginning with the interventionist crisis in 1915. At war's end, even while he was studying in Florence, he maintained his friendships with some of the members of the original *fascio* and supported their efforts. According to one account, during the autumn of 1920 he accompanied a friend, Alberto Montanari, to a night meeting that had been called to plan a raid on the socialists.[61] Another friend, Gualtiero Finzi, recalled Balbo's hesitations about leaving the republicans and joining the fascists. In a late-night conversation at a hotel near the railroad station in Ferrara at the beginning of January, 1921, Balbo worried aloud about "looking like a fool" if he made the switch, Finzi recalled.[62]

In joining the *fascio*, Balbo claimed that he never abandoned his republican principles, his "republican nature," as he sometimes referred to it. He had a point. At the beginning of 1921, fascism posed no ideological conflicts. Asked at that time what he stood for, a fascist would have been hard pressed to answer. The movement was a complex of patriotic passions and anti-socialist sentiments, a reaction to the sudden appearance of the "red tide," a "technique of political fighting."[63] Since fascism was not a formal party at the time, it was perfectly acceptable to belong to political parties and also to be enrolled in a *fascio*. Balbo tried it. He formally left the republicans only after they ruled that he could not—as he requested—retain membership in both organizations.

Balbo's letter of resignation to the republicans, dated February 12, indicates that he thought carefully about maintaining a coherent political philosophy.[64] He also took care not to burn his bridges behind him. In the letter Balbo admitted that he knew full well that the republican central committee opposed his membership in both organizations. However, Balbo insisted, fascism did not conflict with Mazzinian ideals, "especially so far as the Fatherland, socialism, and the agrarian question are concerned." Hence, Balbo explained, he felt no qualms about belonging to both organizations. The problem with the republicans, Balbo wrote, was that if they continued to remain locked in the circle of their narrow prejudices, "the republic will not be made by us." It "is our duty to live among youthful energies," like those of fascism, in order to carry forward Mazzinian criticism, he concluded. The Mazzinian faith that he had nourished in his heart for ten years remained "whole." He was, he concluded, ready to rejoin the party when it had once again taken up the principles indicated by the Master.

Although Balbo clearly cared about maintaining a certain ideological coherence, it would be naive to pretend that he was as idealistic as the fascists of the "first hour." He must have understood quite well what lay behind the "fascism" he was to head in Ferrara—the "agrarian fascism" that even Mussolini once described as representing "the private interests of the most sinister and contemptible classes in Italy."

Unfortunately, Balbo's relations with the *agraria* remain obscure.[65] Strictly speaking, *agrario* simply means "landowner." However, the term was generally reserved for those with a considerable amount of property—more than 200 hectares. Perhaps sixty such landowners lived in the province before World War I. Of these, no more than twenty made up the active nucleus of the *agraria*. These landowners, together with a handful of limited companies with extensive investments in land and sugar, controlled about 60 percent of the cultivable surface of the province. A few were well known, like Giovanni Grosoli, landowner, banker, and prominent figure in the national Catholic political movement; Giuseppe Vicentini, also a banker and Grosoli's right-hand man; and Vico Mantovani, landowner and founder, director, or important shareholder in half a dozen banks, credit institutions, and land companies. He founded the landowners' formal organization, the Association of Ferrarese Landowners, also known as the Agraria. In 1921 he ran on the same list as Mussolini and was elected to the Chamber of Deputies. In 1934, he was nominated a senator. Mussolini's police could find nothing to fault either in his politics or in his personal life.[66] Reports described him as a "constitutional monarchist" who nevertheless became a "fervent fascist" and enrolled in the party from the time of its founding. "He lives with much ease thanks to the considerable financial means at his disposal"; his personal life was "irreproachable." The police report characterizes Mantovani as well-informed, interested, and capable in dealing with the major agricultural problems of the province.

The identity of the rest of the *agraria* remains shadowy. Here and there they appear publicly as benefactors for fascist causes. For example, they contributed heavily to a fund for the "victims" of the Castello Estense shootings. For the most part, they were a cautious, reactionary, indolent lot who lacked vision and shunned modern, mechanized, competitive agriculture, today's "agribusiness." They preferred to rely on traditional methods to insure their profits: government protection in the form of tariffs and subsidies, and a labor force that could be exploited mercilessly. Although Balbo obviously had dealings with them (especially with Mantovani), he did not socialize with the *agrari* often and did not include them in his circle of friends.

There is no simple answer to the question of how and why Balbo supported the *agraria*. Perhaps, like Mussolini, he concluded that without them, fascism would remain only a fringe group of romantics and crackpots. With the support of the *agraria* the socialists could be crushed. Afterwards, "fascism" might turn out to be anything—perhaps even a positive, progressive, revitalizing force for the nation.

While these negotiations took place at the beginning of January, 1921, both the *agrari* and the fascist central committee in Milan carried on their own talks and found they had much in common. The *agraria*, determined to make a last desperate attempt to break the power of the socialists, devised a twofold plan. First, they would try to woo the agricultural workers with their own program for land reform. If the program did not prove attractive enough, they counted on the *fascio*'s squads to provide further encouragement. Through violence and intimidation, the squads were expected to uproot the socialist leaders and drive them into exile. Meanwhile, the socialist offices and meeting-places were to be destroyed. Without leadership, without institutions, without the guarantee of jobs, the agricultural workers would quickly capitulate and join the fascists, the landowners reasoned.

The social program of the *agraria* consisted in creating a land office where those who aspired to become small landowners could apply.[67] The program was announced in a menacing tone, as if the big landowners had their choice between a socialist and a fascist revolution. The author of the program, however, was Vittorio Pedriali, a landowner himself, a fact that gives an indication of the true nature of the plan. In practice, very little land was available and often in ridiculously small tracts. Those who applied to the land office found that they were not "given" the land. They received it under long-term lease at best, and in other cases under conditions that were a regression from what the socialists had achieved. In short, the program harmonized perfectly with the aims of the big landowners; their only interest was to create a bulwark of small landowners who would resist the socialist organizations. The land office was also designed to avert the internal crisis within Ferrarese fascism. The *agraria* hoped that through the land office program, the idealistic "radical" fascists who had pioneered the movement would be won over.

To publicize the program, a new weekly newspaper, *Il Balilla*, appeared for the first time on Sunday, January 23, 1921. The three editors were Ferruccio Luppis, a member of the *fascio*'s executive committee; Vittorio Pedriali, who had drawn up the land office scheme; and Italo Balbo.

Balbo most probably contributed to the opening issue. Under the pseudonym Fantasio he wrote an article entitled "The Gospel of Facism: Why We Aren't Socialists."[68] True to its title, the article revealed much more about the author's anti-socialist phobias than about what fascism stood for. Worker and peasant could become part of the middle class, for the "bourgeoisie . . . is nothing more than the elite of the working class," the writer argued. An attack followed on the "vulgar demagogy" of practical socialism, which stressed workers' rights based on their numbers and said nothing about their moral duties—a leaf taken straight from Mazzini. The article concluded with an expression of sympathy for the workers in the name of the trio of Christ, Marx, and Mazzini. Of Marx, however, only the necessity of the workers to organize was acceptable; all the rest had been denied by Kautsky anyway, claimed Fantasio. He contributed two other short articles two weeks later. In them he demolished strawmen and stereotypes with great sarcasm and irony; he was notably short on concrete programs and ideas.[69]

On the same Sunday that *Il Balilla* first appeared, Balbo made his debut as a *squadrista*.[70] For the first time he led fascist squads on punitive expeditions into the countryside, against socialist leaders and sympathizers. Thus, well before he formally joined the fascists and before he resigned from the republican party, Balbo was deeply involved in the workings of the *fascio*. His nomination to secretary of the *fascio* occurred during a series of meetings held February 3–7. It coincided with a new executive committee that was elected by the membership as a whole on February 13–14. Balbo's name was not contested. The central committee in Milan imposed him on the Ferrarese *fascio* as part of the process of disciplining, restructuring, and "purifying" the local organization. The emissary from Milan, Lieutenant Ottavio Marinoni, described Balbo as "a young man full of enthusiasm and equipped with the necessary qualities to occupy the position of secretary."[71] Chief among these qualities—although Marinoni did not say so—were Balbo's abilities as a *squadrista*.

Chapter Three

Squadrista: Campaigns 1921

For an ambitious young man eager to launch a political career, the position as political secretary of the Ferrarese *fascio* presented an opportunity—but certainly no sinecure. No one, least of all Balbo, anticipated how quickly fascism would develop, or, indeed, that it would develop at all. Mussolini himself had doubts about fascism's potential: if the movement did have a future it lay, he was convinced, in the cities.[1] Yet, due in large part to Balbo's leadership, fascism captured the province of Ferrara with astonishing speed. Even more important, the example of Ferrara spearheaded the spread of agrarian fascism throughout northern Italy—and perhaps kept Mussolini's urban-based fascism from sinking into oblivion.[2] Thus, Balbo and his squads played a key role in transforming fascism from an amorphous movement into a major political force.

About his debut as secretary of the *fascio* and his activities during the first months of 1921 Balbo is uncharacteristically reticent. He refers generically to that year as one of organization and harvest, as the period when the masses first flocked to the fascist standard.[3] With pride and nostalgia he recalls the first massive fascist rallies in Bologna, on April 4, and in Ferrara on the following day when 60,000 greeted the Duce. Such memories, of course, paid tribute to one of Balbo's major contributions to the development of fascism: his ability to rally masses. In his diary he refers to another: "My vocation was, and remained, that of a soldier. I took on the task of bringing discipline, hierarchy, and responsibility to the flying squads who were to crush the red terror forever."[4] What the connections were among the new enthusiasm for fascism, the "flying squads," and Balbo's "vocation" as a soldier, he never quite explained. The links are worth exploring to appreciate what Balbo's contribution to the growth of fascism in Ferrara and then throughout Northern Italy really was. The great novelty of fascism lay in its military organization—the military organization of a political party. The "flying squads" that Balbo referred to, however, originated neither with him nor in Ferrara. In April, 1919, Mussolini created the nucleus of fascism's military organization when in Milan he assembled a band of unemployed *arditi* to guard his newspaper and then to attack the rival socialist *Avanti* in a much-publicized raid. He then encouraged *fasci* throughout Northern Italy to develop groups of 200 to 250 well-armed individuals—perhaps with the idea of supporting D'Annunzio's coup at Fiume. Other vigilante movements fed into the development of what came to be known as *squadrismo*. During the spring of 1920, with the support of the local authorities, civilian "volunteers," composed largely of students and *arditi*, appeared in Milan, Bologna, and Rome. They attacked socialists on the streets and helped break a municipal-employee strike in Rome. The real training ground for the *squadristi*, however, proved to be Venezia Giulia. In this border area, during the summer of 1920, the enemy was not socialism but Slav Nationalism. With the active support of the military authorities, squads sprang up throughout the province and systematically destroyed Slovene clubs, trade unions, and newspapers. By the autumn of 1920, the *squadre* had spread south to Emilia.

By the time Balbo took office in Ferrara the local *fascio*'s pioneers had resolved many of the organization's financial, publicity, and recruiting problems.[5] The squads were established by October, 1920. At first they patrolled elections to guarantee "electoral freedom"; by December they had begun erratic attacks against the socialists. Financial support for the *fascio* from landowners and businesses began to flow in November. And arms presented no difficulties. On January 5, 1921, the socialist paper *Avanti* reported that 200 pistols, most likely from military sources, had been distributed to the fascists. The fascist newspaper *Il Balilla* and the first fascist league for agricultural laborers were founded in January of 1921. Well before Balbo took office, the local prefect demonstrated his fascist sympathies. While the fascists brandished their guns in public, the socialist leader Gaetano Zirardini could not get a permit to carry a pistol. The fascist practice, which became standard, of kidnapping and beating up communal officials and forcing them to resign had begun at the end of December, 1920.

Balbo developed and expanded these institutions and practices. Under his leadership, squads, leagues, and financial support grew; violence became more organized and systematic; public authorities came more and more under fascist control. Balbo first organized the scattered squads on a provincial level, then regionally, and finally on a national scale.[6] By the fall of 1922 he had become one of the major commanders of a private army that destroyed the socialist organizations and opened the way for the March on Rome. In developing the squads into a much larger, coherent organization, he set a pattern that he followed throughout the rest of his political life. During each phase of his career, he took command of an institution in its infancy and developed it into a mass phenomenon: first the Blackshirt squads; then the Aeronautica; finally, the colonization in Libya.

Balbo's activities as a *squadrista* have been interpreted in many ways. Anti-fascists viewed the squads as simply hired thugs of the *agraria* or the "white army" of the bourgeoisie. American newspapers likened the *squadristi* to gangsters and suggested that Balbo would have found himself quite at home on the streets of Chicago.[7] Still other critics ridiculed Balbo's military organization and the "victories" of the squads. His campaigns were little more than costume parties or daytime balls. The guests enjoyed parades, speeches, and mass rallies—a technique learned from the socialists—and flirted with the pretty girls. "How many of Balbo's 'sieges' end in genuine military victories?" taunted journalist Leo Longanesi.[8]

Balbo, of course, would have protested vigorously at this. His campaigns had nothing in common with Chicago underworld wars except their violence. Unlike a gangster, Balbo had no interest in illegal "business" enterprises and he was not content with sharing power at a municipal or a regional level by corrupting local officials. His ultimate goal was for fascism to govern the nation. He was not fighting for a class or a group of special interests like the *agraria,* he claimed. He and his men were patriots struggling to save Italy. That gave his "army" legitimacy—in his eyes, at least. The war against the "reds" demanded the same courage, commitment, and violence as the war against the Austrians. His men, he wrote in his diary, had to know "the pride of peril" and the "consciousness of carrying out a military duty" in their missions. Violence he exalted quite frankly as "the quickest and most definitive way of reaching the revolutionary goal. . . . No bourgeois hypocrisy, no sentimentalism; action, direct and sharp, carried out to the end, at whatever cost," he proclaimed.[9]

Despite his military pretensions, as Longanesi and others pointed out, Balbo was more a politician and a showman, a provincial political boss and a *ras,* than a general. He claimed to be concerned with purely technical military matters. Instinctively, for every political question that Mussolini and the fascist leadership posed, he worked out the offensive and defensive capabilities of the squads, Balbo wrote. Yet, strictly speaking, Balbo was not a professional military man. Prior to the March on Rome, his formal training consisted of the brief course he had completed before being sent to the front. There were plenty of others in the fascist ranks—for example, his fellow *quadrumvir,* General De Bono—who were better qualified and more experienced in military affairs than Balbo. Nor did his squads ever reach the discipline and competence of a professional army. Their "victories" reflected the political paralysis of the Liberal state; the violently anti-socialist sentiments of local bureaucrats, police officials, and magistrates; the often sympathetic attitudes of army commanders; and the divisions within the socialist movement. Balbo avoided putting his squads to the ultimate test: they never faced a pitched battle with regular troops.

Balbo's campaigns certainly constitute part of the fabric of civil wars and violent political struggles that have plagued Europe during the twentieth century. Yet against such upheavals as the Spanish civil war and the Russian revolution, Balbo's campaign—indeed, the entire fascist struggle for power in Italy—appears curiously tame. Balbo fits in best with a local tradition. The Risorgimento artist and politician Massimo d'Azeglio defined it when he commented that Italy was a land of factions and in every Italian can be found a bit of civil war.[10] Garibaldi agreed. "To bring harmony among us Italians, hard knocks are necessary and nothing less will do," he concluded.[11] Balbo's friends placed him in this Italian tradition when they referred to him as a "Carolingian knight" or a "hero of the Renaissance."[12] They meant to stress Balbo's sense of chivalry; they forgot the factionalism and feuding that such a parallel implies.

Rightly or wrongly, Balbo preferred to see himself as a descendant of the *Garibaldini:* they, too, although they were often dismissed as renegades and bandits, fought the good fight in the name of a higher ideal—Italy. Like the *Garibaldini,* Balbo was an adventurer and a romantic. For him, battles and military life were "not only action but also poetry."[13] Through "gatherings, oaths, songs, military rituals," he sought "to drape" his campaigns "with poetry." He wanted the fascist raids to be carried out with "boldness, daring," but also with "open-mindedness, a chivalry not lacking in gaiety." If a march was likely to be peaceful, he invited his sister Egle along to share the good times. New tricks, pranks, and practical jokes—often cruel ones—delighted him.[14] The classic torture of the *squadristi,* dosing an enemy with castor oil, probably originated among the Ferrarese fascists, perhaps among war veterans who recalled that Italian army doctors sometimes dispensed castor oil in place of aspirin.[15] There is no evidence that Balbo was the first to suggest the castor oil treatment, but it fits into his notion of having "fun" while playing politics. Another prank was the "stockfish club." When a prefect temporarily forbade the fascists to arm themselves with ordinary clubs, Balbo substituted dried cod or stockfish from raids on a socialist fishermen's cooperative. When the "clubs" had outlived their usefulness, they joined the soup at a jolly Blackshirt beach party. Another of Balbo's favorite tricks was to lead a small convoy of trucks through a village and gun the engines until they backfired; the terrified villagers thought they were hearing pistol shots.[16] The black shirt was probably another of Balbo's ideas. Black shirts were traditional among the working classes in Emilia and Romagna, for a dark-colored garment hid the dirt. Although the shirt was also traditional among the *arditi,* Balbo claimed that the Ferrarese fascist squads were the first to use the shirt as a uniform.[17]

Disciplined and military, yet humane and courteous, with a sense of goliardic humor—so Balbo wanted to see himself and his campaigns. The reality was considerably more brutal. He made his debut as a *squadrista* even before he was formally appointed as secretary of the *fascio*.[18] On January 23–24, 1921, for example, he organized a series of raids on villages south and east of Ferrara, nearly all within a radius of about ten kilometers of the city limits. At San Martino, according to the prefect's report, a socialist threatened a fascist with a knife. The fascist replied by firing three pistol shots, seriously wounding the socialist. Fascists then set fire to the furniture in the offices of the local league. At Aguscello, according to the prefect's report, two fascists suffered slight gunshot wounds. A socialist newspaper saw matters differently: four trucks full of fascists and two cars of the *agraria*, escorted by trucks full of *carabinieri*, did the shooting. They invaded the headquarters of the league and destroyed or carried away all the furniture. The *carabinieri* then arrested fourteen socialists and charged them with resisting the invasion with their hunting rifles. At Denore, Balbo, accompanied by the *agrario* Giuseppe Chiozzi, attacked the league. In the shooting that followed, Balbo, Chiozzi, and Arturo Breviglieri, who two months later became one of Ferrarese fascism's martyrs, were slightly wounded, according to one account.

Three weeks later, on February 17–18, just a few days after Balbo's appointment as secretary, a second wave of violence followed, this time around Rovigo. The fascist attack left three dead: two socialists and a sixteen-year-old fascist, Edmo Squarzanti. During the latter half of March and the first week in April, Balbo's squads went on a third violent rampage. They were now operating within a radius of about thirty kilometers of Ferrara. Over a period of about three weeks, the headquarters of the leagues at Dogato, Reno Centese, Consandolo, Gaibanella, Quartesana, Copparo, Jolanda di Savoia, Portomaggiore, Sandolo, and Portarotta Maiero were burned or destroyed and the communal councillors were forced to resign.

One socialist source estimated that between January and March of 1921 alone, the fascists engaged in fifty-seven sorties, including twenty-five in which there were fires or other damage to leagues, cooperatives, labor exchanges, or political headquarters.[19] A fascist historian declared exuberantly that there were so many raids between March and May that he stopped counting them all.[20]

Mixed with these violent attacks were others that reflected Balbo's streak of whimsy and goliardic humor. At the end of January or the beginning of February, 1921, Balbo and four companions sought to kidnap a socialist leader who had taken refuge in San Marino. The man was said to be one of those responsible for the Castello Estense affair; Balbo's goal was to capture him and "present him as a gift for Epiphany" to the *fascio* in Bologna. Disguising themselves as "self-indulgent Florentine bourgeois on a pleasure trip," the young fascists hoped to catch their prey on an evening walk. At the last moment, however, the plot failed. Suspicious socialists, some of whom appeared armed, surrounded Balbo and his friends; they narrowly escaped in their car down the winding dusty roads to the safety of Ferrara.[21]

On April 10–11, Balbo led a larger expedition of the same type to Venice. According to a sympathetic chronicler, the fascists, forty strong, with two hundred in reserve, travelled to Venice to confront socialists who had allegedly insulted the flag and certain sailors. A hatless Balbo, fearless, "like Napoleon, like Garibaldi," directed his men in a forty-minute gun battle before the authorities intervened. From the center of the fight, where the firing was heaviest, he threw hand grenades and fired a pistol with admirably sure aim, all the while "smiling and calm as if death were not facing him." When the Royal Guards arrived to reestablish order, their commander wanted to meet the leader of the Ferrara fascists. "Two young men, two noble hearts, two brave Italians. . . . They did not exchange a word, but their two right hands met in a mute outpouring of mutual sympathy."[22]

Many years later, a veteran of the expedition recalled the incident in considerably more prosaic terms. An angry Balbo, frustrated that he could find so few recruits, led a group of around three dozen to Venice to help break a rumored general strike. By the time they reached the city, the socialist-led strike was over and the expedition became a tourist excursion, with picture-taking and feeding of pigeons in Piazza San Marco. The fascists were disappointed that there had been no skirmish with the socialists. The statue of Garibaldi, draped with a red flag, provided

Fig. 4. Balbo (top center with cane) and *squadristi* in Venice (April, 1921) (G. Bucciante, ed., *Vita di Balbo*)

the occasion they were looking for. As they walked along Via Garibaldi, shots rang out from the windows flanking the street and the Royal Guards intervened with more shooting, mostly to keep the snipers away from their windows. There were no casualties. In the end, the fascists seized the flag from the monument and paraded with the banner to Piazza San Marco. There Balbo gave a little speech and the Ferraresi, well satisfied with their efforts, returned home.[23]

Balbo's expeditions yielded impressive results. Between February, when he assumed control of the *fascio*, and the general elections in May, Ferrara "the red" turned into Ferrara "the black." The socialist labor and political organizations, cooperatives, and employment offices lay in ruins. At best, the socialist leaders, terrorized and physically and morally beaten, fled into exile; at worst they were murdered. Duly elected communal or provincial officials resigned or fled. The mass of agricultural workers, terrified by the fascists or indifferent to the political struggle, abandoned the socialist organizations and enrolled in the newly created fascist ones.

Violence alone does not explain the success of Balbo's campaigns. He knew the limits of beatings and burnings. In a circular printed in *Il Balilla* on March 13, 1921, he made it clear that fascists were authorized to respond only to socialist "provocations"; Blackshirts were not to indulge in violence without specific authorization from the secretariat and the squad leaders.[24] There were few casualties. Even a militantly anti-fascist historian has estimated that during the spring of 1921 within the province of Ferrara, the fascists killed no more than a dozen of their enemies.[25] More significant than the number of casualties was the psychological effect of these raids, the climate of terror and desperation that they created among the socialists.

Balbo conquered the countryside both psychologically and aesthetically.[26] His sense of personal daring, bluff, and showmanship often served as an effective substitute for violence. One evening, for instance, armed with nothing more than a little swagger stick and a smile, he confronted a potentially explosive meeting of four hundred socialists in the village of Francolini, where his sister taught school. After addressing the meeting, he asked the audience to go home; he refused to leave until the hall was emptied.[27]

His ability to stage massive pageants and displays proved to be a major factor in the fascist conquest of the countryside. The public funerals that Balbo arranged for fascist "martyrs" demonstrate his talents as a showman and choreographer. More than twenty years after the event, "Everyone remembers Alberto Tognoli's funeral, at which thirty thousand people were present," a friend of Balbo's recalled.[28] What everyone remembered was the team of oxen, the same team that the "martyr" had once used to plow his rented land. Their last service to their master, who had been killed by a socialist March 13, 1921, was to pull the cart bearing the coffin. When the procession reached the edge of the cemetery, Balbo commanded, "Fascists of Italy, attention!" Ten thousand men, it was claimed, snapped to attention; a forest of flags dipped in homage to the fallen.[29] Tognoli's funeral was only one of many that Balbo arranged that spring. Others recalled the final rites for Rino Moretti on March 28. As the funeral procession wound through the countryside, hundreds dropped to their knees as the wagon bearing the casket rattled by. A band played fascist hymns, usually spritely and martial, at a dirgelike tempo. On this occasion Balbo, reflecting his Mazzinian beliefs, spoke of the fascists as "an army of missionaries of Liberty . . . and most of all the liberty to love one's own country."[30] In their simple hearts, he continued, the people no longer heard the "distant songs of social hatred, of the bloody banner, but instead the solemn song of the new hymn of love sacrificed for the Fatherland." At Breviglieri's funeral in April, the body was placed in a glass-enclosed case and displayed like that of a saint. Balbo contributed his own tunic from his days as an *Alpino*. At the funeral of another fallen comrade, Balbo publicly placed his ceremonial *ardito*'s dagger in the victim's hands.

The funerals, with their religious and patriotic overtones, their displays of the Cross and fascist flags, spoke deeply to the peasantry.[31] For a generation they had listened to the rationalist and materialist arguments of the socialists, arguments that remained only abstractions. Balbo appealed to the peasantry with "the most basic of human rites: religion, Fatherland." Fascism also had the advantage of novelty. The socialists had triumphed, and for the peasantry there was little more to be gained. Fascism appeared to represent something "new, exceptional, powerful, human."

Balbo and his squads could not have triumphed so quickly without help. A major factor in the fascist victory in Ferrara, as elsewhere, was the collaboration of local authorities. These ranged from the prefect to the local police and security forces. The prefect during this period, Samuele Pugliese, was openly pro-fascist.[32] He slanted his reports to his superiors. For him the socialist leadership was recruited only from the "most violent elements"; in reporting the incidents of Castello Estense he claimed that the fascists suffered one more victim than even the *fascio* had claimed. In 1924, when the *Gazzetta Ferrarese* praised him for being pro-fascist, he thanked the newspaper for its kind words. The fascists themselves sometimes gave credit to the local police authorities for their help. *Il Balilla* noted that what really crushed the socialists at S. Bartolomeo in Bosco was the work of the secretary of the local *fascio* and the local sergeant of the *carabinieri*.[33] Official police statistics on

Fig. 5. Balbo (right) personally intervenes to break a strike of agricultural workers in the Ferrara countryside (G. Bucciante, ed., *Vita di Balbo*)

violence and arrests also indicate that the authorities generally discriminated against the socialists. A national report of May 8, 1921, for example, noted that in incidents of fascist-socialist encounters more than four times as many socialists as fascists were arrested.[34] Ferrara reflected the national pattern. In a total of forty-nine incidents during the period, thirty-three fascists were arrested, and one hundred ten socialists.

Many local officials did more than offer a sympathetic nod and a wink to the Blackshirts. At a raid on Portomaggiore at the end of March, 1921, trucks full of police singing fascist songs joined the fascists.[35] The police doled out guns and ammunition to those Blackshirts who were not armed. Night attacks, beatings, bombings, and burnings ensued under the eyes of the police. Fascists searched houses and made arrests, and for two days a combined picket of fascists and police searched everyone coming into the area and allowed only fascists to enter. Balbo liked to compare his campaigns against the socialists with the violence of a battlefield, but there was little to compare: the fascists, with their monopoly of "protected violence," clearly enjoyed the upper hand.

The mistakes of the socialists also contributed to the speed and ease of the fascist triumph. Too often they failed to collaborate and unify their organizations as the fascists did. Nor did the socialists create a military arm parallel to fascism's squads. The Arditi del Popolo provided such an opportunity, but the party officially disavowed them and most local organizations followed the party's national directives. The socialists made another major mistake in ignoring the variety of social categories and aspirations within their ranks. Rentiers, small landowners, and day laborers all received the same treatment. This led to resentment and defections, especially among the small landowners, who stood to lose by collectivization.

The national elections of May 15 confirmed the triumph of fascism in Ferrara and the effectiveness of Balbo's squads. The elections were held in an atmosphere of violence. Nevertheless, the outcome was indisputable. The socialists, their organizations smashed, won only a third of their total in the previous election of 1919. The "national bloc," with Mussolini and the *agrario* Vico Mantovani heading the local slate, increased their totals sevenfold over 1919, easily dominating the socialists.

Balbo basked in the reflected glory of the electoral victory. Within three months of having assumed the leadership of the Ferrarese *fascio*, his political career had taken wing. From an unknown provincial war veteran, he had become a figure of importance to the fascist central committee in Milan. He had proved his abilities as a leader of the squads. He had also demonstrated, especially during the final weeks of the electoral campaign, that he could conjure up huge crowds, and he presented them proudly to Mussolini.[36] On April 4, on the grassy field of the Palazzina di Marfisa, twenty thousand people, about half of them peasants, gathered to hear the future Duce speak.[37] Balbo was one of the speakers at the receptions and dinners following the public meeting, gatherings at which fascists, *agrari*, businessmen, ex-syndicalists—the peculiar and explosive mixture that was fascism in Ferrara—all congregated. The following day, with Mussolini, Balbo rushed to Gardone to pay homage to D'Annunzio, who at that time had far more influence on the

squadristi than the future Duce.[38] A final example of Balbo's
influence in Ferrara came on May 26, when he was arrested for
carrying a pistol.[39] As soon as the word was out, fascists from the
countryside rushed into town; church bells rang the tocsin; columns of fascists roused the population with patriotic songs;
crowds besieged the Castello—and the authorities released
Balbo. With funds raised by public subscription, he was presented with a new weapon to replace the confiscated one.

Throughout the summer of 1921, Balbo continued to enlarge
and improve his organization. In June and July, squads from Ferrara began to operate in Ravenna and in the Veneto. In July Balbo
became secretary of a newly created provincial federation. In the
new organization, the power of the town *fascio* declined before the
more numerous rural nuclei. As secretary, Balbo enjoyed broad
powers. A circular published after the provincial organization's first
meeting shows Balbo's priorities. His primary concerns were to
streamline the squads and to build and enlarge his army. He gave
detailed instructions on the composition, training, and armament
of the squads. He wanted monthly reports on the quantities of
weapons and ammunition. Finally, he informed the *squadristi* that
they should prepare uniforms for themselves—military trousers,
and the black shirt that many had already been wearing for some
time. All of this was to be done as quickly as possible. "Everyone
must get to work . . . without sparing energy. By next September,
the fascist regiments of Ferrara must already be magnificently
drawn up in their ranks." He added, "Only with a disciplined army
shall we win the decisive victory."[40] What the mission of these
regiments was to be, and what he meant by "decisive victory,"
Balbo never made clear.

The May elections left many questions unanswered about the
nature of fascism. Apparently fascism would survive. But in what
form? As an amorphous "movement" or as a formal party? What
was to be the role of the squads? Was fascism to return to its
ideals of the "first hour," or was it simply the instrument of the
"agrarian slavers"? Could fascism now move beyond the provinces, perhaps even capture the nation? If so, what strategy
would prove most effective: the violence of the squads, or politicking in the halls of Montecitorio? More than once these difficult, volatile issues threatened to split the movement. During the

summer of 1921, fascism's enemies gleefully spoke of the "crisis of fascism," and they were right.

On the national level, during the summer and fall of 1921 the major issue was Mussolini's decision to make a peace pact with the socialists. Fearing a popular backlash against fascist violence, Mussolini now explored the parliamentary road to power. The provincial *ras* and the squads had little to gain by a parliamentary solution to fascism, so Mussolini maneuvered carefully. Fascism was "republican in its tendencies," he declared on May 21.[41] Such a statement, with its revolutionary overtones, momentarily placated the squads and their leaders, but the phrase also implied an opening toward the reform socialists and the Popolari. The government, eager to check the violence of the *squadristi* and reassert the authority of the state, encouraged such an understanding. On August 3, an agreement was signed. The General Confederation of Labor, the Socialist Party, and the Fasci di Combattimento pledged mutual respect for their economic organizations and agreed to end violent reprisals.

Like most of the other provincial *ras*, Balbo opposed the "peace pact."[42] His career of smashing socialist political and labor organizations and his work of building and organizing the Blackshirt squads appeared on the verge of ruin. Before the pact was signed, he acted as if no truce was possible; in mid-July the squads stepped up the pace of their burnings and beatings. Balbo also protested the pact at a flurry of meetings and conferences, and he published bristling polemics in *Il Balilla*. Two days before the pact was signed, he attended a regional meeting in Bologna of *fasci* from Emilia and Romagna. There Balbo declared himself to be inalterably opposed to the Mussolini initiative. He was the third to sign the final resolution of the meeting. In the resolution, the harshest denunciation of the pact to that point, the delegates declared themselves totally divorced from the negotiations and promised to maintain an attitude of "vigilant defense." On August 14, the provincial federation in Ferrara, which Balbo headed, declared that so far as the province was concerned, the pact had "no practical or substantial value."[43] Two days later, at a congress in Bologna of *fasci* from the Po Valley, opposition to the pact was so strong that Mussolini submitted his resignation from the national executive committee of the *fasci*. Balbo's delegation of ninety-four *fasci* was by far the largest and also the most intransigent in its opposition to the pact, a prefect reported.

Mussolini's resignation did not perturb Balbo. He proposed that Grandi and Marsich visit D'Annunzio to see if he would be willing to head the fascist movement.[44] When Marsich became ill, Balbo took his place. At Gardone he asked D'Annunzio to participate in a fascist commemoration to be staged at Dante's tomb in Ravenna. He probably also sounded out the poet's willingness to lead a march on Rome. When D'Annunzio's answer proved to be equivocal, Balbo muted his opposition to Mussolini. To denounce the pact was not necessarily to denounce Mussolini, he wrote to the *Popolo d'Italia*.[45] Yet in *Il Balilla* his tone was scathing: Mussolini was acting as if he were in a stupor; he was frozen into positions that were illusory; his analysis of the political situation was of a "grotesquely infantile superficiality."[46]

Balbo's most spectacular gesture against the peace pact, and undoubtedly the one that most filled him with pride, was the March on Ravenna, September 10–12.[47] With Grandi, Balbo marched at the head of three thousand men across the dusty roads of the Romagna to occupy the former Roman and Byzantine capital, the site of Dante's tomb. The expedition lasted three days and Balbo was especially proud of its organization. The squads represented the provinces of Bologna and Ferrara. Balbo divided the men into two columns. Each column was subdivided into companies and platoons; each unit had its chief and his subordinate ranks. The men were perfectly organized and "not so badly armed."

Balbo described the demonstration as a purely patriotic gesture. The dates of the march conveniently encompassed both the anniversary of D'Annunzio's march from Ronchi on Fiume in 1919 and the anniversary of Dante's death six hundred years earlier. The peculiar juxtaposition did not bother Balbo in the least. He and his men were paying homage to two great symbols of *italianità*. His sister Egle remembered the march as a sort of grand communal outing. The men trudged along the white dusty roads or pushed or rode their bicycles in the heat of early September. Each day they covered roughly twenty-five kilometers. To break the monotony, they sang patriotic songs and listened to speeches. "For the first time then I had a sense of the future

Fig. 6. Balbo directs squad leaders during the March on Ravenna (September, 1921) (G. Bucciante, ed., *Vita di Balbo*)

Fig. 7. Balbo (in Alpine hat) with Dino Grandi (with riding crop) leads *squadristi* in the March on Ravenna (September, 1921) (G. Bucciante, ed., *Vita di Balbo*)

possibilities," Balbo wrote. "The squads could act not merely as isolated and detached units, but as disciplined masses, like real units in a real army."[48]

But his squads did not behave like disciplined units in a real army.[49] On the contrary, even pro-fascist accounts describe the expedition as simply another occasion for the squads to rampage against the socialists. For the *squadristi* the march was a reply to the socialist Arditi del Popolo, who had staged a demonstration in the city a week before. The Blackshirts also settled old scores with socialists in the villages located near the path of the march. The occupation of the city was no more peaceful. "Subversives" reportedly fired shots at the fascists; in retaliation, the fascists attacked and burned "subversive" buildings in the city. At the official ceremonies, Balbo hinted that the legions were ready to "leap to their feet" and take to the "national road . . . which leads to Rome."[50] D'Annunzio might still provide the spark and leadership for that march, Balbo suggested; the *squadristi* awaited the poet's "inspiring word" to attack everything that "made them feel strangers in their homeland." Balbo pointedly made no mention of Mussolini in the speech.

The march proved that the squads could and would go on violating the peace pact and that the authorities were unwilling or unable to maintain order. Reports prior to the march indicated that the prefect would not allow the legions to enter the city; in practice, the authorities did nothing. The imposing size of the march reminded Mussolini once again what a potentially valuable asset the squads were. For their part, Balbo and Grandi learned that for the moment, at least, the squads could get along without Mussolini. Finally, for Balbo, the march was an occasion to test the organization he had been building since early in the summer.

The struggle to shape fascism was as fierce at the provincial as at the national level. In Ferrara as in many other towns and provinces, the split between the fascists of the "first hour" and the latecomers, between the idealistic, radical "urban fascists" and the reactionary "agrarian fascists," was never satisfactorily resolved. During the spring electoral campaign, the two groups papered over their differences. After the great electoral victory, however, the cracks reappeared. Barely two weeks after the election, a fascist from Ferrara wrote to Mussolini about the "bitter quarrel" between Balbo and Barbato Gattelli, the head of the "dissident movement."[51] According to the dissidents, Balbo had not sufficiently supported Gattelli during the electoral campaign. All would end well if an outside authority like Mussolini ordered the two men to make up, the letter concluded optimistically.

The split, however, went far beyond personal feuds: it reflected a fundamental difference in ideology and goals. The dissidents believed that fascism had a truly revolutionary future. They had pledged themselves to genuine economic and social reform in the Ferrarese countryside, and they were appalled by a movement which so far had done nothing except the bidding of the *agraria*. The socialist peace pact, the dissidents reasoned, offered an unusual opportunity. With Mussolini and the *squadristi* at odds, the dissidents might have a chance to prevail.

On his return from Ravenna, Balbo confronted the first of a long series of dissident revolts.[52] Gattelli had purchased the *Provincia di Ferrara* and transformed it into a rival fascist newspaper. The lead article of the first issue, "The Crisis of Fascism," spelled out clearly the aspirations and demands of the dissidents.[53] According to the article, fascism, like socialism, was suffering from "elephantiasis." Too many joiners from too many different camps had swollen the movement. Now was the time to purify the organization and to remember its founding principle and aspiration: agrarian reform. The big landowners had gone back on their pre-election commitments to the fascists. "The undisciplined and the obstreperous" (the squads) had to be expelled; the *agrari* must respect their commitments. An ideology that went beyond "patriotic homilies," one that could seriously rival that of the socialists, must develop, the article concluded.

In the following weeks Balbo fought off a succession of challenges to his leadership.[54] On September 14, at a meeting of the provincial council, an angry Balbo threatened twice to resign. He felt disowned and mortified, he declared. The hostile attitude of Gattelli at a caucus of the fascist parliamentary group a week earlier, the rumor that fascists were waiting to attack him in the streets, the publication of the rival newspaper without authorization of the provincial council, all slandered and humiliated him. When he walked the streets now people called him the "Doge," he said. Grandi, who had been invited to preside over the meeting, tried to rally support for Balbo. Gattelli stood firm. He would not retract his opposition until "certain people" (meaning Balbo) left the province for good. He had talked directly to Milan, he claimed, and he would not give up his newspaper.

On September 17, under pressure from the dissidents at a meeting of the local *fascio* of Ferrara, Balbo admitted that the *agraria's* technical experts were now having doubts about whether the proposed reform programs "could be carried out and the promises maintained."[55] If the land program was not progressing, Balbo said, the fault lay in the current economic crisis. The hemp crop had failed and the market had declined. Olao Gaggioli replied for the infuriated dissidents, "What sort of impression does fascism make today before agricultural workers?"[56] The dissidents warned that they would not be used only as "lightning rods." When the socialist enemy "once again knocked at the door" the dissidents would not allow the "red shame" to revive; however, the *agraria* would find that bargaining with the dissidents then would be "tougher, oh, very much tougher." On September 22 the *Provincia di Ferrara* accused the landowner's federation of "agrarian slavery."

At this point, Mussolini, in *Il Popolo d'Italia* on September 25, issued a call for discipline. Dissidents and *fascio* reached agreement—for a week. On October 2, at a protest demonstration to commemorate eight fascists who had been killed at Modena in a skirmish with Royal Guards, Balbo was notably absent. He was at a meeting with Mantovani of the *agraria*. Outraged at Balbo's conduct, between October 2 and October 7 sixty-four of the "dissident" fascists resigned from the organization. On October 5, members of the Ferrarese *fascio* resigned from the provincial organization. Manifestos on the walls proclaimed their stand. Fascism had hoped to force the rich and powerful classes to carry out their duties in regard both to the grave economic problems that faced the country, and to the poorest classes. Unfortunately, the mentality of the rich and powerful remained as before, "backward" and "egotistically exploitative." For these reasons, the directory had decided to "burn its bridges" and to "reaffirm and save the original and pure fascist idea." The dissidents formed their own autonomous *fascio*.

Balbo fought back in the newspapers—and with the squads. To the *Provincia di Ferrara*'s charges of "agrarian slavery," Balbo replied in *Il Balilla* on September 25 with a "balance sheet" of reforms that the *fascio* had already carried out.[57] On an area of 18,000 hectares, claimed *Il Balilla*, four thousand families had been "transformed." The nature of their transformation—whether into sharecroppers, leaseholders, or small property owners—was not specified. Meanwhile, during the last days of September, the squads resumed business as usual. They beat up socialists and suspected "bolshevik" sympathizers. The Blackshirts forced their way into the house of the socialist deputy Edoardo Bogiankino, past two *carabinieri* assigned to protect his family. The *squadristi* spat on Bogiankino's wife, defaced a portrait of Marx, and on the walls wrote "Death to Bogiankino and Lenin, long live the *fascio*."[58]

In mid-October a new statute for the administration of the provincial federation gave the political secretary more authority than ever. Naturally the autonomists protested. They were promised more freedom of action in the future. In practice this meant only that the local and provincial offices of the *fascio* would no longer be in the same building. Yet, with the National Congress approaching in November, the dissidents once again compromised. At the National Congress, they hoped, the fascist movement would be transformed into a regular party. Party discipline would serve to curb the one-man rule that had been developing under Balbo. As a sign of at least outward harmony, Balbo went to Rome accompanied by no fewer than three members of the "autonomous" *fascio*.

The dissidents ingenuously pinned their hopes on Mussolini. They believed that he would continue to support the peace pact with the socialists and would repudiate the squads and their violence, but Mussolini had no such intentions. Moreover, the dissidents naively ignored the support that fascism enjoyed among the military, the police, the magistrates, and the bureaucrats. None of these elements was ready to collaborate with the socialists.

At the Congress, the dissidents quickly became disabused of their hopes.[59] Mussolini and the *squadristi* understood that they needed each other. Without the squads, Mussolini realized, the party might be only a momentary enthusiasm, and he would have little chance of rising beyond his position as a minor deputy. The *squadristi* realized that only Mussolini could hold the party together. Their cold reception in Rome reminded them that they were still a long way from power. All was resolved on the second day, when Mussolini and Grandi embraced on the stage before the cheering delegates. The fascist movement was transformed into a party in which the squads formed an integral part. The peace pact with the socialists was buried, and Mussolini formally denounced it a week after the Congress.

Balbo's role in the Congress was minor.[60] In addition to proposing a telegram of greetings to D'Annunzio, he was one of several orators who defended the *italianità* of Dalmatia. He was not acclaimed a member of the party's executive committee nor was he one of the regional representatives on the central committee. At the conclusion of the Congress, Balbo paraded through the streets of Rome at the head of his squads. A photograph shows him in black shirt and leggings, his hair billowing wildly, smiling a bit stiffly at an old white-bearded *Garibaldino* who is displaying the colors.

The Congress revealed very little about Balbo's stand on the major issues that fascism faced. His speech to the Second Provincial Congress, held in Ferrara on November 27, is far more illuminating.[61] Balbo's address reflects both his position at the moment and the attitudes that he espoused throughout his career: his suspicion and intolerance—tempered by political realism—of formal organizations like the Fascist Party; his nominal devotion to Mazzini and republicanism; his admiration for a *condottiero* like D'Annunzio; his sense of the limitations of violence, and his chivalrous attitude toward his adversaries; and his vision of society as a paradise of small landholders.[62]

Balbo candidly admitted his initial opposition to transforming the fascist movement into a party. The movement, in his judgment, was still too young, its program too indefinite to be encompassed by the rigid discipline of a party. He yearned for a movement without many presuppositions, ties, dogmas, a movement with a goal on which was written "a single word: Patria." The "will of the majority and a little contact with the reality of events" brought him around to supporting the creation of the party, he declared.

With regard to the program of the new party, Balbo came down decidedly against Mussolini's "economic liberalism" and in favor of the national syndicalism that Grandi and Marsich had proposed in imitation of D'Annunzio's Charter of the Carnaro. The government, with its demagogic and socialistic spirit, ignored the interests of the nation in favor of individuals and "prostituted itself daily to the violence of the parties," declared Balbo. For this reason he held that "we need to march on the Left rather than the Right." Parliament, the "useless areopagus of empty talk," should be replaced by an organization with links to "national syndicalism." Balbo concluded his discussion of the Rome Congress with an enthusiastic endorsement of D'Annunzio, toward whom he professed "affectionate devotion" and "boundless admiration." In the Charter of the Carnaro, Balbo claimed, he found the "philosophic spirit" of Mazzini, the source from which everyone, from Mussolini to Grandi, "must draw."

As for future direction, Balbo urged his comrades to maintain close ties with the agricultural laborers and to defend the small landowners and rentiers. The party must always have the agricultural workers as its basis. The party also needed to continue with its program of "transforming" the day laborers into higher categories. The small landowner, Balbo reminded his audience, provided both the national wealth and the patriotic backbone of France, yet in Italy the government sank millions into protection for industry and ignored agriculture. If the local capitalists, like the government, opposed the work of the fascists, then the fascists would have to battle mercilessly.

Finally, on the struggle with the socialists, Balbo pleaded for an end to violence and for peace with the enemy. A number of benefits would follow from this "demobilization of the spirit." First, the socialists would realize that the fascists were not the "cannibals" they depicted. Second, the fascist army, which was organizing on a national level, would not be "used up in minor skirmishes" while the government's army might be demanding all of fascism's energies. As a minority, fascism enjoyed widespread sympathy; as a majority, it ran the risk of being labelled arrogant. Discipline and good will would now be needed more than ever, Balbo emphasized. With the Christmas season less than a month away, he asked for brotherhood and respect for the enemy. In the same way that soldiers during the war saluted the fallen, both comrades and enemies, fascists should pay tribute to their adversaries, Balbo urged. The rank and file of the enemy was not at fault: "the fault lies with the leaders, the fault lies with the ideology." The dead are best avenged with deeds that destroy hatred, he told his audience.

Following the Rome Congress, the dissidents, reassured by the new party statute, indicated that they would return to the main provincial body. Soon, however, the feuds, the quarrels, the harangues resumed. Supported by the *agraria* and a statute that gave him wide powers, Balbo's position was secure. Nevertheless, the internal quarrels frustrated him. At moments, apparently, he considered resigning. "I am sorry for all the troubles that your false friends create for you," wrote Gino Baroncini, a Bolognese *squadrista,* to Balbo on November 18, 1921.[63] But he urged Balbo to stay at his post. It would be senseless to leave the *fasci* "and give satisfaction to four or five idiots who would then boast that they had forced you to give in," he argued.

Quarrels with the dissidents, agricultural policy, and the problems of provincial administration interested Balbo very little. At the beginning of 1922, the fascist labor organizations and the provincial machinery worked well enough so that fascism in Ferrara "does not take up all my effort," he jotted in his diary. "I am free to take on more general problems."[64] He meant the challenge of perfecting fascism's military arm on a regional and then on a national scale. The squads must be organized, trained, and disciplined for the ultimate test: a march on Rome.

His opportunity came at the end of November, 1921. The fascist central committee asked Balbo to join the four-man general inspectorate that was to command the fascist military forces. With General Asclepia Gandolfo, the former commander at Fiume, who had secretly aided D'Annunzio's coup; Marchese Dino Perrone Compagni, the *ras* of agrarian fascism in Tuscany; and Lieutenant Ulisse Igliori, Balbo was asked to draw up regulations for the organization of the squads and plans for coordinating their activities. The new, tighter organization of the squads reflected the transformation of the amorphous fascist political movement into a formal party.[65] The relationship between fascism's political wing and its military forces had to be defined. Just as important, discipline and hierarchy were necessary to control the random violence of the *squadristi*—a violence that even Mussolini and the party now officially deplored. Finally, more structure was necessary to control the mass base of the party, especially in the countryside. As the squads smashed the socialist organizations, the party had to find ways of absorbing and controlling the thousands of agricultural laborers.

Shortly after the New Year in 1922, Balbo met for three days with Gandolfo and Perrone Compagni at Oneglia to draw up the directives for the "fascist militia," as Balbo called it. In February the party approved the directives, and they were instituted in March. The squads were created with "the sole purpose of checking the violence of the enemy and of being capable, upon command, of rushing to the defense of the supreme interests of the nation." In keeping with a desire to revive "in every way the Latin and Italic tradition," Balbo and his colleagues took their organization and nomenclature from that of the Roman military organizations. The basic unit was the squad, consisting of twenty to fifty men; four squads formed a centuria; four centuria, a cohort; three to nine cohorts, a legion. The chain of command went from the inspector generals at the top, to the consuls who commanded the legions; to the seniores who commanded cohorts; to the squad leaders and their assistants (*decuriones*) at the lowest level. The new uniform was based on the black shirt, with black sash and leather belt, and short pants with long stockings or puttees. A black fez was optional. Roman eagles and the star of Italy figured prominently on pennants and decorations.

The directives also made clear that the squads were ready to contest the authority of the state and to step in if the state was deemed inadequate. Moreover, the power of the regional *ras* was not to be broken. "In dictating these norms, the General Command was guided by the concept of leaving maximum autonomy to the regional organization" under the command of the consuls, the directive declared at the outset. A "mania for uniformity and centralization" was not to destroy everything that was worthwhile and already formed a part of the regional tradition, the directive read.[66]

Naturally, the paper organization and the realities did not always correspond. At the end of January, shortly before the regulations were to be distributed, Balbo reassured General Gandolfo that "our project has been very well received." Yet problems emerged from the outset.[67] Perrone Compagni, in a series of testy letters to Balbo at the end of January, complained about some of the shortcomings.[68] The regulations provided for a leadership based on election. At the level of the squads this might be acceptable, but not at the level of the seniores and consuls, the Tuscan *ras* argued. Inevitably, under the purely elective system, the most violent and adventurous types rose to the top—with disastrous results. A second problem was the conflict of authority between the military leaders and the provincial political leadership. "Here in Florence I have squads that carry out really criminal acts, stupidly conceived and executed," reported Perrone Compagni. But when he admonished them, the provincial organization replied that the local political situation called for such acts, that they were "normal and as such did not concern [them]." Finally, Perrone Compagni pointed out the difficulties of establishing and controlling such a large unit as a legion outside a large urban area. How many *fasci* would be necessary in a province to constitute a legion? How was the consul to deal with such a large number? Who was to reimburse the consul for his expenses and his salary? And most important of all, who was to nominate the consul when more than four hundred *fasci* had to decide? Balbo urged Perrone Compagni to approve the directives anyway, so that their distribution would not be delayed. Any problems could be solved later, he concluded.

The directives remained in force during the spring of 1922. By the summer, however, Balbo himself admitted that they needed revision.[69] The system of zone inspectors was inadequate; the areas of authority had been poorly defined, and discipline "often left much to be desired," he noted.[70]

In the meantime, "the most important part of the armed forces of Italian fascism is under my direct orders," Balbo exulted. Following the January meeting with Gandolfo and Perrone Compagni at Oneglia, he had been given command over Emilia, Romagna, Mantova, Marche, Veneto, Trentino, Istria, and Zara. "I am very proud and now I aim at the goal, so much greater than I am but not greater than destiny: the revolutionary conquest of all the state to all of fascism."[71]

Chapter Four

Squadrista: Campaigns 1922

By the beginning of 1922, Balbo's goal of unity—one fascism, one leader, one Italy—appeared to be within reach. Throughout large sections of Northern Italy, the socialist resistance had been annihilated. The public authorities "are under control" and "the prefect must obey the will that I impose in the name of the fascists," boasted Balbo.[1] Yet fascism was still a local and regional phenomenon, and the fascists still faced enormous obstacles in their quest for power. As Balbo observed, local success meant very little without national success.

During the spring, in a series of mobilizations, occupations, and raids that ranged throughout the Po Valley, Balbo and his Blackshirts incessantly challenged the authority of the crumbling Liberal government. Balbo carried out a piecemeal revolution. First came the occupation of Ferrara in the middle of May; Bologna at the beginning of June; Ravenna, then the notorious "column of fire" march through the province at the end of July. The beginning of August saw the siege of Parma. Each of these occupations became a landmark in the fascist struggle for power. Each hastened the great day when, fulfilling the traditional dream of military commanders, Balbo could direct his forces to march on the capital.

During this period, crucial both to the history of fascism and to his own career, Balbo was in perpetual motion. Eighteen-hour days, sleepless nights were common for him as he rushed about directing his Blackshirt forces. Somehow he also managed to compile an account of his activities and thoughts, the *Diario 1922.*

Despite its title, the book is not a diary in the ordinary sense of the word: frank, intimate, unexpurgated. It is more like Balbo's official memoir of what for him were the great days of 1922. He never pretended that he was writing history—"honor too great and impossible presumption for the hasty scribbler."[2]

According to his sister Egle, Balbo did make daily notes in 1922. The *Diario*, however, appeared in 1932 as part of the celebration of the first decade of fascism. It appeared at a time of considerable tension between Balbo and Mussolini. As the gossips and backbiters remarked at the time: "He mulled it over for ten years before he brought it out; he must have made too many corrections," and "others too" must have insisted on still further changes.[3] The discovery of both the original typescript and the galleys indicates that the gossips were not wrong.[4]

In addition to Balbo himself, two people probably worked on the manuscript. One may have been Nello Quilici, editor of Balbo's newspaper *Corriere Padano* and a close collaborator and confidant. The other contributor was definitely Mussolini. The typescript and the galleys attest to his hand. The Duce apparently asked for certain changes, checked to see that they were made—and asked for more. One of Mussolini's concerns was to tarnish some of the glory that Balbo attributed to himself. For example, in the introduction Balbo had originally written that he had found his "vocation as military head of the future revolution." That phrase became "vocation of finding myself at the head and not in the ranks of the revolution." Mussolini also wanted to avoid offending as many of the other *gerarchi* as possible. Hence he asked for more compliments for some, like Badoglio, less for others, like Volpi; he wanted no attacks on Alfredo Rocco and Bruno Biagi, and more glory for Arpinati, Baroncini, and Grandi as head of Emilian fascism.

Mussolini had good reason to be anxious. Despite Balbo's protests that he was concerned solely with truth, in publishing the book he was building a monument to himself. He wanted to remind Italy, and Mussolini, how important his role in the fascist seizure of power had been. He said as much to certain friends—and in the book's preface. While others, including the great mass of the Italian people, had doubted the fascist revolution, he had believed in it with a "consuming passion."[5] To give the book additional authority, Balbo asked his fellow *quadrumvirs* De Bono and De Vecchi to authenticate his story. In a prefatory "letter," they thank Balbo for his "precise and scrupulous narrative" of the events that led to the March on Rome. The precise scrupulous narrative, of course, contains no hint of Balbo's disagreements with Mussolini, infighting with other *gerarchi*, struggles with the dissidents in Ferrara, failures of plans and operations. Despite these omissions and despite his own role in shaping the book, Mussolini never liked the *Diario* and made sure that when it appeared the reviews were few and lukewarm.

Over time, however, the book has become a standard source for anyone interested in the development of Italian fascism. Even the most committed anti-fascist scholars rank the *Diario* as one of "the most honest and accurate" eyewitness accounts from the fascist side.[6] For insight into Balbo's beliefs, thoughts, and feelings at this time, the *Diario* is invaluable.

Appropriately enough for one brought up as a Mazzinian, Balbo opens his book with a testament of faith. "I do not know how I could not be fascist," he declares.[7] A little less than a year after his adoption of fascism, his new faith shows all the fervor, the zeal, the dogmatic certitude of the convert. To be fascist and enrolled in another party "is impossible"; to be anti-socialist is not enough any more; to accept other ideas or variations on fascism is intolerable. "The truth is only one. Who believes in it has to defend it with his life. And whoever does not believe that he possesses the truth, absolute and sole, cannot be a fascist, that is, cannot challenge death." Only such a faith can justify violence. "How is it possible to practice violence and yet preach respect for all opinions?" he asks rhetorically. "Propaganda is the instinctive need of the convert," he comments. His public speeches are now effortless, second nature, as if "I were talking to myself."

In Balbo's new faith Mazzini and Mussolini appear to be juxtaposed. Balbo praises Mazzini's devotion to the duties of man and not simply to his rights, and the Master's stress on the necessity of both thought and action.[8] Yet equally memorable and influential are the "unforgettable encounters with Mussolini."[9] "The Chief" clarifies and simplifies the most complicated problems—a great virtue for someone in command. Moreover, he is "very affectionate." He "does not let me leave without a hug. His faith is my validation. My ambition is to surprise him, to do more than he expects."

Yet, beyond a generic populism, Balbo is never very clear on the tenets of his new faith. Is a revolutionary movement, such as fascism professes to be, possible without taking into account the needs of the workers? he asks rhetorically. Out of forty million Italians, how many are laborers? The fascists themselves do not come from the privileged classes, he remarks. The vast majority of the fascists are young veterans who want to work: "petty bourgeoisie already proletarianized by the tragic situation of the war and its aftermath."[10] Fascism, if it wants to win, must not create privileges, but must destroy the old ones. In a later entry, he claims he feels more in sympathy with the "humble rural laborer" than with the "sophisticated city politician."[11]

Balbo is much clearer on what he wants to destroy: the Liberal governments and the socialists. For them he has only contempt. The prefects no longer have any direction. "What a scene!" he exclaims. "Let Rome do as it likes. We are in charge here. We will take care of Rome on the day we can fall on that nest of owls and clean it out. We have only one goal: to deprecate, to reveal the absurdity of the state that governs us. . . . We want to destroy it with all its venerable institutions."[12] Agreement between fascism and its enemies is no longer possible, for "an abyss" divides the two sides.[13] The war has transformed everything. "The spirit has changed. The language has changed. The goal of Italy in the world has changed."

The socialists, too, are contemptible in Balbo's eyes. They, who always maintained that private property is theft, want the bourgeois state to protect their own property, Balbo jeers. "What revolutionary fiber these socialists have! To defend themselves, they have no other arguments than the Royal Carabinieri . . . enemies of property, unite in defense of property!"[14] Balbo also ridicules the socialist military forces: the Arditi del Popolo challenge the Blackshirts not on the battlefield but in anonymous letters in the *Avanti;* the socialist "generals" withhold their names in the newspapers, and they certainly have no soldiers—"They're all with us."[15] When the fascists refrain from interrupting a socialist funeral in Milan, the socialists claim the incident as a victory.

"Everyone consoles himself as best he can. The socialists console themselves with funerals."[16]

Despite his hatred and contempt for "bolshevism" and his apparently fanatic embrace of fascism, Balbo remains far from an ideological warrior.[17] When he hears the rumor that Lenin is to visit Italy for the Genoa conference, Balbo distinguishes clearly between Lenin the founder of "bolshevism" and Lenin the head of the Russian state. As head of the Russian state, the fascists will salute him. Russia is a country with which Italy may have foreign policy goals in common, he notes, unconsciously foreshadowing his 1928 aerial cruise to Odessa. The fascists, he concludes, will confine themselves to singing their anti-Leninist and anti-bolshevik songs in their own headquarters.

During this period Balbo's private life was one with his public life. From time to time he worried about the anguish he was causing his family, especially his mother.[18] His fiancée apparently concerned him less, for she did not rate a single line. On rare occasions he noted that he was overextending himself, that the endless days and sleepless nights were taking their toll.[19] Yet never for a moment did he waver or hesitate; he was having far too good a time. He delighted in the excitement, the danger, the comradeship. He enjoyed the parades and marches; he relished the *beffe,* the tricks and practical jokes he invented to outwit the authorities. He rushed about, organizing, drilling, encouraging his men, perfecting his organization. For him, leading the Blackshirts was an extension of his wartime experiences. But the campaigns also contained echoes of his interventionist days, of the teenaged Balbo, the flag-bearer, leading a crowd of his schoolmates in a scuffle with local police. There are even earlier echoes: the six-year-old reciting verses to his mother about the glories of the military life. When the brute realities of death, destruction, terror, intruded on the wonderful game of war, Balbo turned apologetic. His natural sense of gallantry and chivalry led him to empathize with the enemy. The deaths, the fires, the destruction, the terror were necessary, he wrote, in the name of a higher ideal: the salvation of Italy.

Balbo's first major assignment as inspector of the Second Zone ended in something of a fiasco, but the responsibility did not lie with him. The scene was Fiume, the "martyred city," so dear to the hearts of Italian nationalists, "the first revolutionary act of the post-war era."[20] The Treaty of Rapallo (November, 1920) had declared Fiume a "free city," and elections the following spring gave a majority to those who favored autonomy over union with Italy. On March 3, a thousand *squadristi* under the fascist deputy for Trieste, Francesco Giunta, seized the city. They banished the autonomist leader, Riccardo Zanella, and once again proclaimed the annexation of Fiume to Italy.

On orders from the party, Balbo travelled to Fiume on March 6 and joined the new provisional government. The government in Rome, however, organized a successful countercoup. On March 15, the provisional military forces—a mix of legionaries, Nationalists, *arditi,* republicans, and fascists—turned against the provisional government. Luigi Facta, the prime minister, installed another provisional Italian administration. For Balbo there was nothing more to do. He cancelled his projected mobilization of two thousand reinforcements and left the city—not before firing a parting shot in the form of one of the practical jokes that he loved.[21] "This evening I had a good time teasing the new governors" by spreading the rumor by telephone that the English fleet was about to enter the port.[22] On March 16 he was in Trieste, having barely evaded arrest at the border. Back to the "major task," he noted in his diary, "the conquest of Italy. Fiume will be redeemed by redeeming Rome."[23]

During the next few months Balbo's efforts met with greater success. The fascists had badly crippled the socialist labor organizations. Agricultural laborers now depended on the Blackshirts and on the fascist unions to provide them with jobs. Yet in certain areas the socialists still successfully contested the fascist unions. Balbo's goal was to break that resistance, to ensure that fascist unions were treated on a par with the remaining socialist ones. His tactics in these operations were similar. In Ferrara, Bologna, and Ravenna, the Blackshirts surrounded municipal or government offices or captured socialist headquarters. When the socialists recognized the fascist labor unions or when the government provided public-works jobs, Balbo ordered his men to disperse. The reasons for Balbo's successes were also similar. Certainly his skills as a leader and organizer and his personal daring played a

role. Yet he and his troops won mainly because no one—neither
the local police, nor the military, nor the socialists—seriously
challenged them.

Of his sieges, Balbo was proudest of the first, the four-day
occupation of Ferrara. From May 12 to May 16, according to his
estimate, 63,000 laborers invaded the city in a demonstration for
government public-works projects. Balbo jubilantly described the
operation as "a decisive stage in my life and perhaps in that of the
fascist revolution."[24] Three weeks earlier he had begun planning
the operation. Unemployment in the countryside of Ferrara was
highly seasonal, he explained to Mussolini in outlining his plans.
Spring was the worst time. In April and May the unemployment
rate reached the "astronomical figures" of 50,000 to 70,000. In the
past the government had always provided relief in the form of
public works. This year, to discredit the fascists and to punish the
masses who had deserted to the fascist side, the socialist deputies
blocked the programs. Balbo's solution was to take the city hostage until the government provided relief.

Balbo acted as if he were taking the initiative. In reality, like
fascists all over Italy, he was being pushed as much as he was
leading.[25] With the socialist unions smashed, the fascists now had
to provide for the restless, disorganized mass of agricultural laborers; their demands accounted for much of fascism's apparent dynamism. Ironically, the socialists were now in a stronger position.
They had fewer workers to deal with and they often had the
support of the government. The fascists had to take care of their
own or lose their constituency. Local, piecemeal arrangements
were no longer enough. Some fascist leaders argued that seizing
the government in Rome was now an absolute necessity.

Ferrara was a case in point. To resolve the problems of unemployment, the fascists nominally had two options, the *agrari* and
the government. The *agrari*, however, were not a true alternative. They had gotten their way and were not about to give up all
they had won. Vico Mantovani admitted publicly that the landowners never thought of "self-expropriation" of "Lenin . . . without Lenin."[26] If the landowners agreed to sign new contracts with
the fascist syndicates, they did so under conditions that were far
worse for the laborers. Now unemployed, the laborers literally
faced starvation, the socialists claimed. That left the government

as the only alternative for the fascists—a solution that pleased the landowners.

Mussolini pondered the risks of Balbo's plan. To be sure, it would revitalize the image of the fascists as protectors of the unemployed masses. Yet such a challenge to the government could lead to serious repercussions. The warring factions within parliament—the Popolari, in particular—might decide to form a united front with the socialists and provide a government with a backbone. Another possibility was that the government would decide on military intervention and crush the fascist forces, as had happened a year earlier when twelve *carabinieri* routed five hundred *squadristi* at Sarzana. Mussolini decided to take the risk, but he made clear that Balbo had to assume full responsibility.[27]

For three weeks Balbo worked feverishly to organize the demonstration, tirelessly crisscrossing the province to meet with the leaders of the local *fasci* and the fascist unions. "We also work at night. Now we can no longer keep track any more of our sleeping and waking hours," he noted.[28] His greatest worry was that of maintaining secrecy. If word got out to the authorities about his plans, he feared that the entire operation would be paralyzed from the beginning. Accordingly, he sent out sealed orders to be opened only at the time specified. His circulars, often minute and pedantic in their detail, reflected his origins as the son of a schoolmaster. Like the circulars and memoranda he was to write as head of the air force and as governor of Libya, these demanded perfect behavior and discipline. Alcohol, visits to houses of prostitution, and beatings even of the "worst enemy" were all expressly forbidden. The laggards, the irresolute, and the shirkers were threatened with expulsion.[29] "I am under pressure, but quiet. I am confident that I am preparing a demonstration that will be a milestone in the history of Italian fascism. . . . It is like being on the eve of a revolution."[30]

On the evening of May 11 the great mobilization began. From the most distant corners of the province, on foot, by bicycle, by wagon, by boat, the army of laborers began to converge on the city. By seven o'clock in the morning, according to Balbo's estimate 63,000—others put the number at 40,000 to 50,000—were at the gates of the city.[31] As Balbo knew, politics is, in part, spectacle, and with the eye of a movie director assessing a crowd scene, he described his army.

Colorful sight. The Ferrarese laborer drawn up in columns, with his mantle or with a blanket over his shoulders. A haversack with slices of polenta and pieces of cheese slung around the neck. Emaciated from the privations, faces darkened from the sun and hardened by the dust, but confident and enthusiastic. Extraordinary effect of the dawn march: badly clad feet. Moving spectacle: the army of the barefoot.[32]

To Balbo's delight, his logistics and his plans for security worked perfectly—or so he thought. As each unit reached the city, they received orders for their food and lodging. The communal oven had put in an extra supply of flour. Water supplies were secure. Schools served as barracks and sleeping quarters for part of the crowd; the rest slept in the open. One of his lieutenants, Giulio Divisi, had cut the telephone lines. At the city gates, fascist pickets controlled all traffic. Hotels, restaurants, and stores were closed and the trams were shut down. As of seven o'clock in the morning on May 12, the fascists were in complete control of the city.

At ten o'clock Balbo reviewed his army, assembled at the Montagnone, a park in the southeast corner of the city, bounded by the old walls.[33] Then he marched them down Corso Giovecca and surrounded the Castello. A company of Royal Guards appeared on one of the side streets. According to Balbo, he sent the captain a message to stay out of sight in order to avoid incidents. He disposed of the *carabinieri* and the police in the same way. At eleven o'clock, flanked by representatives of the *fasci* from throughout the province, Balbo presented himself on the castle drawbridge. The crowd, with a "roar that rattled the windows in all the surrounding buildings," yelled, "Down with the government, long live Italy." Balbo marched in to see the prefect, Gennaro Bladier. "Without any preliminaries, speaking with military firmness, I delivered my ultimatum," he wrote: the fascists would not disband until the government had guaranteed a public-works program. Bladier had forty-eight hours to contact Rome and meet these demands. The prefect wore his usual white vest with a gold chain across his "round, honest little belly. But his face was whiter than his vest. . . . He's a good and honest man and within me I regret that I have to give him this terrible problem." Pale and looking terribly burdened but fully aware of the gravity of the moment, in Balbo's presence Bladier telephoned the ministry of public works in Rome. Balbo's demands were met—and within the deadline he imposed.

For two days Balbo did not sleep. Day and night he followed the process of negotiation with Rome, calmed the often unruly crowds, guarded against desertions. In the evenings he dashed from camp to camp throughout the city, greeting comrades, raising morale, checking for infractions of discipline. Except for a "foolish and futile" plot by a group of "undisciplined fascists" to kidnap and hold the prefect hostage—a plot which Balbo personally thwarted—there were no incidents, he declared. "Not even a window in the public schools was broken," he claimed.[34] Nor were there any defections. On the morning of May 14, with his demands fulfilled, Balbo gave the order to demobilize.

Balbo and his comrades, including Mussolini, naturally hailed the occupation of Ferrara as a great victory, proof that the fascists had truly gained a mass following. Otherwise, Mussolini challenged, why did the 50,000 "slaves" not revolt against their handful of masters? In a private letter, a participant with obvious socialist sympathies explained some of the reasons for this "mass following."[35] In the villages and communes the fascists announced that any "traitor" not present at the demonstration would be excluded from any future job—and declined any responsibility for what might happen to him. The crowds that surrounded the Castello in Ferrara were motivated by pistol-waving Blackshirts who screamed, "If you move you're dead!" The lapses of discipline were probably more frequent than Balbo admitted. For example, on May 13, to put pressure on the prefect, truckloads of "slavers" drove round and round the castle dragging empty cans and producing an infernal noise. A crowd of fascists jeering, screaming, whistling, and shouting obscenities followed a car bearing the prefect's wife. Two bombs exploded, the prefect reported, fortunately with no serious injuries or damage.

Balbo's example in Ferrara sparked imitations elsewhere—but success was not automatic. In Rovigo, for instance, a three-day occupation to protest the refusal of the government to validate the election of a fascist deputy failed. Balbo spent the afternoon of May 20 there and left in disgust. The ends did not justify the means, he commented, and added, "Fascism unfortunately falls in love with gestures and tends to mime."[36]

A more substantial protest began in Bologna a little more than a week later. As in Ferrara, nominally at least the issue was jobs and recognition for the fascist hiring halls. The occupation of Ferrara had not cured the problem of unemployment, and laborers streamed across the border from Ferrara to seek jobs in public-works projects around Bologna. Socialists and fascists soon clashed. Beatings and deaths on both sides became a daily routine and Balbo was called to organize another mass mobilization.[37]

The occupation began on May 29. Fascists from Ferrara, Bologna, Mantova, and Modena were called, numbering, according to Balbo, a total of 20,000. As in Ferrara, the fascists besieged the prefect in his offices and demanded that the government cease to favor the socialists. As in Ferrara, although the demonstration sometimes became rough and unruly, the police and the military never seriously challenged Balbo's men.[38] Balbo's goal was to discredit the prefect, Cesare Mori—later to become famous for crushing the Mafia in Sicily—by ridiculing him and reducing him to impotence. Balbo called on his repertoire of goliardic stunts and his sense of showmanship. The stage was highly public: the main piazza in front of the Palazzo d'Accursio, the seat of the government. Here every day Balbo and his Blackshirts challenged the authorities for possession of the square. The police and military, mounted on horseback, tried to maintain order. The fascists fought back by waving flags, hats, handkerchiefs, by clanging trolley car bells, by setting off small bombs, firecrackers, and fireworks—anything to terrify the horses. "Getting the best of the authorities has become an amusing exercise in which the squads are highly experienced," boasted Balbo. But the squads never triumphed except in the most superficial sense. As Balbo admitted, the authorities never seriously resorted to force—such as using an armored car that was parked nearby. On the contrary, according to Balbo, "many of the army officers sympathize with us and they reproached the police who were roughing up two fascists who had been arrested." Confrontations took on the air of practical jokes. When fascist squads fell asleep the Royal Guards disarmed them, confiscating their rifles, pistols, and clubs, but never arrested them. The next day, the fascists surrounded a like number of Royal Guards and disarmed them. In his campaign of ridicule, Balbo's crowning inspiration was to march his men at regular intervals to a spot beneath the prefect's windows—and have them all urinate there.[39]

The occupation ended in a truce. Mussolini, fearing an incident which might force the government to interfere or might turn public opinion against them, advised demobilization. Balbo negotiated with the local military commander. Prefect Mori, after a decent interval, was transferred and demoted to a position in Bari. Once again, as in Ferrara, the government gave in.

Balbo conceded that his triumph reflected the weakness of his opponents. A "strong and coherent government of the extreme right" might have blocked the fascist path for the next few months, although it would not have saved the Liberal regime, which was really in pieces, he wrote.[40] Nevertheless, he claimed grandiosely that Bologna had provided an important experience for his Blackshirts and a "general test of the revolution."[41]

In Rome the government went into crisis, and Mussolini maneuvered skillfully in the parliamentary morass.[42] "This man who comes from the streets knows the game of eluding his adversaries and reaching his goals like an old master pilot," Balbo wrote.[43] For himself, however: "The devil with the crises! I go back to the provinces where the questions are simpler and the means far quicker."[44]

Six weeks after the occupation of Bologna came troubles in Ravenna.[45] As in Ferrara and Bologna, the issue was a labor dispute. The Labor Alliance, an anti-fascist front composed of socialists, communists, republicans, and anarchists, sought to exclude the fascist unions from sharing in the work of transporting grain. The police failed to keep order. In clashes between fascists and anti-fascists, an angry mob seized a fascist who happened to be passing, and beat him to death. Balbo ordered the mobilization of squads from Ferrara and Romagna.

His first task was to split the republicans from the Labor Alliance. In deference to his old party, at first he tried to negotiate with them. When that failed, he resorted to one of his *beffe*. Before dawn, his men snatched their "martyr's" body from the hospital. Balbo then demanded that the prefect guarantee public order while the fascists held a public funeral procession. While the police were occupied with the funeral, other fascist squads easily seized the republican headquarters and held the building

hostage. Meanwhile, as the negotiations with the republicans
went on, in nearby Cesena a fascist was wounded and at Cesenatico one was killed. "Above all, we have to strike terror in our
adversaries. A fascist cannot be killed with impunity," declared
Balbo.[46] In reprisal he burned down the Hotel Byron, the headquarters of the socialist cooperatives. This was one of the great
socialist landmarks, representing two decades of work, an institution that Balbo himself admitted operated according to essentially
"honest" guidelines. Even he showed pangs of conscience and
sympathy for Nullo Baldini, the socialist organizer:

When I saw the socialist organizer come out with his hands in his hair and
the signs of despair on his face, I understood all of his tragedy. Going up
in ashes at that moment . . . were his life's work and dreams. . . . I
cannot conceive of battle without respect for the adversary. . . . Unfortunately, civil strife doesn't allow for half measures.[47]

Negotiations with the republicans dragged on. Balbo probably
would have burned their buildings too if he had not received a
telegram from Bianchi in Rome appealing to his "sense of balance
and restraint" and ordering him not to undertake any new operations until Grandi arrived.[48] In the capital, Facta was trying to
piece together a new cabinet. The fascists might have joined, but
the violence of the squads was compromising Mussolini's efforts.
At Bianchi's telegram, in Balbo's own words he became "un-
hinged." "Today the game is being played outside of parliament,"
he had written three days before the crisis in Ravenna began.[49]
With Grandi's negotiations that led to a peace pact on July 28,
Balbo had nothing to do. He would honor the pact, he declared,
but with so many factions involved he doubted that the agreement would hold. In fact, when a group of fascists ventured into a
working-class quarter of the city—with peaceful intentions, Balbo
claimed—they were greeted with pistol shots, and one fascist was
killed. The fascists responded by burning socialist, anarchist, and
communist headquarters. The troops, which included cavalry and
two armored cars, did nothing to stop the destruction. Nine fascists had been killed since the beginning of the operation.[50]

Balbo now organized his most notorious operation, which became known as the "column of fire."

I went to the police chief. . . . I announced that I would burn down and destroy the houses of all socialists in Ravenna if within half an hour he did not give me the means required for transporting the fascists elsewhere. It was a dramatic moment. I demanded a whole fleet of trucks. The police officers completely lost their heads, but after half an hour they told us where we could find trucks already filled with gasoline. Some of them actually belonged to the office of the chief of police. I asked for them on the pretext that I wanted to get the exasperated fascists out of the town. In reality, I was organizing a "column of fire" (as it was defined by our adversaries) to extend our reprisals over the whole province.[51]

For twenty-four hours, beginning at eleven in the morning on July 29, "no one rested for a moment or ate." Balbo and his men passed through Rimini, Sant'Arcangelo, Savignano, Cesena, Bertinoro, through every town and center in the provinces of Forlì and Ravenna, destroying and burning the headquarters of every socialist and communist organization. "It was a terrible night. Huge columns of fire and smoke marked our passage. The entire plain of the Romagna all the way up to the hills was subjected to the exasperated reprisal of the fascists, who had decided to end the red terror once and for all," wrote Balbo.

Resistance was minimal. "Countless episodes. Clashes with the bolshevik rabble, in open resistance, none." The leaders had all fled. The leagues, the socialist circles, the cooperatives were all semi-abandoned. Although Balbo claimed that "we often had to face the resistance of the armed forces," the military did little more than threaten. Balbo himself gives an example. Along the provincial road from Cesena, he encountered a road block—an armored car. "Fire if you have the courage," Balbo yelled at the officer in charge. The Blackshirts then drove around the car, which had not completely blocked the highway, and proceeded on their way. "Not a shot was fired." In the morning, Balbo returned to Ravenna and gave the order to demobilize. "Endless parade of cyclists. Sultry weather. Dust. We pay for the work of the past few days. But I am pleased with the Ferrarese squads. Not a single infraction of discipline. Everyone gives beyond his powers."[52]

Balbo's campaign affected the political situation in ways that he probably did not anticipate. The violence put an end to Facta's negotiations, and it spurred the socialists to call a nationwide protest strike. For the socialists, the walkout on July 31 proved to be suicidal—"our Caporetto," as they themselves acknowledged. Few obeyed the strike, and the fascists seized the opportunity to extend their control. Major cities, including Milan, Genoa, Leghorn, and Ancona, now came under fascist rule. One of the few cities to withstand the fascist assault was the socialist stronghold of Parma. The city's resistance meant little politically, but it provided a real military test for Balbo's squads: "For the first time, fascism faced an organized and seasoned enemy, armed and equipped and determined to resist to the end."[53] All the most prominent leaders of "terrorist subversion" had gathered there. If they succeeded, "subversives all over Italy would once again raise their heads," Balbo warned.

When Balbo arrived in Parma during the early hours of August 4, a general strike had been going on for three days, which the fascists had been unable to break. Balbo mobilized 10,000 men from seven provinces throughout Northern Italy. With no resistance from the police or the military, he went about occupying the city. The socialists had entrenched themselves in the Oltretorrente, the oldest quarter of the city. Some four hundred well-armed Arditi del Popolo formed the nucleus of the socialist forces, and they were supported by the population. As he had done during his previous occupations, Balbo marched to the prefect's office and presented his demands. Within four hours the workers were to be disarmed, their barricades removed, and their barbed wire, machine guns, and bombs confiscated. Otherwise the fascists would take control from the state, declared Balbo.

The prefect seemed to give in but then attempted a maneuver of his own. He made an agreement with the socialist leadership. The soldiers would enter the working-class areas, where the revolt was concentrated, and confiscate a few token weapons. The fascists would then demobilize. The socialists would have scored a double victory: they would have forced the fascists to leave, and they would have forced the government to deal with them. Moreover, by welcoming the troops the socialists would have made it appear as if the army sympathized with them. Infuriated, Balbo declared that he no longer recognized the prefect's authority; the fascists would not leave, he vowed, until the army had taken control of the city.

The socialists, however, were well entrenched. Repeated fascist attacks on the Oltretorrente failed. Moreover, for once the army appeared ready to fire on the fascists, and Balbo had orders from Bianchi not, under any circumstances, to battle with the army. During the morning of August 5, Balbo personally led a hundred of his best men for an hour and a half in an attempt to break into the city. Sympathetic cavalry officers only pretended to oppose them, and the fascists managed to cross the bridges.[54] At the entrance to the quarter, however, the fascists found a squad of soldiers barring their way. The officer in charge refused to surrender. He would order his men to fire, he told Balbo—then shoot himself. Behind him, "from the rooftops and the windows," the enraged socialists screamed, "Let them by! We'll kill them." Balbo ordered a retreat.

For once, bluffs and the support of the authorities failed, but Balbo refused efforts by the local bishop and others to mediate the dispute. At midnight, the prefect agreed to the fascist demands and turned over authority to the military. Balbo proclaimed victory and ordered the fascists to demobilize. The casualties, according to Balbo, totaled 14 dead and several hundred wounded—mostly fascists; other sources put the total at 39 dead and 150 wounded.[55] In a political sense Balbo had won again, but militarily his Blackshirts had been checked. The socialists agreed to lay down their arms, but only after the army had brought up two cannons and fired a first round into the Oltretorrente. As Balbo left the city on the afternoon of August 6, "the subversives gave me a military farewell by firing their pistols at my car in front of the hotel."[56]

By fiat, Balbo turned defeat into victory. He plastered the city with posters explaining why the fascists had triumphed.[57] He also treated his troops to a ceremonial victory parade. Yet Balbo knew that this rang hollow and that explanations were in order. In his diary, in passages that Mussolini ordered him to strike, he alternately praised his enemies for their valor and denigrated them for their underhanded tactics.[58] To avoid dealing with Balbo's embarrassment, *Il Balilla* did not appear for three days. Finally, Balbo plotted a rematch; only the March on Rome interrupted his plans.

Meanwhile, he went directly from Parma to Ancona, where workers were reportedly still holding out against the fascists. By the time he had arrived, however, even that resistance had ceased. All spring Balbo had been asking himself, "Has the moment for the general insurrection arrived?" At this point even some of fascism's enemies favored a fascist government, if only for the sake of peace, Balbo remarked.[59] But how should the fascists take power? Mussolini's parliamentary maneuvers provided one relatively safe and unglamorous avenue. However, in joining the parliamentary game the fascists risked being co-opted. Balbo favored a more drastic alternative—one that carried higher risks but also provided opportunities for greater glory and greater revolutionary potential. After the experiences of Bologna, Ravenna, and Parma, his Blackshirt legions were ready, he claimed. They only awaited their orders to march on Rome.

Chapter Five

Quadrumvir: The March on Rome

The March on Rome, like so many of fascism's other "milestones" and "achievements," was misnamed. The Eternal City never succumbed to the tramping feet of Blackshirt legions. The fascists did not seize power; they came to it by royal invitation when Mussolini accepted the king's offer to form a new government. If there was a march on Rome it was the parade through the city on October 30, 1922, when Mussolini and the king reviewed a display of Blackshirts—and anyone else who felt like joining in. "A carnival-like procession . . . a parade of youths sure of the garlands and kisses given to heroes, without any fear of having to fight for them," observed a foreign journalist. "We heard these holiday-making history-makers singing on far into the night."[1]

In many ways, Balbo had made all this possible. The March on Rome—as Grandi pointed out—was largely a continuation of the mass mobilizations and sieges that Balbo had directed so successfully against the provincial capitals.[2] Of course, this siege was on a larger scale and for larger stakes. This time the mobilization was nationwide; this time the prize was not a provincial capital but Rome itself. This time the issue was not one of labor organizations or removing the local prefect; it was nothing less than control of the national government. Nevertheless, the fascist strategy remained the same: bluff. They threatened to occupy the capital and negotiated—hoping fervently that the military and the police would not be called out. Once again the government backed down. The king preferred accepting Mussolini to risking a civil war. An old prelate who had watched the Italian army claim the city from the papacy fifty-two years earlier observed contemptuously, "We in 1870 defended Rome better."[3]

Such were the realities of the March on Rome. Mussolini accepted them. In retrospect, he claimed that the march was an insurrection that failed to end in a genuine revolution.[4] Bottai agreed. The March on Rome, in his view, began as little more than a catchphrase to unite the various factions within fascism.[5] Only after the failure of the socialist general strike in August of 1922 did the phrase become a concrete program. By then fascism no longer needed to conquer power, but only to assume political responsibility. Balbo, however, differed vigorously. In his *Diario 1922*, he claimed that from the beginning fascism was destined to seize power and this seizure was both integral and revolutionary. "Integral: that is, without compromises and encompassing all of Italian public life. Revolutionary: that is, with a violent insurrectional act, that marked a sharp break, an abyss, between the past and the future."[6] Such a radical interpretation appears to be a product more of Balbo's romantic imagination than of his experiences. His argument flies in the face of the facts, including those recorded in his diary. What makes that book lively reading is precisely the uncertainty of it all: can such a madcap adventure as the March on Rome succeed? the reader asks himself.

Why, then, did Balbo make such claims? In part, the book reflects its moment of publication, during the *Decennale* celebrations of 1932; in part, the interpretation gave Balbo and his squads full credit for their role, justified and vindicated their sacrifices, answered the charge that the fascist accession to power was nothing more than the usual parliamentary shuffle. In calling the March an insurrection and a revolution, Balbo was describing the event as he experienced it. As one of the *quadrumvirs* responsible for the military aspect of the march, he knew little about the backstairs intrigues; during the March, communications between Rome and the Blackshirt forces were almost nonexistent. Finally, Balbo's interpretation was a declaration of faith, a statement of how the March should have been. For him, fascism could not come to power by "the servant's entrance," through a series of ignominious intrigues; his fascism, as an authentically revolutionary movement, had to seize power.[7]

In practice, there were definite limits to his notion of "seizure." Most likely, he neither anticipated nor desired a real March on Rome—a full-scale military operation that would pit his Blackshirts against the regular army.[8] Despite his confident reports about the readiness of his troops, he probably had no illusions about the outcome of such a confrontation. But such a clash would not be necessary. The army was already in sympathy with fascism's ideals. The more powerful the Blackshirt army, the more the regular troops would respect them and the more reluctant the troops would be to precipitate a clash that could develop into civil war. In Balbo's mind, his army served another purpose: as a symbol that fascism was to be taken seriously, that the fascists would not be bought off with another ministerial reshuffling. For these reasons, in the period between the collapse of the socialist general strike at the beginning of August and the March on Rome at the end of October, he strengthened his forces and pushed for a "radical" solution to the political crisis. His efforts paid off. Mussolini became not simply a minister in another ministry, but prime minister. He owed this in part to his own political gifts, but also to Balbo's determination and to his Blackshirts.

The catastrophic defeat of the socialist general strike opened the way to Rome for the fascists. Their accession to power, however, was far from inevitable and they faced a host of pressures.[9] The entire fascist organization— political, labor, military—had to be kept occupied and financed. Subsidies or extortions from landowners and businessmen no longer sufficed. Only the state could provide such resources. Another major problem was maintaining peace and harmony within the organizations. Agricultural laborers and landowners were at loggerheads. Without sieges and marches to occupy them, the thousands of Blackshirts became restive. Rival organizations such as the Nationalists challenged the fascists. In Taranto and Genoa, for example, Blackshirts and Blueshirts came to blows. Even the fascist grip on Northern Italy was not secure. Balbo's occupations of Ravenna and Parma concluded in "peace pacts" that threatened to break down at any moment. While the fascists had little to fear immediately from the govern-

ment in Rome, autumn would herald the return of a powerful
government under Giolitti, a government that would not hesitate
to use force. Mussolini's goal was to block or at least delay Giolitti's return. Through the end of the summer and the beginning
of the fall, Mussolini negotiated brilliantly. Liberal politicians in
and out of office, the Vatican, the Freemasons, D'Annunzio, the
monarchy—Mussolini cajoled and threatened them all. Meanwhile, he strengthened his military force, though he preferred
never to use it. His fondest hope was for everything to happen "as
if" a March on Rome had taken place.[10]

Balbo had very little to do with Mussolini's negotiations in
Rome. "We know that the Chief is maneuvering with his characteristic energy and ability."[11] "Nobody knows exactly what will
happen," but he was satisfied that "we haven't locked ourselves
into rigid programs." In any case, Balbo's primary goal was insurrection. For about a year he had been building and training his
armies with that aim in mind. He was not about to be cheated of
his supreme moment. "But the moment of insurrection is inevitable. The insurrection is now underway. It is in the air. For my
part, I am convinced that the decisive moment is not far off."[12] To
colleagues such as Grandi, who argued that the means and ends
no longer corresponded, that insurrection was not necessary in
the current political situation, Balbo replied furiously that he no
longer recognized the "revolutionary" in Grandi.[13]

Balbo's absence from the political negotiations in Rome was not
entirely voluntary. Partly by temperament, partly out of a desire
to keep all options open, Mussolini confided his thoughts and
plans to very few of his intimates. In his diary, Balbo revelled in
his closeness to Mussolini, boasting of having received an autographed picture. The inscription, "To my fraternal friend Italo
Balbo, magnificent commander of the Fascist Militia, in expectation of the Supreme March! With admiration," was indeed remarkable, for Mussolini never wrote "with admiration" on his
dedications.[14] However, Balbo was rarely privy to Mussolini's
plans. Even when Mussolini's secretiveness had consequences
embarrassing to Balbo, he apparently did not complain. For example, on October 4, shortly after a September 29 meeting in
which Mussolini discussed insurrection plans with Balbo, Blackshirts occupied Bolzano and Trento. Despite Balbo's position as

one of the triumvirate that headed the fascist armed forces, he "learned the news from the papers."[15] His fellow triumvirs De Bono and De Vecchi protested violently that they had been kept in the dark. "This is not the way to make war nor even revolution," De Bono grumbled.[16] Balbo merely dismissed the incident as excessive zeal on the part of the squads. When the moment came, they would show the proper discipline, he declared confidently. In another case, Balbo knew nothing of an agreement that Mussolini had made with the former prime minister, Nitti, in which he was to give a speech that would prepare the way for a government crisis. Unaware of the understanding, Balbo noted in his diary that even Nitti was becoming more reasonable in his attitudes toward fascism, even though the "old pirate" had nothing to expect from them except a "firing squad."[17]

Rather than fret about such intrigues, throughout the crucial two months that preceded the March on Rome Balbo devoted himself to strengthening the organization, discipline, and armament of the squads. He fretted about the status of the occupations he had carried out at the beginning of the summer, especially Parma, and he planned further operations. "For my part, I have only one proposition: dare everything," he declared.[18]

His first task was to reorganize the fascist militia. At a meeting on August 13, the leaders of the party met to discuss the political situation following the collapse of the socialist strike. Balbo, like the others, rejoiced over the fascist triumphs, but he declared himself worried about "isolated actions," about the poor coordination among the various military and political units.[19] The party needed a far more unified and centralized command structure. The system of zone inspectors that he had created in January was no longer adequate, he felt.

Almost immediately he was assigned the task of creating a new general command of the militia. He was to nominate two others to serve with him as commanders. Cesare Maria De Vecchi (1884–1959), the fascist boss of Turin, was his first choice and posed no political difficulties. A dozen years older than Balbo, De Vecchi sported a shaven bullet head and fierce mustachios. He had joined the cause of fascism in 1919, after having earned a distinguished war record—a record that later earned him the title of "di Val Cismon." He was a clerico-monarchist who, throughout

his subsequent career as colonial governor and minister to the
Holy See, maintained close ties with the royal family. The wits of
the day summed up De Vecchi's chief defect: "He was a child
prodigy; at five he thought the way he does now."[20]

The third member of the triumvir posed greater difficulties.
Balbo probably would have preferred Attilio Teruzzi, but he was
already vice secretary of the party, a job that included acting as
liaison between the party and the squads. Another prime candidate was General Gandolfo, who had collaborated in drawing up
the first set of regulations for the militia, but illness and family
problems made him unsuitable. No other satisfactory candidates
came to mind, until quite casually that day a member of the
Milanese *fascio* suggested Emilio De Bono (1866–1944). Thirty
years older than Balbo, De Bono was a career officer and a veteran of both the Italo-Turkish war and World War I. Although
during this latter conflict he served as a brigade commander,
fought on the Grappa, and was decorated for his valor, De Bono
became known as the composer of the popular "Songs of the
Monte Grappa" rather than as a military hero. Bored and disappointed with his career, for two years after the war De Bono
dallied with political possibilities ranging from the Fiume expedition to the Popolari and the socialists. Then, impressed by Mussolini, he settled on fascism.

For the fascists, De Bono's chief assets were his prestige as a
general and his monarchist ties. During World War I, he had
developed good relations with the ambitious Emmanuel Philibert, Duke of Aosta, cousin to King Victor Emmanuel III and a
favorite fascist candidate to replace him. Beyond these connections, the thin, balding, white-bearded De Bono offered very
little. Balbo's enthusiastic portrait of him in the *Diario* is, to say
the least, idealized: "Open, brilliant. He has a particular, unique
charm that conquers immediately. A fresh spirit, rich with inci-
sive wit. A broad vision of life, an iron memory; he breathes
energy and humanity."[21]

With the triumvirate chosen, the next task was to draw up a
new set of regulations for the militia. The main difficulty with the
set promulgated the previous January was lack of clear lines of
authority between the political and the military organs of the
party. Discipline also "often leaves much to be desired," Balbo

commented.[22] At a meeting on September 15 at Torre Pellice, De Vecchi and De Bono drafted new regulations. Despite his interest in the matter, Balbo missed the meeting. He was far too busy quelling the dissident factions in Ferrara.

The regulations, finally published on October 12, made no difference from a military standpoint. As the occupation of Trento and Bolzano—the first major test of the new guidelines—proved, the militia's activities did not become better planned and coordinated. Nor, during the March on Rome a few weeks later, did the fascist command show any more unity. The real importance of the regulations was political and became evident in the code of conduct.[23] Mussolini, who had been negotiating with Giolitti and Facta, first published the code in the *Popolo d'Italia* on October 3. The code's turgid rhetoric—the work of De Bono—about the fascist militiaman serving Italy "with his spirit pervaded by a profound mysticism, supported by an unshakeable faith and dominated by an inflexible will" meant very little.[24] It was less easy to ignore the militiaman's oath "to devote himself to the well-being of Italy." This was Balbo's work and it carried overtones—according to Mussolini—of Mazzini and the Risorgimento.[25] Even more important was the absence of any reference to the king or the state. The militiaman's obedience was to his commander and to the party and its leader. Officially and unequivocally, the fascists were announcing that they had created their own private army that rivalled that of the state. That declaration, coupled with the occupation of Trento and Bolzano, dealt a last blow to the prestige of the government in Rome. Their only reaction was to consider disciplining De Bono for having participated in drawing up the militia regulations.

On October 6, Mussolini summoned Balbo to Milan. "The conversation I had with him will remain indelible in my memory. I felt my soul vibrate in harmony with his," rhapsodized Balbo in his diary.[26] Mussolini questioned him closely about the possibility of success in case of a military action against Rome. "He did not want general assurances, but precise information, accurate details." Technical aspects of the operation absorbed them: the number and quality of the men, their leaders, their armaments. One of Balbo's main concerns was the uncertain situation in Parma, the last major anti-fascist stronghold in the Po Valley. In a letter to Balbo of September 25 and at a meeting of the party directorate four days later, Mussolini agreed that the problem of Parma had to be resolved before any action against Rome would be possible.

Accordingly, for the next five days, October 7 to 11, Balbo retired to plan a second operation against Parma. He made his headquarters in a farmhouse five kilometers from Borgo San Donnino, a place known today as Fidenza.[27] During these days of seclusion, Balbo met with provisional leaders from Parma, Piacenza, Mantova, Reggio Emilia, and Bologna, and drew up a military plan. In a letter written late at night on October 9, Balbo partially outlined his strategy.[28] The operation, which was to involve two thousand men, was to begin at midnight, October 14. It would end—after old people, women, and children had been evacuated—with the "clearing out of old Parma and flames that would reach to the sky."[29] From Mussolini, Balbo requested supporting propaganda—stories in the *Popolo d'Italia* and other local newspapers about the vicious anti-fascist activity in the city.

Balbo, who never missed an opportunity for adventure, based his plans on firsthand information. "Suitably disguised, I enjoyed the thrill of living for a few hours in their lair," he wrote to Mussolini.[30] A mixture of fear and "thuggish defiance" pervaded the working-class quarters, he claimed. Anti-fascist sentiment ran so strong that anyone who appeared "decently dressed," that is, in middle-class clothes, ran the risk of being beaten. Rumors swirled about the city that the fascists would return and would kill women and children, Balbo noted angrily.

He prepared in detail for the battle of Parma, down to the text of the manifesto demanding that the enemy surrender.[31] Then, abruptly, on October 11, Mussolini gave orders to suspend the operation and to meet in Milan the following Monday, October 16. He called off the Parma operation partly because of its risks. Success—destruction of the working-class quarter—might bring a backlash; failure might encourage fascism's enemies. More important, Mussolini decided that the time for action had come.[32] On the whole, he judged, the political ground had been prepared. On October 6, he had consulted with Balbo about the indiscipline of the squads. However, to improve them substantially would take a long time, and time was running out.

This was Mussolini's position at the meeting on October 16. Those present included the military triumvirate of Balbo, De Bono, and De Vecchi; also attending were generals Gustavo Fara and Sante Ceccherini, and Ulisse Igliori, the head of the Roman fascists. The presence of two other generals infuriated De Bono, who was sensitive to issues of rank and precedence, and he threatened to leave the meeting. Balbo, who cared nothing for Fara and Ceccherini, calmed De Bono so that the meeting could proceed.[33] As the most junior member, he had the "honor" of keeping the minutes. In a "very clear" exposition, Mussolini declared that at any moment fascism might be forced to begin its insurrection. This would lead to a march on Rome and an occupation of the city. The goal was to force the government to relinquish its powers and to induce the Crown to appoint a fascist government. A purely parliamentary solution was "contrary to the spirit and the interests of fascism."[34] The negotiations in Rome had been mere diversions both for public opinion and for the government. Now was the time for action. On October 21, Mussolini proposed, the party would transfer its powers to a quadrumvirate—the three military triumvirs and the party secretary, Bianchi. Fascist forces would then overwhelm Turin and Milan and move down the Po Valley from Piacenza to Rimini. Three armies would mass at Orte, Civitavecchia, and Ancona for the assault on the capital. In the meantime the party would hold its meeting in Naples on October 24 and present its demands to the government. Were the fascist forces ready, materially and morally, for their mission?

De Bono and De Vecchi, supported by Fara and Ceccherini, replied negatively. De Vecchi proved especially vehement. The troops were not at all prepared, he declared, and he favored postponing the action for a month. Balbo and Bianchi seconded Mussolini. Balbo pressed for action as soon as possible. Any temporizing would be "very dangerous." Fascism ran the risk of bogging down in the parliamentary swamp in Rome. "I believe that if we do not attempt the coup d'état now, in the spring it may be too late." A new, more energetic government might easily take stiff police measures and turn the army against the fascists. Now was the moment, while the fascists could still take advantage of the element of surprise. "No one believes seriously in our insurrectionary intentions." In six months the problems would be "ten times worse." Fascist military preparations might be more complete, but so would those of the enemy. The legions of Emilia were perfectly organized and filled with a "magnificent offensive spirit." Balbo personally guaranteed their fighting efficiency, including their armaments. The Tuscan legions were more restless, but they too were ready for action. These legions, ready and battle-tested in the various mobilizations, would form the heart of the fascist forces. The legions from other areas, too, would turn out better than anticipated, Balbo declared. "In conclusion: act, and act now"—so Balbo ended his statement.

Bianchi supported Balbo and Mussolini. According to Balbo's account, Mussolini carried the day without further opposition from De Bono and De Vecchi. However, in deference to their objections, the Duce compromised. He agreed to postpone setting the exact date of the insurrection until the meeting in Naples the following week.

Two days later, on October 18, Balbo, De Bono, and De Vecchi met at Bordighera, a seaside resort not far from the French border. They posed as vacationers seeking rest and sun; in reality they were drawing up final plans for the insurrection. "From dawn to dusk" they examined, region by region, the state of their forces; they designated commanders for the columns that were to march on Rome; they selected leaders for the lesser units. The choice was not easy, Balbo noted, because they carried their files in their heads. "Fortunately, I have an iron memory that astonishes my friends," and that made their task easier, he wrote.[35]

Probably De Bono and De Vecchi had their own reasons for choosing Bordighera.[36] The Queen Mother was there. She was known for her fascist sympathies and De Bono and De Vecchi, who opposed a march on Rome, wanted to sound her out about other possible solutions. The Queen Mother invited the three fascist leaders to lunch, most likely at De Vecchi's request. Balbo declined. He had nothing to wear other than his "little gray suit," which was not fit for the royal presence.[37]

His reputation as a republican might have been more pertinent, but Balbo appears no less admiring, deferential, and sentimental toward the queen than his monarchist colleagues. "We all know the high and vibrant patriotism of the old queen, whose charm has enchanted the poets."[38] With her "sensitive intelligence, rich with intuition," she undoubtedly had understood the purpose of the fascist gathering. However, she said nothing directly—so far as Balbo knew. Balbo, the fiery republican, concluded, "This episode ennobles our work and gives a sort of poetic aura to our spirits." Moreover, two months earlier he had made clear in his diary that so far as he was concerned, the monarchy was not an issue for fascism. "Even the stones know today that fascism's republican tendency is an ideal aspiration which ties our movement to the great currents of the Risorgimento, but practically does not constitute an obstacle to our actions."[39] His decision not to visit the queen, then, had little to do with modest gray suits or principles. He probably understood that his colleagues could cultivate the sympathy of the monarchy better if he were not present, and royal favor was essential to fascist success.

During the ten days that preceded the March on Rome, Balbo was in constant motion. There was nothing new about this state of affairs: "For two months now I've been spinning like a top. My regular bed is on the train seats." He had to call on all his strength, he admitted, "but my nerves are solid."[40] Nor, at this crucial juncture, could his pace slacken.

Military problems occupied Balbo's visits to Florence on October 20 and 21 and to Perugia the following day. In Florence, together with the other *quadrumvirs* and the fascist deputy, Giovanni Giuriati, he instructed the other zone commanders. They were to put aside all political issues and to concentrate on their military tasks. Balbo was particularly concerned about the fourth zone, which comprised Italy's eastern borders (Venezia, Treviso, Udine, Trieste, Pola). During the insurrection, he feared, the Yugoslavs might take the opportunity to advance on Fiume. Worried about keeping the real purpose of their meeting secret, the *quadrumvirs* issued a statement to the press that they were drawing up plans to maintain order and discipline at the Congress in Naples. "There is some alarm over Naples. But in general it is believed that fascism is concerned only with making a grand political demonstration at the Congress," Balbo noted with satisfaction.[41]

The following day, in Perugia, he reviewed a rally of 10,000 fascists and administered the oath to the new inductees in the legion. "I review the squads: superb. Umbrian fascism, with its fervor and dash, resembles that of Emilia. First-rate people."[42] But the city was important for more than simply its legion. After informing himself about local political sympathies and the strength of government forces, Balbo became convinced that Perugia would make an ideal headquarters for the *quadrumvir*s during the insurrection. He even fixed on a location: the Hotel Brufani. Too late, Balbo realized that his choice was a poor one. The city was not on a major rail line. Access roads were long and tortuous. Telephone and telegraph lines were very limited. With such bad communications, during the march, Balbo and his *quadrumvir*s seldom knew what was happening outside the city.

The following day, Balbo was in Rome at party headquarters caught up in the flow of dispatches, orders, messages, letters. "This eve seems interminable," he noted restlessly.[43] But at last, on the evening of the twenty-third, he boarded the crowded train for Naples with De Bono and De Vecchi. "It seems as if all Italy is heading for the Parthenopeian metropolis. The station in Rome is flooded with Blackshirts."[44] For the first time, the three generals showed off their uniforms as militia commanders—black shirt with rank on the sleeve: an eagle with three stars. "I wear my trousers from the war and around the waist the sash which the women of Molinella gave me, on which a mill is embroidered," Balbo wrote. The sash also bore a motto derived from the revolutionary French *Ça ira:* "today the mill grinds events for the future." The uniform, admittedly "a bit theatrical," became the butt of some good-natured teasing. As they had all learned during the war, Balbo replied, a uniform was a symbol of order, organization, hierarchy—necessary conditions if the fascists were to succeed. "Revolutions cannot be made with improvisation and disorder: our fascists need to be convinced of this and they have to become accustomed to looking at reality with different eyes."[45]

In Naples, an honor guard and a band greeted them, and then the *quadrumvir*s rushed off to the Hotel Excelsior to continue their planning. The problems seemed both endless and urgent. Could the fascist railway workers command the railway lines? The logistics for the columns massing for the March on Rome had to be worked out to avoid any "ravaging and looting, which unfortunately are quite frequent during revolutionary periods and ruin the most sacred causes."[46]

"I will not write anything about the gathering today, because it belongs to history," Balbo noted for the following day, October 24.[47] "Triumphant day for Mussolini, who felt the soul of the whole nation vibrate around him. He has pronounced the fateful words that will decide the destiny of our movement. He can do what he pleases with the fascists." The day had been a good one for Mussolini. In the morning, at the San Carlo Opera House, he gave a well-crafted speech. He was careful not to alienate the conservative Southerners who knew little of fascism. He also avoided offending two vital institutions that could block his way to power: the monarchy and the army. At the same time, he fueled the excitement and fervor of the thousands of Blackshirts, who sensed that they were on the eve of revolution. Fascism had sought a peaceful political solution: five portfolios in a new government, including the foreign ministry. The Liberal politicians had made absurd counteroffers, about ministers without portfolios and about subportfolios, sneered Mussolini. Luigi Facta had forced the fascists to consider the use of force. A peaceful solution was still possible for those who truly wanted peace, but not for those who threatened the fascists or the nation.

Following the speech, thousands of *squadristi* gathered in Piazza del Plebiscito to swear allegiance to Mussolini "to the death." From his position on the speaker's platform, Balbo watched the milling crowd and reflected that with a nod Mussolini could have launched them toward Rome: "What force could have held them back?" Leaving the platform, Balbo joined his comrades from Emilia and led them in chanting "Ro-ma, Ro-ma." "Very soon the whole piazza repeated the great word. Enormous effect. Throbbing of a multitude. Supreme expression of the will of a people."[48]

The question still remained: when would the order be given for the insurrection? When would the mobilization begin? That evening the matter was decided at last.[49] At the Hotel Vesuvio, Mussolini presided over a meeting of the *quadrumvirs* and the three party vice secretaries, Attilio Teruzzi, Giuseppe Bastianini, and Achille Starace. As he had at the crucial October 16 meeting in Milan, Balbo kept the minutes—a few notes on telegraph

forms. Within seventy-two hours, at midnight between October
26 and 27, the party would yield its powers to the quadrumvirate
and the insurrection would be launched, he noted. The goal of
the movement: a government with at least six fascist ministers in
the most important cabinet posts.

According to Balbo's notes, this was to be achieved in three
major stages. First would come the mobilization and occupation
of public offices in the major cities of the north. The mobilization
would begin clandestinely on the twenty-seventh and openly on
the twenty-eighth. With the northern cities conquered on the
twenty-eighth would come the second stage on the same day:
concentration of the Blackshirt forces at Santa Marinella, Monterotondo, and Tivoli. Balbo's notes indicate that all efforts were
to be dedicated to strengthening the columns. In case of an easy
victory in the occupations of the northern cities, the fascists were
to leave only a minimal force behind and send the rest to rein-
force the columns pointed toward Rome; in case of serious resistance, the fascist forces should not truly engage the army, but
should rush to support the columns surrounding Rome. On the
morning of the twenty-eighth, the plan was for a synchronized
march of three columns on the capital. That same morning the
quadrumvirs would issue their proclamation from Perugia, demanding that the government in Rome give up its powers to the
fascists. In case of armed resistance, the fascists were to avoid
engaging the army. They were to show sympathy and respect for
the troops whenever possible. However, the squads were ordered
to refuse aid from friendly regiments. In any case, the squads
were "not to yield before any opposition" and were to reach
Rome "at all costs." To secure a supply of arms, the *quadrumvirs*
had singled out two or three deposits that could be taken quickly,
and the fascists could always disarm small detachments of *carabinieri* in the countryside. As of Saturday, all work was to cease
throughout Italy; during the days of the insurrection, the cities
were to be decorated with flags. Special precautions were to be
taken along the eastern frontier to guard against any sudden move
by the Yugoslavs. Balbo noted that he would provide a unit of
arditi who would operate as terrorists. If Rome resisted the
Blackshirt invasion, his special unit would sow panic in the city.
The meeting ended, Balbo noted, "without ceremony, with a few

blunt sentences by Mussolini. Everyone leaves giving the Roman salute in silence. But their eyes sparkle."[50]

Balbo's sketchy minutes suggest that the *quadrumvirs'* eyes sparkled less from excitement and anticipation than from hallucinations. On the train to Naples, Balbo had solemnly reminded his comrades of the seriousness of their venture. Yet the military plan that he and his fellow *quadrumvirs* had drawn up was as theatrical as his militia general's uniform.[51] In essence, the fascist military plan amounted to a series of stage directions by which Mussolini and the Blackshirts could make a grand entrance into Rome. The plan's basic premise was that the government would not put up a fight; if there was any resistance, it was somehow to be treated as if it did not exist. The possibility of defeat was not even considered in Balbo's notes. The question of arms was mentioned only casually. Other accounts of the meeting do not change the picture substantially. One summary considers the possibility of a military defeat: in that case, the fascist forces were to retire to strongholds in Central Italy, form a government there, reassemble their troops in the Val Padana, and once again march on the capital. But such an option was absurd. Government forces were stationed everywhere—not only in Rome. If the government intended to put up serious resistance, Central Italy was no more secure than the capital.

For Mussolini and some of Balbo's colleagues, the absurdities of the military plan were irrelevant. Mussolini counted on the threat of the squads rather than on their real military capabilities. He and Bianchi hoped to win the battle in parliament. De Vecchi, the ardent monarchist, worked feverishly behind the scenes to avoid a military clash. He hoped that the fascist mobilization would pressure the king to intervene and form a new government that included the fascists. Balbo appeared unconcerned about the shortcomings of the military plan. His *Diario* is devoid of critique. "The army does not worry us. It is much more ours than Soleri's [the war minister]," he wrote.[52] He also claimed to have a contact inside the ministry who would advise him of the army's plans.[53] As he had done in the provincial capitals, he would seize a few police stations or prefectures, occupy some telephone and telegraph offices, and force the government's hand again. Faced with his bluff, his ingenuity, his daring, the army and the authori-

ties would not risk a fight. Before that most invincible of weapons, the fascist spirit, Rome, too, would fall. So he concluded—at
least in retrospect. Those who accused the Facta government of
cowardice in surrendering to the Blackshirts had "very little understanding of the nature of the fight," Balbo wrote five years
later.[54] Critics underestimated the material forces of the Blackshirts, "but most of all they ignored the moral elements of the
revolt, over which arms and soldiers could have only a relative
hold," he concluded.

Grandi found Balbo the following day at the Hotel Excelsior
"euphoric, smiling, surrounded by his usual group of trusted
friends."[55] During a private moment in Grandi's hotel room,
Balbo flopped exuberantly on the bed and declared, "The insurrection has been decided. *Decided,* you understand?" Grandi,
whose revolutionary stance had moderated considerably during
the previous year, was shocked. He listened patiently to Balbo's
account of the meeting the evening before and asked again
whether Mussolini was really in agreement. Balbo regarded him
with surprise. "Certainly Mussolini is in agreement. The insurrection is now decided. Mussolini wants it, finally he wants it.
His goal is the conquest of power with a government that will
have at least six fascist ministers in the most important posts."
All this was madness, Grandi interrupted; no one risked an insurrection for the sake of six cabinet posts. "I don't recognize
you any more. Parliament has really contaminated you," Balbo
replied contemptuously.

Balbo's enthusiasm was fortunate, for the fascists possessed
little else. They were badly outnumbered, poorly equipped, and,
as Balbo acknowledged, miserably financed. Claims of fascist
manpower vary.[56] The king claimed after World War II that he
had been told the fascists numbered 100,000. Against them,
Rome could count on only 5,000 to 8,000 police and troops. Only
later did Mussolini admit to the king that total fascist strength
numbered 30,000. Even that figure appears optimistic; about
26,000 is probably closer to the truth. The government could
count on 28,000 troops, and police and reservists had applied to
assist in the defense of Rome. The fascists' rivals, the Nationalists,
had called out their own Blueshirts, 4,000 strong, and placed
them at the disposal of the authorities. For the most part the

Blackshirts were armed with nothing more than pistols, rifles, and clubs. On the morning of the twenty-eighth, when the march on the capital was to begin, about 9,000 men had joined the three columns, but only two of these, with 5,000 men between them, had reached their assembly points at Tivoli and Monterotondo. The third column was blocked at Civitavecchia. Meanwhile rain poured down on the Blackshirts; food, shelter, transport were all lacking.

The insurrection in the northern cities did not go well for the fascists, either. Turin, Genoa, and even Bologna, supposedly a fascist stronghold, were firmly under military control. In Milan the military commander was notoriously pro-fascist, and the prefect, still hoping to arrange an agreement between Mussolini and Giolitti, had ignored his strict orders from Rome to act against the Blackshirts. Nevertheless, the city was not in fascist hands. Mussolini left his barricaded office at the *Popolo d'Italia* only with the tolerance of the army. In Rome the government remained in full control. Barbed wire blocked bridges and other key points. The public buildings and the royal residence were under heavy guard. The office of the Roman *fascio* had been occupied and searched.

Balbo knew only fragments of all this. During the days of the insurrection, he formed part of a "supreme command" that commanded very little.[57] On the twenty-fifth the *quadrumvirs* gathered at the *fascio* in Naples to give orders for the clandestine mobilization of the twenty-seventh and to disperse the available funds to the zone commanders. Each one received 25,000 lire (about 5,000 pre-war dollars) for the expenses of mobilization—a small sum for the enormous task of transporting thousands of Blackshirts to within a day's march of Rome.[58] "Will power will make up for it," Balbo declared.[59] The Congress was held before a semi-deserted hall, with Bianchi presiding impatiently. As Balbo noted, the farce of the Congress had to continue at least through the twenty-sixth. "Only in this way will we be able to mislead the government and public opinion."[60] Meanwhile the fascists, thanks to their contacts inside the war ministry, learned that the government was mobilizing very slowly.

On the twenty-sixth Balbo left for Perugia and the *quadrumvir* headquarters. On the way he stopped in Rome. In Piazza San Claudio, near the party's headquarters, he assembled his secret band of terrorists.[61] They numbered 250, divided into 25 squads. No one, not even the heads of the Roman *fascio*, knew their names or their missions. Armed with bombs of various types and four flame-throwers, their job was to attack, if necessary, the vital centers of government resistance, beginning with the Palazzo Viminale. They were to sow panic and disorder in all the government offices. To protect their secrecy, they were to circulate throughout the city "dressed elegantly" and lodge at the best hotels. More money was necessary to finance them but "here we fight for pennies," Balbo noted; "I do not have a cent in my pockets." The revolution was being financed by promissory notes. The day before, together with De Bono and De Vecchi, he had signed a note for three million lire. That evening Balbo travelled from Rome to Perugia. To evade police surveillance, he and De Bono went to the station separately and then met on the train. "Our beards are too easily recognizable," explained Balbo, and De Bono, in particular, was being carefully watched. On the other hand, Balbo commented, he could not see much reason to keep their movements secret. "Tomorrow all of Italy will know of them."[62]

The twenty-seventh was the day scheduled for clandestine mobilization. While his colleagues directed the local operations in Perugia, Balbo followed developments in the northern cities. The local mobilization went well, "in perfect military style." The news elsewhere was alarming. In Tuscany, especially in Pisa and Florence, the fascists had moved prematurely. The police and the army had been alerted. The road to Florence was blocked. While De Bono and Bianchi remained to direct the mobilization in Perugia, Balbo rushed off to Florence.[63] The weeks of frantic activity had taken their toll on his body: a painful infection had invaded his right ear. Nevertheless, he leaped into a waiting car which had been transformed into "a tank that can move at a fantastic speed." Two machine guns, manned by two fascists, were mounted on the fenders. Through the clear warm night "at crazy speeds," the vehicle roared toward Florence while Balbo cat-napped. Once the car stopped for a government road block. Startled, Balbo awoke. "I ordered the machine gunners to fire . . . four or five meters above the heads of the men. . . . The whistle of the bullets produced the miracle," and the car sped on to Florence.

In the city, everything had gone wrong. The fascists, led by Tullio Tamburini, had taken some army officers prisoner. Blackshirts were about to assault the prefecture, but inside the prefect was hosting a banquet. The guest of honor was Marshal Armando Diaz, the war hero. In the meantime, the fascists had failed in their most elementary missions. They had not even occupied the city's vital points. The railroad station was still open. The postal and telegraph office had been surrounded, but inside the building government troops remained in control.

Balbo took charge. "I personally went to open the door of the room where the army officers had been locked up, shook their hands, and apologized for their treatment."[64] He transformed the assault on the prefecture into a parade and street demonstration in honor of Marshal Diaz. He also ordered the fascist railwaymen at the station to prepare a train that would be at the marshal's disposal. Finally, with Tamburini, Balbo marched into the post office. Backed by his own guards, he ordered the Royal Guards to disperse. "The tone of my voice, my threatening manner, the presence of the fascists induce the Royal Guards to leave without protest."[65] Before racing back through the night to Perugia, Balbo reassured the mayor of fascism's peaceful intentions toward Marshal Diaz, and then telephoned Mussolini in Milan. All was proceeding according to plan, Balbo assured him. On the return trip to Perugia, he rode in a sedan; his ear was too painful for a ride in an open car.

He arrived in Perugia at dawn on October 28, the day of the insurrection. By bicycle, by truck, by car, the Blackshirts had invaded the city. Machine guns guarded the entrance to the Hotel Brufani, and there were sandbags at the windows. Balbo snatched a couple of hours' sleep. In Perugia the insurrection had gone successfully. The prefecture had been occupied without incident, but the Blackshirts had come perilously close to a fight at the post office. So far as anyone knew in Perugia, everything was going according to plan. The columns were forming for the march on the capital.

In the afternoon, Balbo went off to inspect the five thousand reserves gathered at Foligno, which "could represent the decisive card in the revolution."[66] The presence of two generals who had defected to the fascist side—who did not fail to heed the nation's call, as Balbo put it—and a squad of eight hundred Blackshirts from Copparo near Ferrara heartened him. High spirits did not affect his evaluation of the situation: "I realize that the reserve forces are a bit limited." Moreover, "the news that we are receiving about how things are going cannot be said to be excellent, and it appears that the government has decided to put up a fierce resistance," he noted. He gave orders to one of the generals to seize two nearby arms deposits, one at Spoleto and the other at Terni. "But this is very serious!" the general wavered. Nevertheless, with a written order in his pocket, he went off on his mission.

The situation was indeed serious. Yet in Perugia the commanders of the insurrection knew virtually nothing. As Balbo admitted candidly, "We in Perugia are in absolute darkness with regard to the government's intentions." De Vecchi, whose job it was to maintain communications with Rome, returned to Perugia with little more than rumors—"mostly bad news," from the fascist view. The government planned to resist and had stepped up its military preparations. "At headquarters there is much nervousness. We know that not all the fascist leaders until yesterday were committed to action. Some judged it premature; others thought that a parliamentary solution was preferable," Balbo worried in his *Diario*.

What he did not say in the *Diario*—because De Bono and De Vecchi were testifying to the veracity of his account—was that the hesitations and divisions extended to Perugia. De Bono completely lost his nerve and would have fled if Balbo had not locked him in his room.[67] De Vecchi swore while he was alive to the truth of Balbo's *Diario*, but an account by him published posthumously gave a very different version.[68] What he had seen between Rome and Perugia appalled him. In the mud and rain, along the often impassable roads, units of the Blackshirt army, mostly on foot, lurched toward the various staging areas. They were poorly armed, if they were armed at all. These irregular, unpredictable bands, De Vecchi feared, could easily have stumbled into a clash with the army that would have dashed all hope of negotiation. The scene at the Hotel Brufani was no more reassuring. On his return from Rome, De Vecchi found an air more of "nocturnal revels than of soldiers." On the floor, four drunken *squadristi*, surrounded by empty wine bottles and cigarette butts, snored peacefully.

De Vecchi also accused Balbo of thwarting his efforts at a negotiated solution. When De Vecchi received a telephone call from
General Arturo Cittadini, one of the king's military aides, offering
Mussolini a position in a Salandra ministry, Balbo's response was,
"I'll shoot! I'll shoot to the last bullet. I don't make revolutions by
telephone." This was more than bravado. Up to that point, the
army had not intervened and was not likely to do so. Balbo realized that the game was over and the fascists had won. There was
no reason to be satisfied with a few seats in a ministry presided
over by a nonfascist. In the meantime, however, the local garrison threatened to attack the fascists in Perugia. According to
De Vecchi, he convinced the general in charge, an old friend, to
postpone any operation at least until sunset. De Bono was ready
to give in, while Bianchi vacillated and feigned ignorance. Once
again Balbo stood firm. "You go ahead and drop your pants," he
told the others.[69] He would give in only after he had fired his last
bullet. In a rage, De Vecchi left for Rome. Balbo's stubbornness
probably saved the day for the fascists. If word had reached Rome
that the *quadrumvirs* were wavering or ready to surrender, their
bid for power would have failed.

At the request of De Bono and Bianchi, Balbo left to inspect
the column at Monterotondo—one of the three that were poised
for the assault on Rome—and to gather information in the city.
Before leaving, however, he and the other *quadrumvirs* signed a
declaration that they would not lay down their arms before a
government headed by Mussolini had been formed. The purpose
of the declaration was twofold: to indicate that the *quadrumvirs*
were holding firm, and also to pressure Mussolini to hold out for
the prime ministership.

Balbo's inspection tour reassured him that at Monterotondo, at
least, the column was at full strength and efficiency. Nor, despite
the government's security measures, did Balbo have any difficulty
visiting Rome.[70] A pass—procured or faked—signed and stamped
by the ministry of the interior got him past the soldiers and police
at the bridges and even allowed him to drive about the city in a
car. Rome appeared to be in a state of war, he wrote. But the
crucial problem, the political news, remained as vague as ever.
Until late at night the king had continued his consultations. Had
he declared a state of siege or not? The news had been announced
and then denied. But in the city armed patrols, barricades, and

Fig. 8. Balbo *quadrumvir* (second from right) during the March on Rome (October, 1922) (G. Bucciante, ed., *Vita di Balbo*)

barbed wire defended vital points: declared or not, a state of siege
was in force.

Balbo returned to Perugia without incident. On the twenty-
ninth the political situation remained as uncertain as ever. A
passage from the *Diario* that Mussolini suppressed described how
the *quadrumvirs* received a call from Federzoni in Rome.[71] Unless the Blackshirts were demobilized, the king threatened to
abdicate both for himself and for his son, Federzoni told them.
De Vecchi screamed that according to his conversation with the
king the previous evening, Victor Emmanuel had nothing of the
sort in mind. "Here we are again in chaos," observed Balbo. The
quadrumvirs pressed ahead with their military preparations. According to Balbo, the columns massed against Rome now totaled
52,000. De Vecchi and Grandi arrived from Rome with the news
that the political crisis was to be resolved during the day. "Good,"
Balbo noted bravely. "Otherwise . . . today . . . we'll unleash the
columns to march on Rome!"[72] But throughout the day he, like
the other *quadrumvirs*, could do nothing except wait. The air was
heavy with rumors. Doubts about the commitment of allies and
friends preyed on him. For the final assault, the command was to
be shifted to Narni, where they were all to meet at midnight.

Balbo rushed off on another inspection to satisfy himself about
the state of the Blackshirt army. At Foligno again, the site of the
reserve column, he first heard the news: the king had asked
Mussolini to form a government. "A thrill of joy courses through
the fascist squads. Radiant faces, fezes flying, songs of triumph."[73]
With only a few dozen dead, the fascist revolution had ended
"with the most glorious victory."[74] Church bells rang out in Perugia when Balbo returned, and the city "lived one of the greatest
days in its history." Among the fascists, "Evening of victory. Evening of rest."

On the following day, October 30, along the narrow roads
crowded with "thousands and thousands" of fascists, Balbo
headed for Rome. At seven in the evening he reached the city
and went directly to the Hotel Savoia, where Mussolini was staying. "In a room upstairs I find our Chief, surrounded by Bianchi,
De Vecchi, De Bono and many politicians. His face is radiant.
Not even a word. A hug."[75]

Chapter Six

Ras of Ferrara:
The Intransigent

The campaign over, Balbo, like a good soldier, ordered his men to return peacefully to their homes, and he returned to his. In Ferrara a grateful citizenry presented him with a gold dagger.[1] His ear infection continued to torment him. Gaunt and exhausted from the tensions and pressures of the preceding months, he took to his bed for the first half of November.[2] When he recovered, he found himself at loose ends. Mussolini did not ask him to join the government, and it was not clear how Balbo's talents as an organizer and military leader would fit into the new direction fascism was taking.

The March on Rome had apparently swept away the "nest of owls," as Balbo called the Liberal state. Yet, in reality, the "revolution" amounted to little more than a change of ministry. All the traditional institutions of power in Liberal Italy were still in place: the king, the constitution, the army, parliament, the church, industrialists and landowners. Like passengers on a crowded bus, they had made room for a new rider; then the bus continued along its usual route. Such had been the "transformist" tradition in Italian politics ever since the days of Cavour; the Italian ruling classes in 1922 had no reason to assume that matters would develop differently. Optimistic observers even accepted the fascist claim that Italy's body politic would be invigorated by the transfusion of new blood.

For his first eighteen months in office, Mussolini did nothing to dispel the notion that fascism could be woven into the fabric of the state. His cabinets were coalitions in which fascists shared power with their former enemies. He tried to curb violence and he did not abrogate the constitution.

The nation's traditional ruling groups applauded Mussolini's policies; the fascists, for the most part, were appalled. They had marched and fought for a revolution, not for a continuation of the Liberal state. Nevertheless, they divided on what was to be done. As Bottai pointed out, "an atmosphere of passion" held the fascists together; "calm revives their disagreements."[3] The moderates or revisionists attacked Mussolini for failing to create any new, distinctively fascist institutions. The extremists or intransigents spoke ominously of a "second wave" that would culminate in a "real revolution." As they had prior to the March on Rome, they again took matters into their own hands. Despite Mussolini's warnings, the local *ras* led their bored, unemployed squads in crushing the last islands of anti-fascist resistance. For example, in Turin on December 18, 1922, twenty-two workmen were killed during fascist assaults on working-class institutions. In Brescia, the local bishop appealed to Mussolini to stop the violence. The local *ras*, Augusto Turati, replied that in Rome Popolari and fascists might collaborate; in Brescia there was only fascism. Between the March on Rome and the end of 1923, victims of fascist violence totaled about two thousand.[4]

Balbo appeared to fit in with the intransigents. His republican origins, his rise to prominence as the *ras* of Ferrara, his reputation as the most extreme of the *quadrumvirs*, and his position as leader of the militia all suggested that he sided with the extremists. Balbo's stance, however, depended on the context.[5] In his provincial setting, Balbo defended the established order. From the beginning he had allied himself with the *agraria*. Once he had destroyed his enemies, he ruled unchallenged. Personally, he made every effort to join the traditional local political and social establishment—the big landowners and the town bourgeoisie. In 1924 he married the Contessa Florio. His enemies accused him of receiving lavish wedding presents from members of the *agraria* and of later benefiting financially from his association with them. The only intransigent or extreme aspects of Balbo's policies were his methods. Violently, ruthlessly, he destroyed the real subverters of the social order, the socialists and the "dissident fascists."

Viewed from Rome, however, Balbo looked, and sometimes acted, like an intransigent. To maintain his autonomy and his power base, Balbo spoke out for *squadrismo* and for provincial fascism. It was his way of calling attention to himself, of reminding Mussolini who his allies really were, of pressuring the Duce when he appeared too willing to compromise with the king, the army, or the politicians. Mussolini responded with statements like "Whoever touches the militia will get a dose of lead."[6] In practice, to ease fears that he aspired to a dictatorship, he made efforts to encompass the Blackshirts within a regular military organization. Any such transformation of course threatened Balbo's power. Nevertheless, as his role in the militia illustrates, his intransigence had definite limits.

From their inception, the Blackshirt squads and their organizational extension, the militia, served Mussolini as a useful threat when negotiations and compromises failed; but the Blackshirts also posed serious problems. Their loyalties were always uncertain. Nominally they owed allegiance to Mussolini. In practice, they followed their consul or the local *ras*. Mussolini could never be sure that a group of militia commanders, disgruntled with his leadership, might not decide to stage a coup. Then there was the matter of maintenance. One reason for the March on Rome had been to provide for the squads, numbering some 300,000, at public expense.[7] Before the march, only those from the rank of consul upward were on permanent paid service. With the fascist triumph, the junior officers and the rank and file clamored for more permanent positions.

After considerable controversy and compromise, the militia, now known as the Milizia Volontaria per la Sicurezza Nazionale (MVSN), emerged on February 1, 1923.[8] The army welcomed the new force as a relief from security duties, but the militia also became a rival for funds and power. For their part, the militia commanders balked at sacrificing their status, rank, pay, and privileges in any fusion with the army. Balbo himself was appointed a commanding general of the militia. He had the pay and bureaucratic status of the commander of an army corps—no mean feat for one who had risen no higher than lieutenant in the regular army. Naturally, his peers in the regular army resented his meteoric promotion.

At first Balbo's position was not nearly as powerful as the rank suggested.[9] He shared authority with De Bono and De Vecchi. Moreover, De Bono was named first commanding general and sole commander. Yet De Bono, director general of internal security, devoted little time to the militia, and in October of 1923, De Vecchi was appointed governor of Somalia. "Generalissimo" Balbo—as he was sometimes called behind his back—was left in charge. In his uniform of black shirt, gray-green trousers, *ardito*-style jacket with black flame insignias, and the *Alpino* hat (later changed to a fez), he spent much of his time in 1923 and 1924 promoting the organization.

On paper, he headed an impressive force. In 1923 the militia numbered nearly 190,000; in 1924 Balbo tried to increase the organization to 300,000 men. Yet the militia lacked military substance. For example, there were not enough rifles to arm each of the 189,852 men enrolled in August, 1923. The militia also lacked a mission. Most of the men performed security duties. They guarded ports, railways, roads, and post offices and were called out in cases of national disaster. Some four thousand were sent to Libya to help with the reconquest of the colony and a few settled there as colonists. Balbo, when he was appointed as undersecretary to the minister of national economy, occupied some as forest wardens and gamekeepers. Others served as political police at the order of the prefect.

If Balbo had plans to turn the militia to revolutionary purposes or against Mussolini, he kept them well hidden. His position was a unique one. He was still a provincial *ras*, the boss of Ferrara; like the other *ras*, he fought to preserve local autonomy. At the same time, as commander of the militia, he had to support Mussolini and his attempts to centralize his authority. Balbo's oration "Lavoro e milizia per la nuova Italia" (Work and Militia for the New Italy), delivered in Milan on April 21, 1923, just two months after the founding of the militia, gave every indication that he supported Mussolini and the current political and military establishment.[10] In his speech, which was reprinted and widely circulated, Balbo attacked various rumors and suspicions about Mussolini's relationship to the militia. The MVSN was not Mussolini's private army, Balbo argued. If that had been Mussolini's goal, he could easily have followed a Napoleonic model. He could have replaced the regular army with Blackshirts, raided the public treasury to pay them off, and then transformed the heads of the militia into the marshals of Italy. Balbo also tried to dispel rumors about tensions between the militia and the regular army. The regular army's job was to provide the technical means for the nation's defense. The militia was to provide the "granite-like base" of the new state. It was to serve not as a police force but as a spiritual model for the nation, to stimulate a "new military spirit in Italy." A people who wanted to live as a great and powerful nation had to know how to "march in ranks" and live a disciplined life, Balbo proclaimed.

Behind the public declarations, was Balbo planning to turn the militia to his own ends? His enemies charged that he was forever plotting. In practice, he behaved no differently than he had before the March on Rome. In moments of crisis that threatened fascism or the militia—for example, during the Matteotti affair at the end of 1924—he rallied the squads to pressure Mussolini. Beyond that there is no convincing evidence that Balbo sought to replace Mussolini or to stage a coup of his own. On the contrary, at the time of the Matteotti affair rumors flew that Balbo was among those who threatened Mussolini's life if he stepped down. After 1925, Balbo lost interest in the militia, and the MVSN, though officially held in high esteem, degenerated into a weak and discredited organization.

Balbo's real concern was his chronic problems with the dissidents in Ferrara, which the March on Rome had failed to resolve. The program of the dissidents remained a theoretical muddle.[11] Barbato Gattelli hoped for a revived and invigorated Italy under a dictatorship based on a new social hierarchy. Property and wealth would no longer be the dominant values and sources of power; landowners would no longer exploit manual laborers. Thus, the dissident fascists—like the socialists—appeared to champion the agricultural laborers and the workers in small urban enterprises, at the expense of the bourgeoisie. Yet the workers were still to respect and to recognize the superiority of the *uomo di pensiero,* the "man of thought." This meant intellectuals in the ordinary sense, but also bureaucrats who worked for the communal gov-

Fig. 9. Balbo as commander of the fascist militia (Caproni Museum Archive)

ernment or the state, and managers of workshops. How this differed substantially from the present system, Gattelli never made
clear.

If the dissidents were vague in theory, they were precise about
who their enemies were: first, the landowners; second, the fascist
provincial federation—Balbo's seat of power. Arguments alone,
they realized by the spring of 1922, would not change the nature
of fascism in Ferrara. Nor did they have the power to challenge
Balbo directly. Gattelli and Gaggioli, however, knew Mussolini
personally and vowed to keep him informed about local affairs and
to continue their fight as dissidents within the movement.

Balbo dismissed the dissidents as nothing more than a nuisance. "With regard to the situation in Ferrara, it is excellent," he
assured Mussolini in a letter of September 27, 1922, a month
before the March on Rome.[12] Balbo asked only that Mussolini
break all ties with the dissidents. "Once they were completely
isolated, they would be even more dead than they are now. In
any case, they are breathing their last and they do not give
trouble." In his diary, the dissidents are never referred to by
name; their activities are mentioned only obliquely, and Balbo
naturally focused on "unforgettable demonstrations" of fascist
unity and solidarity. Nevertheless, the dissidents probably worried him more than he admitted. Mussolini, he remarked with
admiration, had a talent for inducing his followers to rise above
their local interests and petty jealousies. "He makes us feel that
now there are higher duties incumbent on us."[13]

The dissidents failed to hear this call. During the summer of
1922, a series of grave incidents rocked the province.[14] During
the third week in August, for example, workers in the sugar
refineries rebelled against wage cuts that their fascist union representatives and the employers had agreed upon. Gattelli and Gaetano Ulivi supported the workers and organized a strike. Balbo,
vacationing with his family in Cattolica on the Adriatic, had other
tasks on his mind: the occupations of Ravenna, Ancona, and
Parma, preparations for the long-term goal of seizing Rome; but
an attack on the sugar industry struck at the roots of his power in
Ferrara. He succeeded in preventing the strike and jotted sarcastically in his diary, "That is all we needed—an anarchistic tomfool
of a strike right in Ferrara."[15] That the workers might have had

legitimate grievances apparently did not interest him. On August 27 and 28 the province was on the brink of a bloody conflict, according to reports from the prefect.

To contain the troubles, Balbo contacted Bianchi in Rome and demanded that the party immediately constitute a commission of inquiry.[16] The commission, composed of Cesare Maria De Vecchi, Teruzzi, and Gino Baroncini, issued a report on September 5. Three of the dissidents, Gattelli, Alberto Montanari, and Ulivi, were expelled for "moral incompatibility" (a reference to their keeping mistresses). A fourth, Guido Torti, was expelled for denigrating fascism and for "oblique maneuvers." But the dissidents also got their due. Balbo was formally censured. He had failed in the interests of peace to exercise in full his authority as head of the provincial federation, the commission declared. In addition, the commission agreed that the landowners had been too free to pursue their own economic interests at the expense of the nation. A syndicate of the landowners, over which the party would have authority, should be instituted, recommended the commission.

The inquiry and report failed to resolve the situation. On September 12, a week after the commission report was issued, about a hundred *squadristi* from Copparo descended on Ferrara and beat up the dissidents. In a gun battle between the two groups, three fascists were wounded. The March on Rome temporarily healed the breach. The dissidents, eager to share the glory, put themselves at the disposal of the general command. They were given positions of responsibility in the occupation of Ferrara. The station, the post office, and the law courts were all occupied without incident. Once this had been accomplished, 4,870 *squadristi* headed for Rome and approximately 1,900 for Milan—an effort that temporarily ruined the provincial federation financially.[17]

Triumph in Rome did not make for fascist comradeship in Ferrara. For about eight months after the March on Rome, the dissidents remained active.[18] The glaring fact of the *agraria's* unbridled power in local political and labor matters outraged not only dissidents but also Balbo's closest collaborators. Clamorous resignations marked the spring of 1923. At the end of March the schoolmaster Francesco Brombin, one of the original founders of the *fascio* in Ferrara, quit. He preferred to give up his positions as president of the provincial administration and secretary of the town *fascio* to being a "slave of the clique of fascists and Masons," he announced. In May, Enrico Caretti, political secretary of the provincial federation and commander of the local MVSN, resigned. As a fascist, he had no intention of being "the servant of that plutocratic bourgeois class which has profited from the bloody sacrifices of hundreds and hundreds of our brothers," he proclaimed. [19]

Revolts against the directorates of several rural communes followed. From Bologna, Baroncini, who had served on the commission of inquiry the previous September, telegraphed to De Bono, "Situation Ferrara very serious." [20] Elements of the MVSN sided with the dissidents and were promptly arrested by the prefect.

By the middle of June, anti-Balbo and anti-Mussolini slogans began to appear on the walls of the town. Demonstrators protested police searches of the houses of leading dissidents. Balbo concluded that medicine against the socialists could also be medicine against the fascist dissidents. He called in a gang of *squadristi* from Perugia. Relatively few of the dissidents suffered at the hands of the squad that appeared at the end of June. Nevertheless, the expedition had its effects. Further protest was pointless, the dissidents realized. Their movement died slowly in July and disintegrated entirely over the next three months. [21]

With the collapse of the dissidents, any lingering doubts about who ruled the province disappeared. A former revolutionary syndicalist organizer from Ferrara, Luigi Granata, put the matter succinctly: "Agrarian slavery rules supreme, completely suppressing contracts and wages." [22] "Yesterday you were in power; today, we are and you will pay for it"—this was the attitude of the landowners toward the agricultural laborers, according to Granata. He discussed in detail how, in certain zones, proprietors sacked their workers with no regard for the conditions of the families involved. Some of the landowners organized their own armed guards to protect themselves from reprisals, and on at least one occasion these guards had clashed with the fascist militia. Much of the responsibility for this state of affairs lay in the hands of Italo Balbo, the political boss who dominated the political and economic life of the people of Ferrara for the next seventeen years.

A disgruntled former collaborator, Tomaso Beltrani, revealed the extent of Balbo's authority in a notorious memorandum published in 1924.[23] According to Beltrani, whose account seems to be generally trustworthy, there seemed no limit to Balbo's influence. The newspapers, the police and the magistrates, the communal and provincial governments, party protocol, elections—all came under his scrutiny. His methods as a political boss were often ruthless, and he identified the "honor" of Ferrarese fascism with his own. When the *Gazzetta Ferrarese* showed a bit of sympathy for the dissident cause, Balbo sought to have the editor expelled from the party. When prefects or magistrates or police officials did not act according to Balbo's liking, he threatened to remove them. "Phrases of this type were typical of him: 'I'll send the police chief [of the province] to Girgenti if he doesn't toe the mark' or 'The prefect already knows that I have his replacement ready.' " When Balbo chose to rough up certain enemies, he told Beltrani to inform the local police and political authorities that there were to be "neither arrests nor trials as a result of the beatings." Reports and protocols within the party were passed on only with his approval and revision. He kept a close watch on communal and provincial relations with private contractors, and he chose candidates for the city government of Ferrara. His natural possessiveness and clannishness reinforced an atmosphere that must have been suffocating for his friends as well as his enemies. When Beltrani offered even the mildest dissent to Balbo's directives, Balbo usually burst out, "Don't you want me to take care of the Ferrarese any more? I'll just stick to being a general of the militia and I won't pay attention to anything else any more. But beware that things will go worse for you and everyone else; you won't have anyone who can easily obtain public works and other things for you."

Like Mussolini, Balbo knew how to keep his subordinates in line. He studied their strengths and weaknesses. When necessary he resorted to pressure and blackmail. Beltrani, for example, had boasted publicly that his war record included winning two silver medals. Balbo found out otherwise. As a result, Beltrani, who in January of 1923 had vigorously attacked the *agraria* for their dilatory tactics in negotiating a province-wide agricultural contract, changed his tune. Nor did Balbo hesitate to crush his enemies. In general, he dealt with them much as Mussolini did with his—he "exiled" them. Once they were harmless, Balbo often made peace and even reinstated them or helped them.[24] The major dissidents, Gattelli, Gaggioli, Ulivi, and Torti, all ceased their opposition. Gattelli dropped out of politics but remained in the province; after a few years, Balbo helped him get a technical position in Egypt. Ulivi left the province and, though expelled from the party, found another political position as secretary of the fascist syndicate in Bergamo. Gaggioli became a consul in the militia and was posted to Ancona. When Balbo married, Gaggioli was invited to the wedding, and he later returned to Ferrara. Guido Torti, a postal employee, and the teacher Francesco Brombin never made their peace with Balbo. Both were state employees and both found themselves transferred deeper and deeper into provincial exile and dead-end positions. When all else failed, Balbo turned to violence. A prime example was the attack of the Perugini on the dissidents.

Nevertheless, Balbo's powers had limits, partly self-imposed, partly political, and partly institutional. The self-imposed limits reflected Balbo's style and personality. Basically, he was a power broker, a political boss. He operated unethically and perhaps at times illegally in ruling the province. In his mind, "fascist law" took precedence over the laws of the state. Yet Balbo always considered himself a *galantuomo*, a man of honor. Unlike other *ras* or *gerarchi*, who, through fraud and corruption, used their positions to enrich themselves, Balbo remained honest. Even Beltrani, in the examples he discusses, admits this. By the end of his life, Balbo was financially secure, but he owed his position in part to his marriage and in part to his connections with the *agraria* and to such major figures of the financial and industrial world as Vittorio Cini, not to shady financial dealings.

There were also political limits to Balbo's control. Just as Mussolini ruled Italy with the tacit consent of the monarchy, the church, the military, and big business, Balbo ruled the province with the consent of the *agraria*. Regardless of their political coloration, Catholic or Liberal, the big landowners and their allies for the most part cared nothing about the day-to-day operations of the province or its relationships with Rome. These were left in Balbo's hands so long as his directives did not conflict with their interests. The support of the *agraria* was self-serving.[25] Balbo could not count on their help in personal struggles; they were willing to confront Rome only when their own affairs were concerned. This left Balbo powerful in Ferrara, but considerably more vulnerable in the capital, so that when Mussolini removed him from his position as head of the Aeronautica and appointed him governor of Libya, Balbo was powerless to resist.

Finally, there were institutional limits to Balbo's power. He was often blustering and impulsive. His subordinates were wise enough not to take his words too literally. Beltrani gives numerous examples of directives that he either carried out in milder forms or ignored completely. Thus, Balbo's grip on the province was probably no more totalitarian than was Mussolini's over Italy.

In addition to largely controlling the province's political life, Balbo ruled Ferrara's cultural and economic development. Wherever he reigned, whether in his native city or, later, in Libya, Balbo enjoyed his role as patron of the arts. He liked cultivating the friendship of artists, writers, and intellectuals. He delighted in passing references to him as the last of the Estes and once autographed a cartoon of himself as "nephew of Borso d'Este."[26] Under Balbo the province's cultural life flourished. He arranged or presided over academic congresses, art exhibits, literary symposia, and folk festivals during the late 1920s and early 1930s. Among the best remembered was the series of symposia between 1928 and 1933 known as the Ottava d'Oro. The meetings celebrated one of Ferrara's most famous Renaissance sons, Lodovico Ariosto, and his famous epic, *Orlando Furioso*. Balbo personally inaugurated the cycle of readings and commentary in May, 1928, with a comment of his own, "Il volo d'Astolfo" (The Flight of Astolfo): with much charm and humor and many asides about his own flying career, Balbo described the heroic Astolfo's journey to the moon on his winged horse.[27] In 1932, thanks to Balbo's friendship with Bottai, Ferrara hosted the important Congress on Corporative Studies. Meanwhile, important literary and artistic figures contributed to Balbo's *Corriere Padano*. Other journals and magazines on politics and the arts developed as well. Ferrara's architectural grace as a Renaissance city suffered very little from the intrusion of new muscular buildings in the fascist Littorio style.

The province's economic development was considerably less bright.[28] Balbo came to power promising the impossible. To the barefoot armies of agricultural laborers he spoke of land reform; to the big landowners who financed him, he promised the destruction of the incipient rural revolution that the socialists had fostered during the *biennio rosso*. The revolution died. By 1926, Balbo admitted that "exchange rates cannot be dominated by clubs nor the Stock Exchange by castor oil" and that singing "Giovinezza" is "not enough to galvanize an agricultural sector in crisis."[29] In 1927, at Mussolini's request, the industrialist Vittorio Cini drew up a plan to resolve the province's economic problems. His solutions were familiar ones: more credit for the landowners, and more public works to take care of unemployment. There was also some talk of developing industry. In practice, Balbo delivered the fascist regime's usual stopgap measures to deal with unemployment: public funds for local public works, and organized emigration. As he had promised in 1921, he found new land for the peasants—in the Pontine Marshes and in Libya. In Ferrara, the big landowners reigned supreme. The laborers, organized in fascist syndicates, were at the mercy of their employers. To ward off popular dissatisfaction caused by chronic unemployment and low wages, the fascist regime built public housing in Ferrara and introduced programs for industrialization and urban renewal in communities such as Tresigallo. Nevertheless, spontaneous demonstrations of the unemployed in the late 1920s and early 1930s indicated that all was not well.[30] The industrialization program in Ferrara developed in the late 1930s was too small to take care of the jobless there.

Once he had established himself as *ras* of Ferrara, Balbo tried to shed his image as a violent Blackshirt and gang leader; he cultivated the air of a princely dissident. In August of 1923, however, he was implicated in the murder of an obscure provincial archpriest, Don Giovanni Minzoni. That affair, more than any other, ensured that his unsavory origins as a *squadrista* would never be forgotten.

Born in Ravenna in 1885, Don Minzoni came from a petty-bourgeois background that resembled Balbo's origins. During World War I, he volunteered to serve as a front-line chaplain.

For his services and bravery, this "soldier of Christ and of Italy," as D'Annunzio called him, received, among other decorations, the silver medal—much as Balbo did.[31] After his discharge, the priest returned to Argenta, where he had begun his mission. There he dedicated himself to economic and social reforms and to educational programs. At first he avoided involvement with the Popolari; finally, in April, 1923, in an act of anti-fascist defiance four months before his death, he joined the party.

His major contribution to the anti-fascist cause came in organizing the youth of Argenta. Under his direction, the Young Catholic Scouts (Giovani Esploratori Cattolici) developed so extensively that the fascists were unable to establish their own Balilla organizations. At first the local fascists attempted to co-opt Don Minzoni. They offered him the position of chaplain in the local MVSN. He declined. For the sake of keeping the peace, he declared himself willing to resign from the Popolari. However, he refused to give up his work in the youth groups.

When accommodation failed, the fascist leadership of Argenta decided to resort to other tactics. A first attempt at the beginning of August was aborted. A second one on the night of August 23 succeeded too well.[32] During an evening walk, about 10:45, Don Minzoni and a young companion, Enrico Bondanelli, were ambushed and beaten. The assailants, Giorgio Molinari and Vittorio Casoni, were two fascists recruited from the nearby community of Casumaro. Bondanelli survived; Don Minzoni, his skull fractured, died about two hours after the beating.

In retrospect, it seems clear that the attack was not intended to be fatal.[33] The assailants chose ordinary heavy walking sticks as their weapons rather than lead-reinforced clubs. They selected a site that was dark but close to the center of town. Immediately after the attack it was easy for Bondanelli to call for help. The assailants struck Don Minzoni only once and then turned on Bondanelli before they fled. Had Don Minzoni been wearing a hat, like his companion, the priest might have survived the blow.

Officially, Balbo deplored the attack, and the fascist provincial federation, in wall manifestos, mourned Don Minzoni's death and paid tribute to him as a "courageous adversary." The regrets were undoubtedly sincere, at least in political terms. Political violence was on the upswing again and the fascists, too, had their "mar-

tyrs" in the region. Nevertheless, Don Minzoni had been a popular figure and the fascists feared a backlash. Two weeks after the
priest's death, *Il Balilla* warned anti-fascists not to exploit the
case. They should stop spreading rumors that orders had come
from on high to "bury" the tragedy; "that Italo Balbo himself went
to Argenta to quiet everything."[34] Yet the official inquiry did not
produce results. Balbo and the fascists obstructed the investigation. Although the authorities identified the murder suspects by
April of 1924, the case was dropped for lack of evidence.

But anti-fascists did exploit the case—and very successfully. On
the first anniversary of Don Minzoni's death, on August 23, 1924,
the anti-fascist *La Voce Repubblicana* published an article accus-
ing Balbo of involvement in Don Minzoni's murder. Balbo read
the article during an outing in Rome with Grandi and Mussolini's
brother, Arnaldo. He turned red and roared impulsively, "I'll sue
them."[35] Both his companions advised against it and pointed out
that the attack was politically motivated. During the summer of
1924, the Mussolini regime appeared to be on the verge of collapse over another fascist brutality, the murder of the socialist
deputy Giacomo Matteotti. Anti-fascists hoped to exploit that case
and others, including the Don Minzoni affair, to reveal the corruption, violence, and brutality of Mussolini's regime and bring it
down. Balbo ignored his friends' advice and filed suit for libel.

For Balbo, the trial, which began November 19 and lasted for
five sessions, went badly. The defense never proved Balbo's direct implication in the murder. But that was not their purpose.
"We never asserted that the Honorable Balbo ordered the assassination, but our conscience will not permit us to deny that there
was some responsibility on [his] part," declared the defense
lawyers in their summation.[36] Meanwhile, the trial produced
revelations that blackened the reputation of both Balbo and the
fascist regime. Naturally, *La Voce Repubblicana* published the
most sensational testimony.

Most damaging was the Beltrani memorandum. Tomaso Beltrani, the ex-secretary of the provincial federation and one of
Balbo's most trusted lieutenants, was from Trieste, a war veteran
with frustrated ambitions.[37] Disappointed that his fascist career
had done little to improve his material circumstances, he quarreled
with Balbo and attempted to blackmail him. For 60,000 lire, Bel-

trani first offered Balbo a compromising memorandum and a series of forty letters. When Balbo turned him down, Beltrani sold the material for 7,000 lire to contacts he had in the Popolari. The material came into the hands of the anti-fascist journalist Giuseppe Donati, who began to mount the campaign in his paper, *Il Popolo*, and in others as well. Balbo claimed that the memorandum was fraudulent. Nevertheless, the evidence indicates that the document is substantially correct. Beltrani did not hesitate to make self-incriminating statements; independent police investigations corroborated his accounts; the document was notarized, and independent witnesses vouched for its authenticity.

Beltrani's memorandum did not prove that Balbo was directly involved in the murder.[38] "I have absolutely no indication" of Balbo's "complicity in the actual execution of the crime," noted Beltrani. But if the dispositions that led to the murder almost certainly did not originate with Balbo, how much did he know? On this point, Beltrani's testimony conflicts. In the memorandum he stated that Balbo followed everything that went on in the province, down to the minutest detail. Yet Beltrani also claimed that two days before the murder he himself—the party's provincial secretary—knew nothing of Don Minzoni and his activities nor of the plans to intimidate the priest. In testimony elsewhere, Beltrani declared that he was present twice when the fascists from Argenta complained to Balbo about Don Minzoni's work and discussed plans "to teach the priest a lesson." A post-war hearing in 1947 concluded that Balbo probably knew little about the affair and took no direct interest in it.[39] Unlike, for example, the attempted strike against the sugar refineries in August, 1922, Don Minzoni's activities presented no major threat to Balbo's power, so Balbo advised the local fascists to handle the matter themselves.

Once the murder had been committed, however, according to Beltrani, Balbo tried to protect the fascists involved. "We are talking about Maran, Forti is implicated, we cannot abandon them: one is a consul, the other the best fascist and the most loyal one in the province," Beltrani claimed that Balbo told him.[40] Balbo then used his influence to suppress the story in the newspapers and to influence the investigation. In the prefect's presence, for example, Balbo called in the correspondent of the *Avvenire d'Italia* and advised him to be more vague and cautious about the details of the murder. The affair had nothing to do with politics, Balbo declared. Don Minzoni had been involved with a woman, Balbo claimed; he had proof, in the form of dressmaker's bills, that the priest had been making presents to her.

Beltrani's evidence, then, did not show that Balbo was directly involved in the murder of Don Minzoni. What Beltrani's testimony established was the climate of violence and intimidation in Balbo's Ferrara. Here Beltrani produced Balbo's own letters detailing his pressures on magistrates and government officials. In one letter dated August 31, 1923—more than a week after Don Minzoni's death—Balbo raged at the acquittal of eight socialists tried in Mantova for the Castel Estense "massacre" of December, 1920. "Explain to them," Balbo wrote Beltrani, that "it would be healthy for them to change air and establish themselves in another province." If they insisted on remaining in Ferrara, they should be beaten

without exaggerating, but with regularity until they decide [to leave]. Show this part of my letter to the prefect, to whom you should say in my name that I have good reasons to justify my desire not to have such scoundrels in the town or in the province. The police would do well to persecute them with arrests at least once a week and it would also be well for the prefect to make the state prosecutor understand that in the event of beatings (which should be done with style), we do not want troubles with trials. . . . If I write this letter from Rome, it is a sign that I know what I am talking about.[41]

Beltrani also testified to Balbo's violent interference in the spring, 1924, elections. According to Beltrani, Balbo disdained subtle means. The fascists should repeat their performance of 1921, when they controlled the elections with their clubs, Balbo urged. Who could stop the fascists from stationing two Blackshirts at the entrance to the booth—or right inside it, for that matter? Balbo demanded. Or perhaps the voters should be instructed to emerge from the booth with their ballots open. The surest method of all would be to grab the first voter out of the booth and make an example of him. "Let us take, therefore, this privileged elector and break his head open—even if he has voted for us, too bad for him—shouting, 'Bastard, you voted for the socialists.' " These methods would not displease the government. "I come from Rome and I know what I am saying and doing; I would not take on certain responsibilities if I were not perfectly aware of the government's thinking," Balbo declared.

The trial proved to be an expensive mistake for Balbo. The court ruled against him—thus implying that the paper's attacks had not been libelous—and he was ordered to pay court costs. Still worse, his reputation was so damaged that on November 27 he felt obliged to give up his position in the militia. In his letter of resignation to Mussolini, Balbo alluded to the letter of August 31 and explained that it had been "provoked by a moment of exasperation" with the acquittal of the "assassins" of his comrades.[42] Nevertheless, he did not intend to engage in polemics or to create difficulties for the government. "If I was wrong, I shall pay, as all gentlemen, all fascists, must." Mussolini accepted his resignation; but, as *La Voce Repubblicana* pointed out, the Duce did not in any way condemn Balbo's activities. On the contrary, Mussolini praised Balbo's faithfulness and devotion to the fascist cause. He had sacrificed himself for the sake of the Duce; he had not been brought before the bar of justice.[43]

The Don Minzoni affair did not end there. A second trial took place in Ferrara in July of 1925. By then Mussolini had openly declared his dictatorship and the courtroom atmosphere was such that the assassins were acquitted. Nevertheless, the anti-fascists continued to exploit the case whenever they had an occasion. At a lunch in London in 1928, for example, the Lord Mayor in good faith read in Balbo's presence the following congratulatory telegram: "Unable to participate at your luncheon in the flesh, I am present in spirit. Don Minzoni."[44] In the publicity surrounding his triumphant flight to the United States in July, 1933, a few dissenting voices recalled the Don Minzoni episode—sometimes inaccurately—and one commented, "While millions cheer, a few remember."[45] Nor has the affair completely died. The inquiry of June, 1947, was conducted in an anti-fascist climate. The investigation was minute and the court ruled that Balbo was not directly involved in the murder and was not legally responsible for it. The available evidence supports this conclusion. The courts have upheld the Balbo family in suits against anyone—usually some overzealous journalist—who proclaims otherwise.

Balbo's resignation from the militia—a low point in his career—

coincided with another scandal, that of the Matteotti affair—a low point in fascism's fortunes. Giacomo Matteotti, a reform socialist deputy, had the temerity on May 30, 1924, to stand up in the Chamber of Deputies and denounce the intimidation and violence that had marked the elections during the previous month. For that act, he became one of the most famous of the anti-fascist martyrs. Fascist thugs kidnapped him in Rome on June 10 while he was on his way to parliament and beat him fatally. No direct link with Mussolini was ever established, but the scandal nearly caused the downfall of the regime. Among those forced to resign because of his alleged complicity in the murder was Emilio De Bono.

As head of the militia and as one of the leading provincial *ras*, Balbo represented a significant force in determining how fascism overcame the Matteotti crisis. His rank in the militia, his *squadrista* background, his republican origins, and his impulsive personality all suggested that he favored the intransigents, that he stood with the partisans of the "second wave." For papers such as *Il Selvaggio* or *La Conquista dello Stato*, intransigent newspapers that sprang up to exalt provincial fascism during the summer of 1924, Balbo, "symbol of courageous and intelligent *squadrismo*, was sacrificed to normalization but embodied the will of extremism." Whether Balbo really "embodied the will of extremism" is debatable. What he knew was that to save his own career, fascism had to survive. Thus, he pressured Mussolini and appeared to outflank him—thereby pleasing the intransigents. Yet he was careful not to commit himself completely to the extremists, whom he knew would not be acceptable to the Italian political establishment.

During the Matteotti affair, Mussolini mobilized the militia in early June to make a show of force.[46] By June 19 two complete legions were in Rome. The anti-fascist threat subsided, but the militia mobilization acquired a momentum of its own and there were rumors of a coup. This suited Balbo. In Bologna on June 19 and again on June 22, the militia staged massive rallies—the second attracted 50,000 to 60,000—as a show of force and to boost morale. These rallies recalled the demonstrations three years earlier against Mussolini's "peace pact" with the socialists. At the Bologna rally Balbo mentioned the earlier protests and declared that at the time "we affirmed that fascism was an idea and not a man." But then he hedged his anti-Mussolinian jab with the comment, "Not fascism but Italy now has a single face . . . that of Benito Mussolini." The message was clear: as in 1921, the provincial fascists did not intend to allow Mussolini to conclude peace at their expense. After the rally, the leaders held a secret meeting in which there was talk of a "second wave," but more cautious counsel prevailed.

A week later Balbo organized a "grand review" of the militia commanders of Emilia, Tuscany, and the Veneto. This was partly a demonstration against the possibility that the army might absorb the militia. Afterward he telegraphed to Mussolini, "The militia remained the guardian of the Duce and of fascism." Yet in a July 5 circular, Balbo urged his officers to be patient; they should not fear for either their jobs or their political function. On August 1, he was justified. A decree appeared modifying the regulations of the militia but in practice changing the previous system very little. The militia still remained under the direct control of Mussolini, except when performing functions of paramilitary training. Uniforms, symbols, nomenclature remained untouched. Recruitment, although nominally open to nonfascists, remained in the hands of the consuls.

Balbo's resignation in November, in the wake of the Don Minzoni affair, raised old anxieties among the militia officers. They had faced a double shock: first De Bono's resignation because of the Matteotti murder, and then Balbo's.[47] Under pressure from the army, Mussolini would in any case most likely have replaced Balbo, who was "interim commander in chief," with a regular army officer. Balbo's successor, General Gandolfo, who could boast of both a regular military and a fascist past, did not reassure the militia officers. They worried, with good reason, that Mussolini would succumb to army pressures. The disaffection in the militia was such that an anti-Mussolinian "movement of the consuls" began to form.

Some have argued, on the basis of slim evidence, that Balbo organized the movement, at least during its initial stages.[48] Three days after his resignation, on November 30, he advised his supporters to prove their obedience "one last time," but if the opposition did not accept this "last message of peace," then "we are ready

to make the war cry of the first days of fascism sound again." After
this, his trail becomes obscure. The military continued to pressure
Mussolini. In the army's view, the reforms of August were inadequate; a militia that was too independent always presented the
specter of a civil war. Concerned about losing their positions, the
Emilian consuls met in Ferrara on December 9 and in Bologna on
the following day. Balbo was not present even in Ferrara, where,
as it turned out, the chief topic of concern was the position of Raoul
Forti, implicated in the Don Minzoni murder. *La Voce Repubblicana* on December 17 reproduced a significant telegram from
Grandi to Balbo: "Yours received. Remain Ferrara. Keep very
calm. Show yourself able to wait in silence. This is what one must
do at the moment. Your faithful friend Grandi embraces you." The
same paper on December 21 alluded to "the more or less clandestine meetings of the higher officers of the militia, presided over by
Balbo." On December 20 came the order that the militia leaders
feared. General Gandolfo announced that he would replace all the
zone commanders who had not attained the rank of colonel in the
regular army. The consuls anticipated that they would be next.
They acted to forestall the move in what became known as the
"revolt of the consuls."

On December 31, a group of thirty or so consuls—Balbo was
not present—called on Mussolini on the pretext of wishing him a
happy new year. Their real object was to protest the changes in
command in the militia and to demand that Mussolini suppress
opposition criticism. If he did not, they threatened to launch a
"second wave." Some have interpreted this meeting as a genuine
confrontation, a showdown between the rebellious militia and the
embattled Duce; others have argued that the meeting was a
Machiavellian charade agreed upon ahead of time, with the purpose of intimidating parliament and the king.[49] Perhaps the meeting contained elements of both. In any case, three days later
Mussolini's speech of January 3 marked the end of the parliamentary regime and the beginning of the dictatorship.

Balbo's role in the "revolt of the consuls" remains obscure.
That the consuls should turn to him for leadership was natural: he
was head of the militia and he enjoyed a reputation as a man of
action. Many of the consuls owed their positions to him. If what
they had in mind was a Night of St. Bartholomew, a night of

terror that would force Mussolini to support them, Balbo was an excellent candidate to lead them. After all, he had organized operations such as the "column of fire" march through the Romagna in 1922. Nor would it be surprising if, while remaining in the background, he maintained links with the conspirators and knew of their plans. Yet nowhere are there concrete indications that Balbo was ready to accept the leadership of the movement and to act.[50] His republicanism and his reputation for "rashness" mean very little. Throughout his campaigns of 1921 and 1922 he had taken great care not to alienate either the army or the king. At times he had sought alternatives to Mussolini, but failing to find them, he quickly mended his fences with the Duce. Most likely, in the uncertainties that swirled around the "revolt of the consuls," Balbo had no clear plan. He knew only that he intended to defend his own position—which included the militia—and to ensure that the fascist regime did not collapse.

The pressures of the intransigents were enough. Mussolini publicly assumed full responsibility for the Matteotti affair, cracked down on the opposition, and openly declared a dictatorship. Balbo was not optimistic about the new regime's prospects. Mussolini had been forced to become a dictator "without having what it takes," he observed.[51] A dictator should have no scruples and must not be afraid of blood, declared Balbo; personally he would have made an example of Matteotti's murderers and had them shot. Mussolini faced "troubles," Balbo predicted, yet his pressures had helped save Mussolini, fascism—and his own career.

One of the first signs that Balbo's career was on the rise again was the founding of his newspaper *Corriere Padano*.[52] The first issue of this "newspaper of the fascist revolution" rolled off the presses on April 5, 1925. The *Padano* quickly gained a reputation as one of the liveliest, most intelligent, and most independent of the provincial dailies. For nearly two decades it appeared virtually without interruption. During its early days the *Padano* expanded rapidly. As the circulation grew from an initial 3,000 copies to 40,000 by 1931, so did its coverage. The paper boasted four bureaus (Faenza, Forlì, Ravenna, Verona) and offices (Rovigo, Padova, Bologna, Rimini) throughout the Po Valley and one bureau in Rome. The *Padano* absorbed two local Ferrarese newspapers, the Catholic *La Domenica dell'Operaio* in 1925 and the Liberal *Gazzetta Ferrarese* in 1928.

Balbo was the *Padano's* first editor. Throughout his life, he followed the newspaper closely—sometimes minutely—regardless of his other obligations. From time to time he contributed signed articles. Seven months after the paper first appeared, however, he became undersecretary to the minister of national economy and the editorship passed to his longtime friend and collaborator Nello Quilici.

Quilici was a major factor in the paper's prestige and success.[53] Six years older than Balbo, he had begun his journalistic career before World War I with the *Resto del Carlino* as a foreign correspondent in Germany, Switzerland, and Austria. After war service, he joined the fascists in 1921 and resumed his journalism. In 1924, he inadvertently became involved in the Matteotti affair when he unknowingly stored the kidnap car in his garage. As a result, he was momentarily ostracized from his profession, and Balbo hired him. For the next fifteen years Quilici directed the *Padano*. He also taught at the University of Ferrara, published two historical studies on aspects of Liberal Italy, edited a political journal, *Nuovi Problemi*, and collaborated with Balbo on his books and articles. Despite many attractive offers to head larger and more prestigious papers, including the *Corriere della Sera* and Mussolini's own *Popolo d'Italia*, he stayed with the *Padano*, "like a colonel who is faithful to his regiment and can never become a general," he wrote. His lifelong friendship with Balbo was a major reason he continued to edit the paper. Balbo was also close to Quilici's artist wife, Mimì Quilici-Buzzacchi, and to his sister, Mariula, a publicist who shared Balbo's passion for aviation.

When the *Padano* first appeared, the intransigents welcomed it as a new "integralist daily." *La Conquista dello Stato* proclaimed confidently that the *Padano* "would be the voice of the old and glorious integral fascism of the Po Valley."[54] The *Padano* itself, after six months of publication, claimed that the paper was supported by the comrades of Emilia-Romagna.[55] The truth was quite different. The investors in the paper were Balbo's usual supporters, the big landowners and industrialists of Ferrara. In addition to Balbo's wife, the Countess Florio-Balbo, the major investors included the Società Eridania of Genova, a sugar company;

the Fondazione Cevasco, a foundation supported by the Cevasco family, one of the four major families who dominated the Italian sugar industry; the tourist bureau; and the *agraria*.[56]

Nevertheless, in his programmatic statement in the first issue of the paper, entitled "From the Trench of 1921," Balbo insisted that the newspaper would be faithful to "the original fascism."[57] The article touched on three themes that went to the heart of Balbo's fascism at this time: syndicalism, the militia, and the fascist "revolution." His name, he told his readers, should be enough to indicate where he stood. Many of them had followed him in the enterprises "courageously undertaken and which are known as syndicalism and fascist militia." He recalled proudly that in January and February, 1921, "it was I with a valiant group of friends who wanted them and it was I who created them despite the diffidence of many fascists." A second achievement that he recalled proudly was the March on Ravenna. Finally, he explained what he meant by "the original fascism." That fascism, he cautioned in a manner that must have disappointed the intransigents among his readers, "does not ask to have its hands untied and does not ask for impunity to complete the vendettas that were generously not carried out at the end of October, 1922." That fascism, Balbo continued, had carried out a genuine revolution and not merely "a wretched coup d'état." What he wanted to see now, Balbo affirmed, echoing Mussolini's congratulatory message to the paper, was the revolution translated into laws.

The *Padano* was never conformist. From its first number, Balbo polemicized against the regime. The only important innovation the fascist regime had made was the militia, he charged on April 7. A few weeks later he attacked the finance minister and the regime's fiscal policies in taxing the communes. This provoked a sharp telegram from Mussolini—the first of many complaints.[58] Even during the worst periods of the dictatorship, the *Padano* took daring stands and made shows of independence. Most widely recognized were the *Padano*'s opposition in 1934 to anti-Semitism and later to Italy's alliance with Nazi Germany.

The *Padano*'s nonconformity was certainly not unique. Many other provincial papers, magazines, and journals, either because of their traditions or because they served as a mouthpiece for a local *ras*, showed a similar degree of independence.[59] In the

Padano's case, as long as the paper did not challenge the local status quo, the landowners and sugar kings of Ferrara did not care whether the paper flouted Rome's official line. The *Padano*, however, was unusually lively, as Mussolini admitted with grudging admiration.[60] In part this reflected the highly original and non-conformist staff that Balbo attracted—"anti-fascist residues," Mussolini called them.[61] They included Giulio Colamarino, a Liberal who admired Pietro Gobetti; Pio Gardenghi, the son of one of Mussolini's former colleagues in the Socialist Party and a contributor to *Avanti;* and Massimo Fovel, a radical socialist economist whose writings interested Gramsci. Throughout the fascist period, these men discreetly but persistently debated the ideas of Marx, Lenin, and Gramsci, and they challenged and educated future generations with these forbidden ideologies. The contributors to the paper's *terza pagina*, dedicated to culture and the arts, included Michelangelo Antonioni, Giorgio Bassani, Salvatore Quasimodo, Mario Soldati, Giuseppe Ungaretti, Elio Vittorini, and many others, all either well known at the time or stars of Italy's post-war cultural renaissance.

Over the years, the paper faithfully mirrored Balbo's nonconformist brand of fascism. "Balbo's nonconformism is congenital. In his blood he has the ferment of rebellion," and the paper reflected, as well as it could, "the spirit of its founder and first editor," Quilici wrote.[62] If the newspaper had no other merits, at least "it was neither a phonograph nor a cage of trained parrots," he noted wryly.

A second indication that Balbo's career was reviving came in the fall of 1925 when he was chosen to investigate, on behalf of the party, the "incidents in Florence." The Matteotti affair prompted a revival of *squadrismo* throughout Northern Italy, including the area around Ferrara.[63] In Florence, the outbreaks of October 3–4 were especially serious and widespread. They were directed against the Masons and other secret societies. Mussolini was preparing for the Locarno conference—one of his rare visits abroad—and the anarchic outbursts humiliated him and threatened his image internationally. "The most anarchic party in Italy is the fascist," he declared, and added, with reference to the tourist industry in Florence, "and all this under the eyes of 10,000 Englishmen and Americans."[64]

Balbo's appointment to head the party's investigation was a real test of his loyalties. He had been a Mason, a member of the Loggia di Piazza del Gesù (Scottish Rite), until 1923.[65] He had joined them because their secret rites appealed to the romantic in him—and probably because his fellow Masons helped him establish himself in Ferrara, where the organization had a long tradition. Balbo's Masonic connections were not unusual. At least a dozen out of twenty-eight members of the Grand Council in 1923 belonged to the Masons. They had given considerable moral and financial support—especially Balbo's Piazza del Gesù order—to the fascist cause during the March on Rome. Yet Mussolini opposed the Masons once he came to power. In part, he distrusted their cosmopolitanism, their anti-clerical and democratic traditions; in part, he feared that the lodges might become centers for conspiracies against him. In February of 1923, the Grand Council ordered its members to choose between fascism and Freemasonry. Balbo, unlike some of his fellow *gerarchi*, chose fascism and gave up his lodge membership. Nevertheless, his enemies often referred to his Masonic past, as Mussolini did in 1939 when he spoke of Balbo as "that democratic swine" who was once the orator of the Girolamo Savonarola lodge.[66]

Balbo dealt with the crisis in Florence by making intransigent declarations, then acting decisively to reestablish discipline. The enemies of fascism should share the same fate as the Albigensians, he proclaimed.[67] The direction of the party was "not a subsidiary of the Viminale [the ministry of the interior]" but a genuine revolutionary committee that wanted, at last, to carry out the will of fascism against all obstacles.[68] Then, over a period of about two weeks, between October 9 and October 24, in a series of meetings and hearings Balbo purged the *fascio*. He appointed new leaders and ordered measures against corruption. The outcome proved to be a clear victory for the "normalizers." Moreover, in the Florentine *La Nazione,* he declared that, for him, intransigence was not the periodic eruption of the *squadristi* and must not be confused with episodic violence, damaging to the party and the government. Intransigent fascism meant an uncompromising devotion to the construction of the fascist state.[69]

Less than a month after his investigation of the outbreaks in Florence came a third indication that Balbo's career was on the rise again—and that his days as a *squadrista* were over. On November 3, he was sworn in as undersecretary to the minister of national economy. Balbo had no particular aptitude for financial affairs, but the appointment made political sense. With a single stroke, Mussolini quieted the intransigents by appointing one of them; he also pleased those who favored "normalization." Buried in the bureaucracy, Balbo was unlikely to stir up much trouble. Above him as minister was Giuseppe Belluzzo, a well-known technocrat and prominent civil servant, later responsible for major economic policies such as the Stabilization of the Lira and the Battle for Grain.

The appointment also offered some stopgap answers to the perpetual nuisance of the militia and the squads. Mussolini wanted no more embarrassments like the "Florence massacres"; Balbo realized that there was no real future for him in *squadrismo*. The ministry of national economy had jurisdiction over the royal corps of fish and game wardens; Belluzzo, a month before Balbo's appointment, proposed creating a "forest militia" (Milizia Forestale) that would integrate units of the MVSN.[70] When Balbo joined the ministry, he took on the task—familiar to him—of founding a military-style organization and drawing up regulations for it.[71] His experience with the MVSN he now applied to the Milizia Forestale. The new organization, which was created by royal decree on May 16, 1926, also provided Balbo with ample opportunities for patronage. The old Royal Corps had numbered 2,000; the new Milizia Forestale numbered 5,000, and Balbo used the new positions to reward some of his followers.[72]

As undersecretary, Balbo represented the ministry on official occasions. He used these opportunities to exalt the regime and to urge his listeners to carry on the war to save Italy's natural resources, just as they had fought the Great War. In addition to making speeches, he chaired at least two committees that wrestled with thorny economic matters.[73] In January and February of 1926, he directed an inquiry into the tourist industry. A second committee, over a two-year period beginning in September of 1926, studied the problems of tariffs and Italy's import patterns. The young provincial *ras* presided over committees that included the top figures in the Italian financial and industrial world. Among them were the economist Felice Guarneri, the industrial-

ists Vittorio Cini and Antonio Benni, and the agricultural special-
ist Filippo Cavazza.

Once the Milizia Forestale was created, the ministry offered
few outlets for Balbo's talents as a military organizer and a man of
action. The routine of a bureaucrat never appealed to him; he was
always glad for opportunities to escape—for example, to North
Africa. His first visit to Libya came in 1924, when he accompanied Luigi Federzoni, then minister of colonies, to inspect the
first tentative attempts at land settlement. During the spring of
1926, Balbo made two trips to the colony. The second one, in
particular, proved to be controversial. He accompanied Mussolini
on a highly publicized tour of Tripolitania in April. The visit was
designed to arouse the nation's colonial consciousness and also
served notice to other Mediterranean powers, especially the
French, of fascist Italy's expansionist ambitions.

Following the sojourn in Libya, on April 14 Balbo flew to Tunis. Engine trouble lengthened a scheduled two-day visit into
four. During that time Balbo and his party mingled with the
colony's more than 100,000 Italian immigrants and stirred Italian
nationalist sentiment in a way that was bound to irritate the
French authorities. On his return, in an effusive interview with
the *Corriere della Sera* Balbo praised the patriotism of the immigrants and their faith in Mussolini. By implication, he urged Italians in the colony to resist French naturalization. The French
press accused Balbo of impertinence and discourtesy.[74] In the
meantime, the trip and the polemic had served their purpose of
displaying Italy's military power and expansionist aims.[75]

Balbo had appeared for the first time in a role for which he
eventually became world-famous. The intransigent *squadrista*
gave way to the heroic aviator. The ruthless Blackshirt became
the passionate emissary to Italian immigrant communities overseas and the cosmopolitan ambassador from Mussolini's "new Italy." Six months later, on November 6, 1926, Balbo was appointed undersecretary in the air ministry.

Part Two

The Aviator (1926–1934)

Chapter Seven

Undersecretary: Douhet's "Disciple"

Balbo's seven years with the Regia Aeronautica were among the best of his life. First as undersecretary (1926–1929), then as minister (1929–1933), he was responsible for all phases of Italian aviation, military and civil. The position offered everything he loved: politics, adventure, glory, patriotism, showmanship, military service. "Everyone knows how I loved [it] here," he told his friends at the end of his term in 1933; "I'm leaving my heart behind here"; and "Naturally, I leave this house, this creation of mine, with death in my heart."[1] Eventually he came to enjoy the power and regal splendor of his new position as governor of Libya. He continued to fly and he enthusiastically promoted aviation in the colony. Yet, in his heart, nothing ever replaced the Aeronautica.

The years in the Aeronautica were critical to his personal development and to his reputation. His achievements as an aviator transformed him from a provincial Italian politician with a dubious Blackshirt past into an international celebrity. He joined Charles Lindbergh, Wiley Post, Amelia Earhart, Jean Mermoz, Antoine de Saint-Exupéry, Francesco De Pinedo, Umberto Nobile, Wolfgang von Gronau, and Charles Kingsford Smith as one of the great pioneers of aviation's "golden age," the late 1920s and early 1930s. Like the astronauts of the 1960s, Balbo in his day ranked among those who had "the right stuff." Unlike today's astronauts, who are brave, brilliant, superbly trained, but not always personally memorable, Balbo with his colorful personality and sense of showmanship left a vivid impression. Today's astronauts generally shun publicity. Balbo, in his dual role as minister and aviator, courted it. His long-distance flights prompted frantic celebrations wherever he touched down, Rome to Rio de Janeiro, Chicago to Odessa. His familiar goateed face appeared in advertisements for aviation products. The Marx brothers' film *Night at the Opera* celebrates him generically in a brief sequence that pokes fun at bearded Italian aviators. His very name became part of the flying fraternity's vocabulary, at least in English. A *Balbo* came to signify "a large flight or formation of airplanes."[2]

In the Aeronautica, Balbo created his most enduring monument. All the other institutions that he headed—Blackshirts, militia, the colonial regime in Libya—perished with the fall of fascism. The Aeronautica remains. Yet, for political reasons, even today the Aeronautica acknowledges him as a founding father only with difficulty. For example, an official ministry pamphlet published for the Aeronautica's fiftieth anniversary in 1973 celebrated De Pinedo, Ferrarin, Del Prete, Nobile, Agello, and many other great pioneers of Italian aviation.[3] Conspicuously missing from the list is Italo Balbo. In the massive air ministry building in Rome, one of Balbo's proudest achievements as minister, public tributes to him are muted. The most conspicuous one is over the entrance. There a marble inscription originally read, "Built while Vittorio Emanuele III was king, duce Benito Mussolini, minister Italo Balbo." Only Balbo's name has survived. A careful search also reveals his name on a column dedicated to Italian aviators who died in combat. The Aeronautica's undersecretaries still use his former office today, but nowhere in the modest room is there any indication that it was once Balbo's.

The ministry's equivocal position toward him today reflects the varied attitudes toward his work and achievements. Judgments have ranged from bombastic praise, under the fascist regime, to denigration or, at best, grudging admiration among contemporary critics. Federzoni, though sympathetic to his friend, summarized the case against Balbo. His contribution was characteristic of so many fascist endeavors: far too superficial, far too hasty in his technical development of the service. Yet he did wonders for the prestige and morale of the Aeronautica. "It was *his* because the

spirits of the aviators were *his*."[4] Other critics are not so charitable. Balbo placed far too much emphasis on showmanship and
prestige, they argue.[5] "Sporting events" such as record flights and
air races promoted Mussolini's regime, the Aeronautica, and
Balbo at the expense of the Aeronautica's development. The result was the Aeronautica's disastrous showing in World War II.

These judgments contain a measure of truth—but also a good
deal of exaggeration. They ignore the world in which Balbo
worked, a world where aviation was still in its infancy. The great
task of the pioneers was to prove that flying was more than a rich
man's sport and that aviation had enormous commercial and military potential. These pioneers struggled against enormous odds to
reach the public, to overcome suspicion, fear, indifference. In the
military field, the Aeronautica in Italy was like air forces in other
nations: unknown and untried, lacking traditions, a second-class
service, behind the army and navy. By the end of his term in
office, Balbo could justly claim that he had built a service with a
sense of esprit, high morale, and purpose. His records, his
trophies, his sporting successes all contributed to this and to
creating an "air-minded" Italy.

Too often Balbo's critics also ignore the means available to him.
Italy was a poor country to begin with. Furthermore, for political
reasons, at least during the period of Balbo's ministry, Mussolini
kept the Aeronautica's budget substantially lower than that of the
army and navy. With more funding at his disposal, Balbo might
have done more. He made mistakes—for example, he was more
interested in planning the next aerial cruise than in the long-term
development of the service—but in general, he did the best he
could with what he had. To lay the disasters of World War II on his
shoulders is ludicrous. By 1940 Balbo had been out of office for
seven years. He was not solely responsible for the muddled doctrine and uncertain techniques that hampered the Aeronautica's
performance during the war. There was very little he could have
done to compensate for Italy's weak industrial base. If the Aeronautica was not ready technically, the responsibility lay not with
him but with his successors. Balbo was acutely aware of Italy's
military weaknesses, opposed the war, and predicted disaster if
Italy intervened on the German side. The decision to match the
Aeronautica against a far more powerful enemy was Mussolini's.

Mussolini's motives for appointing Balbo to the Aeronautica resembled those for appointing him to the ministry of national economy: a good dose of politics, with a dash of consideration for his qualifications.

For Mussolini, Balbo was always a source of anxiety, a "buried mine" that could explode at any time. Yet he was one of fascism's most glamorous and competent leaders. Mussolini could never afford to dispense with him. Aviation suggested a promising outlet for Balbo's restless energies. Mussolini wanted fascism and flying to be intimately linked. Like Balbo, Mussolini as a young man had followed aviation's first halting achievements. In 1919, he had begun flying and defined himself as an "aviation fanatic."[6] When he was first elected to the Chamber of Deputies, he founded an "aeronautical parliamentary group," a caucus of deputies interested in the development of aviation. He was a competent pilot who was not shy about showing off his skills to visiting dignitaries.

From Mussolini's point of view, then, Balbo, with his reputation for action, courage, and audacity, seemed a good appointment. As undersecretary, Balbo would stay busy; as minister, Mussolini believed he could keep him under control. In practice, Balbo did as he pleased. What Mussolini failed to anticipate was that Balbo would take to the Aeronautica with as much enthusiasm as he did—or that the position would turn him into such a hero. Yet a close look at Balbo's background shows a long and consistent fascination with flying and the development of aviation. As a boy he had written the Roberto Fabbri pamphlet. During World War I, his aspirations to become an aviator were thwarted only by the Caporetto disaster. In May of 1922, he tried to form a flying squadron of Blackshirts in Ferrara. When he became general of the militia, he flew a great deal around Italy and wrote in 1923, "I believe that the future of Italy is in the sky."[7] In 1924, he was selected as the party's representative to look into the development of emergency landing fields throughout the country. After he founded the *Padano,* one of the paper's first projects was to sponsor a local aerial exhibit. In May, 1926, he accompanied Mussolini to Libya by air, and the trip reaffirmed Balbo's position as "one of the most fervent promoters" of flying in Italy.[8] The *Padano* also contributed to Balbo's reputation as aerial hero.

When Balbo arrived in Ferrara by air, even though he had flown only as a passenger, the paper described his face as "glowing" from the excitement of watching the panorama unfold beneath the wings of the aircraft.[9] Thus, even before his appointment to the Aeronautica, Balbo was known for being air-minded. Such a reputation did not mean that he knew how to fly. He did not get his first pilot's license until the spring of 1927. He became a competent pilot, but never a great one. Nevertheless, in Italy as elsewhere, the "flying minister" image was popular and a pilot's license became an informal badge of office. In 1933, Balbo's French and German colleagues Cot and Goering were aviators; the Marquess of Londonderry, the English minister, also took flying lessons.[10]

Flying, popular as it was becoming, also harmonized with the development of fascism as a movement and as an ideology. Fascism proclaimed itself to be a new and revolutionary political movement, a break with the past, a path to the future; so was aviation. Fascism exalted courage, youth, speed, power, heroism; so did flying. Hence, many ex-pilots joined the fascist movement after World War I. Finally, Mussolini sensed aviation's potential for propaganda. The wonders of fascism could literally be written in the skies.

Because aviation developed so rapidly during the 1920s and 1930s, the Aeronautica acquired a reputation for being *the* fascist service, the one that Mussolini created literally from the ground up. Naturally, Mussolini encouraged this view. Italy came out of World War I, he claimed, with five thousand aircraft at the ready, thousands of motors and spare parts, several thousand properly trained pilots, and a bureaucratic structure that was adequate to the organization. Yet, by the time he came to power in 1922, Mussolini declared, Italian military aviation had been reduced to a hundred obsolete aircraft, only a dozen properly trained pilots, a couple of flying schools, eight or ten wretched airfields, an unreliable meteorological service—and the same huge bureaucracy. The fault, of course, according to Mussolini, lay with the incompetent and corrupt post-war Liberal governments. Under their rule, unscrupulous businessmen speculated on surplus aircraft; peasants who lived adjacent to airfields freely cannibalized the planes. Wings and tails became the walls and roofs of chicken

coops; fuselages were turned into firewood. Officials responsible
for civil aviation wandered from the ministry of transport to the
ministry of merchant marine to the ministry of war seeking a
bureaucratic home.

Mussolini was exaggerating, although how much is difficult to
say. Between 1919 and 1922, Italy, like the other European
powers, demobilized. The Aeronautica's squadrons were reduced
from seventy to thirty-five, and the budget shrank from 600 million to 90 million annually. Estimates of ready aircraft in 1923
range from forty to as high as one thousand. When the fascists
came to power, Mussolini did expand the budget rapidly from 90
to 500 million lire annually. He also reorganized the Aeronautica
as an independent air arm, much as the British did with the RAF.

However, Mussolini glossed over Liberal Italy's role as a pioneering air-power. The Italians could claim the distinction of being the first nation to put airplanes to military use. The occasion
was the Italo-Turkish war of 1911 when Italy wrested Libya—
Balbo's future colonial domain—from the Ottoman empire. During World War I, as in other countries of Western Europe, Italian
aviation developed rapidly. Italy produced her share of aces and
heroes such as Francesco Baracca and D'Annunzio, and she developed a fledgling aircraft industry. Italians pioneered such tactics as mass bombings in huge trimotor Caproni bombers. When
the United States entered the war in 1917 American pilots, including Fiorello La Guardia, the future mayor of New York,
trained in Italy under Italian instructors. Thus, Liberal Italy
ranked among the most advanced of the air powers.

Mussolini's example of denigrating his predecessors was not
lost on Balbo. When he became undersecretary, he, too, claimed
that he had inherited a disastrous situation and that Italy could
not face a conflict with even a minor power. Of all the armed
services, the air force should in theory be the best prepared, for it
would be the first to enter combat at the outbreak of hostilities.
On the contrary, according to Balbo, the Aeronautica was the
least ready of the services.[11] Balbo clearly had a vested interest in
such a view: the worse the situation, the more he could justify
requests for budget increases. Ironically, among the world's air
powers, Italy ranked very high. Balbo's predecessor, General Alberto Bonzani, claimed to have left approximately 800 ready air-

craft and another 800 in reserve. According to one estimate in a parliamentary report of 1926, this would have made Italy the second most powerful air force in the world.[12] Only France, with 1,500 aircraft and 4,000 in reserve, was more powerful. Great Britain and the United States, it was estimated, had only 700 ready aircraft and 700 in reserve. Since one-third of the French and British forces were dispersed in the colonies, Italy's air power appeared even more formidable. "Italian aviation . . . holds a place in world aeronautics that is unsurpassed. The organization and spirit of the Italian Air Force is making it admired by every nation in the world," declared an American aviation magazine.[13] In the hierarchy of air powers, Italy was challenging the United States for second place after France.[14]

Bonzani's numbers were optimistic. Balbo first declared that as of October 31, 1926, a few days before he took office, the number of ready aircraft totaled 551.[15] After a few days of studying the records, Balbo reduced the number to 405 and then prepared an acid test. He ordered all aircraft to take to the air on November 28. Fighters were to stay up for two and a half hours and all other aircraft for three hours. Only 200 completed the test, Balbo wrote to Mussolini, and most of them lacked armament and were not suitable for combat. Of the 405 originally declared ready, 335 took off, yet 104 did not complete the exercise, for various reasons. At the beginning of his term with the Aeronautica, then, Balbo could really count on only 300 aircraft. How many of them were combat ready is uncertain.

The number of aircraft was only one measure of the Aeronautica's efficiency. The status of ground facilities, such as airports, was highly uncertain. Some offices and shops lacked electricity; others had no water. Meanwhile, rain poured into the leaky hangars.[16] Flying suits were in short supply, as were spare parts, fuel, lubricants, ammunition, and bombs. The ordnance problem was downright comical.[17] Only one contract existed to provide explosives to the Aeronautica; delivery could not begin for two years, because the manufacturing plant had not yet been built. A desperate letter from a young pilot to Balbo in June, 1926, contained a catalogue of inadequacies and concluded with a plea to Balbo to correct these "errors and horrors" and to "electrify" the discouraged and despondent personnel.[18]

As minister of aviation, Balbo was responsible for all aspects of aviation's development, including commercial and general aviation. As a military man in a militaristic regime, however, he devoted most of his energies to developing Italy's military force. In his own mind, when he took office, he had to build from the ground up. "Our Aeronautica was nothing more than an office for propaganda, . . . indispensable" to promote air-mindedness among Italians. "Now it is necessary to begin building military aviation and its weaponry has not even been studied."[19] He planned to proceed by stages: "First of all it is necessary to build a sporting air force, then one that is disciplined, and, finally, one that is militarily efficient," Balbo remarked to a fellow student pilot.[20]

Balbo, of course, had no intention of returning to the days before World War I when flying was a sport for rich dilettantes. To Balbo the term *sporting* summed up the mentality and spirit of the new service. Like champion athletes, he wanted each of his men to give his best, to dare everything. He was also pointedly contrasting the Aeronautica's mentality with that of the established services. Unlike the "sedentary," traditional ways of the army and navy, the Aeronautica would be supple, athletic, open to new military techniques and strategies, to new training, technologies, and styles of warfare.

In discussing his ideas about military aviation, some writers have described Balbo as a "follower" and "intellectual protégé" of Giulio Douhet (1869–1930), the famous Italian theorist of air power.[21] Balbo acknowledged Douhet's influence. In the preface to a posthumous collection of Douhet's writings Balbo commented that the two men developed a cordial relationship and had many talks together about the problems of aviation.[22] In the doctrines of the theorist, Balbo found powerful arguments for building the Aeronautica into an independent service that would have equal rank with the army and the navy; in Douhet's ceaseless polemics about the value of air power, Balbo found a useful source of publicity. In his policies, however, Balbo followed a far more pragmatic path. In 1933, General Erhard Milch, architect of the resurgent Luftwaffe, observed, "Nowhere was the strategy of air warfare heeded less than in the native land of General Douhet."[23] Balbo himself remarked caustically in his 1933 report to the Chamber of Deputies that other countries, especially France, took Douhet more seriously than Italy did.[24]

Douhet has often been described as a prophet of air power. The description is appropriate, for Douhet was an odd combination of military engineer, professional soldier, visionary, and literary man. He is remembered for his contributions to the theory of air power, but his interests ranged far beyond aviation and military affairs. His writings include autobiographical works, dramas, comedies, and anti-military satires.

Douhet's experiences in World War I on the stalemated Italian front deeply influenced his thinking. In Douhet's view, air power was the flexible "ultimate weapon" that his country needed. "Command of the air" was the key to Italy's military problems. Against the airplane, Douhet maintained, there was no effective defense. A fleet of "battle planes" could make decisive bombing attacks against enemy industries and population centers. As a result, civilian morale would collapse. The role of surface forces in such a conflict would be purely defensive. Eventually the army would serve as a police force to control the country that had succumbed to aerial attack. In addition to being decisive, air power was cheap—or so Douhet thought—and thus ideally suited to Italy's limited resources.

Douhet proposed a number of specific institutional and technical measures to carry out his ideas. First, he called for a unified command for all three armed services. Under such a scheme the air force would of course have equal status with the army and the navy. Second, he insisted that the air arm should be independent both in its organization and in its role in future wars. Finally, he favored the development of aircraft like his "battle planes." These giant aircraft—in his mind something like flying dreadnoughts— would be employed as strategic bombers. Douhet also predicted a brilliant future for commercial aviation in Italy. Civil aviation would once again transform the nation into a great commercial center as in the days of ancient Rome, he claimed. He maintained that the peninsula was ideal for developing a major aircraft industry. Such an industry, according to him, required a minimum of raw materials and an abundance of skilled workmen—requisites that suited Italy perfectly.

Balbo's chief concern, however, was military aviation. From

Douhet's ideas Balbo chose those themes and doctrines that he found congenial and practical. He concentrated on three points. First, Balbo insisted that the Aeronautica had its own war to fight. The Aeronautica would cooperate with the other services as needed, but it would no longer be limited to serving as an auxiliary to the army and navy. In future wars, the role of the air force would be predominant, he predicted, and he believed that the development of aviation had revolutionized strategy and "diminished the absolute value of the other forces."[25] Second, in Balbo's view, the Aeronautica should have a first-strike capability. Given Italy's strategic position, neither the army nor the navy could carry out this mission. Finally, as one who made a career out of organizing and leading masses, whether Blackshirts or colonists or aviators, Balbo naturally seized on Douhet's idea of aerial fleets. The day of the "single machine fighting raids" as in World War I had ended, Balbo argued. He pictured "hundreds and hundreds" of aircraft engaged in colossal air battles among the clouds. Hence there was a need for a "completely new doctrine and technical strategy" for the Aeronautica that specifically recognized the characteristics and needs of aerial warfare.

In developing a doctrine for the Aeronautica, Balbo was a pragmatist. In certain of his aerial cruises and in maneuvers like those of 1931, he experimented with Douhetian mass flights and exercises in strategic bombing. Yet he also supported those, like General Amedeo Mecozzi (1892–1971), who advocated tactical uses of air power. Both in his declarations and in his policies Balbo made it abundantly clear that he was not committed to either side. "Neither of these theories can be altogether discarded. . . . I think there is virtue in both," he told an English newspaper while he was still undersecretary.[26] As early as 1929, with Balbo's encouragement, the Aeronautica organized tactical units and practiced maneuvers based on Mecozzi's ideas. Balbo expressed his theoretical doubts about Douhet most extensively in an authoritative *Enciclopedia Italiana* article, "The Art of Aerial Warfare," published in 1938.[27] "Aerial warfare, properly understood, could not be applied in all circumstances," Balbo argued. Douhet's ideas were suitable for a struggle between two industrialized powers, but they were not valid, for example, in colonial warfare. To date—Balbo referred to the Ethiopian war, the Spanish civil war, and the Sino-Japanese conflict—Douhet's ideas had never been put fully into practice. The closest that anyone had come to adopting them was in certain limited actions during World War I such as Italy's mass bombing of Austria's Adriatic port of Pula. Balbo also cited technical reasons in explaining why Douhet's principles had been only partially accepted. Bomber speeds had increased enormously; the accuracy of bombing had not kept pace. Furthermore, no nation to date had sufficient faith in Douhet to commit its resources to massive bomber fleets. Douhet had great importance as a theoretician, Balbo concluded. He was the "precursor" of the "new" and "purely Italian" concept of "total aerial warfare." Yet Balbo added, "Naturally, not all of Douhet's affirmations are to be taken literally, because the development of aircraft and the continual evolution of experiments and applications are such as to exceed every expectation."

In general, Balbo developed a broader, more flexible vision of the potential of air power than Douhet did. For instance, Balbo never believed in the infallibility of Douhet's "battle planes." As William Mitchell, the great publicist of air power in the United States, observed on a visit to Italy, Balbo still allocated aircraft to defensive work.[28] Nor did Balbo believe, as Douhet simplistically did, that military and civilian aviation were interchangeable. Hence, he fought for more investment and development of military aircraft and for more modest appropriations for civil aviation. In addition to encouraging tactical uses of aircraft as Mecozzi suggested, Balbo foresaw the logistical capabilities of aircraft. For instance, in 1938 in Libya, he directed an exercise in which two hundred parachutists "captured" an enemy airport.[29] Reinforcements to secure the objective arrived by air in the form of one hundred transports carrying two thousand troops and equipment.

Douhet's theories, then, served as a base from which Balbo expanded his own ideas and policies, but Balbo never acted as Douhet's devoted disciple. Neither Balbo nor Mussolini gave the theorist a position of authority. Even if Balbo had intended to follow Douhet closely, he would have had a difficult time. Douhet constantly changed his ideas. In his writings of the early 1920s, he allowed for an auxiliary aviation force for the army and navy. In 1927, he renounced that position as being too "cowardly."[30] Significantly, on the tenth anniversary of the Aeronautica's founding,

March 28, 1933, Balbo's main theme was not the creation of a Douhetian air force. He stressed his success in eliminating the "excessive spirit of individualism" from the service. Similarly, in his annual speeches to parliament, Balbo rarely mentioned Douhet as the inspiration for the Aeronautica's development. With monotonous regularity that honor went to Mussolini. Such tributes were ironic. Mussolini posed as a daring aviator and as a progressive statesman who appreciated the potential for air power and favored building a Douhetian air force. When it came to concrete policies—especially appropriations—the Duce acted quite differently. The Aeronautica remained the poor relation among the armed services.

"Honorable Comrades, 'l'argent fait la guerre,' " Balbo declared pointedly in French—at least, it allows a nation to make its defensive preparations, he added hastily.[31] For the last time—although he did not know it—he was delivering his annual message as minister of aviation to the Chamber of Deputies on May 3, 1933. The phrase in French, to remind his colleagues of their powerful neighbor's policies, summarized Balbo's single greatest frustration as minister: the Aeronautica's limited budget. For four years in a row, the appropriation for aviation remained fixed at approximately 700 million lire (between 35 and 40 million pre-war dollars). Year after year, his voice brimful of sarcasm, frustration, and fury, he pleaded for more funds. "We cannot eternally use good will to make up such a large financial shortage," he declared in his message of 1930.[32] He had to balance being thrifty with his matériel against being thrifty with his personnel. "It is a policy—let me tell you— that has me in anguish every day," he told the Chamber in 1932.[33] The only policy he was really allowed to carry out, he said, "and here we do real miracles," was that of personnel.[34]

Perorations in parliament were only part of Balbo's campaign for more funds. He appealed directly to Mussolini. In a polite note in September, 1927, Balbo asked the Duce to give the aviation budget "the special treatment that I have so often pleaded for."[35] Two months afterwards, he most likely presented a memorandum that Douhet had drawn up. In the interests of national defense Italy should prepare to take "command of the air even at the cost of reducing the power of the army and the navy."[36] In a more belligerent and sarcastic mood five years later, Balbo wrote to Mussolini's mistress, confidante, and biographer, Margherita Sarfatti, that he could write an interesting article for her journal, *Gerarchia*. "Here is the title: 'How we are getting ready to lose the future war.' "[37]

To understand what the 700-million-lire budget meant, it is useful to put it in comparative perspective. Balbo did so regularly when he addressed the Chamber of Deputies and contrasted the Aeronautica's budget with that of the other air powers, especially France. "We are moving among giants: giants in wealth, in finance, in raw materials, in technical and mechanical plant and equipment," he told the deputies in 1928.[38] The figures support him. In 1930, Italy's national income (400 billion lire) ranked from a quarter to a third of those of France (1,350 billion), England (1,650 billion) and Germany (1,450 billion), and one-sixteenth of that of the United States (6,650 billion), according to an estimate used by the army chief of staff, Federico Baistrocchi.[39] Inevitably, the Italian aviation budget reflected the nation's relative poverty. In equivalent lire, the French budget (1,341 million) and the English budget (1,900 million) ranged from nearly two to two-and-a-half times larger for 1928/29.[40] Even worse, while the Italian budget remained fixed, those of the French and the English increased sharply during the years of Balbo's ministry. In 1928 the English budget grew by 71 percent over the previous year and in 1929, another 79 percent over 1927; the French increased their 1928 budget by 14 percent over the previous year, and in 1929 by 144 percent over 1927.[41] By 1932, Balbo pointed out in frustration, the French budget had climbed to the equivalent of 3,252 million lire, or more than four times the Italian budget (754 million lire) for that year.[42]

Balbo not only wanted a larger budget in absolute terms, he also sought a larger share of Italy's defense pie. He wanted to match rival services as well as rival air powers. In his annual speeches before the Chamber, he reiterated his views on the Aeronautica's critical role in national defense. Again and again he pointed out Italy's vulnerability to air attack. A narrow peninsula with 4,000 kilometers of open coastline and a few strategic centers was peculiarly susceptible to aerial incursions, he argued—as did foreign military experts such as B. H. Liddell Hart. It is only necessary to draw a compass circle representing a distance of 300 to 400 kilometers—the range of a bomber—on a map from Ajaccio, Corsica, or Ljubljana, Yugoslavia, to show how easily Italian industrial centers could be bombed, Balbo told the deputies.[43] The only effective defense was an efficient air force that could retaliate with a lightning stroke, perhaps even a decisive one. The air force was the most cost-effective of the services, he argued. The issue went beyond division of the budget. Italy's defense strategy and the structure of her armed forces, too, had to be revised. The air force's "real capacities" to contribute to the nation's defenses had to be appreciated and to be seen in the general context of the nation's armed forces. On that day the budget issue would be definitively settled, Balbo declared in 1930.[44]

In his campaign for an equal share of the budget, Balbo alluded frequently to how the Aeronautica's appropriation compared with that of the army and the navy and how this ratio compared to other countries. In Italy during the years that Balbo was minister, the Aeronautica's budget remained at about half of the navy's and a quarter of the army's.[45] As Balbo's supporters in parliament pointed out, in France the defense budget was divided far more evenly among the services. In 1930, the Aeronautica claimed about 14 percent of the total defense budget. France devoted about 22 percent of her military budget to aviation, and England devoted a little more than 17 percent.[46] In their plea for an increase in the budget, Balbo's supporters argued fruitlessly for a percentage that would equal that of France and would push the Italian appropriation over the 1,000-million-lire mark.

Naturally, Balbo's lamentations have to be taken with a grain of salt. He was right about the order of magnitude. In competing with France, Great Britain, and the United States, Italy was jousting with giants. Yet like any good service chief seeking a bigger budget, he had a vested interest in making things out to be worse than they were. Just how bad they really were is as difficult to determine today as it was then.[47] Accounting practices varied enormously from country to country; nations exaggerated or understated their budgets as it suited them. Moreover, as everyone knows, it is easy to do tricks with statistics, and Balbo and his supporters conveniently picked those that would best make his case. For example, Balbo claimed that the British and French apportioned more of their defense budget to aviation than Italy did. That depended on the year. The Aeronautica's share of the total defense budget at 15.1 percent in 1932 was very close to that of the United States (15.2 percent), France (15.5 percent), and Great Britain (17.8 percent).[48]

In depicting the Aeronautica's sad state, Balbo also argued as if Italy's case were unique. The reality, of course, was quite different. The inter-war period was difficult for all air forces. Economic depression, inter-service rivalries, and anti-militarist sentiment among the public all contributed to reducing appropriations. Technological considerations also played their part. Battleships, artillery, and rifles, for example, were expensive to design and to develop, but they had a longer life span before they became obsolete. Aircraft, highly expensive to develop in the first place, quickly became outmoded. Maintenance and training expenses were also very high.

Yet, like anything else, the question of development costs must be kept in context. After all, as a contemporary writer has argued, perhaps Balbo's budget was small, but aircraft at the time were not nearly as complex and expensive as they are today.[49] Aviation was still considered a relatively cheap form of defense. In 1929, with rapidly rising costs, the price tag for a military aircraft ranged between 200,000 and 500,000 lire (about $15,000).[50] Douhet and other defenders of the air force, including Balbo, made the same argument. In the late 1920s and throughout the 1930s, small nations such as Poland, Yugoslavia, and Czechoslovakia could afford to produce their own fighters.

Finally, in presenting the Aeronautica's budget, Balbo ignored or downplayed where, on her "shoe-string" budget, Italy really stood in contrast to the other air powers. Whether in terms of budget, number of first-line aircraft, or number of personnel, Italy ranked only fourth among the world's top air powers, after France, Great Britain, and the United States.[51] Moreover, on a beer budget, Balbo managed to give Italy's Aeronautica a champagne reputation. "The Italian air force of well over one hundred squadrons, smart and well trained, appears to show more results for money spent than probably in any other nation," wrote a *New York Times* correspondent on November 29, 1929. In a world where the limits of air power were still not understood, where

there was plenty of room for fantasy and for grand visions about
the airplane as the ultimate weapon, Balbo did a remarkable job
of filling in his material shortages with showmanship. In this he
was not unique, but he was unusually successful.

Balbo failed in his struggle to increase his budget. He admitted
as much in his last brief, dispirited speech in 1933. The fault did
not lie with him, although on occasion his salesmanship lapsed.
During his 1927 budget speech, for example, he read his text in
such a monotonous tone that a number of the deputies napped and
Ciano gibed with delight that this was a wonderful example of *vol
plané*, of flying with your motor off.[52] To some degree the problem
lay, as Balbo declared, in the nation's lack of "air-mindedness."[53]
The deputies, the public, and the military establishment could not
or would not understand the issues involved. In France, he
pointed out enviously, in addition to the minister and the rappor-
teur, twenty-two speakers discussed the entire program for four
consecutive days. In Italy, however, the newspapers preferred to
concentrate on sporting aspects of aviation, such as races and records, or resorted to sheer rhetoric in reporting Balbo's speeches.[54]
The rival army and navy regarded Balbo's requests with a jaundiced eye. Badoglio dismissed military aviation as nothing more
than "bluff" and called Douhet "a madman."[55]

In a dictatorship, however, the public's lack of air-mindedness
and the inter-service rivalries could have been overcome in the
Aeronautica's favor. Mussolini chose not to intervene. Superficially, he appeared to be air-minded. He created the Aeronautica
as a separate service in 1923; he boasted of building a Douhetian
air force, and for the first four years of the Aeronautica's existence
he supported a sevenfold increase in the aviation budget. Any
further increases, however, at the expense of the army and navy
would have alienated these senior services and eroded the basis of
his political support. Mussolini maintained power by balancing
the new fascist institutions such as the party and the militia
against established ones such as the bureaucracy and the armed
forces. The party could not triumph over the state. The Aeronautica, the most fascist of the services, could not gain the edge over
the army and navy. Fears of strengthening such a rival as Balbo
perhaps entered into Mussolini's decision to limit the Aeronautica's budget. In 1936/37, after Balbo had left the service, for the

first time the Aeronautica's appropriation was greater than that of the navy. In general, the air ministry's budget from 1935 to 1940 grew at a faster rate than that of the other services. These increases reflected the "special" appropriations prompted by Italy's involvement in Ethiopia and Spain. Without them the Aeronautica would have continued to lag behind the other services, and indeed the Aeronautica never came close to matching the army, which always claimed close to half the defense budget. On the other hand, the "special" appropriations were a vindication of Balbo's policies. The Aeronautica had arrived as a legitimate military service with a major contribution to make to the war effort.[56]

The subsidiary issue of whether Balbo spent his limited funds well was a matter of debate in his day, as it is now. In August, 1929, Francesco De Pinedo (1890–1933), then the Aeronautica's deputy chief of staff and one of Italy's most famous aviators, sent to Mussolini a devastating critique of Balbo's work as aviation minister.[57] Personal rivalry and animosity colored De Pinedo's report, but he was well qualified technically to judge the state of the Aeronautica. In his opinion, nearly every fighter, bomber, and reconnaissance plane with which the Aeronautica was then equipped was either totally outmoded or barely acceptable. He made an exception of only two reconnaissance planes. Nearly forty years later, a contemporary critic with no personal animosity toward Balbo echoed De Pinedo's critique.[58] At the end of 1929, Balbo's fighter squadrons were still equipped with the Ansaldo AC.3, copied after the French Dewoitine D.1 and the Fiat CR.1. Squadrons were only just being reequipped with the Fiat CR.20, which was comparable to contemporary fighters of other air powers. The bombers, the Fiat BR.1 and BR.2 and the Caproni CA.73, were as outdated as the older generation of fighters. Furthermore, according to this analysis, Balbo based his personal fame on two outmoded designs. The first was the Savoia Marchetti SM.55 seaplane, with which he made his most famous long-distance flights; the second design involved the record-breaking series of Macchi seaplanes. The SM.55 was already obsolete in Balbo's day. The Macchi series won the Schneider Cup and set seaplane speed records that have never been equalled. Yet neither the airframe nor the engines were translated into production models. By extension, Balbo established a tradition that by 1940 left the Aeronautica unprepared for World War II. While the British and the Germans developed fast, heavily armed monoplane fighters like the Spitfires and Messerschmitt Bf.109, the Italians found themselves armed with the highly maneuverable but much slower and completely outdated biplane Fiat CR.32s and CR.42s.

Such evaluations are unjustified. They show little understanding of how aircraft designs developed during the inter-war period. Two factors restricted the design of military aircraft during the 1920s and early 1930s.[59] One was simply the limitations of budget. With an eye to economy, air forces tried to keep down the number of specialized aircraft, to standardize as much as possible and to build all-purpose models. A second factor, at least in England, was the "ten-year rule." Under this assumption, an impending war would be clear at least a decade ahead of time. This meant that it was enough to build only a few advanced prototypes to keep up design and production facilities; there was no need to manufacture these aircraft in quantity. Production would begin when the war was well in sight. As a result of such assumptions and budget restrictions, by the early 1930s the major air powers were all admirably equipped to fight the air battles of World War I over again. The first-line aircraft were still the same as those that had proved successful in 1918—biplanes with fixed undercarriages and limited armament. No country had a clear advantage and no country had fallen behind. Thus, a more recent Italian military historian, no admirer of Balbo or his policies, has concluded that, on the whole, the aircraft with which Balbo equipped the Aeronautica were certainly as good as, if not better than, those of the other air powers of the day.[60]

Two simple and compelling arguments support such a view: first, Italian aircraft during these years established an extraordinary number of records; second, Italy became an important manufacturer and exporter of aircraft beginning with Balbo's ministry and continuing through the early years of World War II. Between April 1, 1927, and November 1, 1939, Italians set 110 records, though some were held for only a short time. At the end of 1939, Italy still kept 36 of the 84 records established by the International Aeronautical Federation.[61] Between 1937 and 1943, Italy exported aircraft to no fewer than thirty-nine countries.

Many orders came from Latin America and Eastern Europe, but included were such air powers as Germany, Japan, England, and the United States.[62] Balbo did not always achieve everything that he claimed, but there is no evidence that he seriously neglected the Aeronautica's technical development. Balbo equipped his Aeronautica with aircraft that in their own day stood up favorably against their competition. A glance at specific types substantiates this view.

The standard fighters under Balbo's ministry were the Fiat CR.20s and CR.30s and 32s.[63] By 1931, Balbo had equipped his squadrons almost completely with CR.20s. This was a single-engine biplane of metal construction armed with four machine guns. Powered by a 400-horsepower Fiat A 20 engine, the CR.20 had a top speed of 250 kilometers per hour, a ceiling of 6,500 meters, and a range of two and a half hours. While it was not a particularly innovative or advanced design, the CR.20 had good flying characteristics and exceptional maneuverability, which made it a reliable pursuit plane as well as a crowd pleaser in aerial shows. From planning to prototype to production in those days was about a three-year cycle. The prototype of the CR.20 had been tested in September of 1926, shortly before Balbo took office. The CR.20's successors, the CR.30 and the CR.32, appeared in 1932 and in 1933. The CR.32 became the most famous Italian fighter of the inter-war period and ranked among the best—some claim it was *the* best—of its day. It was used in the Spanish civil war and was still in limited service during World War II, ten years after its first flight. Furthermore, the CR.32 was exported to Austria, China, Hungary, Paraguay, and Venezuela. The aircraft went into mass production in 1934, just as Balbo left the Aeronautica.

Critics have argued that since their biplanes performed so well, the Italians were slow in developing the monoplanes that triumphed in World War II. This is probably overstating the case, and such an argument misrepresents the thinking in Balbo's day. In the early 1930s, the superiority of the monoplane over the biplane was not established.[64] Most veteran fighter pilots felt that the key qualities of a fighter were rate of climb, speed, and maneuverability, with emphasis on extremely short radius turns. The monoplane, with its high wing loading, greater turning radius, and greater speeds in takeoff and landing seemed to be seriously disadvantaged. The situation began to change only after Balbo left the air ministry. Messerschmitt, for example, began working on the Bf. 109 in the summer of 1934 and the plane made its first flight in September of 1935. Similarly, R. J. Mitchell developed the Spitfire in 1934/35 and the prototype flew for the first time only in March, 1936.

The bomber situation under Balbo was less satisfactory. In 1931 Balbo claimed in his annual message to the Chamber of Deputies that the bomber problem had been "fully confronted," that bombers made up the "foundation" of the air arm, and that "worries over our inferiority had by now dissipated."[65] The reality was considerably different. Balbo's day bombers were mostly BR. 2s and 3s, part of a long series of designs that had begun in 1919. Both the BR. 2s and BR. 3s were known for their records and distance flights. In 1931 a BR. 3, together with a Fiat A. 120, won the Prince Bibescu Cup with a flight of 710 miles (1,433 km) at an average speed of 156.6 miles per hour (252 km/hr.). Nevertheless, an aerial armada of these machines scarcely had the capability of dealing decisive blows to the enemy.[66] The BR. 2, for example, was a single-engine, two-place, open-cockpit wooden biplane that could deliver a half-ton (metric) bomb load over a 300–400 km range at a speed of about 240 km/hr.—about the same speed as a fighter. The night bombers, slower, and therefore theoretically unable to face fighters, were mostly Caproni Ca. 73s and 74s. By 1931 these were being replaced by Ca. 101 trimotors and twin-engine Ca. 102s, aircraft with a much greater range (1,000 km) but no greater speed.

Every specialized land plane had its counterpart in a seaplane, for Balbo's ministry coincided with the golden age of the seaplane. In those days, retractable landing gears had not been perfected; fixed ones buckled and broke. Landing fields were literally nothing more than that—open fields. Today's modern runways and standardized airports developed as a result of World War II. Both military and commercial aviation in Balbo's day utilized a well-established institution: harbor and port facilities.

The Aeronautica's standard bomber and reconnaissance seaplane under Balbo's ministry was an odd-looking twin-hulled flying boat that he made famous: the Savoia Marchetti SM. 55.[67] This unusual "flying catamaran" became one of the most famous and best publicized aircraft of its day. As Balbo's critics point out, the SM.55 was an old design. It was first planned in 1923 and flew for the first time in 1925. Its ruggedness and dependability made it a favorite for long-distance record flights, and Balbo used it for three of his aerial cruises. A larger variant of the SM.55, the SM.66, was used as a fourteen-passenger flying boat on commercial runs between Rome and Tripoli or Alexandria. The SM.55 proved so durable that it was not withdrawn until 1939, when the Italian navy still had thirteen in service.

If the Aeronautica's first-line aircraft under Balbo's ministry were not inferior to the standards of the time, their quantity and availability were a different matter.[68] In seven years Balbo ordered 2,000 aircraft. This was actually fewer than the 2,300 that his predecessors, Bonzani and Finzi, had ordered in the four years of their administration. The types of aircraft that Balbo ordered also differed. He contracted for about half as many military aircraft as his predecessors and many more planes for tourism, general aviation, and training. Nor could he meet his goals for expanding the number of squadrons. In 1930, for instance, he had funds enough to outfit only two-thirds of his squadrons with CR.20s; the rest had to wait until the following year. In 1932 he noted that lack of funds prevented him from completing his three-year program. It is no surprise that he never came close to his "wish list"—a total of 3,600 aircraft, including auxiliary forces for the army and navy, for which he estimated he needed a budget of 3 billion lire. "The absurdity of this sum can save us from taking it into consideration," he commented.[69]

During Balbo's ministry, Italy's aircraft industry, on which he relied to equip the Aeronautica, developed and expanded. Italy became a major exporter of aircraft. On the surface, these look like commendable achievements. Post–World War II, however, the Italian aircraft industry has come in for some harsh criticism. No one questions the skill and inventiveness of individual designers such as Celestino Rosatelli, Filippo Zappata, Giovanni Pegna, Mario Castoldi, Giuseppe Gabrielli, Alessandro Marchetti, or Gianni Caproni. Individually they produced aircraft that won races and prizes and established a host of records. The industry as a whole, however, failed to deliver, the critics argue.[70]

Despite a multitude of inducements—protective tariffs, subsidies, prizes—the major aircraft companies did not, on a regular basis, produce the equipment the Aeronautica needed. The classic example is the issue of engine design. While Italy built beautiful engines to set world speed records and win the Schneider Cup, the industry did not create a reliable 1,000 to 1,500 horsepower engine that could power fighters and bombers. As a result, the Italians had to rely on foreign engines or clumsy expedients such as trimotor bombers.

According to the Aeronautica's semi-official historian, much of the responsibility lay with the ministry, which gave the industry directives that proved to be "weak and uncertain and in many sectors erroneous."[71] In the relations between the ministry and the industry, the industrialists had the upper hand. If they did not receive as many contracts as they wished for, they raised the specter of unemployment, and the ministry satisfied them.

Such a critique undoubtedly applies at least partially to the years of Balbo's ministry. However, it seems doubtful that stronger direction from the ministry would have resolved the Aeronautica's problems. Such an argument ignores a much larger question: should Italy have developed an aircraft industry in the first place? As one writer has argued, the myth of Italy as a major industrial airpower was merely one of the many myths that the fascist regime fostered and to which Balbo contributed through his policies.[72] He devoted much of his energy to building a national industry, independent in its designs, raw materials, and financing. Since Italy's domestic market was far too small to absorb the national production, foreign sales became an absolute necessity. Italy needed to trade for raw materials or for hard currencies with which to purchase materials. Balbo's mass flights around the Mediterranean and his transatlantic crossings served as publicity and sales trips to promote industry.

From a purely economic point of view, these policies appear ludicrous. On a long-term basis, Italy could not possibly compete with France, England, and Germany. The individual brilliance and intuitions of her best designers and engineers were not enough to sustain an industry. Italy lacked managerial skills, technical facilities, and the necessary huge amounts of capital and raw materials. Production figures from World War II illustrate how absurd Italy's pretensions were. In 1941, her peak year, Italy produced 3,503 aircraft; during that year the English and Americans, working far under their maximum capacity, produced nearly six times as many. As their production expanded, by 1944 the Americans produced 96,370 planes annually, and the English 29,220.[73]

Balbo knew that Italy could not continue to compete. On his aerial cruises he visited all the major air powers except Japan. Air attachés and the Aeronautica's intelligence service kept him informed of aerial developments abroad. Nevertheless, in his mind political and patriotic considerations outweighed economic ones in promoting Italy's aircraft industry. Such a nationalist economic policy, with its emphasis on autarchy and self-sufficiency, was typical of fascism and reflected the protectionist trading policies of the inter-war period. Balbo's one faint hope was that through a restructuring of the armed forces the Aeronautica would enjoy a larger budget and thus would be able to sustain Italy's aircraft industry.

Like the aircraft industries of the other air powers, Italy's first developed as a crash program during World War I.[74] From 382 aircraft and 606 engines in 1915, the industry boomed to produce 6,523 aircraft and 14,849 engines by 1918. Most of these were of French or English design, although the first Italian designs began to appear during the last years. The expansion of the Balbo era, despite the Aeronautica's limited budget, helped pull the Italian industry out of its post-war slump. In 1926, Italy's aircraft sector consisted of about 14 aircraft companies and engine manufacturers. The airframe companies employed about 4,300, and the engines, 2,200. In his annual message as minister, Balbo announced that the industry had produced 420 aircraft and 900 engines during the year—a level not much higher than that of 1915.[75]

Despite Balbo's efforts to expand the industry, Italy's productive capacities came nowhere near those of its competitors.[76] In 1932/33 Balbo made some estimates of Italy's wartime productive capabilities. Within six months, production could increase to 700 aircraft a month and eventually reach a maximum of 1,000 aircraft a month. Aircraft engine production could increase from 120 units a month to 1,300 or 1,400 units after eighteen months of mobilization. Balbo was proud of his industry's response to a concrete test for summer maneuvers in 1931. Three of the largest companies working alone, Aeronautica d'Italia, Caproni, and Breda, in three months had produced and repaired 600 aircraft and delivered 600 new engines and repaired 550.

In their productive capacities, however, the other major air powers dwarfed Italy. Germany, although restricted by the Treaty of Versailles, had seventeen aircraft factories, six for engines and three for dirigibles and balloons. In 1932/33 the Italians estimated that their current monthly production was 250 aircraft and 275 motors. After a month of mobilization, it was estimated that Germany could produce 750 aircraft and 860 motors and after a second month could expand to 3,000 aircraft and 4,000 motors. The French and English, too, overwhelmed Italy in scale. In 1932/33, France, the largest manufacturer in the world, boasted forty aircraft companies and ten engine manufacturers with an estimated monthly productive capacity in peacetime of 200 aircraft and 450 engines. England, with thirty aircraft companies and twelve engine manufacturers, produced 70 aircraft a month, but its capabilities were much larger.

In producing commercial aircraft, estimates ranked Italy (350) with France (373) and Germany (200) in 1932.[77] This was well below Great Britain (470) and the leader, the United States (1,582). The Americans regularly accounted for close to half the world's commercial aircraft.

A national industry meant independence in raw materials. Balbo worked toward this end. His annual messages to the Chamber of Deputies are full of optimistic indications that Italy could become self-sufficient.[78] Italian researchers experimented with tar as a source of airplane fuel and castor oil as a lubricant. Italy reduced her dependence on Japan for parachute silk and produced her own fabric. New provisions were made to protect her domestic supplies of wood. These efforts failed. The costs of producing substitutes—when that was possible—proved uneconomical. The aircraft companies themselves, despite regulations against buying raw materials abroad, did so regularly, because of lower costs.[79]

Despite these obstacles, Italy took on the appearance of an industrial air power. She exported aircraft, engines, spare parts, and parachutes throughout the world.[80] In 1931 her sales included seven aircraft and forty-four seaplanes for a total of nearly 16 million lire. Her customers ranged from Japan to the Belgian Congo. The largest order that year came from the Soviet Union, which bought sixty-two Isotta Fraschini Asso 750-horsepower engines. In 1933, the Germans considered buying Italian fighters until the German aircraft industry could rebuild and produce its own models.

In his procurement policies Balbo appears to have been demanding. At first he looked like an easy mark for the industrialists, for he lacked a technical background. In his first annual message to the Chamber of Deputies in 1927, for instance, he clumsily defended the validity of wood construction airframes against those built of steel and aluminum. "He is in the hands of the usual meddlers and intriguers, because he knows nothing of the technical aspects and thinks he knows," snickered Antonio Locatelli, a gold-medal winner with D'Annunzio's squadron in World War I, and a deputy.[81] But Balbo relied on highly respected technical experts such as Rodolfo Verduzio, Giulio Costanzi, and Arturo Crocco, and he learned quickly.

In public, he praised the industry and Italian designers who produced aircraft that won the Schneider Trophy and flew the Atlantic.[82] If Italian designs had not always been highly original in the past, he blamed the government's "excessive restrictions." In asking for future bids, Balbo promised that the government would require only a few basic characteristics so that designers would be free to exercise their ingenuity. He also promised—following Verduzio's advice—that in drawing up contracts with the companies, the ministry would not haggle excessively over prices. Such a policy was only an apparent saving; in reality, it led to the use of inferior materials, he claimed.

Despite these declarations, he earned a reputation for dealing with a firm hand. He described himself as being "fairly tough with the industrialists and rigorously demanding what industry can and must give me."[83] At the beginning of his ministry, he took a hard line. On November 19, 1926, he held an important meeting with the major manufacturers, including Caproni, Piaggio, and Macchi, in which the two sides sounded each other out.[84] The manufacturers complained about a long list of difficulties with the ministry: slowness of payments, penalties for late consignments, and other bureaucratic problems. In turn, Balbo attacked the industry for its tardiness in making deliveries and fulfilling specifications. He warned them that the ministry would not subsidize ailing companies and he demanded "without discussion" that the industry form a consortium for exports. Over the years, he insisted on competitive bidding and the construction of prototypes. Test pilots for the ministry no longer accepted gold watches and other little gifts from the companies for overlooking flaws in the prototypes and failures to meet contract specifications.[85]

In the politicking over contracts, many gossiped about whether Balbo favored one manufacturer over another.[86] Some thought he was partial to Fiat because Fiat had helped finance the *Corriere Padano*. Others thought he was partial to SIAI because of the SM.55. Yet Balbo's personal integrity was such that it became the subject of an often-repeated anecdote. On a visit to Fiat, the story goes, he was offered a sports car. The president of Fiat, scrupulous about regulations against bribery and favoritism, asked for a symbolic payment of one lira. Balbo drew a two-lira coin from his pocket and presented it to the official. "I'm sorry, I don't have any change," the official said. "That's all right," Balbo replied. "Just give me another car."

Although Balbo generally relied on the advice of his technical experts in making procurement decisions, he was quite capable of taking matters into his own hands and riding his own hobbyhorse.[87] One example was the affair of the MF 5. In August of 1930, the ministry asked for bids on a design for an Italian seaplane that could become standard equipment on civilian airlines. A Fiat subsidiary, CMASA of Marina di Pisa, designed a twin-engine, all-metal, ten-passenger flying boat developed from the German Dornier "Wal," which the company produced under license. Although the designer claimed that the MF 5 met all the contract specifications, Balbo rejected it in 1933. The MF 5, derived from the Dornier models, looked too "German" for Balbo and he preferred the SM.66, a larger passenger version of his beloved SM.55.

His most colossal—in every sense of the word—procurement blunder was the DO X. The DO X was the jumbo of its day, a monster flying boat whose twelve engines generated 7,500 horsepower and were theoretically capable of lifting an airframe with a capacity of 150 passengers. Dornier's dream, with this giant, was to supersede dirigibles in transatlantic travel. From its inception in 1926, the project was plagued with engine troubles. Balbo's technical advisers, Costanzi and Verduzio, were divided on the DO X's merits. Nevertheless, Balbo ordered two of the giants in 1931 at a cost of more than 30 million lire—a significant drain on the budget. The DO Xs proved to be white elephants. They were far too large to be used economically on civilian airlines; they were far too unwieldy and unreliable to be used for military purposes. In 1933, the planes were used for training purposes; by 1934 they were no longer flying, and by 1937 they had been scrapped.

As air minister, Balbo was responsible for the development of commercial as well as military aviation. During the seven years of his leadership, Italy established and developed her first regular commercial airlines. Thanks to generous government subsidies— up to half their costs, in some years—airline traffic doubled, tripled, and quadrupled during the first few years of operation. Very quickly, commercial flights linked all parts of Italy, extended throughout the Mediterranean, and stretched north to Berlin. Balbo encouraged this growth and took pride in it as yet another example of how Italy was marching in the vanguard of "civilization." Yet he resented the diversion of funds in his budget away from military purposes, and he doubted whether commercial aviation would ever pay for itself.

Italy was the last of the major European air powers to develop commercial airline service.[88] The first regularly scheduled airline began service on April 1, 1926, on the Turin-Trieste run. By the end of the year, five airlines had established routes over a 3,700-kilometer network. They had carried 4,000 passengers, 1,500 kilograms of mail and 50,000 kilograms of baggage. From these beginnings, in his annual messages, Balbo proudly cited the statistics of growth. By 1931 the network totaled 16,249 kilometers, four times what it had been in 1926; the number of kilometers flown in 1930 was eight times what it had been in 1926, and the number of passengers had increased tenfold. By 1930, with 40,000 passengers carried that year, Italy ranked third in Europe, after Germany and France—and ahead of Great Britain. It was a remarkable achievement.

In addition to expanding Italy's domestic net, Balbo branched out to establish international and colonial routes. These were problems that required Balbo's personal attention, for together with commercial advantages, the international routes raised issues of national prestige. To highlight the importance of the colonial tie, Balbo personally flew a trial of the Rome-Tripoli line with fourteen passengers on October 2, 1928.[89] He also negotiated the "line to the Orient" with the British and French.[90] His goal was to share the "India mail" traffic to Egypt. For prestige reasons, he sought to tie Libya into the network and to secure landing rights in Tunis. "Thousands and thousands of Italians who live on the African coast in conditions of almost complete isolation from the mother country" would now be an hour from Sicily, two hours from Sardegna, and four hours from Rome," he told the Chamber of Deputies. In March, 1928, the French agreed to grant landing rights in Marseilles and Tunis. In return, the Italians gave the French rights to stop in Naples and Castelrosso (Dodecanese). Balbo broke a stalemate in negotiations with the British and inaugurated the Genoa-Rome-Alexandria route at the end of March, 1929. Balbo also investigated expansion in China and routes to Latin America. The Chinese venture never bore fruit; the Latin American routes were established in 1938–1939, long after Balbo had left the ministry.[91]

Despite his pride in the development of commercial aviation in Italy, he had serious reservations. "Civil aviation is not a field that can develop without limit," he told the Chamber of Deputies in 1929, just after boasting that the industry's statistics had doubled over the previous year.[92] "Today, all the airlines in the world are in the red" and "much caution" would be necessary to establish commercial aviation as a public service that would meet the needs of the nation. In taking this stand, he was undoubtedly following his own convictions, but he may also have been following Mussolini's lead.[93] In a brief memorandum to the minister of finance, Senator Antonio Mosconi, the Duce commented that "the further progress of commercial airlines (important most of all from a *military* point of view)" required 18 million lire in additional funds for the year 1929/30. However, the airlines had already reached their maximum development, Mussolini concluded.

Balbo's chief concern was the financial drain of commercial

aviation on his budget. "Since I am convinced that it will be very difficult to utilize civilian aircraft in war, I must focus financial efforts above all on military aviation," he declared in his 1931 budget message.[94] His skepticism was justified. Although both passenger and freight service had grown by leaps and bounds, the airlines were not carrying anywhere near their capacity, nor were they close to making a profit.[95] As in other European countries, the Italian airlines could not have developed without heavy government subsidies. Between 1927 and 1929 these nearly doubled, from 35 million lire annually to 68 million, from 5 to 10 percent of the Aeronautica's annual appropriation. The subsidies in 1928 amounted to about half the cost of operations. In addition, the government took part in the capitalization of the companies and exempted them from customs and other taxes on fuel, lubricants, and necessary imported equipment. In 1931 Balbo commented that the first period of explosive growth was now over and he wanted to establish stable, practical, efficient public service. Passenger and tourist service, he was convinced, would always have only secondary importance for civil aviation. The mails, Balbo felt, would provide the chief rationale for commercial aviation. "Everything will have to depend on the postal service . . . whose development already is the pride of all great civilized nations," he declared.[96]

To ease the financial straits of the airlines and the drain on the budget, in November of 1933 Balbo drew up a plan to consolidate the competing airlines into a single state-operated airline.[97] At the end of October, 1934, the new organization, Ala Littoria, emerged with an operating capital of 18 million lire and seventy-nine aircraft. By that time, Balbo had already been governor-general of Libya for ten months.

Chapter Eight

Minister: Father of the *Aeronautica*

"The problem in aviation is above all the problem of personnel. It is infinitely more difficult to create a pilot than to build an airplane."[1] So Balbo defined his greatest challenge as air minister. He began with a brand-new service—one with no clear sense of mission, traditions, or discipline. The Aeronautica's spirit and traditions were derived from the individualistic, often anarchic, experiences of World War I. Its relationships with the other armed services were confused and uneasy, and its bureaucracy was not even housed under a single roof. In his seven years as minister, Balbo changed all this. By the time he left, the Aeronautica's blue uniform had captured the imagination of the public and the hearts of young Italians who sought to join its ranks. The men who wore the uniform knew that they belonged to a legitimate service with traditions, regulations, and a mission. Naturally, Balbo did not always succeed. For example, his struggle with the other services left bitterness, confusion, and uncertainty about the Aeronautica's mission—but this was not unique to Italy.

Recruitment for the Aeronautica was a difficult task at first. Without the prestige and traditions of the army and the navy, the Aeronautica had a hard time attracting young men inclined to a military career. To fill the ranks, many pilots—and other personnel as well—came from the other services.[2] During 1926–1927, for example, the Aeronautica held no fewer than six special competitions for officers and NCO's needed to fill the ranks. These included 200 sergeants for ground crews, 400 for flight crews, and 100 officers for reserves. Other competitions sought officers from the army and navy to fill both active duty and reserve positions. These last would be eliminated as soon as the service's immediate needs were met, Balbo promised. For the sake of morale, an air force career had to begin at the bottom and not at the top, he declared.

Another personnel problem, to which for obvious reasons he did not refer, was the conflict between cliques and the inter-service rivalry within the Aeronautica. An anonymous "Commander Nemo" informed him regularly of the feuds between former navy and former army men.[3] Balbo tried to attract pilots from World War I to the Aeronautica's reserves. With his instinct for publicity, he thought of new ways to promote the Aeronautica and flying, both civilian and military. The office of civil aviation, the ministry's press office, and the Aero Club d'Italia all dispensed information. Aerial cruises, displays and pageantry, air races, and flying tours of Italy generated interest in aviation and attracted recruits. By 1932, Balbo claimed that the Aeronautica had so many aspirants to become pilots that the service could afford to reject 80 percent of them on the basis of a physical examination.[4]

Thanks to these efforts, the Aeronautica grew in size and began to take on the composition of a professional fighting force.[5] The 1925 Bonzani regulations provided for 2,340 officers; Balbo's regulations of 1931 provided for 3,060, an increase of about a third. Within the flying branch between 1925 and 1931 there was also a notable increase in the numbers of officers from captain to general and in the noncommissioned officers. The numbers of subalterns and enlisted men diminished. This reflected the large increase in professional men in the ranks—those who were committed to a career in the Aeronautica or who had, at least, voluntarily signed up for a long-term period of service. By 1930, Italy could claim 3,000 pilots, three for every one of her available military aircraft—without counting those in the reserves, Balbo claimed proudly. This was almost quadruple the cadre provided for in 1926.

The organization also began to show increased specialization. For example, the 1931 regulations created a service section within the flying branch. This was to employ personnel who, for various reasons, could no longer fly but could still serve usefully on the ground. A special section of medical officers was also created. Nevertheless, if numbers of support personnel for every pilot are an indication of an air force's sophistication, Italy lagged well behind the other air powers. In 1927 Balbo reported that Italy had the lowest ratio of personnel per plane and the lowest ratio of nonflying to flying personnel of any of the major air powers.[6] For every aircraft in service, England had fifty-three support persons, France twenty-nine, Germany thirty-four. Italy had only seventeen.

While the Aeronautica's numbers increased steadily, Balbo lobbied for an even larger service. For example, in the 1931 regulations the Aeronautica was allowed 3,060 officers, with 1,750 of them to be assigned to the flying branch. In practice, when parliament voted appropriations, it authorized personnel increases on a year-to-year basis. For 1931/32, parliament authorized 2,160 officers, 4,000 NCO's, and 18,000 enlisted men. The Aeronautica's real strength fell short even of that. As of January 1, 1932, there were 1,700 officers (1,100 of them in the flying branch), 3,100 NCO's, and 16,000 enlisted men.[7] Was the Aeronautica short-handed? Probably not. The staff that Balbo sought had little to do with the Aeronautica's real needs and capacities at the moment. He wanted to create openings for future development and to show the Aeronautica's emergence as a power under his direction.

Critics sniped that those who aspired to join the Aeronautica came for reasons other than simple love of flying. They wanted to take advantage of faster promotions and special medals and honors for those who took part in activities such as the aerial cruises. While this may have been true initially, by the early 1930s the ranks had filled and the easy careers and fast promotions had disappeared.[8] Sixty percent of the officers, Balbo declared in 1932, would complete their careers as captains. The other 40 percent, who reached the higher ranks, had to meet stiff standards both of technical competence as pilots and of leadership ability. As Balbo pointed out, the age limit for the highest rank, *generale di squadra aerea*, was 55; the average ages for the few generals in the next two ranks below were 48 and 46, respectively.

Filling the ranks, of course, was not enough; Balbo also sought to imbue his men with pride in their organization and with ideals worth fighting for. As the newest of the services, created under fascism, the Aeronautica gained a reputation for being the most fascist of the armed forces. Balbo had molded a fascist air force while Gazzara had created an anti-fascist army, sneered Farinacci.[9] He was wrong. One of Balbo's great achievements was that under his direction, the Aeronautica came to be accepted as a legitimate armed service on a par with the army and the navy. Balbo used his political position to advance his career in the military and to become a minister. Once he had reached the top, however, he behaved like a professional soldier. The military, in his view, had no business mixing in politics, except as private citizens.

Balbo made his stand clear in two ways. First, he refused to allow politics to affect promotions. He personally decided on those whom he felt worthy of party membership and restricted the number severely. He urged the party secretary to ignore any requests that did not come directly from him. He protested when a local party secretary publicly distributed party cards to officers on active duty.

Second, Balbo made his attitudes toward politics and his ideas about the proper conduct for an officer explicit in a circular of December 6, 1927.[10] Under the heading "Moral and Political Education of Airmen," he urged his officers to speak out in favor of fascism. In doing so, he referred to no specific organization and no particular personality. He equated fascism quite simply with national pride. To speak of fascism, of the abyss from which it had saved Italy, of the goals toward which Mussolini was striving "was not carrying out political intrigue in the barracks because fascism today is identified with the nation." "An unlimited pride in being Italian" must be instilled in young people. Admiration for foreign achievements must be considered a "shameful relic" of Italy's dark past, when she was unjustly held in subjugation.

Balbo's code of behavior for his officers was thoroughly conventional. He expected them to behave like gentlemen, with "that aristocratic distinction which must form the chief trait of the person who comes from a good family, who is well educated, who at every moment of his life feels that he represents not only himself but the corps to which he belongs." Irregular relationships—illegal marriages or mistresses—would not be tolerated, he warned. Those who were involved in such relationships, and he knew of several, he claimed, had two months to resolve them. In addition, officers must be discreet. They must not publicize their feats or records without prior authorization. Gossips and critics were admonished to control their tongues, for, Balbo noted, foreign air attachés were not only up on the latest developments in the Aeronautica, but also knew all the gossip. Finally, off duty and away from their bases, officers might participate in social life as much as they liked, but air bases were for training, not for aerial joy rides, dancing, teas, and tennis with girl friends and wives, he admonished.

Balbo did not always live up to his own standards. When it came to demonstrating physical courage, to risking his life, few faulted him, and most people enjoyed his boyish charm. But there was another far more difficult side to him that friends and close collaborators had to deal with. The suave, cosmopolitan aviator and politician gave way to the provincial boor. To a faithful subordinate, for example, he might say with a malicious grin and his familiar slight lisp:

"How long have you been with me?"
"Ten years, excellency."
"Bravo. Now pull off my boots."[11]

As he approached middle age, his friends and collaborators had to endure his obsession about getting fat—a preoccupation that he shared with Ciano and many of the other *gerarchi*. Like Ciano's friends, Balbo's often had to put up with attending him while he took a bath. Invariably, he asked them if they thought he had put on weight. Then he would tell them:

"You suffer from the lamb's ill."
"What?"
"Your belly's growing and your pecker's over the hill."[12]

More disturbing to those who worked closely with him was the ease with which Balbo the free spirit gave way to Balbo the pedant, the inflexible enforcer of petty regulations—at least for others. He gained a reputation for punishing infractions severely, and he turned down appeals. "I know that the punishment you had was stiff, but you know, and not from today, that the minister, even though it pains him, is inflexible when it comes to duty," Balbo's personal secretary replied to a former flying instructor for whom Balbo had a soft spot.[13] In the case of an old comrade from the *Alpini,* Balbo intervened so that the man was able to rejoin the army and then the Aeronautica after he had been medically discharged. Nevertheless, in his recommendations to the army, Balbo always scrupulously added that he did not want to violate any regulations. After twelve years in the Aeronautica, despite the man's pleas and appeals, he had not risen beyond the rank of captain.

One of Balbo's major battles in the Aeronautica was with the aces and *prime donne.* With them he was even more demanding and inflexible than with the rank and file. He played a major role in ruining the careers of De Pinedo and Nobile. Lesser personalities such as Mario De Bernardi and Arturo Ferrarin preferred not to tangle with him. Even Stefano Cagna, his personal pilot for many years, a veteran of all Balbo's major aerial cruises, got a cold shoulder when he violated Balbo's sense of duty. In April of 1940, on the eve of the war, Cagna had resigned from the Aeronautica to take a position in civil aviation. "Your departure, even if it left me with a bad impression, certainly has not changed my feelings with regard to you," Balbo reassured him. Nevertheless, "I really cannot wish you anything in your new activity except that very soon you will give it up for an important command or a delicate military mission where a young general can best serve the service and the Fatherland."[14]

Balbo's great goal, he declared in his annual message to the Chamber of Deputies in 1929, was to imbue Italian aviation with "a military spirit, which . . . would take into account the wholesome individualism of every flyer." Nevertheless, each pilot must develop a sense of duty that would go beyond mere individual achievements to include a feeling of belonging to a larger organization.[15] On March 28, 1933, the tenth anniversary of the Aeronautica's founding, and six and a half years after Balbo became head of the Aeronautica, he declared that he had "definitively eradicated the excessive spirit of individualism that diminished the military character of the service"; he had created a healthy and high esprit de corps, and he had restored discipline. This was his greatest achievement.

To judge by their world records, their victories in air races such as the Schneider Cup, their aerobatic teams that performed throughout Europe and the United States, Balbo's disciplined Italian pilots ranked among the best in the world. Critics, however, wondered aloud how typical these displays were. Too much of the Aeronautica's training was devoted to special events, they claimed, and not enough to preparing the rank and file.

Balbo frequently declared that he was committed to eliminating *divismo* and to building an Aeronautica in which every man would be extraordinary. He did work hard to overhaul the chaotic system of training.[16] Until 1929 seven civilian aviation schools (all private enterprises) used about thirty different types of machines to carry out a three-stage training program. In that year Balbo appointed a military commission that standardized both the program and the machines and reduced the training costs. Flying in these schools in 1927 totaled 33,000 hours, about half the total hours of military pilots for that year, and more than five hundred students successfully completed the civilian courses in 1929.

Balbo also introduced several specialty schools.[17] The Scuola di Alta Velocità at Desenzano (Lake of Garda) for research and development at high speeds began operations in April, 1928, and the Scuola di Navigazione Aerea di Alto Mare at Orbetello began operations on January 1, 1930, as a center for training crews for long-range oceanic cruises. At Roma-Ciampino, he also developed a center to test and train pilots in Mecozzi's assault tactics; at Udine-Campoformido he supported a unit that specialized in aerobatics; and at Montecelio he favored a center for research in high-altitude flying. The fates of Desenzano and Orbetello, in particular, support the argument that Balbo had created these programs for very limited purposes. Desenzano's mission was really to pursue the Schneider Cup with greater method; Orbetello's, to train crews for the Atlantic cruises. Once Balbo left the Aeronautica, the programs faded away—Desenzano as early as 1936.

Meanwhile, those who were not involved in these special projects flew relatively little, as the statistics illustrate.[18] To be sure, flying time in the Aeronautica increased more than two and a half times, from 50,400 hours in 1926 to 139,400 in 1931. However, so did the number of aircraft and the number of pilots. The Aeronautica's flying time in 1931 was only about half that of the estimates for the French air force (250,000–400,000 hours) and the RAF (325,000 hours) and about a third of the total for the American army and navy (670,000 hours). The Aeronautica's flying time per aircraft was also relatively limited. In 1930, for example, fighters averaged 150 hours a year, bombers 70 hours, land reconnaissance 190 hours, and sea reconnaissance 170. Accidents were relatively frequent. In 1927, for example, there were 581 accidents, with 58 dead, 19 seriously injured, and 260 aircraft destroyed. In 1931, 25 officers and 38 NCO's had to leave the service because of accidents. Conscious of this problem, Balbo eagerly pointed out signs of improvement. In 1933, for the period up to May 1, there had been only 8 flying fatalities, compared to 30 the previous year with the same number of flying hours, he proclaimed.

With his taste for display, Balbo emphasized aerial shows such as the two Wing Days (Giornata dell'Ala) held on June 8, 1930, and May 27, 1932.[19] These exhibitions were consciously patterned after the RAF displays at Hendon that were held annually from 1920 to 1938. Like their Hendon counterparts, Wing Days were nominally staged to raise money for air force charities—in the Italian case, an orphanage under the protection of the Madonna di Loreto, the patron saint of aviators. To prove that the Wing Days were not a "slavish" foreign imitation, Italian journalists distinguished between the British aviator, who was only a "sportsman," and the Italian aviator, who "remains a soldier even when he is an artist."

The programs were elaborately choreographed. Spectacular aerobatics and elaborate formations, mock attacks on an "Arab village" and a mass parachute jump comprised the program of the first Wing Day. For the grand finale, 200 planes attacked an "enemy" airport and chased each other around in vivid dogfights. The "curtain" came down when a squadron of fighters laid down a smoke screen. "It was a triumph for Balbo," De Bono noted in his diary. With the exception of the parachuting, the show was "brilliantly conceived and carried out and we were treated to a show rivalling that of the Royal Air Force Pageant at Hendon," wrote a foreign guest attending Balbo's 1932 Congress of Trans-Oceanic Aviators. "I doubt if any pilots of any other nation could have surpassed them," he concluded.[20]

Balbo also experimented with large-scale aerial maneuvers such as those of August, 1931.[21] The exercise was intended to test the Douhetian thesis of the effectiveness of massive aerial attacks. Taking the model of army or navy maneuvers, Balbo wanted two aerial armies or fleets to clash in the sky. Two aerial divisions of 70 squadrons each, totaling 860 aircraft, participated in the maneuvers, which lasted from August 26 to September 3. For three days, each side carried out day—and sometimes night—bombings against major Italian cities including La Spezia, Ancona, Genoa, Florence, Bologna and Terni. For the finale, 300 planes carried out day and night attacks on Milan.

Officially, Douhet triumphed. A nation that experienced such an aerial invasion surrendered unconditionally, according to the official communiqué. However, Badoglio, then chief of the supreme general staff, still denied the value of air power and bitterly criticized the official communiqué. More significantly, the conclusions of the experts and the official results were never made known. Most important, Balbo never repeated such maneuvers. The following year, in August and September he cooperated with the army in maneuvers, and in October the Aeronautica carried out an experimental bombing of Rome.

Wing Days and aerial maneuvers were ways of showing off the Aeronautica's prowess before a domestic audience. For the international stage, the major display was for the Schneider Cup.[22] With the famous American competitions, the Thompson, Bendix, Pulitzer, and Gordon Bennett, the Schneider ranked as one of the great air racing classics of the pre–World War II period. The French steel and munitions baron Jacques Schneider (1878–1928) first offered the cup in 1912. His goal was to stimulate the development of flying boats, and he dreamed of linking the world by means of flying fleets that did not require expensive airfields.

By the time Balbo first became involved, the Schneider had evolved into something quite different from what its founder had intended. In the Cup trials between 1926 and 1931, the entries were no longer flying boats but racing float planes, more advanced than their land-based counterparts. Like racing cars, the Schneider entries demanded enormous amounts of money and effort to develop. The competition, the critics complained, had degenerated into a madcap struggle for speed supremacy—and national prestige. The planes were built exclusively for racing.

Balbo took office a week before Italy's greatest triumph in the series, the 1926 competition held at Hampton Roads, Virginia, on November 13. The Italians, with three Macchi M.39s, captured both first and third places. Mario de Bernardi piloted the winning entry at an average of 396.689 km/hr. In less than nine months, the Italians had produced a design that set the standard for future seaplane racers—slim fuselage, low-set monoplane wing, liquid-cooled, in-line engine. Four days after the Schneider competition, De Bernardi set a world speed record of 416.618 km/hr.

For the next five years, Balbo pursued the Schneider Cup fruitlessly. The 1927 competition in Venice was particularly humiliating for Italy, and for Balbo. A quarter of a million spectators jammed the length of the fashionable Lido. Of the three M.52s prepared for the race on September 26, not one completed the course. Mechanical failures plagued each one. The British, the only other competitors, had only to complete the course to claim victory. As a consolation that year, on November 4 De Bernardi set another speed record of 479.290 km/hr., faster than the winning Schneider time.

The failure was particularly bitter because on paper the Italians should have won. They had made some excellent test runs, in some cases easily surpassing the eventual winning time. On the other hand, both Italians and foreign observers agreed that the Italians, perhaps overconfident from their startling success the year before, had not prepared seriously and methodically enough for the race.[23] The aircraft companies were contacted too late about building a new engine. Balbo should have agreed to a two-week postponement of the race, as the Americans requested.[24] The Italians would then have had time to test their engines, which proved so unreliable. Even Balbo admitted to Mussolini that the engines had not been sufficiently tried. Balbo's informants hinted that rivalries among the pilots also contributed to the poor preparation.[25]

Undaunted, Balbo made two decisions to improve Italy's chances in future competitions. First, in agreement with the English, the race was scheduled for every other year. Second, he established the research and testing center at Desenzano. Matters did not improve at the 1929 competition held September 7 at Calshot on England's south coast near Southampton. Four companies, Fiat, Macchi, SIAI, and Piaggio, prepared four different models for entry into the race. Fires, crashes, and other disasters destroyed nearly all of them. Dal Molin claimed a respectable second for Italy in an old Macchi M.52R, a slightly modified version of the model that had been victorious in 1926. It was a good showing, considering that his engine produced 900 horsepower less than the winner.

The British needed only one more victory to claim the trophy permanently. So expensive and dangerous had the race become that governments balked at sponsoring it. The 1926 victory had cost the Italians 3,860,000 lire, more than five times that of the previous year; by 1929, the costs had risen to 14,650,000 lire.[26] The aircraft companies bid grudgingly for the Schneider contract and only on the condition that the government provide comfortable subsidies. In parliament, deputies protested that the Schneider cost too much and produced no practical results. The British government, too, refused to subsidize the race in 1931 and it had to be financed with private funds. Balbo defended the value of the Schneider both as a means of technical progress and as a training exercise. British and French public statements about disinterest in the race were merely posturing, he declared. If they thought they had a chance to win it, they would once again show interest, he claimed.[27] With the French, he asked for a postponement of the race to allow time for more training and development, but the British declined. Macchi and Fiat teamed up once again to produce the MC.72. A Fiat AS 6 engine—actually two coupled AS 5 engines—powered the aircraft; the development took longer than expected, and after a fatal crash the Italians withdrew. On September 12, a Supermarine S.6B completed the course at Calshot at an average speed of 547.188 km/hr, and the British claimed the Schneider trophy permanently.

How much the Aeronautica benefited from the Schneider races and the subsequent speed development at Desenzano is still a subject of considerable debate.[28] The research and development for racing engines continued after the Schneider competition ended. Agello continued to set records with the MC.72. On October 23, 1934, at Desenzano, he piloted a 3,300 horsepower aircraft to a record of 709.202 km/hr. (440.681 m.p.h.). That speed, of course, has long since been surpassed, but the record still stands for aircraft of that type. Yet the MC.72 had no real influence on standard Italian fighter design. Some claim that the World War II Macchi 202 and 205 were offspring; others argue that the only factor in common is the aircraft company name. Moreover, in 1933, for reasons that are still unclear, the Italian air ministry decided to give up on the development of in-line liquid-cooled engines in favor of air-cooled radial engines. Thus, all the development that went into the Schneider engines was abandoned. The English, in the meantime, based on experience with their Schneider engines, developed the Rolls Royce Merlin that powered their best World War II Spitfire and Hurricane fighters and even the American Mustang. The Italians in 1940 had to rely on German liquid-cooled engines built under license.

For these reasons, Balbo's critics have dismissed his support of the Schneider races as wasted effort. This hardly seems fair. Balbo gave Italian aviation an opportunity. By participating in the Schneider competition, Italy shared in the wealth of new technical developments in designs, fuels, engines, cooling systems, superchargers, and flying techniques. The Schneider racers were so advanced technically that it took four or five years for the rest of the aeronautical world to catch up. If his successors missed the chance, this was hardly Balbo's fault. The Schneider was important in another way: at a time when there was little money for aviation, the races kept public attention focused on flying. Such benefits may be intangible, yet in evaluating Balbo's participation in the Schneider races they cannot be ignored.

In addition to winning races and gaining public support, Balbo, like the other air ministers of the inter-war period—whether Goering in Germany or Pierre Cot in France—was concerned with establishing an independent Aeronautica equal in every respect to the army and the navy. Training, esprit, and air shows were not enough. The Aeronautica had to have bureaucratic and legal independence. One of his first steps in this direction was to oversee the construction of a new building in Rome.[29] When the Aeronautica was founded, the ministry was scattered in twelve offices throughout the city. Communications between the offices required mountains of paper, squads of messengers, and weeks of time, claimed Balbo. Security was a problem. Finally, and perhaps most important, the physical separation of the offices worked against the creation of a unified spirit within the service.

The new ministry building, located in Rome's Castro Pretorio section, between the railroad station and the university and next to an artillery garrison, was inaugurated in 1931 as part of the celebrations of the March on Rome for that year. Balbo's ideas for the building came from his visits to the United States, where he had carefully studied such facilities. The exterior, spare, bare, and sober, reflected perfectly the interior rule of life, he claimed. "What rule? That of simplicity, clarity, speed, elements of the modern discipline of labor."[30] Whoever carries out the orders is at the disposal of the commander, under his eyes, like "a sort of human keyboard," he explained. He planned bright, open offices where glass replaced walls; he included pneumatic mail service, internal telephones, modern elevators. Everything was adapted to extreme speed and to the silent movement of a complex of 1,200 employees. Visitors remarked on the spareness and simplicity of the furnishings—no armchairs, no rugs, no curtains. Everyone sat on simple wooden chairs.

One of Balbo's great innovations was the American-style work schedule—a great shock to government employees accustomed to lunch at home and perhaps a little nap before resuming their office work. Balbo allowed only forty minutes for lunch; at noon—early by Roman standards—everyone ate in the building's dining hall at the same time. "Long rows of black marble tables, desk high, chromium-trimmed (a glorified Child's restaurant)," according to the American racing pilot Major Al Williams, who visited it in 1936.[31] He, like nearly every other visitor, was astonished at another detail. "There were no chairs in the room—these officers were eating their luncheon standing." His host explained proudly, "We have the chairs, of course—the space for them—but no time for them."

Balbo defended his work schedule zealously. Among its other advantages, he claimed, was that it promoted a better family life. Employees who came to work at eight or eight-thirty could be home with their families at three-thirty or four o'clock in the afternoon. From time to time, he wandered about the ministry to see that employees were observing the schedule. To his undersecretary, who had sent a memorandum that the hours must be respected, Balbo commented tartly, "The warning is excellent but one hundred percent useless . . . if you personally set a bad ex-

ample, arriving at the office not at eight but after ten. Get up
early and at eight make the rounds of the offices. . . . That's the
way to command. . . . This is not just an order but also a friendly
bit of advice." As a postscript he added, "Make your own immediate employees respect the schedule, for they never do so! (I'm
referring to your personal secretary.)"[32]

Balbo not only regulated the hours and the environment in
which the ministry employees ate lunch, he also tried to regulate
how they ate.[33] Each employee received a little handbook on
good table manners. The reader was carefully instructed on the
use of forks and knives: knives were to be used only for cutting,
not brought to the mouth. The reader also learned the correct
posture while eating on his feet and was ordered to stand ten
centimeters from the table. (Predictably, the employees amused
themselves by measuring the distance with their palms at the
level of the stomach or groin, thereby making suggestive or ob-
scene gestures.) The manual discussed the impropriety of sneez-
ing, coughing, or blowing one's nose at the table; the proper use
of a handkerchief; the correct tone of conversation at meals—
"cheerful"—and post-meal dental hygiene. Each employee—at
his own expense—received a toothbrush and toothpaste and was
carefully instructed in the manual, with illustrations, on how to
use them.

On the surface, Balbo's concern with these details appears to
be merely one more manifestation of the tyrannical side of his
nature. Undoubtedly there is some truth to this. Yet it is also
important to keep the context in mind. Balbo was struggling to
give the Aeronautica legitimacy and respect, to mold a first generation of officers and civilian employees who looked and behaved
according to the highest standards of European military tradition
and civil service. For the young officers, in particular, white teeth
and graceful table manners were fundamental. In the 1930s, bad
table manners could ruin the career of officer candidates in the
German *Kriegsmarine*. Unlike the RAF, which he admired,
Balbo's air force could not recruit monied boys from private
schools. Balbo had to create his own officers and gentlemen.

The new ministry building was important as a bureaucratic
symbol of the independence of the Aeronautica. The problem of
the Aeronautica's relationship to the other services remained.[34]

According to the statute of 1925, the Aeronautica was divided into four sections: the "aerial army" proper, consisting of seventy-eight squadrons; army aviation, fifty-seven squadrons; naval aviation, thirty-five squadrons; and colonial aviation, twelve squadrons. The statute was obviously a compromise. To mitigate their jealousies, the senior services retained substantial air forces of their own. At the same time, the Aeronautica had sufficient numbers of its own to create an independent aerial force. Balbo was not satisfied. The Aeronautica was not recognized as an independent force capable of fighting its own battles, he insisted. As soon as he came to the ministry, he laid claim to the air forces assigned to the navy and the army. In doing so, he was behaving like a model disciple of Douhet. "Auxiliary aviation" (those air forces assigned to the other services) was "useless . . . harmful . . . superfluous," Douhet argued in a memorandum to Balbo.[35]

Both theory and experience, Balbo told parliament, had established the organic unity of aerial defense. The air was a theater independent of the other theaters of operation; it must be entrusted exclusively to the "aerial army, in which all the available offensive and defensive forces are united"; he was also quite certain that "the decisive action in future conflicts will be entrusted to the aerial army."[36] The Aeronautica's unity of command and action must not be weakened by dividing up its forces and its missions.[37]

In challenging the army and the navy for their air forces, Balbo was breaking down a door that was already half open. Neither of the senior services had much faith in the role of aviation. So long as their budgets were not cut, they did not oppose Balbo vigorously. First the navy, in a meeting of January 27, 1928, gave in on the issue of the auxiliary forces. The assistant chief of staff for the navy, Romeo Bernotti, engaged in a spirited discussion with Balbo. The relationship of the Aeronautica and naval aviation, he argued, should not be decided on the basis of abstract principles such as Balbo proposed, but according to the concrete military problems that Italy might face. His superior, Ernesto Burzagli, the naval chief of staff, interrupted him: "That's enough. We give in."[38] The army's turn came in April, and once again there was no real opposition. The army assumed that airplanes would play much the same role that they had in World War I—useful mostly as artillery spotters, reconnaissance, and couriers. The navy agreed to cut their aerial forces from thirty-five squadrons to eighteen, the army from fifty-seven to forty-six squadrons. The army also accepted Balbo's demand that their airplanes be used only for reconnaissance. The negotiations with the army dragged on for at least two years, however, and relations between the two services deteriorated.

Balbo, in the meantime, aspired to draw up a statute to reflect the Aeronautica's new status. The army found an ally in the finance ministry, which resented Balbo's cavalier way of dealing with the state's accounting methods. Balbo's proposal was blocked when he brought it before the Council of Ministers in June, 1930. Mussolini, who did not want to show favoritism, preferred to have the service chiefs resolve the matter among themselves. Balbo, however, appealed directly to him in a letter of June 16, 1930. "Today even after so many proofs of competence and sacrifice before you and Italy, I feel clearly that the independence and maturity of the Royal Air Force is not finding among all the ministers its proper recognition. Give me a chance to defend your ideas in your presence," he pleaded.[39] Balbo succeeded, and in January, 1931, his new set of statutes was approved by the parliament. They did not differ radically from those of 1925 except that the forces assigned to the army and the navy were reduced.

Balbo won another struggle with the navy—the battle over aircraft carriers. "You want aircraft carriers, but I shall not let you build them," he told Admiral Bernotti. Carriers were superfluous for Italy, he argued—and he had many supporters.[40] Italy itself— the peninsula, Sicily, and Sardinia—formed a natural carrier, a much cheaper and more secure one than a vessel, Balbo argued. From land bases, the Aeronautica's aircraft had sufficient range to strike all vital points in the Mediterranean. His opposition to building battleships, however, failed. Despite his contention that air power was cheaper and that a battle fleet was too vulnerable in a narrow sea like the Mediterranean, the navy prevailed.

In his struggle with the other services to assert the independence of the Aeronautica, Balbo won. So far as the nation's defense was concerned, however, his was a Pyrrhic victory. In practice, each service prepared for its own war, and coordination among the branches was ignored. The Aeronautica never developed a clear sense of its role. The effects became evident in 1940 when the Italians failed in their attacks on the British fleet in the Mediterranean and in their bombings of English cities. The fault certainly did not lie only with Balbo. The responsibility for coordinating the three services lay with Mussolini. He might easily have created a defense ministry or a general chief of staff with powers over all three services. Balbo made such proposals in 1933, and Mussolini repeatedly turned them down. Such an office, particularly with Balbo at the head of it, as he proposed, posed too great a political threat to the dictator. Italy paid dearly for this decision in 1940. Balbo, too, perhaps paid dearly for his battle with the other services. With better coordination, the antiaircraft batteries might have been aware of who was approaching the airfield at Tobruk on June 28, 1940.

Chapter Nine

Aviator: The Mediterranean Cruises

Balbo's years as air minister coincided with aviation's "golden age"—the great pioneering period of record flights, of air races and long-distance aerial cruises.[1] Those were the days of Lindbergh's solo across the Atlantic, of Wiley Post's record circumnavigations of the globe, of Byrd's and Nobile's polar flights, and of countless lesser transoceanic or transcontinental hops. Those were also the days when daring pilots raced after the Pulitzer, the Thompson, and the Bendix trophies in the United States and the Schneider Cup in Western Europe. Women such as Amelia Earhart, Jacqueline Cochran, and Amy Johnson proved that virtuoso flying was not exclusively a male province.

The record flights and races were more than sporting events. Each new achievement, each competition pushed forward the boundaries of aviation. Racing stimulated new developments in technology: the best in airframes, engines, fuels. Long-distance flights pioneered routes, spurred designers to create comfortable cabins for the pilots, demanded sophisticated navigational techniques. Commercial aviation, especially, benefited from these innovations.

The record flights and races also shaped public opinion. Immediately after World War I, most military men dismissed airplanes as no more than flying artillery spotters; only the most daring and prosperous of businessmen regularly booked flights on the nascent airlines. For the public, flying meant, for the most part, thrilling rides with a barnstormer at a country fair. The record flights and air races helped change all that. They marked the transition from flying as a sport to a major commercial and military enterprise. In much the same way, the pioneering flights of the 1960s and 1970s marked the transition to the military and commercial use of space.

Italy made some remarkable contributions to aviation's "golden age." Francesco De Pinedo and Arturo Ferrarin ranked among the world's top distance flyers. Mario De Bernardi, to the astonishment of the aviation world, snatched the Schneider Cup in 1926. Ferrarin and Del Prete's record-breaking endurance flight in 1928 and their long-distance flight to Brazil "placed the Italians in the foremost place in regard to aeronautical engineering," according to an admiring American aviation journal.[2] Balbo belongs to this Italian and international pantheon. Between 1928 and 1933, he participated in or led half a dozen mass aerial cruises. These achievements gained him international fame and a lasting reputation as one of aviation's great pioneers.

As air minister, Balbo regarded the record and long-distance flights as a mixed blessing. He admired the record men, the aces, the great solo flyers for their courage, their dedication, their skills. He welcomed the publicity they provided for the development of flying in general and for the Aeronautica in particular. Yet he opposed the mentality of the *prima donna* and the *diva,* which he claimed went with such record flights. Unless they were endowed with "truly superior moral qualities," it was very difficult to force the great champions to submit to military discipline, he declared in 1929.[3] There were also personal considerations. Some of the *dive,* such as the glamorous Francesco De Pinedo, aspired to be at least Balbo's equal. Others, like Umberto Nobile, with his dedication to airships rather than airplanes, were, in Balbo's view, leading the Aeronautica down a blind alley.

Balbo's solution to the problem of the *dive* and the record flights was typical of him. "We want to demonstrate that the Italian air force does not have in its ranks only a few exceptional men but that all the personnel can participate or collaborate in the most daring enterprises of our time," he told the Chamber of Deputies in March, 1928.[4] The Aeronautica's new frontiers lay "not in individual flights but in collective cruises of multiple squadrons with no fewer than eighty aircraft."[5] In short, just as he had transformed scattered Blackshirt squads into a militia, now he planned to transmute solo distance and record flights into aerial armadas.

Such was the origin of his famous aerial cruises. In general, each cruise was longer and more difficult than its predecessors and Balbo played a larger role in planning and leading it. His four best-known expeditions spanned oceans. The first two, in 1928 and 1929, covered the western and eastern extremes of the Mediterranean. In 1931, in a far greater achievement, he spanned the South Atlantic from his home base at Orbetello to Rio de Janeiro. In 1933, in his most famous exploit, he led a mass flight across the North Atlantic to Chicago and back—a double crossing.

Like the traditional naval cruises from which they were derived, the aerial ones served many purposes. First, they were training missions. Pilots gained valuable flying time and experience in various types of weather. Balbo also envisioned formation flying as a form of close-order drill that taught the value of command, of discipline, of performing as a group. He denied that he was creating an elite. With proper training and leadership, even an average pilot could participate in these expeditions, Balbo claimed. He also stressed the cultural benefits of the cruises. His men would come in contact with new peoples and new customs. In addition, the cruises showed the Italian flag, publicized fascism, displayed the Aeronautica's technical prowess, and demonstrated the excellence of the Italian aircraft industry to prospective customers.

There were paradoxes in this. The flights, thanks to the fascist propaganda machine, enjoyed enormous publicity. Heroism was not abolished, but instead of being individual, it became collective. Balbo's goals in these flights provided another paradox. He did the extraordinary with the aim of transforming it into the ordinary. The ultimate goal of his transatlantic flights was to make such crossings routine.

Balbo's notion of mass flights was certainly not original with him. Italian aviation had a well-established tradition along these lines.[6] Douhet had first suggested the idea of great aerial fleets, and during the waning days of World War I, at the battle of Vittorio Veneto, the Italians experimented with such formations. Balbo was

also deeply indebted to Francesco De Pinedo, who was internationally recognized as one of the great pioneers of long-distance
flight. De Pinedo made two remarkable long-distance seaplane
journeys. On the first, in 1925, over a seven-month period he flew
from Rome to Melbourne to Tokyo and back, a total of 55,000
kilometers. On his second flight, with Carlo Del Prete, De Pinedo
made a tour of the "Four Continents" or the "Two Americas." On
this 40,000-kilometer flight, between February 8 and June 16,
1927, he flew from Europe to the West African coast, then across
the South Atlantic to Brazil and Argentina. From there he made
his way northward across the Caribbean to the United States and
eventually across the Atlantic again to Italy. What he had proved in
an era before airports were common was that a small flying boat
was an incredibly versatile and durable vehicle.[7] With a good pilot
it could go practically anywhere on earth.

For his aerial cruises, Balbo followed De Pinedo's example with
regard to flying boats. In addition, he depended heavily on De
Pinedo's skills as an organizer and as a pilot, for he was not himself
an exceptional pilot. During a flying career that lasted approximately fourteen years, Balbo totaled about 3,000 flying hours, a
good but not an extraordinary total.[8] Unlike the best airmen, he
did not handle seaplanes as well as land planes. Because he knew
his limitations, for years he kept Stefano Cagna, a truly outstanding
pilot, as his flying aide. At first, in organizing the aerial cruises,
Balbo had the good sense to rely on more experienced and talented
pilots. De Pinedo provided the leadership for the two Mediterranean cruises. For the first Atlantic expedition in 1931 to Brazil,
Balbo called on Umberto Maddalena, who, like Cagna, was personally close to Balbo and one of the Aeronautica's most skilled
pilots. By 1933, for the last of the four major aerial cruises, Balbo
felt experienced and self-confident enough to take charge himself.

Of these four major aerial cruises, the first was by far the
largest in terms of men and equipment.[9] Sixty-one seaplanes
transported a party of nearly two hundred to ports of the Western
Mediterranean from May 26 to June 2, 1928. Beginning from
Orbetello, the huge expedition made six stops: Elmas (Sardegna),
Pollensa (Balearic Islands), Los Alcazares and Puerto Alfaques
(Spain), Berre (France), and Orbetello. The route was chosen
according to specific criteria. The distance between each pair of

Fig. 10. Balbo as pilot (Caproni Museum Archive)

ports was no more than about five hundred kilometers or three to four hours of flying time. Each stop offered a bay large enough to accommodate the entire formation, provided good anchorage, and was easy to supply. The bulk of the aircraft were fifty-one SIAI S.59bis reconnaissance and light bombers with 500-horsepower motors. The remaining ten aircraft consisted of SM.55s like the one De Pinedo used in his long-distance flights, and one Cant.22. These carried the observers: dignitaries, high-ranking officers, journalists, and foreign military attachés, including those from France, Spain, England, and the United States.

The scale of the formation was unprecedented. Prior to this experiment, such flights had usually been carried out with no more than eight aircraft. When the full expedition lined up, wing tip to wing tip, the row of aircraft stretched for four kilometers. Such a large formation was vulnerable to the open sea, and critics predicted that five aircraft would be lost on each leg. Nevertheless, with Mussolini's blessing—and substantive advice that led to rerouting parts of the expedition—Balbo went ahead.

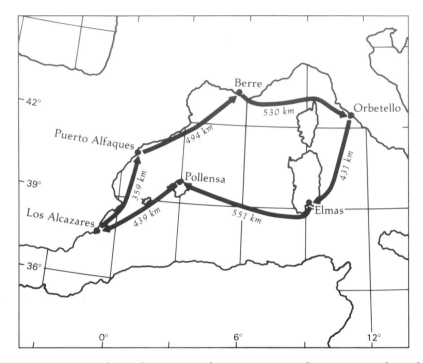

Map 1. Route of aerial cruise to the Western Mediterranean (adapted from G. B. Guerri, *Italo Balbo*)

Except for a storm which led to some minor collisions while the fleet was anchored at Los Alcazares, the operation went smoothly. As the expedition progressed, the pilots became increasingly skilled and confident in their formation work, and the expedition made a great show.[10] In the air they formed four arrowheads around a diamond. So tight was the formation that the planes looked suspended from invisible threads, wrote one journalist; so huge was the formation that in flight the nearest aircraft looked like "eagles" and the most distant like "flies." Even more spectacular were the takeoffs and landings. At Orbetello, the expedition took off squadron by squadron. Nine by nine, as if dancing a quadrille, each squadron taxied into the wind; then, as one, they gathered speed, reached the "step," broke from the water's surface, and lifted off, leaving nine parallel churning white furrows—the wakes—behind them. By the time the expedition reached

Puerto Alfaques, the pilots were skilled enough to take off en masse, and the town marvelled at the spectacle of all sixty-one aircraft lifting off simultaneously. Their tight formation over Marseilles brought cheers from the spectators on the ground.

Balbo's role during the Western Mediterranean cruise was minor. He flew about as he pleased, and while the expedition was anchored at Los Alcazares he lunched in Madrid with the king of Spain. The real leader of the expedition was De Pinedo. Balbo generously acknowledged this in a final press conference: "He is no longer only the great record man, the victor over the toughest aerial circuits in the world, he is also a leader of soldiers, a general in the widest sense of the word."[11] At his own suggestion, as a reward for his role in the expedition, Balbo enjoyed a meteoric promotion. First, Mussolini promoted Balbo to the rank of reserve general in the air force and then called him to active duty. From a militia general, Mussolini had magically transformed him into a real general like the one both he and his father had dreamed of becoming as children. De Pinedo, too, received promotions in rank and position, as well as the title of marquis.

While the sixty-one aircraft of the first Mediterranean cruise flew from success to success, far to the north another Italian aerial expedition, for which Balbo was partially responsible, ended in disaster. The airship *Italia*, under the command of General Umberto Nobile, flew triumphantly over the North Pole on May 24. The following day, on the return flight to its Arctic base, the airship encountered bad weather and crashed on the ice. Nobile and nine companions, including his dog Titina, survived in the cabin; the other six members of the expedition were swept away with the balloon and perished. For a month and a half, the world followed breathlessly the international rescue effort and the saga of the survivors housed in their "red tent." In a decision that became controversial, Nobile allowed himself to be rescued on June 24 before all the rest of the survivors had reached safety. On July 12, the rescue concluded when the Russian ice breaker *Krassin* reached the last of the stranded crew.

Once the rescue operations were completed, the controversies began. Until his death in 1978 at the age of 93, Nobile polemicized about the expedition. He was a victim of political persecution because of past socialist sympathies, he claimed, and he blamed Balbo's opposition to the project in large part for the *Italia* disaster.

As air minister, Balbo was inevitably involved in the *Italia* expedition. Nobile, a brilliant and imaginative designer of airships, held the rank of general in the Aeronautica's engineering corps. With Balbo's support, Nobile might have enjoyed use of Aeronautica matériel, personnel, and financing for his project. Balbo flatly and openly opposed the expedition. First, airships, he felt, had no military value; he refused to support an enterprise that would glorify them. Second, he considered the expedition to be essentially a repetition of an earlier one that Nobile had made with the American aviator and scientist Lincoln Ellsworth, in 1926, and that had come close to disaster. Nobile remembered Balbo saying, "One doesn't tempt fate twice"—an opinion that Mussolini shared.[12] Third, the expedition violated Balbo's campaign against the record men and *dive*. To some extent this may have reflected a fear of Nobile as a rival. Yet, compared to De Pinedo, the threat Nobile posed was minor. Finally, Balbo opposed Nobile, a pre-war socialist sympathizer, on political grounds—so Nobile claimed. Such a consideration was, however, very minor in Balbo's thinking compared to the others.

Balbo's opposition to the *Italia*'s flight was certainly not decisive. He was only the undersecretary; Mussolini was the minister. In the end, Mussolini gave his approval, with the proviso that the expedition take place under civilian auspices. The solution delighted both Nobile and his opponents. In the Aeronautica, some argued that technically Nobile, as a member of the Aeronautica's engineering branch, was not qualified to pilot airships. If he persisted in doing so, his enemies cheerfully declined any responsibility for the consequences. Nobile was happy because he would not be subject to military discipline or direction. When the expedition was approved, Balbo gave it considerable informal support. Balbo himself, apparently, suggested the Royal Geographical Society as a civilian sponsor.

After the *Italia* crash, Nobile complained that the Italians "could have done much more" to rescue the expedition.[13] In effect Balbo dragged his feet, according to Nobile. He took off on the cruise to the Western Mediterranean and ordered the newspapers to focus on it and to downplay the *Italia* story, claimed

Nobile. That was not the case. Balbo quickly dispatched four of his best pilots—Major Pier Luigi Penzo, Lieutenant Tullio Crosio, and two of his personal favorites, Maddalena and Cagna—to help the rescue efforts. In fact, Balbo's pilots were the ones who first sighted the red tent on June 20, and Nobile himself, at the official post-rescue inquiry, testified to Penzo's zeal. In addition, in a letter of June 12 to Mussolini, Balbo proposed that he himself should participate in the search operations.[14] Nobile dismissed this offer as confirmation that the rescue operations were inadequate and that Balbo's offer was purely for propaganda effects. Nobile was not entirely wrong. In the June 12 letter to Mussolini, Balbo wrote that in general the newspapers had blown up the disaster out of proportion and that there were even a "few clowns" who claimed that the Aeronautica was not doing enough for the rescue. "If you think that a gesture would be opportune, even to divert the public's attention, I am very ready to take the second pilot's place and leave tomorrow for King's Bay," wrote Balbo.[15] Such an action would go far to silence the anti-fascist press, he suggested. Yet Balbo was not one to risk his life foolishly, especially in search of an enemy. He volunteered because, as he wrote, he considered that his presence "would not be completely useless" in the rescue operations.[16] Mussolini vetoed Balbo's personal participation. The decision may well have saved Balbo's life; Penzo and Crosio crashed fatally on their homeward flight.

Nobile's charges that Balbo failed to support the *Italia* expedition and hindered the rescue efforts are, then, less than convincing. Despite his opposition, Balbo gave the expedition, including the rescue efforts, reluctant support. Nobile's complaints that Balbo had a hand in persecuting him after the rescue contain more substance. On his return to Italy in the fall of 1928, Nobile faced an official inquiry. Mussolini, of course, had no reason to look closely into an affair that was bound to reflect unfavorably on Italy and his regime, and initially Nobile was welcomed as a hero. The atmosphere changed when Nobile turned to settling scores. He alienated the navy—the service that had supported him with a base ship—by filing a complaint against the ship's captain. He also attacked Balbo, judging that perhaps this was the moment to oust him. Under international pressure to conduct an inquiry,

Mussolini acceded, and Balbo was happy to second him. Unquestionably, the board, stacked against Nobile, made little effort to be impartial and to gather the facts. When Balbo appeared before the board on November 13, 1928, in his fifty-two pages of testimony he did not hide his animosity toward Nobile.[17] The board, for its part, made jokes and disparaging remarks at Nobile's expense and did not bother to question Balbo in any systematic fashion.

In his testimony Balbo made two points. First, he attacked the dirigible program, which he felt was useless to the Aeronautica in an era of collective aerial cruises. Second, he accused Nobile of unmilitary behavior. Nobile had not, Balbo claimed, taken proper leave of him and Mussolini at the start of the expedition. On his return, he had not shown the proper gratitude either to the pilots involved or to Balbo and Mussolini for their parts in the rescue efforts. Rather than seeking to meet with Balbo and Mussolini, Balbo claimed, Nobile first sought an audience with the pope. Nobile also displayed unmilitary behavior in his lack of courage. He had not fought at the front as a dirigible pilot during World War I; even worse, he had allowed himself to be rescued first off the ice pack after the *Italia* crashed. To a journalist friend who tried to defend Nobile, Balbo revealed his attitudes clearly. He disliked Nobile. More important, he felt that the Aeronautica's reputation was always at stake in the conduct of its officers. "You're one of those who wants to keep a virgin wife and at the same time have children. . . . Any one of us soldiers who doesn't keep his nerves under control in the most critical moments can also be shot," he remarked.[18]

In its conclusions, the board of inquiry blamed Nobile for the loss of the airship and found that his decision to allow himself to be rescued first had "no plausible justification."[19] They also found fault with his personal conduct—much as Balbo had suggested. As a technician in his special field of dirigibles, the board concluded, Nobile was excellent. His behavior during the *Italia* expedition, however, was "presumptuous, self-interested, and ungrateful toward those who helped him with his plans and who also gave their lives to save him." In leaving the expedition first, he failed to live up to his duties and his dignity as a general and commander. Finally, with his behavior and his words, and in newspaper articles, the board concluded, Nobile attacked some of his followers on the expedition, and denigrated the Aeronautica's rescue work in comparison with foreign rescue efforts. The board was not empowered to impose any sanctions or punishments, but Nobile's career in the Aeronautica was finished, and he resigned.

Unlike the ill-fated *Italia* expedition, Balbo's flight to the Western Mediterranean under De Pinedo's leadership was a model cruise. Less than a month after his return from it, Balbo led a parody of an aerial cruise. The trip came to be known euphemistically as the Cruise of the European Capitals.[20] A better name for it might have been "the scattering of the *dive*." The cruise's main destination was London, to attend the RAF annual air display at nearby Hendon. The expedition violated all Balbo's carefully enunciated principles about aerial cruises. The twenty-four pilots were all senior men with long experience, not ordinary pilots from regular units; the dozen planes were not seaplanes but twelve land planes—six A.120s and six R.22s; the expedition did not train together for formation flying; Balbo apparently gave no thought to logistics and ground support. He sent one of his aides ahead by train to determine the location of the London airport. The expedition left June 28 for the 1,600-kilometer flight to London via Paris. Only half the aircraft arrived that day. Four landed in France, two in Belgium, and one in the Netherlands. The remaining six straggled in at various intervals, "like sheep." How so many experienced pilots became so lost, Balbo never explained. In any case, the air show was "magnificent"; Balbo hobnobbed with the English sovereigns, and with the king of Spain, whom he had met during the Western Mediterranean cruise.[21] The air minister, Sir Samuel Hoare, and the chief of the air staff, Lord Hugh Trenchard, hosted Balbo. He toured major aircraft factories. The Italian community in England turned out enthusiastically for the visit. Balbo sang the praises of fascism and the London *fascio* registered eighty new members.

According to one story, Balbo proselytized beyond official gatherings. In response to a challenging note from the local antifascist Circolo Garibaldi, he cut short an official ceremony. In full uniform with all his decorations, he confronted the anti-fascists at their meeting-place in Soho. As he told the story, many of the anti-fascists were ex-*Alpini* and "I won them over immediately."

Soon they were singing songs of the Great War and talking of Italy.[22]

The cruise next flew to Berlin where, showing no symptoms of his later Germanophobia, Balbo politely toasted the president of the German Republic, the German people, and German aviation.[23] Finally, the aviators returned to Rome on July 10, completing the 4,000-kilometer tour. Balbo, who should have arrived first in Rome, straggled in fifth. Fortunately for him, there was little publicity about his first attempt to lead such an expedition. Six months afterwards, he brazenly boasted of the cruise.[24]

In December of 1928, Balbo embarked on a trip that influenced him deeply and inspired him to plan his famous Atlantic crossings. For the first time, he visited the United States. He was invited to give a paper at an international conference on civil aviation in Washington, D.C., and then went on to visit an aeronautical exposition in Chicago. He had obviously been thinking about such an American trip for at least a year beforehand. As early as January 14, 1928, he had questioned the American naval attaché in Rome about the possibility of such a visit.[25]

The trip developed in two parts: first the conference and the visit to Chicago, then a tour of military installations throughout the United States. Balbo was not present to deliver his paper in Washington; he had caught a bad cold at a banquet in Chicago. The speech was largely a reiteration of his annual messages to the Chamber of Deputies. Despite her restricted aviation budget in comparison to the other air powers, Italy "in these last years has made a contribution which I would dare call significant to the general progress of aviation,"[26] he wrote. He cited De Pinedo's long-distance flights and his own aerial cruises to Spain and to the capitals of Europe. He stressed that the cruises led to concrete results. Commercial Rome-Barcelona and Rome-Milan-Munich-Berlin flights had been inaugurated the previous October. He also gave hints of Italy's widening aerial interests. The Mediterranean, with many Italian colonies scattered along its shores, was a natural region for aerial expansion, he said; however, Italy "could not forget the Atlantic, the route that the genius of Columbus had opened to world traffic."[27]

When Balbo, his wife, and a small party of aides resumed their tour, they stopped in Dayton, Ohio, where he met Orville

Fig. 11. Balbo (second from left) next to Henry Ford in Detroit (December, 1928) (Caproni Museum Archive)

Wright; then in Detroit to meet Henry Ford, a charmer whose directness in appearance and manner Balbo found delightful.[28] From Detroit they travelled by train to the West Coast to tour military bases in San Diego. This visit, Balbo told his hosts twice, more than justified his trip to the United States, and he repeated his conviction in a telegram to Mussolini.[29] At the naval air station he reviewed six squadrons of the Fleet Air Force. Technical matters did not interest Balbo, but the virtuosity of American pilots sent him into raptures. After watching six squadrons demonstrate their skills in close formation flying, he declared, "Their tactical exhibition was the best I have ever seen."[30] The organization of the separate naval air arm also impressed him; it was a system that he favored, he told his hosts.

Throughout his travels, Balbo noted the reception the Italian-American communities gave him, and he looked for signs of anti-fascist demonstrations. Both considerations were important in planning a return trip, and he was reassured on both counts.

Everywhere he went, beginning in Chicago, he was delighted to sense the "fervid passion for Italy and for the man who governs it" and the "mystical union with the great distant Fatherland."[31] He was proud to hear what model citizens Italian-Americans were. The anti-fascist demonstrations were minimal.[32] Balbo encountered a group of perhaps thirty or forty—by his count—protesters on January 4 when he visited New York's City Hall. Many of them were not even Italian, he claimed. Some demonstrators directly in front of him waved placards urging, "Join the Anti-Fascist League." Since they appeared to be asking him if he would join, Balbo replied, "I'll think about it, I'll think about it."[33] "I have the impression that anti-fascism in New York is of very limited importance when it is given no weight," he telegraphed to Mussolini.[34]

The trip impressed him deeply. He marvelled at the enormous power, wealth, and size of the country; at the millions of Italian-Americans making new lives so far from their homeland; at the simplicity and modesty of many high officials, from the president on down. Among the aviators, he was surprised to find that many of the most famous American long-distance flyers had not capitalized on their achievements. A pilot who had made a round-the-world flight was handing out programs and pamphlets at the aviation exposition in Chicago when Balbo visited it.[35] The Old World had much to learn from this "sense of limit, [as] a preventive medicine for rhetoric and vainglory."[36] His direct contact with the United States "increased my old fascination with her," and the "desire to lead an Italian aerial squadron across the Atlantic" became a concrete design.[37] On the voyage home aboard the *Conte Grande,* Balbo began to lay plans that he carried out in the summer of 1933 in his most famous flight, the Decennial Air Cruise.

Even before he left for his visit to the United States, however, Balbo, with De Pinedo, had been outlining a second Mediterranean cruise, this time to the east.[38] Three possible routes were considered before the final one evolved. Originally Balbo proposed a flight to Smyrna, Alexandretta, and Beirut. The Turkish government denied permission to land in the latter two ports, but it did offer Istanbul. Then, largely by coincidence, a new and daring possibility developed. Through contacts first with two officers of

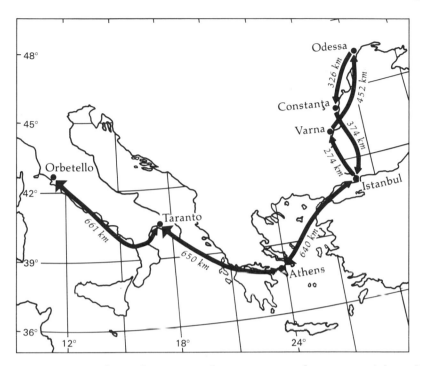

Map 2. Route of aerial cruise to the Eastern Mediterranean (adapted from G. B. Guerri, *Italo Balbo*)

the Krassin who were in Rome to testify at the Nobile inquest and then with the Russian ambassador, Balbo received permission for his expedition to land in Odessa. The final plan ran: Orbetello, Taranto, Athens, Istanbul, Varna (Bulgaria), Odessa. The return flight was almost a repetition of the outgoing one: Odessa, Constanţa (Rumania), Istanbul, Athens, Taranto, Orbetello.

The new project was a little longer than the Western Mediterranean cruise—about 5,300 kilometers of flying. However, in men and equipment the expedition was about half the size of the first. This was in part to cut costs, for the Western Mediterranean cruise had turned out to be enormously expensive. This time the expedition consisted of 32 SM.55s, 2 S.59bis's and a Cant.22, a total of 35 aircraft and 136 persons. Costs also dictated the timing. The plan was to make the outgoing flight as quickly as possible and then return in leisurely fashion in order to exploit the publicity aspects to the full. On the return leg, the Italians also planned to do some hard selling: Greece, Turkey, Bulgaria, and the Soviet Union were all clients of the Italian aircraft industry.

In its technical aspects the expedition proved uneventful—a sign that it had been well prepared. Accidents and mechanical failures were few. A storm, while the expedition was anchored at Constanţa, tore three aircraft loose from their moorings, causing enough damage that Balbo postponed departure for a day. One of Balbo's speeches provided another minor bit of drama, a small ripple on the international diplomatic scene. At the Bulgarian Black Sea port of Varna, he gave a fiery speech that appeared to encourage Bulgarian irredentist claims on Macedonia.[39] Despite Balbo's protests that he had been misunderstood, the Rumanians muted their welcome when the expedition reached Constanţa.

The real drama of the cruise lay elsewhere: in the meeting with the Soviets in Odessa, and in the bitter rivalry that developed between Balbo and De Pinedo.

When two ostensibly mortal enemies, communism and fascism, embraced, contradictions and ironies were bound to occur—and they did. The first was the contradiction in the Soviet reception.[40] When the Italian aviators stepped ashore in Odessa, their hosts hailed them as heroes. For the occasion the Soviets had erected a triumphal arch, built a new wharf, repaired the roads, refurbished two old hotels, and even baked white bread. At the same time, the Soviets kept the visit as secret as possible. On their arrival, the planes were not allowed to approach within ten kilometers of the city. To keep away curious spectators, guards patrolled the hills above the lake where the planes were anchored. In town a young French-speaking officer served as Balbo's guide. Perhaps he also reported to his superiors on Balbo's activities, but the guide made no effort to limit his charge's movements. During their day-and-a-half visit, the Italians roamed the city as they pleased. When the expedition departed, the authorities inexplicably lifted the ban on flying over the city, and the expedition circled it three times before proceeding toward its destination.

The reason for the ambivalent Soviet welcome was easy enough to understand. The Soviets and the Italians had a common interest in the visit. Both craved recognition and respect from the Great Powers; both thought the occasion would enhance their

diplomatic status. For this occasion, then, both wanted to minimize their ideological differences.

This was easier said than done. As Balbo put it, the Soviets
were both the masters and the slaves of the Third International.
The Soviets had to consider the reaction of the anti-fascist press
and the more orthodox adherents to the Third International.[41]
Particularly galling to the anti-fascists and the orthodox communists was a photograph widely published in the international
press, of Balbo and Red Army officers saluting the Red Flag.
Balbo showed no ideological qualms. To his mind, he was merely
carrying out his obligations as a guest. Only in a sly aside did he
make reference to his past as a Blackshirt. He was no stranger to
the "Internationale," he wrote, for he had heard the "subversive"
peasants of Emilia and Romagna sing it at the top of their lungs
during the tumultuous rallies of the post-war period.[42] In the
present context, he claimed to hear something completely different: a "mystical" spirit that was above parties and street brawls
and expressed the Russian national will to power.

So eager was he to find a common ground with his hosts that the
hated "bolsheviks" whom he had battled for so many years now
became fellow soldiers and fellow revolutionaries. "They are good-
looking soldiers. They have made a revolution: now they defend it.
Whoever professes a political faith strongly respects that of others,
most of all when he opposes it," he noted.[43] Balbo even found a
point of convergence between fascism and bolshevism: an antipathy toward the Western democracies, "rotten to the bone, lying
and false, with all the wiles of a superior civilization."[44]

Nevertheless, Balbo did not minimize the enormous cultural
and political abyss that divided Soviets and fascists, Italians and
Russians. His account of the expedition reflected Balbo's own nationalist, patriotic, middle-class upbringing, and his vision undoubtedly appealed to his Italian readers, who were largely nationalist, patriotic, and middle class. Clichés about the bloodthirsty
and totalitarian bolsheviks and the imponderable mysteries of the
Russian mind, more Oriental than European, abound in his book.
At an official lunch an Italian dignitary commented on the comparative lack of bloodshed during the fascist revolution. Why had the
bolsheviks shed so much blood? he asked. A Soviet general replied

calmly, "Very simple. The reason is this: we are not vegetarians."
"The reply makes our blood run cold. What a strange vision of life
these Russians have!" Balbo remarked.[45] He was also glad to see
traces from time to time of pre-revolutionary Russia. They allowed
him to escape from the "oppressive atmosphere of bolshevik uniformity" that gave the city a barracks-like air; he wondered at the
"perverse mania" that the revolution had for rendering life "un-
comfortable, ugly, squalid."[46]

As a final irony, the trip to Odessa revealed clearly how Balbo's
attitudes toward fascism and toward revolution had changed. His
apparent sympathy with his fellow revolutionaries, even if they
were Soviets, was polite humbug. Balbo the radical republican
had disappeared. On this cruise, as on the previous ones, he
mingled easily with royalty, with middle-class statesmen, even
with churchmen. In his patriotism, his military courtesies and
chivalry, his requisite display of classical culture, he behaved
liked a traditional Piedmontese general. In Rumania, for example,
Princess Ileana greeted him, and as a well-behaved general
should, Balbo described her as a "charming princess," tall and
slim, whose large dark eyes dominated her serene face.[47] For
Balbo, at this point, fascism was nothing more complicated than
patriotism and Mussolini. When the children in the streets of
Odessa call out "Mussolini" to the aviators, it is the same as if
they were calling us "Italians," he wrote.[48] He delighted in finding signs of *italianità* everywhere. The mouth of the Danube
reminded him of Porto Garibaldi, one of the mouths of the Po
near Ferrara. Shortly afterwards, on spying an Italian ship from
the air, he exclaimed "Where don't our sailors reach!"[49] To his
great joy, in Bucharest, the wife of the Italian military attaché
greeted him in Romagnolo dialect: *"Cum l' dvante magher! ach
faza bruseda!"* (How thin he's become! what a dark face!)[50] At a
dance, when the military attaché's wife asked him who the most
beautiful women in the room were, Balbo replied gallantly, "That
Italian woman with the velvety eyes." Finally, to the delight and
relief of his readers, Balbo showed that he was not all pilot and
military man. He might concentrate on his instruments and his
navigational calculations, but his head was crammed with poetry.
As he flew over Ithaca, he recognized it from Homer's description. Over Mytilene, he asked, "Where is Sappho of the violet

hair?"[51] Leaving Negropont, he recited Foscolo's "I Sepolcri." His wife had transcribed the verses for him on slips of paper. In Constanţa, he gazed at the statue of the exiled Ovid, whose melancholy observations on the fragility of friendship he had read in school.[52]

A drama of the cruise second only to meeting with the Soviets was Balbo's deteriorating relationship with De Pinedo, one of the "four nails in my cross during the years I spent with the Aeronautica," Balbo once remarked.[53] The reasons for the falling out between the two men are not always clear.[54] When Balbo first became undersecretary he deeply respected both De Pinedo's achievements as a long-distance ace and his prestige within the service. He did not consider De Pinedo to be a rival; the two men became good friends. Indeed, Balbo defended De Pinedo when malicious tongues and police reports alleged that he was a gambler.

Following his triumphant tour of the Two Americas in 1928, De Pinedo wanted to resume his long-distance flights and proposed making a round-the-world flight to be financed with funds that an Italian-American paper in New York, *Il Progresso Italo-Americano*, had collected in 1927. Balbo vetoed the project and ordered De Pinedo to prepare the cruise to the Western Mediterranean. In November, 1928, Balbo appointed De Pinedo assistant chief of staff of the Aeronautica, with the duties of chief of staff. He then asked De Pinedo to prepare the aerial cruise to the Eastern Mediterranean, with the understanding that if it succeeded, De Pinedo would become chief of staff of the Aeronautica, the technical counterpart to Balbo's position as minister. The "half promotion" to assistant chief of staff enraged De Pinedo. He was also disappointed when for the second time he proposed a round-the-world flight and for a second time Balbo turned him down.

De Pinedo's ties with the monarchy may have provided another irritant in the relationship. De Pinedo, a Neapolitan, came from a family of patrician origins, and he was highly ambitious. Before joining the Aeronautica in 1923, he had begun a promising career in the navy that had included commanding the royal yacht, where he met the royal family. According to rumors, he developed a romantic relationship with the princess Giovanna, who was flattered to have a glamorous aviator courting her. The sentimental link probably did not interest Balbo as much as De Pinedo's access to the monarchy did, for Balbo had begun cultivating his own ties with the royal house. With the king, for example, he discussed the projected expedition to Odessa. For a subordinate like De Pinedo to enjoy the same access to the monarchy violated Balbo's sense of hierarchy.

During the two months before the cruise to the Eastern Mediterranean was scheduled to leave, the relationship between the two men deteriorated rapidly. De Pinedo's career was still on the rise, but Balbo, at the end of May in his annual message to the Chamber of Deputies, had launched his campaign against the *prime donne*. The cruise degenerated into a series of running feuds and petty squabbles between the two men, disputes over protocol in the seating arrangements at dinner, over regulations about the proper wearing of the uniform, over landing sites—disputes that became arguments about who was in charge of the expedition. More than once De Pinedo threatened to leave the cruise and return to Italy immediately. Balbo ordered him to stay at his post. De Pinedo obeyed, but he declared that from the moment the expedition reached Italy, Balbo could consider him as having resigned.

Such a state of affairs could not continue. When the expedition ended, Balbo decided to eliminate his rival. On August 12 he sent De Pinedo an urgent letter.[55] During De Pinedo's flight to the United States in 1927, Italian-Americans had reportedly raised $30,000 for future aerial expeditions. Balbo wanted an accounting of the funds, and he wanted an immediate reply, he said, for he had to report to the Duce. The letter was apparently friendly in tone, but in context Balbo's intentions were unmistakable. His timing was deliberately offensive: De Pinedo was taking a vacation with members of the royal family in Northern Europe. Balbo was also raising the issue at an odd time. He had collected rumors about the De Pinedo funds while he was on his trip to the United States the previous winter. Why had he waited for eight months before taking action? Furthermore, the documentation about the funds was in the Aeronautica's files. Balbo, as minister, should have known about the money instead of claiming, as he did in the letter, that he knew nothing.

De Pinedo replied on August 22.[56] He sent Mussolini a series of letters and reports resigning his position and unleashing a violent attack against Balbo. De Pinedo complained bitterly about the slights and humiliations to which Balbo had subjected him during the cruise to Odessa. Then he turned to the state of the air force. "With great effort," he claimed, the Aeronautica could put together for an aerial cruise or for a maneuver about fifteen squadrons, enough to maintain the air force's reputation. Its combat readiness, however, was "something quite different." In a detailed critique of the service's state of readiness, he charged that too many of the nation's resources were going into projects like the Schneider Cup, light aircraft for tourism, and the gigantic Do X transports. Meanwhile, the Aeronautica lacked the aircraft it needed; industry was far from ready for mobilization; foreign-designed aircraft dominated Italian commercial aviation, and no effort was being made to replace them with Italian ones. "There can be no doubt about the cause of all this," De Pinedo concluded. The Aeronautica was a highly technical service. It needed leaders with a high level of experience and technical skills, men who had come up through the ranks. It could not be operated successfully on the basis of "improvisations" and whims. De Pinedo tendered his resignation as assistant chief of staff. His critique of Balbo's leadership and the detailed report on the state of the Aeronautica, however, implied that he was ready to take on the position of chief of staff.

Mussolini did not hesitate in choosing between Balbo and De Pinedo. Mussolini admired De Pinedo personally, described him as "the lord of the distances," and declared, "the new Italian is De Pinedo."[57] However, putting Balbo out of office meant unleashing a dangerous enemy. Moreover, despite De Pinedo's often justified criticisms of Balbo's leadership, Balbo's policies suited Mussolini. Balbo had created a "fascist service" that popularized the regime.

Mussolini accepted De Pinedo's resignation. For three years De Pinedo served as air attaché in Buenos Aires and then retired officially from the service on October 1 at the age of forty-two. Free at last from his service obligations, he resumed his plans for long-distance flights. His first project was a solo nonstop 10,000-kilometer New York-to-Baghdad record flight. The attempt ended disastrously on September 2, 1933, when De Pinedo attempted to take off from New York's Floyd Bennet Field. De Pinedo's Bellanca, overloaded with fuel, veered off the runway and burst into flames; De Pinedo died in the wreckage.

Balbo's enemies held him morally responsible for De Pinedo's death and De Pinedo's brother hinted at sabotage, at least "moral" sabotage. The expedition was a private one. Nevertheless, De Pinedo wanted his flight to be an Italian triumph. He chose to fly an Italian-designed Bellanca monoplane; he planned to fly under Italian colors. De Pinedo counted on paying tribute to Mussolini by dropping a message over Rome. Nevertheless, the Aeronautica refused to give him any help with weather information and replied to his requests only with bureaucratic quibbles.[58] De Pinedo's friends pointed out that Balbo did not even attend the funeral. But Balbo was neither so unfeeling nor so unforgiving as they made him out to be. For the funeral, he sent a telegram of condolences and dispatched Valle as his representative. He would have sent a funeral wreath and perhaps even marched in the procession had he not been afraid of offending the family, Balbo declared. Balbo's friends hinted that before De Pinedo's last flight, he had become mentally unbalanced. He had appeared at the airfield wearing a blue business suit with a gray bowler hat and a long silk muffler.[59] On his feet were a pair of light blue bedroom slippers. The small crowd laughed at these unorthodox flying togs, but De Pinedo's friends claimed the clothes were carefully chosen for comfort and safety. In the cramped cabin, for instance, the bowler protected him from protruding instruments and equipment better than a regular flying helmet.

Balbo summed up his struggle with De Pinedo when he said that De Pinedo was the best pilot in Italy, perhaps in the world, but "there wasn't room for both of us in the same cockpit."[60] Balbo was consistent. For years he had declared that he would not support individual record flights, even if they were attempted by great pilots. On the other hand, in his behavior toward De Pinedo, Balbo abandoned the chivalry he valued so highly. By 1933, Balbo was not only the Italian Air Minister. Like De Pinedo, he was a world-famous aviator, a member of the international flying brotherhood. In denying De Pinedo weather information, for example, Balbo violated that brotherhood to which he so often professed to belong.

The Mediterranean cruises accomplished many of Balbo's goals and confirmed his ideas about the Aeronautica's development. They brought prestige both to the fascist regime and to Italian aviation. The great powers were forced to take notice of Italy's expansionist aims in the Mediterranean. The cruise may also have helped to sell Italian aircraft, as Balbo claimed, although the connection is less evident. In September of 1931, the Turkish government bought twenty-eight Savoia Marchetti flying boats for use against smugglers. The contract was particularly gratifying to the Italians because the Turks had formerly purchased French aircraft.[61]

The military value of the cruises was more uncertain. Neither Italian nor foreign military experts could fathom the significance of these flights. Paradoxically, they were at the same time swift and mobile, and inflexible and cumbersome. Once in the air, the squadrons moved quickly. However, the preparations, the weather, the refueling, and the inability to deviate from their established routes made the flights vulnerable to attack.[62] "For demonstration and spectacular effects the self-contained aerial fleet is naturally more impressive than the same number of aircraft concealed within the walls of an aircraft carrier," noted an American naval journal.[63] Yet the same aerial fleet operating from a carrier provided far greater range and flexibility.

For Balbo the cruises had another unpleasant characteristic. They could be used to publicize the fascist regime, but others understood that such raids could be used just as easily to publicize the anti-fascist cause.[64] The success of Balbo's cruises prompted a number of anti-fascists in 1930 and 1931 to undertake daring flights from Switzerland and France in light planes to bombard major Italian cities such as Milan and Rome with propaganda leaflets. The most famous of these attempts was that of the poet Lauro De Bosis in October, 1931. Taking off from Marseilles, he succeeded in reaching Rome, showered the city with leaflets, and then disappeared over the sea near Corsica. For Balbo, these flights proved to be an enormous humiliation. His vaunted Aeronautica in those pre-radar days could neither prevent these incursions nor catch the culprits. Fortunately for Balbo, De Bosis's feat marked the end of these raids.

The cruises brought Balbo fame and glory. In 1929, the International League of Aviators offered Balbo the Harmon Trophy. Balbo turned it down, modestly pointing out that he was not in the same league as the previous winners. His contribution had been more as an organizer than as a pilot. He suggested that the trophy be awarded to General Aldo Pellegrini, who had been in charge of the expedition—a slap at De Pinedo. In place of the trophy, Balbo accepted a gold medal of honor. His most famous aerial feats were yet to come: the two Atlantic expeditions.

Chapter Ten

Aviator: The First Atlantic Cruise

In the history of aviation Balbo's Mediterranean cruises barely rate a footnote. They served, as Mussolini proclaimed, to teach Italian airmen how to "stroll" about the Mediterranean. Such flights over Southern Europe and the Balkans were too regional to capture the interest of the international press and public. The expeditions that catapulted Balbo to international fame were his flights across the Atlantic. The first, in 1931, crossed the South Atlantic. With twelve aircraft and fifty men, Balbo flew from Orbetello to Rio de Janeiro, a distance of 10,400 kilometers. He lost five men and three aircraft. In men and equipment, this was by far the costliest of the four major cruises. On the last and most famous of his aerial cruises, in July, 1933, Balbo led twenty-five aircraft and one hundred men in a double crossing of the North Atlantic from Orbetello to Chicago and back, a distance of 19,000 kilometers. On this longest and most difficult of his aerial undertakings, he lost only two aircraft and two crewmen.

One grand vision fired Balbo's Atlantic crossings. At the end of his visit to the United States in 1928, homeward bound aboard the liner *Conte Grande*, he stood at the rail watching the New York skyline, "the bizarre, colossal outlines of the chaotic metropolis, wrapped in epic curtains of smoke and fog, barely gilded by the sunset."[1] At that moment, for the first time, "the vision of an Italian aerial squadron, which after having crossed the ocean triumphantly arrived in the sky over New York," seized his imagination.

An Atlantic crossing of any sort was in those days a difficult and dangerous enterprise. At that time there had been forty-seven attempts; only fifteen had succeeded.[2] The North Atlantic, because of fog banks and uncertain weather patterns, presented a greater challenge than the South Atlantic. Yet the North Atlantic, perhaps because of the hope of tying together Europe and the United States, exercised a greater fascination. By the end of 1928, the North Atlantic had been attempted thirty-nine times, with only nine successes. By contrast, the South Atlantic had been tried eight times, with six successes.

All attempts up to that point had been solo flights. With his plan for a mass flight, Balbo was undertaking a project that was technically far more difficult. Preparing and leading a squadron, no matter how good the pilots were, multiplied the difficulties. Moreover, as Balbo pointed out, a mass flight to North America carried different political and military implications. Each transatlantic crossing—the first had been in 1919—reduced American isolation and added to the "bridge" between the two continents. With the solo flights, the structure was still fragile. His flight, Balbo claimed, would create an "entirely new" situation.[3] The "bridge" would support dozens and dozens of people and revolutionize ties between the two continents.

In 1928, however, Balbo had virtually no experience on which to base a plan. He considered briefly and rejected various North Atlantic routes and pondered the advantages and disadvantages of seaplanes as opposed to land planes. He concluded that he needed more experience and better equipment before he undertook the expedition. In the meantime, he joined the cruise to the Eastern Mediterranean and fixed his eyes on the South Atlantic. Italians already had two South Atlantic crossings to their credit. De Pinedo, with Carlo Del Prete, made the first in 1927 as part of his tour of the Four Continents. The following year, shortly after they set a new world distance record for a closed circuit, Del Prete and Arturo Ferrarin flew 7,450 kilometers nonstop from Rome to Natal in forty-four hours and nine minutes. Balbo chose the banquet in March, 1929, in honor of their achievement, to announce, "We'll cross the Atlantic with various crews as soon as the right aircraft is available."[4] With considerably more brashness, he wrote to D'Annunzio on July 26, 1930: "I have to talk to you about the expedition I am preparing. It is an almost mad undertaking, at the limits of what can be dared—however, it has been studied and calculated in the minutest detail."[5]

The right aircraft turned out, once again, to be the SM.55A, slightly modified.[6] The floats on the new aircraft were larger. The cockpit was completely enclosed and sealed off from the fuel tanks so that the crew could now smoke. The aircraft also had a new, larger engine, the Fiat A 22R, derived from the A 22, which first had powered Ferrarin and Del Prete in 1928, and then Maddalena and Cecconi in 1930 in their successful attempt at the world records for distance and endurance in a closed circuit. The A 22R delivered approximately 200 horsepower more than the Asso 500 and was fitted with new propellers of somewhat larger diameter. The SM.55A had a top speed of 215 km/hr., a cruising speed of 165 km/hr., and, most important, a range of 3,100 kilometers, about 100 kilometers more than was needed for the longest segment of the flight between Bolama, in Portuguese Guinea on the extreme tip of the West African coast, and Natal, the first stop in Brazil.

Even with the latest aircraft and equipment, the enterprise was full of hazards. Balbo's instrument panel, for instance, would make a modern pilot smile—or perhaps shudder.[7] In the center of the instrument panel, pilot and co-pilot shared various gauges that monitored engine functions: a tachometer, and gauges for temperature and pressure of oil, fuel, and water. On each side of the instrument panel, pilot and co-pilot had duplicate sets of instruments to control the flight. These included an anemometer or air speed indicator, an altimeter, a variometer or rate-of-climb indicator, an ordinary magnetic compass, a clock, a turn and bank indicator, an attitude indicator, a gas gauge, and an air flow control for the radiators. At that time, "blind flying," flying on instruments alone, was a relatively new technique, but two instruments based on the gyroscope were being developed: artificial horizons supplemented the conventional turn and bank indicators, and directional gyros supplemented the magnetic compasses. Although these instruments were available in 1931, Balbo then described them as "complicated and very expensive" and left them off his instrument panel. For his 1933 expedition, however, he included both directional gyros and artificial horizons—a fact that the manufacturer, the Sperry Company, exploited in its advertising. Balbo's navigational equipment might also strike the contemporary pilot as odd. Balbo's aircraft was literally a flying boat, and he and his crew navigated in the air according to naval techniques and standards. On the little table located in the left float, the navigator laid out his charts, portolans, compasses, chronometers, and sextants and plotted the aircraft's position.

If the equipment of that era seems rudimentary, the standards for being a good pilot in those days and the style of flying were also vastly different. Today's pilots and astronauts are technicians, sometimes with advanced degrees in engineering or physics. In Balbo's day, flying was much more a matter of instinct and of individual heroic achievements. Pilots were judged for their daring and bravery and the elegance of their acrobatic skills. Exhibitionism and bad training took their toll. In Italy, among students of the Accademia Aeronautica between 1923 and 1959, 283 died in war missions, and 426 succumbed to flying accidents.[8] Balbo understood clearly that the development of aviation depended not only on better machines and instruments, but also on more disciplined and sophisticated pilots. He viewed his cruises as contributions to that end.

From a technical point of view, the success of his first Atlantic expedition depended on one maneuver: the takeoff from Bolama with the large load of fuel necessary to make the ocean crossing. Many complex factors entered into this operation, including air temperature and humidity. Theoretical reassurances that the feat was possible did not convince Balbo. From January to March of 1930, Balbo sent Cagna to experiment under the same conditions that the expedition would face a year later. For his crews, Balbo selected thirty-two pilots and thirty-two radiomen and mechanics from the Aeronautica's seaplane units, "chosen by merit from the moral aristocracy of the Aeronautica."[9] As their commander he appointed Umberto Maddalena, internationally recognized as a top distance flyer, holder of various world closed-circuit records, and one of the heroes of the *Italia* rescue mission. For a year, beginning January 1, 1930, the crews trained at the seaplane base at Orbetello on the Tyrrhenian coast about 150 kilometers north of Rome.

The location was ideal.[10] Orbetello was built on a peninsula at

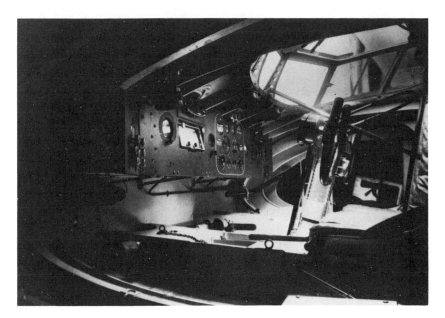

Fig. 12. SM.55X cockpit and instrument panel (Caproni Museum Archive)

the end of which was the promontory of Monte Argentario. The airport was built on a narrow neck of the peninsula between the town and the mainland; large numbers of seaplanes could swing at anchor in the long bay, protected from the sea by a sandbar. Although by air the connection to Rome and its seaplane port of Ostia was easy, Orbetello was relatively isolated by land. At that time the main highway, the Aurelia, was only a white, twisting, dusty track. Much of the surrounding countryside was still wild, for the Maremma reclamation projects (Bonifica Maremma) had barely begun. Those who trained there found few worldly distractions—just as Balbo had planned. Orbetello was to be no ordinary training camp. He spoke of it as a quasi-religious community in which "the souls of the appointed would not for any reason be distracted from concentrating on the goal."[11]

The training was tough and at times costly. The men were given leave only once every two weeks. They became proficient in both academic and practical disciplines. For example, they studied celestial navigation—perhaps far more than they needed.

Such skills had been necessary for solo flights like those of De Pinedo in 1927 and Ferrarin and Del Prete in 1928. They had braved the Atlantic without radios or a system of support ships that advised them of their positions. Balbo's expedition had both—a measure of how much more complex and sophisticated his expedition was, and of how quickly aviation technology changed. Balbo also put his men through a long series of training flights. These included night flights, takeoffs with progressively heavier loads, and flights of up to twenty hours, the time necessary to cover the distance on the longest leg of the flight. The training took its toll. Two died on November 27 while practicing with progressively heavier loads.

Although he spent much of his time in Rome performing his duties as minister, Balbo did not neglect his own training. During July, 1930, he spent several weeks literally camping in a pine grove that extended between Viareggio and Forte dei Marmi. He lived "almost like an aborigine" on the beach, he declared.[12] His notion of an aboriginal lifestyle was a peculiar one, however, for he lived in a large, comfortable tent, furnished—according to the gossips and anonymous letter writers—with lion and polar bear skins. In the evenings he shed his bathing suit for a dinner jacket to receive his usual hordes of friends, journalists, dignitaries—and his current mistress. Nearby, a villa, once owned by D'Annunzio, was at his disposal, although he never used it. He also put in flying hours and looked in on the training at Orbetello. Like any pilot, he had his share of near-fatal accidents. One of the worst came in June, 1930, shortly before he went camping at Viareggio. While taking off near Capri, one of the floats on his seaplane gave way and the plane sank almost immediately to a depth of more than twelve meters. Although injured, Balbo managed to free himself from the cockpit and surfaced after he had been given up for dead. The incident haunted him; he recalled it during some of the worst moments of his North Atlantic crossing in 1933.[13]

In choosing his route across the South Atlantic, Balbo followed the trail of earlier pioneers. The first stop, Los Alcazares, Spain, had been the furthest point for the first Mediterranean cruise in 1928. The ports along the west coast of Africa—Kenitra, Morocco; Villa Cisneros, Rio de Oro (today Dakhla, Mauritania); Bolama, Portuguese Guinea (today Guinea Bissau)—had all been utilized

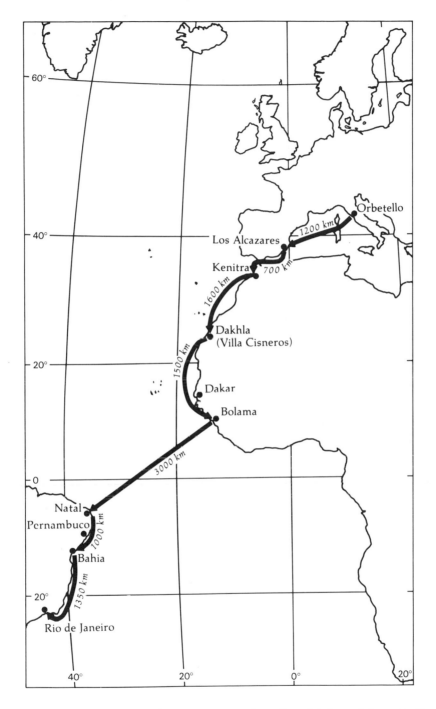

Map 3. Route of first Atlantic cruise, Italy to Brazil (adapted from G. B. Guerri, *Italo Balbo*)

by De Pinedo and Del Prete in 1927, or by other conquerors of the South Atlantic such as the French aviator Jean Mermoz.

By mid-December of 1930, the expedition was ready. It comprised four squadrons of three planes each, with two aircraft in reserve. The crews totaled fifty-six, with twelve in reserve. Balbo had begun with the more modest ambition of only two squadrons totaling six, but when Mussolini assured him that the expedition would work with larger numbers, Balbo cheerfully doubled its size. He moved to Orbetello on December 9 and officially took command of the expedition on December 14. "The greatest formation flight in the history of flying" and the "greatest aerial venture undertaken by Italy since the tragic flight of the *Italia* to the North Pole" was about to begin.[14]

The first leg of the expedition from Orbetello to Los Alcazares nearly turned into a disaster. For two days, Balbo postponed the departure because of the weather. Finally, on December 17, the weather was "not at all prohibitive," Balbo wrote.[15] One cyclone had passed across their route, but another one was forming. Had he postponed his departure another twenty-four hours, he would have had perfect weather. Inexperience, impatience, and the pressures of well-wishers and journalists who crowded around Orbetello all contributed to Balbo's faulty judgment. From Orbetello across the Tyrrhenian and through the passage between Sardegna and Corsica, the weather held. Shortly afterwards, for about two hours, the fourteen seaplanes "engaged in a life-and-death struggle" with the storm.[16] Fierce rains threatened to rip the fabric covering off the wings. Visibility was close to zero. Downdrafts swept Balbo's aircraft from an altitude of two or three hundred meters to just above the wave caps. The radios no longer worked. To maintain some semblance of formation, Balbo ordered his mechanic to peer out the portholes and shout course corrections. Nevertheless, Balbo lost track of time—and of the rest of the expedition. Five aircraft remained with him; eight flew off to the north. Fortunately, at this point he saw land below—the Balearic Islands. Eventually, he and the five aircraft with him landed in the little bay of Puerto de Campo, a fishing village of three hundred people. He had saved half his expedition. He did not learn until late in the afternoon, when he managed to contact

Rome by radio, that the rest of the aircraft had landed safely in Los Alcazares. For forty-eight hours the storm lashed the island. Not until December 19 was Balbo able to rejoin Maddalena and the others. In the primitive lodgings, in wet, cold, humid weather, Balbo developed a fever that plagued him for several days afterwards.

The expedition had been saved, and the aircraft were not seriously damaged; however, the rain and hail had pitted and scarred the wooden propellers. At Los Alcazares, new ones were fitted, but there were not enough for the entire expedition. Those that could not be replaced remained unbalanced. For the rest of the expedition they vibrated and thus put unusual stress on the engines.

This near-disaster raised doubts in Mussolini's mind about the leadership of the expedition. Even today it is not clear where the responsibility lies for the original error in misjudging the weather: with the weather service, with the expedition's collective leadership, with Balbo himself.[17] The error might have been rectified after the expedition took off, for the storm worsened by stages. The expedition might easily have returned to Orbetello or even to Elmas (on Sardinia) before the situation became critical. The wear and tear on the aircraft, especially on the propellers, could have been avoided. Either Balbo or Maddalena could have given the order. There is no evidence of radio messages between the two. Maddalena plunged ahead. His stubbornness and determination might have been appropriate for a race or a solo flight, but not for such an expedition. Balbo, who was not nearly as experienced a pilot, trusted Maddalena's judgment. Balbo redeemed himself a bit when he chose to land at Puerto de Campo, but already Mussolini's confidence in Balbo may have been shaken. The Duce withheld his congratulatory telegram until the very end of the expedition, when he could be certain that the cruise had ended successfully.

On December 21 the expedition resumed, hopping along the northwest coast of Africa from Los Alcazares to Bolama, where they arrived on Christmas Day. For the next twelve days Balbo and his men prepared for the critical flight across the Atlantic. The question on everyone's mind was always the takeoff. Fuel, crew, oil, water, supplies, and food totaled 4,700 kilograms. In addition there was the weight of the SM.55 itself. Listed as 5,200 kilograms, after three weeks of soaking in the water the wooden frame was considerably heavier. Thus, the engines had to lift a total of over 9,900 kilograms. On prior Atlantic crossings in equatorial zones, 1,000-horsepower seaplanes had lifted only two-thirds that much weight. On January 2, Maddalena and Cagna, during the hottest hours of the day and with no wind, lifted off after a run of eighty-five seconds and landed safely again. Balbo planned to leave at night. At a lower temperature the task would be much easier. Nevertheless, to increase the safety margin, he ordered everything feasible done to lighten the load, including jettisoning the rubber life rafts. In case of emergency, the pilots were to stay with their planes to the last moment, to defend their craft as if they were defending their own lives, "but to consider themselves lost at the moment in which the aircraft was lost."[18]

Balbo also waited patiently—after his experience during the first leg of the journey—for the most favorable weather. On this, the longest and most difficult part of the trip, the expedition would fly 3,000 kilometers, from Bolama to Porto Natal. He estimated the flying time at about twenty hours. Since part of the flight had to be at night, he wanted to take advantage of the moonlight and the trade winds.[19] From a study of the past weather records, January 4 at 11:30 P.M. appeared to be the ideal date; three times—January 2, 3, 4—he postponed. On January 5, the weather improved a bit. With no guarantee that it would get any better and afraid of losing the moonlight, he set the departure for 1:30 A.M.

That evening the sunset was dark and the sky was overcast. Night came on with a heavy, leaden hue. The moon was veiled behind a thick layer of clouds. Originally, Balbo had planned for only a dozen planes to make the flight. The two reserve pilots, however, convinced Balbo to include them. Emotions ran high. Aboard the yacht *Alice*, one of the support ships, Balbo's excitement mounted as each succeeding crew boarded. "I want to show myself as indifferent more than calm," he wrote later, and he played an aimless card game until the last crew member was aboard the last aircraft.[20] By then the moon had disappeared entirely and it was impossible to distinguish between water and sky.

At exactly 1:29 Greenwich time, Balbo was in the cockpit of his own aircraft carrying the special civil registration I-BALB, ready for takeoff. "I am very calm. My nerves are submissive to the will that controls them. Never, perhaps, as at this moment, have I felt master of myself." With everyone ready, "into the unknown and toward the unknown we launch the aircraft at full speed." The enormous seaplane, so heavy that the stern was almost entirely underwater, rose abruptly out of the dense water. Faster and faster it sliced through the waves, lifted up on the step. With all their strength, Balbo and Cagna pulled the stick back against their chests. At this moment of top speed, "woe if you look out of the cockpit toward the surface of the water. Woe if you look for the horizon. The slightest indecision, the slightest hesitation . . . guarantees the loss of life and aircraft. Forward, forward straight into the dark." At last they felt the aircraft break from the surface and rush up into the night sky. For the next twenty minutes, in total darkness, their eyes glued to the altimeter, they climbed in a straight line without losing speed until Balbo judged, "We're safe."[21]

The rest of the expedition was less fortunate.[22] Balbo, first in the air, could not follow what was happening. I-VALL, which was part of his immediate squadron, had trouble lifting off, he knew, because of an overheated motor. The other squadrons took to the sky without incident, except for I-RECA, which, like I-VALL, suffered from overheating. About twelve minutes after takeoff, while the crews of the two aircraft waited for their motors to cool off, they saw a great flash and glow on the horizon in the direction that the expedition had taken. It was I-BOER. The plane exploded and sank. No trace of the aircraft or of the crew of four was ever found. The cause of the explosion was never determined. Balbo blamed a short circuit in the electrical system.

At 3 A.M., I-VALL and I-RECA, their motors cooled, attempted another takeoff. I-VALL gained cruising altitude without incident. I-RECA, maneuvering to keep I-VALL in sight, lost airspeed. The big seaplane hit the water, smashing the right float and killing the mechanic who was riding there. In all, during that night in Bolama five crewmen and two aircraft were lost.

For the first six hours of the flight, Balbo's nerves were on edge; then the tension eased. After daybreak, the flight became routine except for the need to maintain formation. For eighteen hours the pilots constantly adjusted their engine speeds and maneu-vered to maintain their positions in the flight. In exasperation, Balbo the arch-enemy of solo flights became their great booster. "I think that if I were to do another Atlantic flight, I would prefer to do it three times from one end to the other solo rather than once again in formation," he wrote.[23]

Only two more incidents marred the flight. At low altitudes the heat of the day made it difficult for the radiators to cool the engines adequately. The mechanics found themselves using all the available liquids aboard—water, drinks, even urine. I-BAIS and I-DONA eventually succumbed to overheating and landed in mid-ocean. A support ship attempted to tow I-BAIS to the main-land, but eventually the aircraft sank—the third loss of the expe-dition. I-DONA was saved and rejoined the cruise at Natal.

At 20 hours Greenwich time (5 P.M. local time), the main body of the expedition, nine aircraft, reached Natal. They had crossed in about eighteen and a half hours at an average speed of 162 km/hr. I-VALL, flying solo, took seventeen hours and averaged 177 km/hr. Balbo's complaints about the difficulties of formation flying were confirmed.

Natal welcomed the aviators with the peal of the city's church bells. In a cosmopolitan spirit, Balbo declared: "This group of Italians, crossing the ocean, has served not only their own coun-try but the cause of humanity, which today feels itself more than ever united across vast distances, tied together by unsuspected bonds of solidarity, ever more confident of its destiny of progress and civilization."[24] In Italy, the expedition's safe arrival stirred patriotic celebrations. Mussolini personally made the announce-ment to the king. Performances at La Scala in Milan and the Teatro Reale dell'Opera in Rome were interrupted to announce the good news.

A tidal wave of congratulatory telegrams from all over the world swept into Balbo's hotel room. "They scare me; I can't escape them."[25] From Italy alone there were more than two thou-sand, from everyone from the king to D'Annunzio. From Musso-lini, however, there was nothing. Mussolini's silence undoubtedly aggravated Balbo's physical and emotional exhaustion. He could not address his report to Mussolini properly: "Gabaeronautica," the air ministry in Rome, became "Pietrogrado." Images of Luigi

Boer and Danilo Barbicinti, the pilots on the lost I-BOER, disturbed his sleep. At dawn, he boarded one of the support ships and sent one last message to Bolama asking about the fate of I-BOER. The immediate negative eliminated any last hope of rescue.

For five days the expedition stayed in Natal, occupied with protocol and ceremony; then on January 11 they flew to Bahia, where huge crowds of Italian emigrants greeted the aviators. Balbo planned the expedition's last leg, the grand entry into Rio de Janeiro on January 15, carefully. The expedition arrived early and circled outside the harbor for about an hour. The magic moment came precisely at 4:30 P.M. The entire expedition, ships and aircraft, entered the harbor simultaneously. The triumphant *atlantici* in a V-formation, with Balbo in the lead, soared above the eight support ships into "the golden sky of the great metropolis." It was a sight worthy of the greatest Italian painters, of Giorgione, Carpaccio, Tiziano, or his fellow Ferrarese, Dosso Dossi, Balbo rhapsodized; and he added that "perhaps God in creating the Bay of Rio wanted to demonstrate that art is descended from him. . . . Forward, forward, winged squadron of Italy. After the run over the ocean, you have earned this scene of beauty and fantasy. Follow me faithfully. In the skies of Rio we'll trace an aerial wreath of joy, of strength, of friendship."[26]

The expedition touched down, taxied to the anchoring buoys, and shut off the engines. The crews climbed out onto the wings of their aircraft and stood at attention. From the eight ships came the first of nineteen salvos from their forty-eight guns. Salutes from Brazilian warships and nearby forts joined in the chorus. The Brazilians had declared a national holiday. Huge crowds gathered to cheer deliriously. "Madame, the good Lord is Italian today!" the wife of an Italian diplomat recalled someone saying to her.[27] Balbo disembarked under an avalanche of flowers. "What ravishing women!" he exclaimed happily and headed for his rooms at—appropriately enough—the Hotel Gloria. "That day, descending from the sky, covered with glory, he stood straight as a sword and he radiated joy," a friend remarked.[28]

One of his first acts that afternoon was to make a radio broadcast to North America. Now that the great South American enterprise had concluded, he declared, he wanted very much to carry out another one across the North Atlantic to bring greetings from the Fatherland to the Italians in the United States. He also found a telegram from Mussolini. "You will understand why I waited until you had reached your goal before I sent you my praise and my applause for the flight that I willed and that you so superbly carried out. Until everything is finished, nothing is finished."[29]

For three weeks Balbo remained in Brazil, visiting the Italian immigrant communities in Rio and São Paulo. On February 7 he sailed for Italy. On his return he received a tumultuous welcome and made a series of public appearances in major Italian cities. He was rewarded with the nation's gold medal for military valor. Two honors, however, escaped him. He was made neither a count nor a marshal. For a lesser flying exploit De Pinedo had been made a marquis, and De Vecchi for his services as *quadrumvir* had become a count. Mussolini, however, decided against ennobling Balbo. "*I conti non tornano*," the wits punned.[30] As for Balbo's aspirations to become an air marshal, "the president," De Bono commented, "got a little annoyed. These youngsters have no sense of proportion." Balbo was in a "bad mood and discontented," he added.[31]

If Balbo did not receive all the accolades he wanted at home, abroad he emerged as one of the giants of the flying world. The International Federation of Aviators awarded him its gold medal for the finest aeronautical undertaking of the year. He had joined the company of De Pinedo, who had won it when it was first given in 1925, and Lindbergh, who received it in 1927. In London and Paris the leading lights of the flying world praised his feat. Many also recalled personal acts of kindness and generosity on Balbo's part.[32] The foreign press was warm in its praise. "A Great Flight" and "Well Done, Italy," commented two English papers.[33] "One aspect of the flight which has given real satisfaction is the warmth of the foreign praise," the *London Times* remarked about the reaction to the flight in Italy. The only negative comment was some surprise in the foreign papers that in Italy the news of the death of the five aviators in Bolama was withheld for two days, until January 8.[34] It was, concluded the English press, in order not to mar the celebrations over the triumph. Balbo, infuriated, declared that the delay was purely for the sake of accuracy—to be sure that there was no hope for the aviators—and out of respect for the families of the dead.

In the meantime, he had already turned his attention to his new project. From the moment he had arrived in Rio de Janeiro, he made clear that the flight to Brazil was only a stepping-stone to a larger enterprise. By May of 1931, barely two months after Balbo's return to Italy from Brazil, pilots and crews were already in training at Orbetello for his second Atlantic cruise.

Chapter Eleven

Aviator: The Second Atlantic Cruise

On Wednesday, July 19, 1933, about 7:20 in the evening local time, "an Italian aerial squadron, having crossed the ocean, triumphantly arrived in the sky over New York."[1] With Balbo in the lead, the twenty-four "silver sparrowhawks" passed in review before the "Babylonian" skyscrapers of Manhattan, soared over the Statue of Liberty, and headed for the Floyd Bennet seaplane base at the tip of Coney Island.[2] The aerial armada cast a "fleeting shadow" over the huge crowds gathered to welcome the aviators. Then, one by one, each aircraft settled smoothly on the water. Overhead, the airship *Macon,* the largest in the world, and a hundred airplanes of various shapes and sizes flew in formation or dipped their wings in salute. This mammoth welcome surpassed even Balbo's original vision of five years earlier and provided a fitting climax to the last and most famous of his aerial cruises.

Dubbed the Crociera del Decennale, the Decennial Air Cruise, the expedition celebrated both the first decade of fascism—one year late—and that of the Aeronautica. For the second time, Balbo headed a successful mass crossing of the Atlantic. Over a period of about six weeks, his aerial armada flew by stages from Orbetello to Chicago and back. This second Atlantic expedition, however, was no repetition of the first: Balbo effectively doubled the risks. This time he led twenty-five seaplanes and about one hundred men—twice the size of the Brazilian cruise. This time he faced the far more difficult North Atlantic—

and crossed it twice. "Legendary," Mussolini declared at the end of the feat. For once the Duce was at least partially right. Balbo's flight never achieved the fame of an accomplishment like Lindbergh's solo to Paris. Nevertheless, Balbo's expedition was a "unique feat in aviation, one whose success not many other countries could have matched at the time."[3]

So great were the technical problems and so serious the consequences of failure that some of Balbo's friends tried to dissuade him. The most tenacious, as Balbo acknowledged, was De Bono, who noted in his diary on May 6, 1933, "In my view this is a mistake . . . a check of any sort would be damaging, while the cruise in essence is of no practical value."[4] The king had his doubts, De Bono added, and "it appears that even he [Mussolini] does not approve."[5] This time Balbo had taken on something "too great for human powers," a journalist friend commented.[6]

Balbo did not think so. For nearly five years he had been planning the expedition. At first he had proposed an even more ambitious scheme: a flight around the world with twenty-four aircraft and one hundred men, a feat that would easily have overshadowed the flights of De Pinedo and other Italian long-distance aviators.[7] The unsettled conditions in the Far East due to the Sino-Japanese war and the prohibitive costs of such a trip served to scuttle the project, but traces survived. These included the North Atlantic crossing and the visit to the United States. Chicago's Century of Progress Fair would be an appropriate showcase for Balbo's aerial armada.

In addition to the missions of his previous cruises—to test the Aeronautica's equipment, to train pilots and crews—Balbo viewed this expedition as a pioneering step toward commercial flights across the Atlantic. The cruise also served the usual publicity and propagandistic purposes. Even in 1933, in the depths of the Depression exported from the United States, fascist Italy was vital and resilient—this was the intended message of Balbo's expedition. His flight would be another triumph in a year that was full of Italian sporting triumphs. Primo Carnera punched his way to the world heavyweight title; the ocean liner *Rex* won the blue ribbon for its Atlantic crossing; Francesco Agello roared to a world record for seaplanes of 682 km/hr. at Desenzano. In soccer, fencing, speedboat racing, and track, Italians scored international victories.[8]

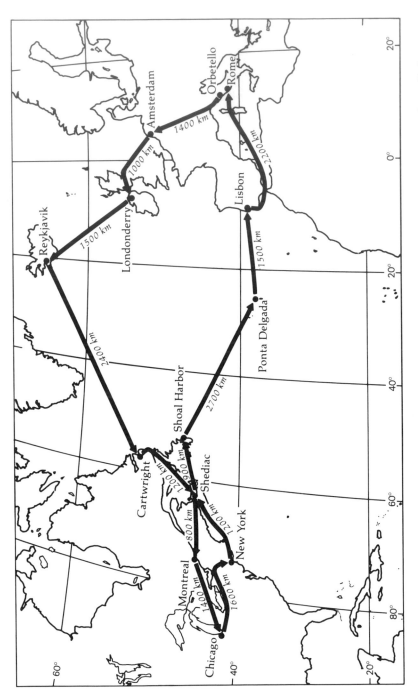

Map 4. Route of second Atlantic cruise, Italy to the United States (adapted from G. B. Guerri, *Italo Balbo*)

Finally, the year had its foreign policy triumph, or so it seemed. Mussolini proposed the Four Power Pact among Italy, France, England, and Germany. In the end, the pact amounted to very little, but many observers noted that Balbo's expedition took off shortly after the agreement was signed.

For Balbo personally, especially after his 1928 visit, the United States had a special fascination.[9] With no new lands to discover, he wrote, there were new civilizations to explore. For him the United States represented "the brilliant anticipator of mechanical progress, the immense reserve of optimism, health, power, the guarantee of a more stable peace." In addition to a fascination with the civilization of the future, he burned with patriotic pride. He wanted the thousands of Italians who had abandoned their homeland for the United States to know that Mussolini and fascism had ended the era of shame and humiliation.

Given the size of the expedition and the technical risks involved, Balbo prepared carefully. He devoted two years—twice the time he spent on preparation for the flight to Brazil—to planning and training. He wanted no repetition of the Bolama tragedy that had marred the trip to South America. Beginning in May, 1931, under the command of General Aldo Pellegrini, pilots and crews began to train at Orbetello. In the past Balbo had chosen pilots from among those who were already familiar with seaplanes. For this cruise, to broaden the experience of his men he selected seventy officers of whom four-fifths had no experience with these aircraft. However, he also included about a dozen veterans of the expedition to Brazil; they provided experience and inspired the younger pilots. The academic program included courses in mathematics, physics, aerodynamics, thermodynamics, navigation, and English. The practical program included flying an average of five hundred hours over two years. The men also worked on their sailing skills, for once on the water, their aircraft became an unwieldy boat. The movements of winds and waves, the fundamentals of handling a small boat, the problems of taxiing up to buoys and then tying up, and the transfer of men and materials at sea were all vital to handling their aircraft. Since the expedition would venture to extreme northern latitudes, the crews trained in snow and ice in Misurina during the winter of 1932/33. To practice formation flying, they flew a series of missions throughout the

Mediterranean. Discipline was harsh. Thirty-five of the original seventy applicants failed and were replaced.

The rigorous training, combined with Balbo's minute planning, paid off. The discipline never dimmed the enthusiasm of the pilots and crews. On the eve of their departure, they felt completely confident in their skills, their machines, and their organization. Whatever the goal of "the great enterprise"—until the end they were not sure of their ultimate destination—they were confident they could reach it.[10] On their return from Chicago, they felt capable of starting regular service across the North Atlantic. Due to the careful training and preparation, Balbo lost only two aircraft and two crew members during the 1933 double crossing. This was an impressive achievement. In the previous crossings, all one-way, twenty-seven out of forty-five aircraft had been lost, with twenty-three deaths.[11]

Balbo methodically organized his logistical support and his weather service. The expedition was promoted as an Italian effort. Certainly, the planning, leadership, crews, and aircraft were all Italian. Much of the crucial support, however, was international, beginning with an international congress of transoceanic aviators that Balbo convened in Rome in May, 1932. Balbo used the occasion to show off the Aeronautica. The guests toured the new ministry building and attended demonstrations and rallies that, according to one visitor, made the "vaunted 'Broadway Parade' fade into insignificance."[12] Balbo's main purpose, however, was to gather all the practical information he could for his own expedition. About the same time, he sent pilots on three separate missions to scout possible landing sites from Labrador and Newfoundland to Greenland and Iceland. On the basis of their reports, he planned a route that would touch on Iceland and Labrador on the initial crossing and would return via Newfoundland and Ireland. Accurate weather information was crucial to the success of the expedition. National weather services that covered the path of his flight— Italian, German, Danish, English, Canadian, and American—all contributed to the effort. He also established special weather centers. In Londonderry, for data on the eastern part of the North Atlantic, he stationed Filippo Eredia, an Italian meteorologist. From Julianhaab, Greenland, Balbo received reports from the German geophysicist, Baumann, an expert on Arctic weather. In

New York, Lieutenant Colonel Mario Infante served as liaison with the United States Weather Service. The International Telephone and Telegraph Company donated radio links among the weather centers, the bases, and the squadron. Balbo also stationed eleven weather ships along the flight path.

Once again, as on his expeditions to Brazil and to the Eastern Mediterranean, Balbo chose the tough, durable Savoia Marchetti SM.55—a flying machine, as he pointed out, that had given the Italians a total of fifteen Atlantic crossings. The SM.55X model (the X did not stand for "experimental" but was a Roman numeral, for the Decennial cruise) was a refinement of the one he had used on the first Atlantic cruise. The most important change was in the engines. Fiat A. 22R engines had powered the earlier SM.55TA model. Balbo wanted larger engines. A competition developed between the Fiat A. 24R, developed from the Schneider engines, and the Isotta Fraschini Asso 11R. Both engines were rated at 750 horsepower. Industrialists, politicians, and even workers at the two companies pressured Balbo, hoping to influence his choice. He declared that he would choose on the basis of test performance. After a test of 500 hours, the Isotta Fraschini won. The SM.55X had a top speed of 280 km/hr., a cruising speed of 225 km/hr., and a range of more than 4,000 kilometers. There were other refinements: larger fuel tanks, modified radiators, metal propellers, and more sophisticated instruments. American aviation magazines noted proudly that Balbo's instrument panel included a Sperry artificial horizon and a direction indicator that permitted controls to be set for any desired direction.[13]

By the beginning of May, 1933, preparations for the expeditions were nearly complete. The aircraft were delivered in April. The crews had reached the peak of their training. Supply bases, weather stations, and communications networks were ready. Everything now depended on the weather. Floating icebergs blocked one of the weather ships from her position off the coast of Labrador. Then from mid-June to the first of July storms buffeted the Alps and northcentral Europe almost continuously. For nearly two weeks, Balbo and his crews waited anxiously. "All we need is a twelve-hour break of weather between Labrador and Iceland and we'll make it easily," Cagna, who was Balbo's personal pilot, told an American reporter.[14]

Rumors began to circulate about the delay: the regime was divided over the flight; the expedition was too costly and the money was needed elsewhere; Balbo, content with his glories from the South American flight, did not really want to fly.[15] Mussolini prodded him to make the trip—and hoped for a disaster. The blame would fall on Balbo, and Mussolini would be rid of a dangerous opponent. Departure dates provided another great subject for speculation. First it was said that the expedition would leave on May 24, then on June 1 at the latest. As the delays continued through the second half of June, cartoons in the European press lampooned the expedition.[16] In one drawing, American girls crossed the Atlantic in paper boats more quickly than the Italian aviators; in another, a crowd of spectators waited so long for the aerial armada that fungi sprouted from their feet.

In addition to increasing tension at the base, delays increased the risk of accidents. Balbo himself had an accident on June 20 at Punta Ala; fortunately, no one was seriously hurt.[17] As days and then weeks passed, Balbo began to consider following an alternate route over French territory, even though that would mean giving up the spectacle of his armada soaring over the Alps.[18] He decided to wait five more days before settling on the alternative.

Despite his anxieties, Balbo revelled in the atmosphere in Orbetello.[19] He was in his element: at the head of a merry band of adventurers, preparing to lead them on a great escapade. He roared with delight when his men, with a few stripes of paint, transformed the base mascot, a patient little donkey named Marco, into a zebra. With his pilots and the press corps, he feasted on fish and the local white wines at restaurants and cafés in the nearby fishing village of Porto Ercole. "He seemed to be feared and respected by his men and at the same time popular with them," noted an American journalist.[20] Despite an official ban on visitors, they came in a steady stream: important diplomats such as the American ambassador, Henry Breckinridge Long, and the British ambassador and his wife, Sir Ronald Graham and Lady Graham; party leaders such as Achille Starace, the party secretary, and De Bono; famous flyers of the day such as Winifred Evelyn Spooner, the English woman aviator who had participated in many Italian air races and air tours.

Finally, during the night of June 30 to July 1, the weather

cleared.[21] "Orbetello was like a town on the Western Front when troops were moving on the eve of an offensive," one reporter recalled. Balbo set reveille at 4:15 A.M. As he frequently did during the cruise, he spent a sleepless night and appeared "worn and nervous," with dark circles under his eyes. Following a flag-raising ceremony at dawn, Balbo gave the order for departure. The men replied with a rousing "Viva il Re!" By 4:37 Balbo's own I-BALB was in the air and by 5:00 the entire expedition was airborne, "disappearing toward Genoa, three by three, like a swarm of well-organized insects."

The aerial armada roared northward in formation: eight flights of three aircraft apiece.[22] The twenty-fifth plane was considered a reserve and assigned to the eighth flight. As with the previous Atlantic expedition, each flight was color-coded: black, red, white, and green. Circles or stars painted on the upper surfaces of the ailerons and on the vertical tail fins distinguished flights of the same color. The leader of each flight had a single star or circle; the right aircraft had two stars or circles; the left had three. As with the flight to Brazil, whenever weather permitted Balbo maintained the formation, both for discipline and for show.

On that first day, Saturday, July 1, the expedition soared over the Alps in a majestic formation that was widely reproduced in photographs, on postcards, and even on a book jacket.[23] After a seven-hour flight the aviators reached Amsterdam. For the first time they experienced the joyous frenzy—and the hazards—that awaited them at each destination. Sixty Dutch aircraft rose to meet them. Ships and boats of all sizes cluttered the harbor. Some belonged to the official welcoming party; others carried fuel and supplies for the expedition; still others were police vessels, trying to control the huge numbers of journalists, well-wishers, and sightseers. The boats in the landing area constituted a major hazard for the twenty-five pilots trying to set down their aircraft; but in the first fatal accident, which occurred here, pilot error rather than the harbor traffic was ruled the cause. The pilot of I-DINI overshot his landing and flipped over. Three of the crew and a passenger were saved; a fourth crewman died, trapped in the wreckage.

With their aircraft safely anchored for the night and refueled for the next day's flight, Balbo and his men faced the second

Fig. 13. SM.55X at anchor (R. Cupini, *Cieli e mari*)

major challenge of their arrival: the public ceremonies and festivities. Exhausted from the flight, their ears ringing from the roar of
the motors, their bodies limp from the vibrations of their aircraft,
Balbo and his men could look forward not to rest and relaxation
but to speeches, anthems, receptions, dances, flowers, telegrams,
keys to the city, and the clamor of the press. An American cartoon summed it up. A cheerful but exhausted Balbo confronts
Mussolini with the comment, "They gave us everything but rest
and sleep."[24] In Amsterdam, however, out of respect for their
dead comrade, Balbo ordered all festivities and celebrations suspended. Nevertheless, courtesy dictated that he receive old
friends and dignitaries from the aviation world. These included
Wolfgang Von Gronau, the German long-distance flyer, who
came as Hermann Goering's personal representative; the English
journalist Lady Drummond Hay, who had just completed a flight
around the world in the *Graf Zeppelin*, and aircraft designer
Anthony Fokker.

Fig. 14. Aerial armada soars over the Alps (R. Cupini, *Cieli e mari*)

The following day, Sunday, July 2, in five and a half hours the expedition crossed the North Sea, flew over Newcastle, Edinburgh, and Glasgow, and landed in Londonderry, Ireland. Howling winds at their next destination, Reykjavik, Iceland, delayed the expedition. Finally, on July 5, the four weather ships, stationed at 340-kilometer intervals along the route, signaled favorable conditions. The weather was good except for half an hour in a fog bank. "The first contact with the fog always produces one effect for sure: my heart jumps into my mouth," noted Balbo.[25] He dropped to an altitude of 30 meters, at which the waves were visible. The slightest dive and I-BALB would plunge into the water; a sharp climb meant the risk of collision with other aircraft. "The strain on my nerves becomes a torture: my eyes hurt," Balbo recorded. As the temperature dropped toward freezing, the aviators watched nervously for ice forming on the wings. Then, abruptly, they emerged into clear weather. By six o'clock that evening, at the end of their 1,528-kilometer flight, they were

Fig. 15. Cartoon: "They gave us everything but rest and sleep" (*Columbus: The Italian-American Magazine*, December, 1933)

tying up in the harbor at Reykjavik. They stepped into a subpolar cold of 5 degrees Centigrade. For the first time, they appreciated the value of their Alpine training—and their fur-lined overcoats and hats.

For the next six days the expedition remained in Reykjavik, waiting for the weather to clear and preparing for the second and most difficult stage of the North Atlantic crossing: from Reykjavik to Cartwright, Labrador. The disasters and near-disasters of the cruise to Brazil had taught Balbo patience. The weather ships had to shift their positions to cover the second half of the route. The weather had to be right. He had chosen Julianhaab, Greenland, as an alternate destination if conditions were not favorable over Labrador, but the chances of becoming a prisoner of the weather in Greenland were much higher than in Labrador. There was a secondary consideration. The hop from Greenland to Labrador was much less spectacular than the direct flight from Reykjavik.

At last, on Wednesday, July 12, the expedition roared off again into skies filled with fog and rain. Outwardly the crossing proved uneventful. In the cockpit, Balbo suffered moments of anguish and uncertainty.[26] As usual, in anticipation of the flight he had been unable to sleep the night before. Light-headed and nervous, he fortified himself with coffee and an occasional nip of cognac as the expedition dodged in and out of fog banks and rain showers. In contrast to flying over land, flying over water, he fretted, stretched on interminably. The hours, especially the last ones, dragged on like months. With nothing for the eyes to focus on, his imagination roamed freely and flying became a nightmare and an obsession. Like the traveller in a desert, he wrote, the pilot's life becomes focused entirely on the concrete things around him—his companions, his instrument panel, the outlines of the wings. Outside, fog banks varied from light and white to dark and opaque, so dark that he could see only the glow from his instruments. Showers of rain battered the aircraft and water leaked into the cockpit. For a moment the artificial horizon went haywire, but a swift kick righted it. Visions of the ocean engulfing him again, as it had almost two years ago at Capri, haunted him. Then a radio message came from another aircraft: five hundred meters higher the weather was clear. Despite the risk of falling temperatures and ice forming on the wings, Balbo ordered the expedition to climb. "The blue!" A childish joy, a frenzy, coursed through him, he recalled—a feeling of liberation, like waking at dawn from a nightmare.

At last, at seven o'clock in the evening, after twelve hours in the air, the expedition reached the coffee-colored waters of Sandwich Bay. They had covered 2,400 kilometers. In Italy an excited radio announcer interrupted a broadcast of Beethoven's Sixth Symphony with the great news. The clouds and fog banks had not permitted the expedition to fly in formation along the route. However, their discipline was so tight that on arrival there were no stragglers. Each flight of three arrived at the same time and in the same position they had occupied during takeoff.

Although they were bone-tired from the flight, the crews followed the tedious and backbreaking routine of refueling their aircraft. In bucket-brigade fashion, they wrestled the heavy cans of gasoline from small boats to the aircraft until the fuel tanks were filled. Then, wearing their black shirts, the men disembarked. Brimful of joy, pride, and satisfaction, they hugged the support crews and journalists who had been anxiously awaiting the fleet's arrival. Balbo, refreshed by nothing more than a glass of lemonade, congratulated each of the ninety-nine crew members who had made the trip. He also checked each of the aircraft for possible repairs. "None. Not even a spark plug needs to be changed." The *Alice*'s cargo of spare parts proved to be unnecessary. That evening at dinner aboard the yacht, "high spirits were

not missing," Balbo recalled. A bottle of grappa di Bassano made
the rounds at the end of the meal "with great success," and soon
everyone was singing.[27] At midnight everyone went to bed. As
one proud pilot with a penchant for statistics noted later, among
the other precedents and records, Balbo's expedition had transported ninety-nine Italians from Europe, eleven more than Columbus and seventy-one more than the twenty-eight aviators who
had previously made this crossing.[28]

Fatigue lay heavily on the pilots and crews the next day, but
they flew for six hours in excellent weather from Cartwright to
Shediac, Newfoundland. In anticipation of Balbo's expedition, the
population of the resort town had temporarily tripled to 30,000.
Balbo and his men missed Charles Lindbergh and his wife, Anne
Morrow Lindbergh, by one day; they were to arrive in Cartwright
on a survey of the North Atlantic for future commerical air routes.
On Friday, July 14, the expedition flew from Shediac to Montreal
in five hours. The day's greatest danger was by now a familiar
one: the swarms of small boats, flitting about in the area where
the armada was preparing to land. "I broke into a cold sweat,"
Balbo recalled, but no one else seemed to care. The bells of
Montreal pealed; sirens shrieked. Above the chaos Balbo vainly
screamed orders to clear the area. At that moment a newsman
approached him with a microphone. In his nervousness and fury,
he let fly a few "unparliamentary invectives" and the microphone
was hastily withdrawn.

On Saturday, July 15, at about 5:45 P.M. local Chicago time, a
boy with binoculars first sighted them.[29] From the ground they
looked like a group of black specks emerging from the smoke and
haze over Gary, Indiana. "Here they come!" the boy shouted as
the armada began to emerge in "neat spearheads of threes." The
crowds that lined the shores of Lake Michigan for miles went
"wild with joy; Italians among them nearly burst." "Viva Italia!"
"Viva Balbo!" Two weeks after they had left Orbetello, Balbo's
armada was in the skies over Chicago. Their elapsed flying time
had been forty-eight hours and forty-seven minutes. They had
flown 9,766 kilometers (6,065 miles) at an average of 200 km/hr.
(124.6 m.p.h.).

I-BALB, of course, led the grand entrance. The armada flew
north past the fairgrounds and the navy pier and then swung back

to alight into the wind. Each pilot, conscious of the mammoth audience, tried to make the landing one of his best. Overhead, forty-three American fighter planes which had escorted the expedition from Detroit paraded above the lake, forming the word ITALY. Here was Balbo's dream realized literally: to see Italy proclaimed throughout the world in capital letters. While the visitors moored their aircraft, the Americans put on a spectacular aerobatics show. At a lower altitude, the dirigible *Macon* hovered over the Italian armada, and at least half a dozen other airships paraded by. One trailed a message that read, "Hail Balbo and the sons of Great Italy." A naval training ship, the *Wilmette*, fired honorary salvos.

Once ashore, Balbo and his men launched into the long round of visits, banquets, parties, speeches, receptions, and religious celebrations. A caravan of fifty automobiles carried the expedition to the "Century of Progress" fairgrounds, where they visited for an hour. Then the procession continued to Soldier's Field. There, before an audience of 100,000, according to Balbo's estimate, Mayor Edward Kelly welcomed the aviators. In a comparison that was certainly popular with the city's estimated 300,000 Italian-Americans, the mayor linked Balbo and Columbus. On winged ships, Balbo had transported more men than Columbus had transported by sea. In tribute to this feat, the mayor proclaimed this day "Italo Balbo Day" and Chicago's Seventh Street was renamed Balbo Avenue—a name it still bears today.

In the evening, the *atlantici* attended a banquet and a dance at the Hotel Drake. Balbo, who did not dance, was more interested in the contingent of plainclothes policemen clustered about his hotel room door. With their straw hats and their huge cigars, they had a Neapolitan air about them, he noted. Better yet, they guaranteed his sleep.

After a day of religious ceremonies, a visit to the fairgrounds, and a radio broadcast, Balbo that evening was guest of honor at the biggest banquet he had ever attended—a five-thousand-plate affair at the Stevens Hotel, hosted by the Italian-American community. Italian and American flags decorated the banquet hall. Two huge black silhouettes against a white background, one of Mussolini, one of the king, formed a backdrop. When Balbo and his men entered the room, many of the guests stood up and gave the fascist salute and yell, "eia, eia alalà"—a gesture that prompted angry letters to local newspaper editors. To Balbo's surprise, Loyola University in Chicago awarded him an honorary degree. In his brief speech that evening, he invited his countrymen "to be proud to call themselves Italians," an invitation he repeated throughout the trip. "I was profoundly moved and waves of emotion swept over the room," for four-fifths of those present had participated in that "tragic odyssey" of emigration, he believed.[30]

The dedication of Balbo Avenue and a monument to Columbus subsidized by the Italian-American community highlighted the ceremonies the following day, July 17. "This monument has seen the glory of the wings of Italy led by Italo Balbo, July 15, 1933," read the inscription. During a visit to the mayor's office, Balbo received a gold key to the city. He in turn presented I-BALB's anchor buoy to the Chicago Historical Society. The buoy was a welcome companion piece to an anchor, in the society's collection, from one of Columbus's caravels. Finally, in a ceremony Balbo found to be one of the strangest of the entire trip, at the fairgrounds he was initiated into the Sioux tribe. Conscious of his image as a public figure and a representative of fascist Italy, Balbo was uncertain whether to accept. Only when he learned that President Coolidge was the most recent to be so honored did Balbo agree.[31] Dozens of newspaper and movie cameramen recorded the event. In the photographs, Balbo in his gray, double-breasted suit looks somewhat stiff and hesitant. He declared himself to be "more amused than moved." But at the high point of the ceremony, when he received his crown of eagle feathers, a timid, half-suppressed smile of childish delight illuminated his face. The games and fantasies of his childhood had become a reality. Appropriately, his Indian name was Flying Eagle.

On the evening of July 19, the expedition reached New York.[32] Millions waved and cheered as the armada flew over Manhattan and landed at the Coney Island seaplane base. The crowd of dignitaries and celebrities that greeted the expedition included the reigning heavyweight boxing champion, Primo Carnera. As in Chicago, a caravan of fifty cars transported the aviators from the base to Manhattan and the familiar round of receptions and dinners. Balbo was exultant. "The name of Italy is on everyone's lips, it throbs like a great flame. . . . With a great lump in my throat, I

Fig. 16. Balbo as Chief Flying Eagle (Italo Balbo, *La centuria alata*)

wave and wave."[33] The Italian neighborhoods in Brooklyn and lower Manhattan particularly moved him. Every house he looked at displayed the tricolor. Nowhere in Italy or in Europe had he seen anything like New York and its crowds. The city's seven million inhabitants and its incredible system of communications, with some streets "100 meters wide and some 40 kilometers long," amazed him. Then, completely forgetting Mussolini's passion for "oceanic crowds," Balbo offered some snide remarks on the American "mania" for mass meetings. America has the reputation for "unbridled individualism," he commented; "What a mistake! In a city like New York, the individual drowns in the mass."[34]

Among the high points of Balbo's stay on the East Coast was an invitation to lunch at the White House on July 20. Balbo chose a select group of his most senior pilots to accompany him. Delays in President Roosevelt's schedule kept the aviators waiting, and it

Fig. 17. New York paper heralds arrival of Balbo's armada (Caproni Museum Archive)

was very hot. Nevertheless, Balbo remembered the encounter with enthusiasm. He found the president to be "like all Americans . . . very cordial and direct in his manners." The president also seemed to agree with a number of Mussolini's social programs, such as battling against urbanization and inducing the excess population to settle in the countryside, Balbo remarked. "I do not know if he is close to fascism," he concluded. "In any case, he is a dictator."[35] To a member of the White House staff, Balbo, "unhappy and weary," was beginning to show the strains of the trip.[36]

Another highlight of the visit was the customary ticker-tape parade down Broadway on July 21. Many times before, New York had celebrated heroic aviators and great aerial feats, but none of the turn-outs "equalled the splendor of yesterday," noted the *Herald Tribune*. "In our lives it would be extraordinary to experience something as grandiose again," Balbo commented. The crowds filled the air with a tremendous "concert": sirens, horns, whistles, screams, the "incredible orchestra with which the American enthusiasm expresses itself," an enthusiasm that has something "primitive, almost savage," about it.[37]

Invitations from Italo-American patriotic and charitable organizations inundated the visitors. If they had accepted them all, two weeks would not have been time enough for their stay. At Balbo's request all the celebrations and demonstrations were concentrated into a huge gathering in Madison Square Garden that afternoon.[38] American newspaper accounts estimated a crowd of 60,000. Balbo exuberantly placed the figure at 200,000, half within the stadium, the other half listening and cheering outside. Two rows of girls dressed in white showered the aviators with flowers as they made their way into the arena and up to the podium. The welcoming applause lasted half an hour, Balbo claimed, though American journalists put it at closer to ten minutes.

When he did speak, it was one of the high points of his life, perhaps even greater than the "Roman triumph" that awaited him on his return home. The rally, Balbo claimed later, had had a political slant that was "decisively, openly, and passionately fascist."[39] Yet, as in Chicago, his speech, despite its obligatory references to Mussolini, was little more than the credo of a patriot, one that a Mazzini or a Crispi might have applauded. "Italians of New York . . . people of my blood and my faith," he told them, his aerial expedition had come to New York to bring them greetings from Mussolini's Italy. "Be proud to be Italians," he exhorted them. "Mussolini has ended the period of humiliations: to be Italian is now a sign of honor." He told his audience to respect the laws of their new land, so that they themselves would be respected. Honor, with the tricolor, the "beautiful star-spangled banner," he urged the cheering crowd; never had the two nations been divided in the past, nor, he added in a bit of bad prophecy, "would the future ever divide them."[40]

A banquet in the evening for four thousand at the Hotel Commodore, sponsored by the Italian-American community, ended the great day. A reception and dance followed at the Waldorf Astoria. As usual, Balbo fled the dance, this time to visit the *New York Times*. In the composing room, to his delight, he found many Italians among the crew. They confirmed his impression that "there is no great American enterprise with which the patient genius of our race does not collaborate."[41]

The New York visit ended Sunday with a mass at St. Patrick's Cathedral. Balbo then met with Wiley Post, who had just com-

pleted an around-the-world flight in seven days. In front of
newspapermen and movie cameras, Post praised the Balbo expedition for its organization and discipline. "I think most generals
are phoney, but you have absolutely proven yourself a general to
have gone out and taken charge of such a flight as you have
made," Post commented.[42] The flight was a real contribution toward the opening of intercontinental commercial flights, declared
Post, and he claimed that Italian aviation was leading the world.

So far as the public knew, Balbo's flight had been a stunning
success, a marvel of organization, harmony, discipline. Yet, inevitably, behind the scenes Balbo had had his headaches. Mussolini
provided a major one. The dictator followed the progress of the
flight minutely, marking each stage with little tricolor flags on a
large map. The Duce, of course, wanted to capitalize personally
on the success of the flight as much as possible. In addition, after
the near-disasters on the South Atlantic cruise, he may have retained lingering doubts about Balbo's leadership. In any case, he
bombarded Balbo with telegrams.[43] Some offered congratulations;
most offered advice and even orders on how to run the expedition. In Rome, Mussolini channelled his communications through
an officer in Balbo's cabinet, Colonel Sabato Castaldi Martelli,
who served as liaison between the air ministry and the Palazzo
Venezia. As Balbo's success became apparent, Mussolini fretted
incessantly about being upstaged. The flight was not a mere
sporting event, he chided, and he urged Balbo to minimize the
party-going and festivities. Sensing Mussolini's jealousy, Balbo
prudently turned down offers to extend the expedition to other
parts of the United States and Canada. To speed Balbo's return,
Mussolini dangled an unprecedented honor: "If all goes well, as I
do not doubt it will, at the Lido di Roma Balbo will receive from
me the baton of an air marshal." In the past, only major heroes of
the Great War, generals Armando Diaz, Luigi Cadorna, and Pietro Badoglio, and Admiral Paolo Thaon di Revel had been so
rewarded. In the fledgling Aeronautica the rank did not exist.
Little wonder that Balbo badgered Martelli about news of the
"project."
    As Balbo began to receive prestigious invitations and honors,
Mussolini too hungered after them. Through Martelli, he grabbed

for his share—or at least tried to limit Balbo's. Balbo's invitation
to lunch at the White House prompted Mussolini to ask for a
telegram of congratulations from President Roosevelt. Protocol,
however, dictated that the president send one only to a head of
state. The king did receive a telegram from the president, but
Mussolini rated one only from the secretary of state. Chicago's
Balbo Avenue provoked a major crisis. Mussolini yearned to have
a major street in New York or Washington named after him.
Failing that, he wanted Balbo to renounce the honor in Chicago.
Balbo had no such intention. To decline the honor would be
discourteous, he cabled back to Rome, and he added that the
Italian ambassador agreed with him. Grudgingly Mussolini proposed an alternative. He offered to send a Roman column to the
city to commemorate the flight. The street or square where the
column was erected was to be named after Mussolini. The following year, Mussolini sent a column; however, the city did not
reciprocate by honoring him. Nor, despite Balbo's discreet hints,
did anything come of a suggestion to name "at least" a skyscraper
after Mussolini.

The ceaseless flow of telegrams from Martelli irked Balbo.
Probably he had his suspicions about who was behind them. At
one point he brusquely cabled Martelli to mind his own business. Then, fearing that the reply would seriously annoy Mussolini, for the rest of the trip Balbo tried to behave like a model
fascist. He refused to meet with Peppino Garibaldi, son of his
old mentor Ricciotti Garibaldi and grandson of the national hero,
for Peppino had become an anti-fascist. In public, Balbo continued his fulsome praise of Mussolini. "Ah, Mussolini! You don't
know what he means to us. Mussolini and God are our religion,"
Balbo declared to the *New York Times* reporter in Chicago.[44] In
his five-paragraph speech to the crowd at Madison Square
Garden he mentioned Mussolini four times.[45] Nevertheless,
Martelli continued to "suggest" that Balbo send more telegrams
to Mussolini of the sort that read "In the name of the Duce we
reach all goals." Balbo complied. The dictator was most pleased
with one, sent after Balbo's lunch at the White House, in which
President Roosevelt was said to express sympathy and praise for
Mussolini's work in reviving Italy and for his efforts in dealing
with international relations.

Another of Balbo's concerns throughout the trip was the possibility of anti-fascist demonstrations. They did take place. In Chicago, throughout the Loop and the fairgrounds, the Italian Socialist Federation and the Italian League for the Rights of Man distributed thousands of "flaming circulars" attacking Balbo, and a light plane flew over the fair dropping anti-fascist leaflets.[46] A united front of anti-fascist organizations demanded that Mayor Kelly refuse to hold a public reception for Balbo, and journalists invoked the specter of Don Minzoni.[47] George Seldes, for example, reminded the public of the priest of Argenta, commenting, "while millions cheer, a few remember."[48] Carlo Tresca, the IWW leader and militant anti-fascist, sent Balbo a telegram, "I am watching you," and signed it "Don Minzoni."[49] Throughout his visit Balbo was under heavy police protection. Nevertheless, the demonstrations were so ineffectual that after the Madison Square Garden rally Balbo telegraphed to Mussolini, "I believe it explodes the myth of anti-fascism abroad. We did not find any evidence of it."[50]

Balbo was right in his assessment of the anti-fascist efforts to discredit the cruise. He then made a doubtful leap to the opposite conclusion: "Nothing succeeds like success and the success of Mussolini's experiment has won over even the most embittered critics in America."[51] He also claimed that his speech at Madison Square Garden had been overtly pro-fascist and that it had been well received. In general, he overestimated his reception in the United States. For the most part, Balbo received a warm welcome. Like the launching of ocean liners such as the *Rex* and the *Conte di Savoia* and De Pinedo's flight, Balbo's expedition impressed growth-minded American industrialists.[52] The crowds in Chicago and New York, thanks in part to the large Italian-American populations, were huge and enthusiastic. President Roosevelt received the aviators. The famed humorist Will Rogers compared Balbo's expedition favorably with Teddy Roosevelt's Great White Fleet and added, "There was a lot of Mussolini in that old boy."[53] Editorials and cartoons in newspapers throughout the United States generally viewed the flight as a gesture of good will and praised its organization and discipline.[54] However, editorial writers and cartoonists associated the flight more with Columbus than with Mussolini and fascism. Some editorials in American papers declared

Fig. 18. Cartoon: Balbo as sportsman of the air (*Columbus: The Italian-American Magazine*, December, 1933)

explicitly that in applauding Balbo, the flight, and Italian-American friendship, they were not endorsing Mussolini and fascism.[55] Letters to the editor complained about seeing the fascist salute as a sign of appreciation during some of the public ceremonies.

Among the critics of the expedition, few saw any military significance to the cruise, except for General William Mitchell, who declared that the flight "revealed how this country is allowing foreign nations to outstrip her in air forces."[56] Others doubted whether the Italian public was happy about spending so much

Fig. 19. Aviation gasoline advertisement based on Balbo's successful second Atlantic cruise (*Aero Digest*, August, 1933)

money on the flight. Some even poked fun at Balbo's heroic image: "It is as though General Grant after Appomattox should simultaneously have taken a course in free ballooning, become president of Vassar and editor of the *Saturday Evening Post*, and having succeeded in all these activities, had then planned to lead twenty balloons across the Atlantic to Italy to be present at the opening of an international exposition."[57]

Most likely, the expedition had its greatest effect on Italian-Americans in Chicago and New York. Yet this was a tiny minority of the American population. If Balbo had barnstormed his way around the United States as President Roosevelt suggested, he would undoubtedly have captured a wider audience. Most Americans probably had difficulty distinguishing between Balbo's expedition and half a dozen competing ones. One editorial cartoon pictured Americans as "bombarded" with flights; another, entitled "Here, There and Everywhere," pictured an airplane labelled *aviation* chasing a butterfly marked *fame and fortune* around the world.[58] On July 15, the day that Balbo's expedition arrived in Chicago, Wiley Post left to beat his own round-the-world record. With him he took to England photographs of Balbo's arrival in Cartwright and Montreal. Post returned in time to share the spotlight in New York with Balbo. On the very days that Balbo was enjoying his triumph in New York, July 22–23, Jim Mollison, the "flying Scot," and his wife, Amy Johnson, having crossed the North Atlantic from Wales, crash-landed in a marsh near Bridgeport, Connecticut. Their accident temporarily overshadowed the excitement over Balbo. During that same period, the American aviator James Mattern, who had been attempting to break Wiley Post's old record, was found in Siberia; in New York, De Pinedo made preparations for a record flight to Persia; two Frenchmen, Maurice Rossi and Paul Codos, on August 5–7 set a world straight-line distance record by flying from New York to Syria, making use of part of Balbo's support network across the Atlantic. Little wonder that the public had a hard time concentrating on Balbo's flight. "A good stunt, a truly remarkable and strictly first class achievement," noted one journal. Yet in the light of what had already been done in the air, the writer concluded somewhat unfairly, Balbo's flight "will seem like nothing more wonderful than Glen Curtiss' flight from Albany to New York in May 1910."[59]

Balbo's return journey began on July 25.[60] The opening was a mirror-image of the flight from Italy. First came two easy stages to the edge of the North Atlantic, then a long and anxious period of waiting for the weather to clear for the crossing to Valentia, Ireland.

The stages from New York to Shediac, Nova Scotia, on July 25, and from Shediac to Shoal Harbor, Newfoundland, on July 26, passed with only minor incidents, but at Shoal Harbor the waiting game with the weather began. Balbo had anticipated a stop of only two or three days, planning to leave on July 29. At the last moment, however, a cyclone blew directly across the expedition's flight path. On July 31, the weather seemed to clear, then abruptly worsened. When the storm finally cleared, a new obstacle developed: fog banks over Ireland in the evening, just at the moment of the expedition's scheduled arrival. Balbo began to consider alternate plans and routes. A night flight was one possibility. The landing in Ireland would then take place in the afternoon before the fog banks formed. The moon was full and the crews had been trained for just such an operation; nevertheless, Balbo rejected the plan as too risky. Another possibility was to change the route completely and return by way of the Azores. Balbo did not like the plan: the route was 1,200 kilometers longer, the winds were unfavorable, the route was less prestigious, and the harbors were not large enough to accommodate the entire squadron. Nevertheless, he had little choice. The days were shortening rapidly, making daylight landings difficult along the northern route. The escort ships were running low on fuel.

While Balbo weighed these technical factors, Mussolini, through Martelli, bombarded him with "suggestions" based on his instincts as a "country weatherman," as he labelled himself.[61] The "suggestions," however, had more to do with politics than with the weather. Mussolini did not want Balbo to set down in London, Paris, or Berlin on his way back. In a cable to Martelli, Balbo ridiculed alternatives based on political considerations. Balbo instructed Martelli to deal with "the Chief" as little as possible and not to communicate anything from Mussolini that was not a direct order. Finally, Mussolini sent orders directly: until August 10 the expedition was to aim for Ireland; after that date, the Azores.

Balbo made his own decision. On August 8, the expedition took off for the Azores. The crossing took place without incident. Nine of the aircraft landed at Horta and fifteen at Ponta Delgada. The following day, however, the second fatality of the trip occurred. I-RANI, in taking off from Ponta Delgada, overturned. Lieutenant Enrico Squaglia, one of the pilots, was fatally injured. The cause of the accident was never determined.

Balbo learned of the fatality only after he had arrived in Lisbon. He took the incident hard, for it seemed to nullify his cautious decision at Shoal Harbor. In sign of mourning, he postponed leaving Lisbon for a day, cancelled all ceremonies, and decided against making a stop at Berre in southern France. On Saturday, August 12, Balbo led his men on the last leg of the journey, from Lisbon to the Lido di Roma, a distance of more than 2,200 kilometers. The futurist poet F. T. Marinetti made a live radio broadcast of the armada's arrival at the mouth of the Tiber at 5:35 P.M.

Listen to the music of the sky with its mellowed tubes of pride, the buzzing drills of miners of the clouds, enthusiastic roars of gas, hammerings ever more intoxicated with speed and the applause of bright propellers. The rich music of Balbo and his transatlantic fliers hums, explodes, and laughs among the blue flashes of the horizon. . . . The cruiser *Diaz* fires salvos. The crowd shouts with joy. The sun mirrors the Italian creative genius. . . . The crowd yells: "Here he is, here he is, here he is! Duce! Duce! Duce! Italy! Italy!" The rumble, rumble, rumble of the motors that pass a few yards over my head.[62]

An ecstatic crowd, including Mussolini and members of the royal family, and a bombastic welcome awaited the heroes. The moment Balbo stepped ashore, Mussolini, in a rapid, spontaneous movement, embraced him affectionately and kissed him on both cheeks. "In this gesture he says everything to me and I everything to him," declared Balbo.[63] But Mussolini had more: a triumphal march under the Arch of Constantine awaited the aviators the next day, Mussolini informed him. "This is too much for us," Balbo protested with the modesty appropriate to a national hero.

Fig. 20. Mussolini greets Balbo on his return from the second Atlantic cruise (G. Bucciante, ed., *Vita di Balbo*)

"No," the Duce insisted, "the *patria* owes it to you." A triumphant motorcade bore the heroes from the Lido di Ostia to Piazza Venezia and Piazza Colonna in downtown Rome, a journey that took about an hour. Four huge searchlights lighted up Piazza Colonna as bright as day. The crowds demonstrated joyously while the *atlantici* waved from a balcony. Above them was a huge mural showing the route of the expedition. White lamps marked the outbound voyage; red, the return. Above the map was a huge portrait of Mussolini. When at last Balbo was able to speak, he made it clear that he intended to keep his head in the midst of the frenzy. In the name of all the *atlantici*, he thanked the crowds for their magnificent welcome. But he added: "I don't want you to lose sight of reality and don't let me and my comrades lose it; we are only modest soldiers of a great Chief in whose name it is sweet and easy to achieve such victories."[64]

For political, and perhaps for personal, reasons, Balbo wanted to remember the day as he recorded it. Not everyone recalled the excitement, joy, and harmony with Mussolini that he did.[65] In Rome it was difficult to tell whether it was Balbo or Mussolini who had flown the Atlantic. Great posters displayed Mussolini in aviator's costume beside a squadron of planes, as if he had done the flying and Balbo had assisted him. The press referred to the "Wings of Mussolini under the guidance of Balbo" and telegrams were published to show that Mussolini had directed the flight from day to day. In Piazza Colonna, a photograph shows Mussolini's portrait dominating the map of the cruise and a huge banner with a quote from the Duce: "For the Aeronautica, the Atlantic will become a Mediterranean." To an American reporter, the crowds at Piazza Colonna appeared to be comparatively small and indifferent. And behind the scenes, Mussolini furiously berated a newspaper editor for publishing a photograph of him with Balbo in which he looked much older than his lieutenant.

The promised Roman triumph came the next day, August 13. Following a royal audience at the Quirinale Palace, the *atlantici* in their white dress uniforms marched to the Forum by way of Via XXIV Maggio, Via IV Novembre, Piazza Venezia, and Via dei Fori Imperiali. Oak and laurel branches covered the Via dei Fori Imperiali, and the crowds cheered and threw flowers as the aviators paraded through the heart of ancient Rome. Finally came the

Fig. 21. Balbo salutes during "Roman" triumphal march under the Arch of Constantine (August 13, 1933) (Italo Balbo, *La centuria alata*)

climax: like a victorious Roman legion, the *atlantici* marched under the Arch of Constantine. For the first time in two thousand years, Balbo exulted, the Via dei Trionfi was no longer an artistic and cultural monument but a "live element in the life of Rome."[66] It was a tribute "beyond our merits," Balbo wrote demurely. On the Palatine Hill, Mussolini addressed the assembled *atlantici*. In time, their expedition would become "legendary," he assured them. They could be proud that during the flight, "hundreds of millions of men, in all the languages of the world, had pronounced the name of Italy."[67] Then Mussolini presented the *atlantici* with their awards. Balbo received the cap of air marshal. His men received promotions according to their ranks. The cruise came to a formal conclusion the next day when the expedition flew from Ostia to their base at Orbetello for a last presentation to the king. Afterwards, Balbo embraced each member of the expedition individually and departed.

About ten days after his return from the expedition, in the seclusion of his villa at Punta Ala, far from the hysterical crowds, the parades, the hero worship, Balbo summed up his thoughts about the significance of the cruise.[68] He couched his reflections in the form of a phantom press conference before a crowd of the "tall and blond" American journalists—the ones who had constantly kept him under fire with their "insatiable desire to know." The expedition had been an enormous success, far greater than he had anticipated. Under normal odds only twenty of the twenty-four aircraft would have completed the trip. How to account for such success? Careful organization, training, careful quality control over the equipment. An example of quality control: he had kept a register with the name of each worker who was responsible for each individual part. Thanks to this system, each worker felt he had a stake in the expedition, and breakdowns of major parts did not occur.

Which leg of the flight was the most difficult? Each one was long. The uncertain weather, especially unpredictable this year, made every stage risky. Did the cruise prove that regular airline service was possible? The North Atlantic was still too tough for regular commercial air service, he concluded. Temporary flights between Iceland and Labrador during the summer were feasible as long as the weather was good; the central route between the Azores and Bermuda might also work during the winter. For the moment, however, he did not see regular service as a possibility. His impressions of the United States? The parallels between Roosevelt's and Mussolini's ideas had struck him most.

What of the costs? The bills were not yet all in, but indications were that the operation had totaled no more than 5 million lire. This included the expense of renting the fleet of weather ships and the costs of billeting his men during the trip, limited as they were. Most likely, he declared, his men would be billed for some of these expenses, just as they had been during the first Atlantic cruise. The cost of the expedition was so modest because private companies such as Standard Oil and the International Telephone and Telegraph Company furnished fuel and the communications

network. Sales of special commemorative stamps issued for the
expedition would further diminish the costs. Indeed, the stamp
sales would even leave a surplus that might be applied to future
expeditions, he claimed.[69]

From the perspective of half a century, how does Balbo's evaluation stand up? Technically, the cruise was a grand achievement. Twenty-four aircraft and approximately one hundred men
had challenged the North Atlantic twice. Two aircraft and two
men were lost, but thanks to careful preparations, just as with the
first Atlantic cruise, Balbo had beaten the odds. Moreover, as he
pointed out, his Atlantic expeditions were in a class by themselves. They were not sporting adventures that depended on an
exceptional pilot with exceptional courage and skills. Like the
space flights of today, Balbo's Atlantic cruises proved the value of
organization, method, routine. They marked a watershed between the pioneering-sporting phases of aviation and the new
commercial-industrial era.

Some critics have belittled the North Atlantic flight by ar-
guing that the Italians were not the only ones who could have
done it.[70] Any one of a dozen other states might have accomplished the same thing if their governments had been willing to
invest the men, money, and time. Certainly others might have
done it. Some did carry out similar expeditions—and with less
fanfare.[71] The American navy claimed that one of its squadrons
flew nonstop from Norfolk, Virginia, to the fleet air base at Coco
Solo, Canal Zone, a distance two hundred miles longer than any
of Balbo's flights. In December, 1933, perhaps in reaction to
Balbo's achievement, General Joseph Vuillemin, chief of the
French air force in Morocco, led twenty-two bombers on a forty-
day, 20,000-kilometer cruise in thirty-six stages from the south
of France around Africa. These were admirable achievements,
but they do not in any way diminish Balbo's.

In addition to its technical brilliance, the flight promised to
make a major contribution to the development of commercial
aviation. In their hearts, many of the *atlantici* felt that they had
the training and the rudiments of a support system that could
have made regular commercial transatlantic flights possible. That
promise remained unfulfilled. Balbo himself concluded that, at
least for the moment, regular service was too difficult. By the

year 2000 passengers would think nothing of crossing the Atlantic at an altitude of 20,000 meters, he wrote.[72] He showed no interest in anticipating the date. Nor did Mussolini. The Duce was far more concerned—as were the other colonial powers—with establishing links with his African empire. The real systematic pioneering of the North Atlantic was left to the Germans in the early 1930s.[73] They linked Europe and the United States, using great airships like the *Hindenburg* and aircraft that were catapult-launched from the decks of ocean liners. In 1938 a four-engine Focke-Wulf FW 200 Condor made a Berlin–New York flight, paving the way for nonstop commercial service. World War II marked the watershed. The war effort in Europe demanded huge quantities of men and supplies from the United States, and so the North Atlantic crossing became a routine occurrence. The war also brought major technical improvements in aircraft: they now flew above the weather, and they had pressurized cabins for the passengers. By the late 1940s, about fifteen years after Balbo's enterprise and more than half a century ahead of his own estimate, regular commercial air traffic across the North Atlantic became a reality.

At his imaginary press conference, Balbo said nothing about the flight as a cruise—as a vehicle for training his men and for promoting the Aeronautica—but he often defended his expeditions on these grounds. His critics argue that he actually detracted from the service's military effectiveness.[74] On balance, Balbo's claims are dubious. The training that his men received at Orbetello was first class and Italian pilots gained a worldwide reputation for their excellence. Whether this cruise, or any of the others, provided effective training for the organization as a whole is another matter. Balbo claimed that he was not training an elite. This was nonsense. The seventy or so *atlantici* who trained at Orbetello for two years were no more "ordinary" than pioneering astronauts in a space program. Balbo liked to boast of his 3,100 pilots, yet only seventy were admitted to the Orbetello course and about one hundred men, pilots and crews, flew with the expedition. Balbo pointed out that after the expeditions, the *atlantici* were distributed widely throughout the ranks of the Aeronautica. They shared their experiences and served as an inspiration to their fellow airmen. Perhaps they did. Nevertheless, such a procedure seems an odd substitute for training the organization as a whole.

Balbo believed that the cruises were good discipline and training and referred to them vaguely as "military maneuvers," although he never pretended that they were full-scale exercises. Since Italian military planning focused on war in the Mediterranean, not against the United States or Latin America, the contribution of the cruises to the nation's defense may appear remote. What Balbo had shown was that Douhet's facile dreams of irresistible aerial fleets were difficult to achieve in practice. Aerial fleets might be possible, but they required a long period of preparation and practice. On the other hand, to charge that Balbo's cruises were somehow responsible for Italy's lack of preparation in World War II is absurd. Three months after the trip to Chicago, Balbo left the Aeronautica. He was responsible for having given the service a good reputation. He was certainly not at fault if his successors overestimated the Aeronautica's real capabilities and made foolish or misguided decisions.

The cruise was plainly not a cost-effective way of achieving Balbo's training goals for the service as a whole. Balbo's cost estimate for the second Atlantic cruise of 5 million lire—about 2 million more than the one to Brazil—was low. The official costs, according to the report that General Valle made in January of 1934, were 7.4 million lire, about one percent of the air ministry's budget.[75] Moreover, this accounting was based only on the immediate expenses for setting up the support network. Included were such items as renting the fleet of weather ships and crews, the costs of maintaining the crews at weather bases, flying togs, and photographic equipment. Excluded were the long-term expenses of training the flight crews and the costs of the aircraft and engines. These expenses formed part of the ordinary budget, it was argued. The fuel and communications network were also excluded, since they were donated. Balbo's great hopes for the philatelic market were never fulfilled.[76] In part this was because the stamps commemorating the cruises had to compete with too many other "special issues" of the day; in part, because the sales were mismanaged. In 1937, some of the remainder were distributed among the *atlantici* and the rest were auctioned as a bloc.

Even if Balbo's accounting was seriously understated, his defenders have argued that the cruises were a bargain. The investment paid off in larger budget allocations and in intangibles such as increased prestige. The budget did increase in absolute terms during the next half-dozen years, from 695 million lire in 1933/34 to 1,285 million in 1938/39; and also modestly—from about 18 percent to about 21 percent—in relation to the defense budget as a whole.[77] But Mussolini, involved in Spain and Ethiopia, had launched a rearmament program and the budget increases would have come about anyway.

Another major goal of the cruise was good will and publicity for Mussolini and his regime, for the Aeronautica, and for Italy's aircraft industry. Certainly the cruise was a success from this point of view, but not always as much as anticipated, nor as much as the fascist propaganda machine boasted. The Italian aircraft industry, for example, probably benefited from the publicity. On the other hand, it is difficult to show a correlation between the flight and increased Italian aircraft sales abroad. The United States had its own aircraft industry and thus never became an important market for Italian products. In 1928, a company in New York known as the American Aeronautical Corporation, hoping to capitalize on Balbo's cruises and the SM.55's reputation, began to manufacture and sell the aircraft. By 1932, however, the company was forced to liquidate.[78]

Undoubtedly the second Atlantic cruise, in particular, generated good will and publicity internationally for Italy, for Mussolini, and for the fascist regime. The expedition made newspaper headlines and news broadcasts throughout the world, and the commentary was largely favorable. In the United States, the flight generated enormous publicity. Yet the impact was probably less widespread than the fascist press or Balbo's own accounts claimed. Mussolini's foreign policy adventures in Ethiopia and Spain, and his alliance with the Nazis, neutralized the good will that the flight had generated.

Balbo's personal star, on the other hand, never really dimmed in the United States. In 1935, both he and his chief aide on the cruise, General Aldo Pellegrini, were awarded the Distinguished Flying Cross. Previous winners included Lindbergh for his flight to Paris, Admiral Richard Byrd for his flight to the North Pole, and Amelia Earhart. The award was all the more unusual in that

Balbo was neither an American citizen nor serving in the American armed forces.

Balbo's ultra-fascist background and the experiences of World War II in no way dimmed his reputation or that of the flight. One of the young American military officers assigned to host the Balbo expedition in 1933 was Dwight Eisenhower.[79] By chance, in 1950 during a visit to Italy as head of NATO, Italian authorities assigned him to stay in Udine with Giuliana Florio, widow of Balbo's nephew Cino. Embarrassed Italian government officials at first wanted to remove family portraits of Balbo from the living room. The officials were doubly embarrassed, for Eisenhower spoke warmly of meeting Balbo in 1933 and of his insistence, as a point of national pride, on always speaking Italian. With his charm, his acute sense of publicity, his passion for doing things on a grand scale, remarked Eisenhower, Balbo was made for Americans even more than for Italians. Nearly two decades earlier, the head of the "Century of Progress" fair in Chicago, Harry S. New, had said much the same thing: "If Balbo were to remain in the United States, he'd get elected President."[80]

In Chicago, Balbo Avenue and the monument to his flight survived World War II and anti-fascist sentiment. After the war, the Italian ambassador to the United States, Alberto Tarchiani, a militant anti-fascist, requested that these tributes be removed. Reportedly, the mayor of Chicago was surprised at the request and replied, "Why? Didn't Balbo cross the Atlantic?"[81]

As a symbol of Italian-American friendship the second Atlantic cruise has proved to be an enduring institution. On the first anniversary of the flight, July 15, 1934, the Roman column that Mussolini had promised to Chicago was unveiled. For the occasion Balbo prepared a radio message of friendship and good will.[82] In the late 1930s, as Italy moved into the German orbit, Balbo's cruise was largely forgotten. Ironically, after World War II memory of the flight that was intended to publicize fascism was revived, as a symbol of Italian-American friendship. For the twentieth anniversary of the flight in 1953, the American air attaché organized a banquet in Rome for the surviving *atlantici*.[83] The fortieth-anniversary celebrations in 1973 were even more impressive. Fifty-eight of the surviving members of the expedition and Balbo's son Paolo flew to Chicago for the city's annual Columbus

Day celebration.[84] As they had forty years earlier, the *atlantici* paraded triumphantly through the streets, accompanied by Mayor Richard Daley and Illinois governor Daniel Walker before cheering crowds estimated at 10,000. The parade was the high point in a series of events, including conferences and exhibits, on the theme of "Italy–U.S.A. Air Progress." Most moving of all to the veterans of the cruise was the reaction of the Italian-American community. Many families had treasured programs and other souvenirs from the original flight. In 1973, the *atlantici* found a new generation, waving the memorabilia of forty years earlier, once again clamoring for autographs.

Chapter Twelve

Air Marshal: The Road to Exile

In the fall of 1933, on his return from Chicago, Balbo was at a peak in his career and in his personal life. At thirty-seven he had, like many of the fascist *gerarchi,* come a long way. He was no longer the petty bourgeois revolutionary, the adventurer from the provinces, the schoolmaster's son who aspired to the status and economic security of the haute bourgeoisie. By the fall of 1933, he had family, friends, fame, and fortune. He loved his work as air minister, and he was recognized as one of the leading aviators of the day. In Italy, as *quadrumvir,* militia general, *atlantico,* and air marshal, he ranked as a national hero—and knew it. He felt himself to be, after Mussolini, "the most popular leader in Italy (and outside of Italy)," Ugo Ojetti—writer, art critic, and good friend of Balbo—remarked in his diary.[1] In his beloved Ferrara, he was the king, "greeted by everyone, knows everyone, calls everyone by name," and "if necessary" to maintain his status, he knew how to deal out "kicks." He was the proud parent of two girls and a boy. He had a fascinating mistress—one in a series of extra-marital affairs—who came from the Roman nobility.[2] His army of friends from the various strata and circles of Italian society ranged from industrialists and financiers such as Agnelli, Cini, Volpi, and Caproni to writers and critics such as Leo Longanesi and Curzio Malaparte. Until Ciano replaced him a year or two later, Balbo was the darling of the Roman nobility who set the tone for the city's social life.

Much of Balbo's success was inextricably linked with the success of Mussolini and the fascist regime. By 1933, after a decade in power, fascism had changed. It was no longer based on the eclectic band of ruffians who had marched on Rome. Mussolini, securely entrenched since 1926, had compromised with all the traditional elements in Italian society: monarchy, church, military, big business. Balbo's attitudes changed too. "Politics doesn't interest me anymore. Let them do as they please. I'm sticking to aviation," he told Ugo Ojetti in 1929.[3] Strictly speaking, that was not true, then or later. Throughout his career Balbo remained involved in politics and in many of the major decisions that affected the fascist regime. Nevertheless, he was serving notice that he had lost interest in the "revolution" and that he no longer believed in it. Fascism had infused the nation with new energy and prestige and had brought him fame and fortune. For Balbo, *that* was the "revolution." For such fascist institutions as the corporative state, the party, or the militia, and for fascist "achievements" such as the Lateran Pacts, he cared very little.

Like Mussolini, Balbo did not have a clear vision of the social order that he wanted to see once the fascists took power. During the immediate post-war period, he praised Mussolini's "positive vision": "the rule of youth, the Italy of Vittorio Veneto in power, the fascist state."[4] At best, this meant little more than the "revolution" as a circulation of elites, an infusion of new blood and energy from the younger generation, room at the top for men like Balbo.

Balbo regarded social experiments such as corporativism with a jaundiced eye. Corporativism, a set of guilds or trade union-like organizations that represented both labor and capital, attracted wide interest and admiration both in Italy and abroad. Many saw in this system a possible solution to the struggle between employer and employee, a "third way" that avoided both the destructive class struggles of capitalism and the revolutionary leveling of communism. Syndicalists such as Panunzio and Bianchi influenced Balbo, and he paid respectful lip service to them and to their ideas.[5] Yet, when Mussolini began to build the corporative state in 1925, Balbo showed little enthusiasm for it. "Fascism does not need the 'corporative state,'" the *Padano* of July 3, 1925, declared. A corporative order was antithetical to all that fascism stood for. Fascism was born as an anti-bureaucratic, decentralizing movement whose goal was to liberate Italy "from the

fetters of a bureaucracy that lacked soul, faith, and principles."
The corporative state, the article predicted, would lead to an
even more complicated and cumbersome system. Corporativism
was not forward-looking; it was a throwback to the past, "to that
same corporativism of the Middle Ages that knew nothing of the
nation." Finally, the *Padano* argued that the corporative state
would not benefit the Val Padana. Corporativism rejected "the
clear division between the only two categories that we would like
to see recognized by fascist legislation: the employers and the
employed." The last phrase, in particular, illustrates how little
interest Balbo had in social engineering—or in upsetting the status quo. His power in Ferrara depended on the support of the
agrari. He was not about to sell them out for social theorizing.

The ultimate goal of the corporativists was to replace parliament with a system of corporations. Balbo opposed any such experiments. As Mussolini did, in 1927 he came down on the side of
"not too much zeal."[6] In the struggle over how to balance "fascist"
institutions—corporations, party, militia—and traditional ones—
monarchy, parliament, army—Balbo took a cautious position. He
opposed dismantling the monarchy or parliament. In his view,
fascism's "revolutionary adherence" to the monarchy had already
transformed that institution; parliament should be governed with
a firm hand but not be abolished. To abolish it would upset the
balance between the fascist government and the monarchy. Corporative institutions such as "committees, technical councils, corporative chambers" he viewed as "institutional snares" that would
increase the powers of the Crown and "reduce to dust" the government's freedom to act.[7]

Five years later, on May 5–8, 1932, Ferrara hosted the Second
Conference of Syndicalist and Corporativist Studies. Balbo intervened briefly twice. First, he claimed that fascism was not just
the White Guard of big landowners and industrialists. Fascism
had built as well as destroyed. He spoke of the "new institutions
for the protection of workers' rights"—presumably he meant the
fascist unions and corporations. What these new institutions had
done or should do he did not specify.[8] In his second comment, he
ridiculed one of the more fanciful applications of corporative theory, *military corporativism*. The supporters of this scheme argued
that military units would benefit if they were made up of indi-

viduals who practiced the same trades or professions and thus could be expected to share many of the same values and experiences. The "military corporativists" also wanted the soldier's military occupation to utilize his peacetime skills. Balbo pointed out that a committee for mobilization whose task was to match civilian skills and military assignments already existed. Then with characteristic sarcasm that brought laughter from the audience, he argued that if military corporativism was to be taken literally, "if individuals are to be recruited as soldiers, that is, to make war, according to their peacetime skills, who will be a soldier?"[9] Another radical proposal, the *proprietary corporativism* of the philosopher Ugo Spirito, favored corporations that actually owned and operated businesses. Balbo could see no difference between this and "bolshevism" and declared that as a Mazzinian he believed in private property.[10]

In a last summing up, in February of 1937, Balbo returned to the same objections to corporativism that the *Padano* had raised in 1925. In a private conversation with a group of friends, Balbo declared that the entire syndicalist and corporativist order as it then existed was "nothing more than the imposition of bureaucrats to whom the workers pay no attention and whom they often tolerate with great discomfort."[11]

Personally, then, Balbo was skeptical about the corporativist experiment as it developed. He protested against the creaky bureaucracy staffed by party hacks, and he had no use for radical theories like those of Spirito. Nevertheless, Balbo the nonconformist, the protector and patron of dissident artists and intellectuals, supported those who took corporativist theory seriously. In addition to hosting the conference in 1932, he opened the columns of the *Padano* to left-wing social theorists such as Massimo Fovel and Giulio Colamarino, and Quilici wrote in the *Padano* that one of the paper's major projects was to illustrate and discuss the problems of corporativism. The University of Ferrara sponsored the first chair of corporative law, and Balbo asked Bottai to see that an entire faculty be recruited.[12]

The Lateran Pacts of 1929, another widely heralded fascist achievement, failed to elicit Balbo's enthusiasm. Under the agreements, the Vatican and the Italian state at last ended more than half a century of schism. For Mussolini, the pacts proved to be a triumph of publicity. Italians could now be both good citizens and good Catholics. Many radical fascists and traditional anti-clericals like Balbo, however, complained that this was a sell-out to an old and wily enemy. "Your Majesty knows that I don't take to priests very easily," he told the king in 1931.[13] Balbo also protested on a procedural point. "Balbo says rightly that in a matter of this sort, the Grand Council could not *not* be consulted," De Bono noted.[14] Balbo took no part in the public celebration of the accords. His name is absent from the list of dignitaries who attended a *Te Deum* at the cathedral in Ferrara on February 13, 1929. Nor did the *Padano* print any notice of congratulatory telegrams or statements of Balbo's on the occasion. The paper took the line that the pacts were a great triumph for Mussolini. Both sides gained, the paper commented. The state had not erred on the side of "excessive generosity," and the Holy See had not made exaggerated demands. Both friends and enemies of the regime had to admit that "the image of the Duce is greatly enlarged."[15]

Balbo was never a great booster of the party.[16] For the sake of his career he had joined it, somewhat reluctantly, in January of 1921. Once the March on Rome succeeded, he lost interest. He preferred a small, elite organization that would give direction to the masses and some substance to fascism. His friend Bottai, too, favored such a structure, a "vanguard of the proletariat." Bottai, the intellectual, however, favored an organization that was internally open to genuine debate; Balbo, the soldier, favored a far more oligarchical structure with a minimum of discussion, one that would defend the privileges of those who had made the revolution.

These differences were academic, for Mussolini made the decision. In the mid-1920s he chose between two diametrically opposed views of the party's role. Farinacci proposed a "dynamic" and "revolutionary" party that would absorb the state. Mussolini favored a more conservative path. The party became a mass institution, bureaucratized and centralized. Balbo predicted disaster. "Who can make heads or tails of this anymore?" he wrote to a friend in December, 1925. "After Farinacci's 'hither and thither' no anti-fascist can be found even if you paid him his weight in gold. And that's the danger, the great, the very great danger."[17] With Farinacci, Bottai, Scorza, and Giunta, Balbo worked feverishly to undermine Turati, the architect of the "mass" party. In the meantime, he made sure that the party did not "contaminate" the Aeronautica. He refused to recommend his officers for appointment to the party, "not only to avoid inflating the party, but also so that the party card would not become an anchor of salvation for the mediocre who would inevitably be bypassed in their careers."[18] To one of his most faithful collaborators, Pietro Tassotti, Balbo once commented about the party, "It's all a swindle. What do you care about being enrolled in the party? You're an air force officer."[19] When he was forced to recommend an officer for party membership or to accept a party leader into the Aeronautica, he assigned him to the P Squadron.[20] This special unit was assigned propaganda duties and had nothing to do with ordinary operations.

By 1933 Balbo had even distanced himself from the militia, the most "fascist" of the military organizations, the one he had helped found, the one to which he owed his rank as general. For a couple of years after the March on Rome, he looked to the militia—which he happened to head—as a means of infusing a new spirit of discipline, duty, and sacrifice into the nation as a whole.[21] However, once he left the organization, he lost interest in it—and expressed his contempt for the mediocrities who comprised it. In October, 1929, a militia consul wrote Balbo a silly letter full of grammatical and syntactical errors, complaining that an Aeronautica officer did not salute him regularly when they met at a restaurant. Balbo replied first by attacking the letter writer's prose, "unclear and certainly not worthy of your rank." Seven years after the March on Rome, Balbo continued, faith, valor, and zeal could not make up for lack of talent or even competence. Balbo asked Teruzzi to reprimand the letter writer. With his characteristic sarcasm, Balbo signed his note with best wishes "for an always stronger and more intelligent militia."[22]

These ideological differences only underscored the personal frictions that made Balbo's relationship with Mussolini so often insecure and frustrating. The Duce boasted of having built a "totalitarian state"—a smooth-running hierarchy with power flowing efficiently from the top. Yet of the three major dictators of the inter-war period, Stalin and Hitler came far closer to the totalitarian ideal than Mussolini ever did. The Duce actually created a "system of all-pervasive political irresponsibility under the guise of an authoritarian dictatorship."[23] Fascism in Italy resembled a modern unitary state less than it did a medieval system of private fiefdoms in which Mussolini acted as mediator. The Chicago gangster Al Capone summed it up neatly when he reportedly remarked, "Mussolini? He'll do all right as long as he takes care of the boys."

Caring for "the boys" was not easy. Each viewed Mussolini differently; each made different demands on him. Bottai, the intellectual, believed in him; Grandi, the diplomat, flattered and courted him; Starace, the party hack, venerated him; Farinacci rebelled against him. Balbo, for the most part, respected Mussolini's superior political talents and genuinely sought his advice and approval on various plans and projects; nevertheless, the relationship between the two men was a difficult one. Bottai, shortly after he heard of Balbo's death, described his friend's ambivalent attitude toward Mussolini and their often tormented relationship:

[Balbo] loved [Mussolini] with a love that was violent and angry, ferocious and contemptuous. He appeared to be loyal for the sake of *omertà*, rather than for friendship. He would have drawn up false papers in order to win him over, to feel that he was "his" or, rather, "one of his." But at bottom, he despised him, would not even recognize his intuition, his sensibility. He conceded him a certain cleverness, a second-rate cleverness, capable of resorting to every means, even the least noble and worthy. And yet he would fall for it, he more than anyone else: all he needed was a word, a gesture, a little pat from the Chief to go into raptures or march off to the most dangerous enterprise.[24]

Balbo was probably less devoted to Mussolini than Bottai made his friend out to be. Yet Balbo believed in loyalty and friendship and paid frequent homage to his chief. In his personal letters to Mussolini, Balbo invariably used the familiar "tu" form and to journalists liked to boast of his closeness to the dictator. At times, he employed the exalted "Mio Duce!" or "Mio Gran Capo!"— although it was not always easy to tell when Balbo was being sarcastic; often, Balbo wrote simply "Caro presidente," as if to remind the dictator of his constitutional limitations.

Balbo was never a sycophant. He sought a relationship with Mussolini on the basis of equality, including an authentic friendship. The two men had some similarities in their backgrounds and training. Balbo was from Ferrara, Mussolini from the neighboring Romagna. Both were steeped in the radical political traditions of these regions. Both came from petty bourgeois backgrounds, although Balbo's family was undoubtedly better off than Mussolini's. The Duce's father was a blacksmith, but his mother, like Balbo's, was a schoolteacher.

Despite these common traits in their backgrounds and a friendship and collaboration that had begun in 1914, the two men remained poles apart in their personalities. Balbo overflowed with self-confidence and security. He loved company, loved to be surrounded by friends, cronies, crowds of followers. Mussolini was just the opposite. Shy, suspicious, insecure, he trusted no one except perhaps his brother, Arnaldo. He was a timid man who forced himself to behave like a lion, Balbo's widow concluded from her few encounters with him. She recalled that even when he came to Libya on a state visit, Mussolini often preferred to eat alone. His tastes were frugal. Material things interested him very little. He had only one obsession: power. He came to fascism from socialism, and certainly did not share—perhaps even resented—Balbo's aspirations toward gentility. During his last years, he spoke of creating a "proletarian Italy" and of breaking with the monarchy. His last political office was as head of the nominally socialist "Salò republic." It is difficult to imagine Balbo making such a break.

The contrasts in their personalities and values served to maintain a certain distance between the two men. And Mussolini had another reason for keeping his distance. Of all the *gerarchi*, Balbo was one of the two (the other was Farinacci) whom the Duce genuinely feared.[25] "A good-looking *Alpino*, a great aviator, but the only one who would have been capable of killing me," Mussolini declared toward the end of his life.[26] Mussolini's attitude toward Balbo emerged clearly at the time of the latter's death. A number of witnesses remarked on the Duce's cold reaction to the news. He received it "without showing the slightest emotion" and made no comment except "to ask who should be appointed to succeed him," according to Badoglio.[27] Bottai was angry at Mussolini's behavior in the Grand Council: to dissipate the rumors and gossip, the Duce explained the circumstances of Balbo's death "and nothing else: not one word of mourning and regret."[28] In one of his last recorded judgments, in November of 1941, Mussolini murmured with reference to Balbo, "We weren't always in agreement, but he was a frank and capable man."[29]

Mussolini maintained his position through his remarkable gifts as an actor, orator, and journalist—and his ability to dominate his subordinates. He encouraged their internecine feuds; he ordered the police to survey them, tapped their telephones, and blackmailed them. Balbo knew something of these methods, for he used them to rule Ferrara. Nevertheless, he chafed at the treatment when it was applied to him. In a letter of January 31, 1928, Balbo complained bitterly about having his telephone tapped, even though Mussolini denied it. The letter is a curious one, for it illustrates the power of Mussolini over his subordinates. The tone is at the same time angry and protesting, defensive, fawning, and diplomatic. It opens with a flattering cliché: "As often happens with great leaders, you have been misinformed," Balbo wrote. He had never boasted, as the gossips intimated, that he had his men planted in the telephone monitoring service. Nevertheless, he insisted that his own line was being tapped. "That is the irrefutable fact." About the propriety of phone taps, Balbo had no qualms. He was afraid only that the eavesdropping was being carried out by "irresponsible" elements who could not always be controlled. "I would not care at all if you were watching me, not only on the telephone but also in my thoughts: what humiliates me as a *gerarca*—and not the least of them—of our revolution" is to be at the mercy of unknown employees who could easily abuse their positions. He concluded, "Your crude letter has upset and pained this old *squadrista*'s heart, which is devoted to you more with deeds than with empty words."[30]

Balbo raged against Mussolini's surveillance of him. From time to time, either in jest or in anger, Balbo threatened and insulted the anonymous eavesdropper. But Balbo also learned to turn the system to his advantage. He used his recorded conversations to send messages to Mussolini. For example, in a 1928 telephone discussion with De Bono, Balbo let Mussolini know how much he disapproved of Teruzzi's nomination as head of the militia and, more generally, of Mussolini's system of picking subordinates.[31]

In addition to phone taps, Mussolini kept track of his subordinates through police reports. For the most part, the Duce probably considered them as gossip rather than as authentic intelligence. However, they were an excellent means of baiting, humiliating, and exasperating his lieutenants. With Balbo, Mussolini made this a regular practice. For example, on September 28, 1928, Mussolini received a report that Balbo, speaking with his friends Bottai, Malaparte, and the *federale* of Florence, had made a long list of heretical observations: the party was not functioning well; the *federale* said the opposite to maintain their positions; the party secretary, Turati, gave long and boring speeches; pellagra had reappeared in some areas of the Veneto where the socialists had eradicated it. Mussolini sent Balbo the text of the police report with a malicious note: "Dear Balbo, the following declarations, which I would describe as singular, to say the least, are attributed to you." Balbo could only sputter in reply, "Is it possible, my dear President, that people invent fairy tales of this sort? I swear that my hands are itching. . . . If I find out who is responsible for this game, fists will fly."[32]

On another occasion, in July, 1930, while Balbo was on vacation and preparing for his first Atlantic crossing to Brazil, Mussolini sent him an anonymous letter—not even a police report—that raised issues about his holidays.[33] While he claimed to be camping modestly in a pine grove, the letter declared, Balbo was actually receiving his mistress in a lavishly furnished tent. Balbo replied with spirit. The lion skins and bear skins in the tent, he claimed, were there in order to receive Mussolini properly, in case he chose to visit. "A few hours of flying, of sea, of tent living can only be good for the Duce of fascism and of Italy."[34] But then Balbo dutifully answered the accusations. The vacation was costing him "less than a stay in a second-class hotel" and his guests at the camp were all respectable ministers and women with their husbands. He had chosen the site, he said, because it was close to Orbetello, where he was preparing his first transatlantic expedition, and he had put in at least fifty hours of flying time during the vacation period.

This often humiliating relationship with Mussolini, combined with Balbo's growing fame and his insatiable ambition, inevitably led to periods of tension between the two men, even to rumors that Balbo was planning to overthrow the Duce. The image of

Balbo as plotter was nothing new. From his first *Garibaldino* expedition to Albania when he was a child, to the intervention crisis and the March on Rome, he was always "plotting" against an established authority. The rumors continued after the March on Rome. First, there was his association with the intransigents around *Il Selvaggio* and his possible implication in the "revolt of the consuls" at the end of 1924. An anti-monarchist coup of December, 1926, proved to be totally fabricated—most likely by Mussolini to impress the king, as Federzoni's unpublished diary shows.[35] But the king himself did not believe the story and two or three weeks after the episode showed his faith in Balbo by going flying with him. Nevertheless, Rome talked of "nothing else for twenty days" and the story circulated widely in the foreign press. Rumors of Balbo's plots continued throughout his life.

The majority of these rumors are without substance. Even those that have the most plausibility are far from definitive, as is the case with Balbo's alleged plots against Mussolini in 1931–1932. Certainly Balbo did not lack motive. He was an ambitious man, and the more he succeeded the more he aspired to new honors. "Balbo even wanted to be made air marshal! These youngsters have little sense of proportion," De Bono grumbled in his diary. "Balbo is still exalted. Today he was telling me that in Italy he is considered a victim. But I ask myself, what does this boy want? Now he says it would be fortunate if Mussolini died," De Bono noted three months later.[36]

The moment seemed propitious for Balbo. During 1931 and 1932 Mussolini was often ill, and the question inevitably arose of a successor. Balbo's star, thanks to his fame as an aviator, appeared to be on the rise. Just what Balbo had in mind is not clear, but between March of 1931 and the beginning of 1932, he may have planned to overthrow Mussolini and replace him, using De Bono as a front.[37] Apparently he made specific proposals to Grandi and to De Bono. Grandi wrote to Mussolini on July 31, 1932, "Balbo is a wretched coward. I know what I'm telling you. At the right moment I'll tell you more. There's time for everything," and Mussolini noted in 1943 that Grandi had violently "slandered Balbo, also on a personal level." There are other bits of confirmation that Balbo's intentions were more overt during this period—or at least that rumors were flying. In Gianni Caproni's unpublished diary he reported rumors that Balbo had made clear his intention of replacing Mussolini. Police reports commented that among the anti-fascists in Paris, "Balbo is becoming popular." Another police report noted that Ludovico Toeplitz, governor of the Bank of Italy, claimed that Balbo told him, "We'll have to see who is more uninhibited, he or I. I know he wants to get rid of me, but I'm not the type who lets himself be eliminated." According to a police informer in an August, 1931, report, Balbo felt assured of the succession, for he had already drawn up a plan for his followers to suppress twenty of his rivals in one night.[38] Finally, the writer Curzio Malaparte, in a letter to Nello Quilici, claimed that "London and Paris are full of rumors of his [Balbo's] plots" and admonished, "Enough, dear Quilici, of these Balbian plots of his disorderly clamoring in the streets."

This evidence is far from conclusive. Balbo tended to strut about and talk too much, knowing full well that he could do so with a certain impunity. Mussolini preferred to avoid confrontations. Nor, for the most part, are the witnesses to the 1931–1932 "plot" unimpeachable. Grandi and Malaparte, for example, had motives for maligning Balbo or flattering Mussolini, and police reports were notoriously unreliable. Yet better evidence probably is not available. Balbo was not the type to leave it around. The rumors, however, illustrate the strained relations between the two men and help explain why, so soon after Balbo's return from his triumphant flight to Chicago, his career suddenly went into eclipse. First, Mussolini turned down Balbo's pet project for military reform; then, at the beginning of November, Mussolini requested his resignation from the Aeronautica and appointed him governor general of Libya.

"Sooner or later it was bound to happen," Balbo's wife commented, when he told her the news of his resignation. There was nothing surprising in Mussolini's decision to transfer Balbo to a new position. One of the dictator's methods of retaining his authority was to shift his subordinates about so that no one, through his office, could develop a genuine power base. The real question was why Balbo remained with the Aeronautica until November of 1933. Mussolini had many earlier opportunities to dismiss him.[39] The most obvious time came with a major reshuffling in July, 1932, when Mussolini took over the foreign ministry and the ministry for corporations and thus displaced Bottai and Grandi. Mussolini's motives for keeping Balbo on for another fifteen months are a matter of speculation. At the time, Balbo was preparing his second Atlantic crossing, and perhaps Mussolini wanted to see the project completed. The Duce may also have been satisfied with Balbo's performance as minister, while he was not pleased with the work of Bottai and Grandi. Finally, Mussolini may have been up to another of his old tricks: promoting feuds among the *gerarchi*. Keeping Balbo on was likely to pit him against Grandi. A disgruntled Balbo in 1932, however, might have joined with Grandi and Bottai. Such an alliance of brains, diplomacy, and action was too big a risk. The Duce had not forgotten their alliance against him in 1921.

An opportunity to promote division came in July, 1932, at the Geneva disarmament conference. Grandi, the chief Italian representative, had been working hard toward an agreement.[40] Early in February, he proposed a radical plan. All major weapons— heavy artillery, tanks, capital ships, aircraft carriers, submarines, bombers—were to be abolished. The nations involved were to find parity at the lowest common denominator. Mussolini disapproved of this "pacifism" and of having "gone to bed" with England and France. On July 20, he abruptly assumed the portfolio of foreign minister and Grandi was packed off as ambassador to London. Balbo, present at Geneva as air force minister, replaced him. Balbo's mission was twofold: first, to interrupt the negotiations: second, to prove his loyalty to Mussolini by attacking Grandi. Balbo carried out both tasks admirably.

Balbo had been suspicious of the League of Nations since his days as a student in Florence when he attacked the organization in his *tesina orale*. Nor, as he made clear in various newspaper interviews and statements, did he believe in disarmament. No matter what happened at Geneva, no one should lay a finger on his beloved air force and "he meant it," commented the Marquess of Londonderry.[41] Balbo shared Mussolini's view that the conference would benefit the French and the English but harm the Italians and the Germans. The goal of the great powers was to "disarm the others while they retained their own military predominance," he told a Polish journalist afterwards.[42] The best he could wish for the conference was that the League of Nations palace would slide into Lake Geneva, he remarked.[43]

In addition, Balbo showed his loyalty to Mussolini by savaging Grandi and his work. The vehicle was an article on July 31 in Mussolini's *Popolo d'Italia,* printed simultaneously in the *Corriere della Sera.*[44] In the article Balbo attacked the "Geneva machine" whose every decision bore the "trademark of the French, English, American group." There was nothing surprising in this. What raised eyebrows was the barely disguised attack on Grandi. He was accused of succumbing to "the compliments, the falsity which is de rigueur in the so-called rules of diplomatic courtesy." In a section that Mussolini deleted, the article charged that to be applauded at Geneva as a political genius and a far-seeing statesman "it was enough, without too much resistance, to fall in behind the wagon of the victors." Many thought that Mussolini himself might have written the article. Yet the piece was so vituperative that it suggested Balbo's hand. Grandi interpreted the vindictive tone as Balbo's revenge for his failure to support him in the alleged plot earlier in the year, and the article soured their relationship until the eve of World War II.

Meanwhile, Balbo had been working on a plan that, if implemented, would have crowned his military career. Between 1931 and 1933 he sought to become military head of the armed forces, either defense minister or at least minister of war and air.[45] He also had plans for modernizing and reforming the armed forces.[46] In his project for reform he had the support of a number of high-ranking officers who were dissatisfied with the current system and with Badoglio's leadership. Badoglio, they argued, was both militarily and politically too conservative to remain at the head of a revitalized "fascist" military machine. Italy needed to devise new strategies and new policies for her armed services. With her limited resources, she should not copy the formulas of the other great powers. As a Mediterranean power, she had to be concerned about controlling the seas and defending her coastline. However, instead of investing heavily in capital ships, she would do better to build up her air force, since aircraft were expected to dominate ships.

Balbo was the leading candidate of the "modernists" who

wanted to replace Badoglio. Balbo's supporters pointed out that he was an air marshal, which demonstrated his military competence; he had led two transatlantic cruises, which demonstrated his abilities as an organizer; finally, he was "a fascist while Badoglio is not."[47] On July 21, 1933, while Balbo was being feted in New York during the second Atlantic expedition, Mussolini abruptly dismissed the minister of war, Pietro Gazzera, who was notoriously devoted to Badoglio. The Duce assumed the portfolio himself. As undersecretary he appointed General Federico Baistrocchi, who had a reputation for dynamism. Baistrocchi, unlike the vast majority of the Italian officer corps, was also an avowed fascist. Balbo and his supporters interpreted the change as a good omen.

In this context, a few days after his return from Chicago, Balbo discussed his ideas for military reform with Mussolini at Piazza Venezia. Balbo proposed to strengthen the navy and the air force greatly, at the expense of the army. With the defeat of Austria in World War I, Balbo reasoned that Italy could now safely retreat behind the "fortress" of the Alps and concentrate on her position as a Mediterranean power. To do so, he favored reorganizing the armed forces into a series of highly flexible and mobile forces. The army was to be reduced in size to twenty divisions, of which five would be Alpine, five armored, and ten motorized. Balbo viewed the new army as an ensemble of "expeditionary forces" ready to embark at a moment's notice, primarily by rail or by sea, for Italy's four shores. These units would be well equipped, armed with the latest weapons, and trained in amphibious warfare. The Aeronautica's budget would be quadrupled (in part to subsidize the aircraft industry and to prepare underground shelters for it). The navy's budget would be increased by a third and would include three divisions of marines maintained on a war footing.

Technically the plan was innovative and sound, claim Balbo's supporters; had it been implemented, they argue, Italy might have been spared some of the disasters of World War II. Yet, from a financial and political viewpoint, the plan was nonsense.[48] Under Mussolini the defense budget had not risen above 6 billion lire a year. Balbo's plan required, for a decade, an immediate annual increase to 10 billion lire of regular appropriations and 6 billion of extraordinary appropriations. This would have absorbed as much as two-thirds of the state's total budget. Nor did the plan make political sense. Such a program of rearmament would have sent shock waves through Europe, for it would have been interpreted as a major challenge to the Anglo-French dominance of European affairs.

Balbo's scheme also implied a major rearrangement of the regime's internal affairs. The plan would have given Balbo, as chief of staff, far more authority over the armed forces than Badoglio had. For an avowed fascist to have so much political and military power would have alienated the king. The army and navy naturally viewed this new program, from a man who had preached the supremacy of air power, with a jaundiced eye. The other service chiefs also balked at giving the highest position in the armed services to someone who was not a professional soldier. Mussolini could perhaps have imposed Balbo on the other services, but it was certainly not in his interests to do so. First, he would have alienated much of the support on which his regime rested. Second, he would have clearly designated Balbo as the second man in the hierarchy and successor—an issue that Mussolini always avoided. Finally, Mussolini was planning the Ethiopian war. That project was not likely to succeed if at the same time he was lauching a major military reform, especially one that would have reduced the size of his army. Little wonder, then, that Mussolini rejected the proposal and Balbo's candidacy—although Balbo suspected that the king had blackballed him.[49] On October 16, 1933, the Duce drafted a letter in which he asked Balbo to resign his position as air minister and informed him that he would be appointed governor general of Libya.

Balbo's new assignment could not have been much of a surprise to him. For some months Rome had been buzzing about it and Balbo had been busy issuing denials, for he feared such a "polite retirement."[50] When Mussolini decided on a "changing of the guard," as he called it, ministers often learned of their "resignations" from the radio or the newspapers. With Balbo, however, mindful of his rank and of his popularity, Mussolini chose to be more tactful. He waited patiently while his old friend and comrade recovered from a bout of malaria—one of the few times Balbo ever fell ill; then, on November 4, the Duce met with him in Rome. In a letter which Balbo received the following

day, Mussolini emphasized that the new position was appropriate to Balbo's rank and reputation; and, perhaps aware that
Balbo had written in his *Diario* sincerely that "Mussolini's praise
is my reward," the Duce added that he wanted to "express my
satisfaction and my praise" for Balbo's contribution to building
the Aeronautica.[51]

Publicly, Balbo replied with a great show of discipline, obedience, and devotion: "My great chief! Always at your orders! . . . I
thank you for the kind words [and] put at your disposal my position as minister of the air force. With complete devotion, your
most affectionate . . . ." Privately, as Mussolini learned from the
transcripts of Balbo's phone conversations with his wife and his
friends, he alternated between blustering and threatening, resignation and heartbreak.

In a conversation, perhaps with his wife, he said, "As things
stand, I don't think there's much to be done. . . . Anyway, we'll
talk about it again! That rascal [Mussolini] wanted to sweeten the
pill . . . but I'm quite capable of busting him in the snout."[52]
With De Bono, in a conversation on November 25, he was explicit about Mussolini's motives in appointing him to Libya:

"He did it specifically to get me out from under foot."
"Are you sure?"
"I know him well. I became aware of it from the day of my return.
When he saw the grandeur and, most of all, the spontaneity of the
tributes to us, he began to glower. It was the same thing with the
manifestations of enthusiasm in the United States. People who are very
close to him told me. He's afraid of my popularity—which I don't care
about—without thinking that the honors are not to my political person
but to the aviator."

And then Balbo blustered: "If he thinks he can do with me as he
does with the others, he's miscalculated."

To his wife and to close friends and collaborators he revealed
his heartbreak. He spoke of "leaving this house of mine, this
creation of mine, with death in my heart," of giving up "a person
I've always loved" and of "leaving my heart behind." Nevertheless, "That's life," he told his wife. He was not so sanguine about
his new post in Libya: "It really bothers me."[53] "Certainly Balbo

doesn't believe he'll have to stay there five years," as his predecessor, Badoglio, had done, De Bono noted in his diary.[54] His friends urged him to look on the bright side. Libya would season him for greater responsibilities. So the king told him when Balbo paid a farewell visit. In miniature the colony was a reflection of the state, the king pointed out; Balbo would learn many things and prepare himself for the future.[55] Just what that future might be fed the rumor mills for the next seven years.

When the news was made public on November 6, it came as a shock to both Italians and foreign observers. Many echoed the anguished cries of Douhet's widow when she wrote, "But, Excellency, what will Italian aviation do without its great leader?"[56] From Germany, Erhard Milch, the architect of the renascent Luftwaffe, "profoundly deplored" that Balbo was no longer head of Italian aviation, but hoped to see the day when Balbo would return in triumph as head of all three defense ministries.[57]

In the foreign press there was surprise at what the Reuters news agency called Balbo's "dethronement," that Mussolini would dare topple him from his "pedestal" as one of Italy's "powerful and vivid personalities."[58] Balbo, however, should not be counted out, a French paper remarked. He was quite capable of "astonishing the world" as governor of Libya in much the same way he had done as air minister.

Despite Balbo's anguish, the politician and the soldier in him quickly surfaced. Knowing that he had no alternative and that Mussolini was watching him carefully, he accepted the change as a soldier would follow orders.[59] He wanted no repetition of what he called the "misfortunes of 1924," no sudden depression in his career as there had been over the Don Minzoni affair. He may also have taken the fate of his friend Leandro Arpinati to heart: forced to resign from the interior ministry in May, 1933, banished to Bologna, harassed by the police, expelled from the party in July of 1934, Arpinati provided a grim paradigm of what a fall from grace could entail. Hence, Balbo stressed that he was leaving "quietly and cheerfully. I'm not one of those who slam the door, so I'm perfectly happy, even if I feel pain in my heart." He instructed Renzo Chierici, the local federal secretary, carefully on how he was to deal with the news in Ferrara:

Be sure that everyone understands: "Italo is happy, he had to go away, this was the best moment, the Chief said some very nice words to him, the Chief himself is taking over the position of minister and for him that's a source of pride. On the other hand, there's a good position out there, at least a big colony, etc." You understand?

Careful as he was not to burn his bridges, to show himself as the Duce's devoted and obedient follower, Balbo enjoyed a measure of revenge. Before he left for Libya, he was formally awarded his air marshal's baton. In the past, a knighthood in the prestigious Order of the Annunziata had eluded him as had the title of count, which had been the rumored reward for his flight to Brazil.[60] Mussolini had wanted to promote him only to general in the Aeronautica. Balbo insisted "proudly" on the marshal's rank. The nomination came about by special decree and violated constitutional procedures, but Balbo prevailed.[61] In Ferrara on December 20, the thirteenth anniversary of the Castello Estense incident, Balbo formally received his air marshal's baton.

In a grand ceremony at the Teatro Verdi, Ferrara honored her greatest contemporary hero. "When one says Ferrara, one says Balbo, and vice versa. There's no country in the world now where the two names are not united," commented the *Padano*. When Balbo made his entrance at 11:20, "delirium" swept through the audience of 3,000 packed in so tightly that "not one more person could fit in." After all, they were not applauding any ordinary hero; this was "Italo Balbo, the Ferrarese with the immortal name . . . that would shine in the imaginations of new generations of Italians."[62]

An old peasant woman, mother of one of the "martyrs" of December 20, made the presentation. The inscription on the baton read: "To Italo Balbo—first Air Marshal—Ferrara—Proud Mother." "Visibly moved," Balbo accepted the baton, then hugged the old woman. The crowd surged to its feet, applauding wildly, while Balbo stood at attention.

Balbo's acceptance speech followed. It was typical of his often sarcastic spirit, a subtle oration full of innuendos and veiled barbs in which he expressed his pride and gratitude for the honor and also the joys and frustrations of his checkered relationship with Mussolini.[63] He began by acknowledging all the dignitaries who were present and the institutions they represented. But as he paid tribute, he evoked his own past deeds. He was surrounded, he said, by the pennants of the first fascist battles fought "on our territory" and by the pennants and the men of the latest fascist battles "fought in the skies of the world" (a reference to the *atlantici*). At his side he had the worthy representatives of the government "in which for eight years I participated"; of the party, "of which I am a faithful member"; of the militia, "that I commanded at the moment of its constitution and during the first two years of its history"; of the army, under whose banners "I battled not so unworthily in war"; of the navy, "which on the sea has valiantly collaborated in my undertakings"; and of the air force, "of whom I feel I am the eldest son." His only merit, Balbo said, was having known how to command one of the state's armed forces by "reconciling the military tradition with my indefatigable fascist spirit."

Then the audience's "fervor reached its highest peak" and the cheeks of thousands of spectators paled and their eyes filled with tears, the *Padano* reported breathlessly. Once again, Balbo snapped to attention. At such a "proud, unforgettable moment," he declared, he felt it was his duty to address "the Chief" symbolically: "DUCE! I thank you for having given me such great missions. I thank you for having believed in my command. I thank you for having allowed me to demonstrate to the world your and our Italy, your and our revolution." It was a performance worthy of a great operatic tenor, recalled the writer Giorgio Bassani, who witnessed the scene as a teenager, and it brought down the house.

The ceremony gave Balbo his moment of glory—and a chance to vent his frustration with Mussolini. Behind the scenes, however, the dictator was taking precautions against his restless lieutenant. If Balbo did not behave himself, the Duce threatened to destroy his reputation as builder of the Aeronautica.[64] In a letter of November 12, a week after he asked Balbo for his resignation, Mussolini wrote him a brief note about the number of aircraft on the Aeronautica's books. In his farewell visit of November 7, Mussolini noted, Balbo had declared that the Aeronautica's strength totaled 3,125 aircraft. This was the official number in the account books that Balbo and General Giuseppe Valle, his undersecretary, had signed. "I proceeded with the necessary discriminations and it follows that the number is reduced to 911 aircraft, combat ready on that date. I hasten to add that I consider the situation satisfactory."

The letter was clearly a form of blackmail and perhaps an answer to Balbo's telephonic outbursts about "breaking his snout." Balbo's reply was dignified, but also subdued, that of a man who had no intention of stepping out of line. Given the nature of the matter, he "could not fail to answer," he began. He insisted that the aircraft, including those that were in production, totaled 3,125. He had always counted those in production because they would appear regardless of his successor. He broke them down into their categories: 703 fighters, 578 bombers, 484 reconnaissance, 59 on ships, 344 trainers, 957 for tourism and training. "May I add with Christ: *est, est, non non.*" As to the number of combat-ready aircraft, he pointed out that the criteria were many and he did not know which ones Mussolini used. In Balbo's opinion, the 1,824 warplanes he had singled out were combat ready.

To add insult to injury, Mussolini gave orders to purge the Aeronautica of Balbian influences. "Balbisti" in the Aeronautica were "suspected and persecuted"; on one of Balbo's first visits to Italy after assuming his position in Tripoli, not a single representative of the air ministry was at the train station in Rome to greet him.[65] Mussolini inquired suspiciously about the "enthusiastic demonstration" with which the aviators at the base at Augusta had welcomed Balbo's visit.[66] At the ministry itself, only with great difficulty did Balbo, as air marshal, maintain an office with a small staff, including his personal secretary, Colonel Agostino Pischedda. The first day that Pischedda reported for duty he was not allowed to enter the building. As a sign of peace, when he arrived in Libya Balbo sent Mussolini a telegram: "I begin my new work with the cry, 'viva il Duce!' " Mussolini's comment, according to his secretary, was "It's too late." Four days after his arrival in Libya, Balbo posted two letters to De Bono.[67] In one letter Balbo listed the humiliations in the air ministry office and insinuated that the OVRA (the secret police) was spying on him. "The Chief, by making me a marshal, should not think that he's given me a cheap decoration. He has given me a very high honor to defend," Balbo wrote. He would defend it like a soldier, with dignity and honor. The letter continued, alternating threats with melodramatic suggestions: "Tell Mussolini, the one of '22, that if he wants proof of my loyalty, I am ready to give it absolutely, perhaps as the samurai do, killing myself tomorrow while I am flying. I disdain life and I do not fear death. But my rank must be respected, because my dignity is everything." If he did not get satisfaction, Balbo threatened, he would retire to private life. The second letter was a cover that asked De Bono to show the first to Mussolini and suggested how, administratively, Mussolini might rectify the insults. "In the meantime, I am getting my suitcases ready. And to think that I was starting to like my work!" Balbo scribbled.[68]

Mussolini might have welcomed a samurai-style proof of Balbo's loyalty—but not a clamorous resignation five days after he arrived in Libya. Nor could Mussolini have relished the prospect of Balbo retiring to private life, where it would have been far more difficult to keep an eye on him. The harassments ceased.

Exiles usually depart their homeland without honor and with no prospect of it at their destination. Balbo left for his "exile" covered with honors. The air marshal's baton was the most important one, but there were a host of other tributes, domestic and foreign. Nor did the gregarious "exile" embark on his journey alone and unattended. Crowds of friends and well-wishers saw him off at the station in Ferrara; in Rome, all the military undersecretaries, various political officials, friends and admirers greeted him; in Naples, Balbo paid homage to the royal family by visiting the palace. When he and his party finally sailed for Tripoli, they did so aboard a destroyer, with another destroyer as escort. Overhead, the Aeronautica paid a last tribute. His own aircraft, I-BALB, with *atlantico* Ranieri Cupini at the controls, dipped in salute and sent a radio message of best wishes.

Shortly before noon on January 15, Balbo's ship docked in Tripoli. In bright sunshine, he and his family paraded triumphantly through the streets. The following day, he issued his first proclamation as governor. After paying tribute to his predecessors, Volpi, De Bono, and Badoglio, he vowed to follow in their paths, which had brought "civilization and well-being" to the colony. His government, he declared, would be one of "Roman justice."[69] But traces of disappointment and bitterness at his "exile" surfaced as quips. Badoglio greeted him with "Dear Balbo, you have no idea how sorry I am to leave this colony." To which Balbo replied, "Dear Badoglio, your sorrow at leaving is nothing compared to mine at arriving."[70] "Balbo left, not resigned," De Bono noted in his diary. "However, I'm sure he'll find himself very quickly."[71]

Part Three

The Colonizer (1934–1940)

Chapter Thirteen

Governor General of Libya: Builder and Colonizer

Balbo's new fiefdom was a huge, impoverished, virtually empty territory, nothing like today's oil-rich nation.[1] The colony was slightly larger than the present state, which encompasses 1.8 million square kilometers and ranks as Africa's fourth largest nation. More than 90 percent of the land is desert; the majority of the population huddles along the Mediterranean coast on less than 3 percent of the country's total area. At Balbo's direction, an Italian geologist made tentative efforts to prospect for oil along the coast and traces were found.[2] However, the Italians had neither the capital nor the technology to explore deep in the Sirte Desert, where the first major strike was made in 1959.

Italy wrested "the big sandbox"—as the anti-colonialists called it—from the Ottoman empire in 1911. Like all of Libya's previous conquerors, from the ancient Greeks to the Ottomans, Italians devoted all their energies to transforming the region's only known resource at the time, the meager agriculture along the Mediterranean littoral. That task was a formidable one, for Libya's climate was brutal, her water resources almost nonexistent, and her soil mostly barren. At the time of the conquest, however, most Italians were only dimly aware of these realities, for Libya in 1911 was as unknown as it was vast. Patriotic rhetoric and poetry filled the void.[3] Giovanni Pascoli, the reigning *vate*, predicted that Italian colonists would transform the barren shores into a paradise; Libya would become a major outlet for emigrants who otherwise would be lost to the New World. As for the local population, Italians were assured that "Arab hostility is nothing but a Turkish fable."

Such visions themselves, of course, proved to be fables. When Balbo became governor, the Italians had little to show for their two decades of effort. Land colonization programs advanced at a snail's pace. The Italian population in 1934 totaled slightly under 50,000, concentrated in Tripolitania and most heavily in the city of Tripoli. Moreover, the colony bore the scars of a long pacification campaign. Tripolitania, which had a strong tradition of city-dwellers and fixed agriculture, was relatively accepting of the Italian invasion of the countryside, and the area was peaceful by 1924. The fierce nomadic tribes of Cyrenaica took another decade to subdue. These twenty years of pacification weakened an already precarious economy. Between 1925 and 1934, trade declined by a third. Financially the colony was nothing but a burden on the mother country.[4] In 1934, Libya's own revenues covered only a quarter of the costs of administering the colony. Italian taxpayers made up the balance.

Balbo's mission was to realize Pascoli's poetic vision: to transform a barren, backward colonial territory into an extension of Italy—a "fourth shore" to add to Italy's Tyrrhenian, Adriatic, and Sicilian shores.[5] To do this, he had to resolve certain concrete problems: provide for Libya's administrative and physical unity, attract colonists, resolve the colony's economic imbalance, and integrate the indigenous Libyans. In carrying out his tasks, Balbo enjoyed certain advantages over his predecessors. First was the internal peace. He could now tender the olive branch to the Libyans and concentrate his efforts on reconstruction and development. Second, the fascist regime gave him full political and financial support, for a strong Libya enhanced Italy's expansionist ambitions in the Mediterranean and in Africa. Libya's development also offered job opportunities for a mother country racked by depression and unemployment. Finally, there was Balbo's rank, his prestige, and his personal good name. He was the second *quadrumvir* (De Bono was the other) and the second marshal (after Badoglio) to govern the colony, and he enjoyed "enviable international prestige."[6]

If the man suited the job, the job also suited the man—eventually. At first "the conquering eagle of the transoceanic flights" felt "caged among the palm groves of Tripoli," according to an admirer.[7] "Have you come here to visit the exile? Because, as you know, I'm here in exile," he blurted to journalists at the opening of the Tripoli Trade Fair in 1934.[8] But then he plunged into his new tasks with his usual gusto. The office of colonial governor still had an aura of fascination and prestige. The parallel with Marshal Lyautey in Morocco caught Balbo's fancy. Cheerfully ignoring the vast differences in age, background, and attitude between himself and the aristocratic, Catholic, royalist Lyautey, Balbo declared enthusiastically, "No one admires him more than I do."[9] The comparison became a cliché with visiting journalists. They remarked on the ability of the two men to inspire fierce loyalty and obedience in their followers. Just as Lyautey loved to be *le patron* and to have his *équipe* around him, so Balbo needed his court of collaborators and close personal friends. Just as red-cloaked cavalry were posted to guard Lyautey's residence, tall, motionless Libyans guarded the old Turkish governor's palace in Tripoli. Those who took the parallel more seriously did not get very far. Giuseppe Daodiace, one of the "old Libya hands" on whom Balbo relied heavily during his first years as governor, prepared excerpts of French colonial manuals and Lyautey's writings for Balbo to read. Balbo may have glanced at them, but there is no evidence that they influenced him. He found his own way.

One of his first tasks as governor was to unite the colony administratively and physically. For centuries Libya's rulers had recognized the deep historical and geographical differences between Tripolitania and Cyrenaica and had governed the territories separately. The Italians, prior to Balbo's arrival, were no different. Under Badoglio each territory had its own budget, its own tax system, and its own administrative peculiarities. The administration was united only in the person of the governor, who ruled from Tripoli with the help of a vice governor located in Benghazi.

Proposals to unify the two territories had been debated from time to time before Balbo's governorship but had been rejected as premature. Graziani, as vice governor of Cyrenaica, turned down one such proposal in April, 1932.[10] Before any such measures were undertaken, he argued, the area needed to be far more fully developed. A coastal road must link Benghazi and Tripoli. Colonization in the Gebel should be well underway. The status and intentions of the Sanusi exiles who had fled to Egypt needed to be clarified.

Balbo argued successfully that conditions had changed.[11] Italy had achieved control over the entire colony, and a separate Cyrenaican government was now both superfluous and costly. Administrative unity did not need to wait for the development of communications and colonization; the two processes could be carried out simultaneously. Balbo's campaign for administrative reform, however, was not simply an issue of bureaucratic efficiency. He wanted to test his authority as governor against that of the minister of colonies in Rome—at this time his fellow *quadrumvir* Emilio De Bono.

De Bono was a veteran of such struggles. Five years earlier he had grappled with Badoglio, who had insisted on being directly responsible to Mussolini. Nevertheless, "Balbo sours my life" and is "always restless," De Bono lamented in his diary.[12] First, Balbo made a major issue of refusing General Guglielmo Nasi as his vice governor and insisting on his own candidate, Dino Alfieri. "What he doesn't want is to be subject to a minister," De Bono noted, and he vowed to stand firm. Balbo persisted, threatened to resign. A compromise was reached: Nasi was named "regent." "A question of name. That boy is hysterical," De Bono grumbled.

Balbo, however, would not be pacified. He tried a grand symbolic gesture. To prove the colony's unity he proposed to review the troops in Tripoli and Benghazi on the same day. For the occasion, he chose Constitution Day, the first Sunday in June. At 8 A.M. he inspected those in the Tripolitanian capital. After a three-hour flight, he presided over the same ceremony in Benghazi. Throughout the summer of 1934, he continued his agitation. Even Mussolini, according to De Bono, asked, "Why does Balbo talk so much?"[13] By the fall of 1934, Balbo pressed for the creation of four commissariats and the abolition of the vice governorship of Cyrenaica. Mussolini, claimed De Bono, told him that he would postpone the question. Then, at a meeting, Balbo "overwhelmed him with a flood of words" and Mussolini "gave in."[14]

A royal decree of December 3, 1934 (n. 2012), formalized Balbo's victory. The legislation fused Tripolitania and Cyrenaica into one colony known as Libya, with a governor general at its head. Balbo, however, was not convinced that all of Libya was suitable to be included in Italy's "fourth shore." For him, the littoral and the hinterland were two separate worlds. The coastal strip belonged to the Mediterranean and could be linked intimately to Europe. South of the Tripolitanian Gebel and Cyrenaica's Gebel Akhdar, Africa began. The December, 1934, decree, therefore, provided that the coastal areas would be administered like metropolitan Italy. The implication was clear. The coastal region would lose its colonial status and be integrated into the metropolitan bureaucracy. The interior, for the foreseeable future, would remain a colonial territory. From the 29th parallel, marked by the oases of Giofra, Cufra, Fezzan, and Ghat to the extreme southern borders, military rule remained in force. To police this vast desert territory, in place of the usual camel corps (*meharisti*), Balbo devised a mixed unit of aircraft, camel corps, and motorized riflemen and machine gunners. To command these units he appointed young air force officers and then bragged enthusiastically that the experiment was "completely new" and also brought "great prestige" to his old love, the Aeronautica.[15]

As he battled for administrative unity for Libya, Balbo also struggled to unite the colony physically by improving its communications. When he first arrived, the chief link between Tripolitania and Cyrenaica was, as it had been for twenty years, a weekly boat. Neither roads nor telegraph lines linked the two regions. Communications with the mother country were equally tenuous. The "conqueror of spaces" and transoceanic flyer was expected to devote much of his energy to breaking the colony's internal and external isolation.[16] He did so. Within the first two years of his governorship, Ala Littoria instituted daily flights to Tripoli, and biweekly flights linked Libya with Egypt and East Africa; the telephone network, especially in Tripolitania, nearly tripled in size; and on April 1, 1935, a radio telephone tied Tripoli to Rome.[17]

These accomplishments did not have the grandeur and visibility of his best-known achievement: the construction of the Litoranea Libica, the 1,822-kilometer coastal highway that stretched from the Tunisian frontier to the Egyptian border. In his honor the road, which was completed in a little more than a year from 1936 to 1937, became known as the Balbia. On the Black Continent to date, "nothing so imposing, so . . . grand had been conceived and carried out in such time and circumstances" as the Litoranea, Balbo trumpeted.[18] There was an epic quality about the project. How to maintain thousands of men in a desert hundreds of kilometers from inhabited areas, with no local drinking water, under infernal temperatures? Balbo relished the challenge and the adventure as much as the administrative and engineering problems.

The need for such a highway had often been discussed before Balbo's governorship. Graziani made the road a precondition for the colony's administrative unity. Others pointed out the economic and cultural advantages that such a road would bring. With the Litoranea finished, North Africa would be open to automobile traffic from the Atlantic to the Nile, and the colony would benefit from increased trade and tourism. What gave the project a sudden urgency in 1934 was a military factor: the possibility of war in the Mediterranean and in Ethiopia.[19] Within a month after he arrived in Libya, Balbo met with Graziani and various military leaders and engineers to plan the road. From a military perspective, the Litoranea offered several advantages: the movement of men and supplies throughout the colony would be greatly facilitated; fixed military outposts could be eliminated in favor of motorized units; and garrisons could no longer be cut off as had happened during World War I. The savings in eliminating the fixed garrisons, Balbo argued, would pay the construction costs of the road.

In their enthusiasm, contemporary accounts sometimes imply that Balbo built an entirely new road, but only 799 of the total 1,822 kilometers were entirely new.[20] In Tripolitania a 320-kilometer section already existed between Zuara and Misurata; in Cyrenaica, a 600-kilometer stretch between Marsa Brega and Tobruk was also complete. Balbo's task was to link these two sections. By far the most difficult stretch was that of 571 kilometers across the Sirte Desert between Misurata and Marsa Brega. In addition to building the new stretches of road and improving the existing ones, the project included the construction of sixty-five houses for maintenance crews. A final major item, to underscore the nature of the achievement and to remind the traveller of the glories of fascism, was the construction of a huge commemorative arch in the middle of the Sirte, one kilometer from the bay at Ras Lanuf. In Tripolitania construction began on October 15, 1935; in Cyrenaica on January 15, 1936. The rate of construction averaged 200 meters a day. The entire project required 4.5 million work days, yet by the end of January, 1937, the project was completed.

The task had posed enormous engineering, logistical, and labor problems. The biggest difficulty was to keep the army of laborers adequately supplied with water, especially throughout the summer of 1936. August proved critical.[21] In some areas, the temperature reached 49 degrees Centigrade in the shade. A fleet of cistern trucks and cars bearing water in tins, barrels, and demijohns struggled to keep a regular flow of water to the nearly 13,000 men on the road gangs. But the trucks and cars bumping over old dirt tracks, *wadi* beds, and dunes broke down, blocking the other vehicles and creating traffic jams. Soon a line of rusting hulks, "the truck cemetery," marked the construction sites, especially in the Sirte. Balbo himself, in pith helmet, khaki tunic, boots, and dark glasses, a cigarette dangling from the corner of his mouth, appeared in the most difficult areas such as the segment from the En Nufilia Crossroads to the Misuratino border. Three thousand men, wearing nothing more than shorts and a shirt, "looking like white shadows in the white blinding blaze of the sun," worked there.[22] The nearest source of water was sixty kilometers away. At times the desperate men threw themselves at brackish water. Soon afterwards, violent spasms wracked their bodies and sometimes they urinated blood. Balbo, sweating, cursing, threatening, and encouraging, visited the site often. He ordered new wells to be dug, and he organized the water convoys so that an adequate supply of water flowed.

Just as critical as the supply of water was the supply of labor.[23] Despite talk that the Litoranea furnished jobs for Italy's unemployed, Italians provided only 330,000 work days of the total 4.5 million required to complete the entire project. The reason was simple: Libyans worked far more cheaply than Italians. Italian laborers, most of whom were recruited in Italy, had their trip paid back and forth from the mother country to the colony. In addition, their wages averaged two and a half to three times higher than those of the Libyans. The Libyans, however, found that they did have a certain amount of leverage on their employers. Contractors were willing to pay a premium in order to finish their projects on time. In addition, high-priority military construction projects along the Egyptian border competed for the existing labor pool. Wages soared. Such a situation destroyed "one of the most important factors of technical progress and a balanced economy": cheap indigenous labor.[24] Faced with potential cost overruns on the Litoranea and disruption of the entire colonial economy, Balbo, in a gubernatorial decree (DG, May 4, 1936, n. 8277), fixed Libyan wages at a level that varied between half and a third of Italian wages.

A second labor problem developed in the fall of 1936 when the rains began in Tripolitania. Libyans abandoned their jobs to return home and plant their crops. Once again the government intervened. A rationalized leave system was instituted; new and faster methods of recruitment and transportation were organized, and the labor supply once again became stabilized.

The completion of the road meant fresh glory for Balbo. To his great joy, Mussolini himself came to inaugurate it in 1937. There were also less public but equally satisfying rewards. He had proved his abilities as an administrator, for the project was completed entirely within the colonial budget. His costs, he boasted, averaged 100,000 lire per kilometer, significantly lower than the costs of the roads built by his predecessors between 1930 and 1934. His comment aroused a furious reply from De Bono and the affair had to be settled by a jury of honor.[25] The secret to his economies, Balbo claimed, lay in subdividing the project into a large number of segments (eventually totaling sixteen) and then inviting the maximum number of contractors to bid on them. The more contractors participated in the project, the quicker the execution and the less likelihood of price fixing among the bidders. As a tribute to his administrative and financial acumen, Balbo particularly treasured a letter from Tommaso Lazzari, a high official in the ministry of finance. Given the difficulties involved, Lazzari wrote, he had fully anticipated a huge cost overrun; instead he had witnessed a technical, financial, and administrative "miracle."[26]

Uniting the colony administratively and building the Litoranea were relatively easy problems to resolve. Far more difficult and crucial was the issue of colonization. On it depended the colony's political, economic, and social future. A vast influx of colonists was politically necessary, to counterbalance the Libyan population, which totaled about 700,000. The colonists were also an economic necessity: Libya had nothing to offer—no important raw materials or mineral resources, no industry, no trade—except her meager agriculture. Finally, the colonists were fundamental to building colonial society. Without them, there could be no "fourth shore."

When Balbo became governor, he inherited a bastard system. Private investors dominated the colonization.[27] A very few believed in the future of Libyan agriculture and were willing to invest in a concession. They developed their huge tracts with cheap Libyan labor and made no effort to attract Italian colonist families. The state intervened. Beginning in 1928, while De Bono was governor, the government offered an elaborate system of subsidies and bonuses. The goal was to encourage the concessioners both to develop their land and to do so with the help of Italian colonist families. The system did attract colonists, especially to Tripolitania. In 1929, some 455 families (1,778 individuals) had settled there. Four years later the number had more than tripled to 1,500 families (7,000 individuals). In Cyrenaica, because the Sanusi rebellion was still active, the colonization proceeded more slowly. At the end of 1931, the Italian agricultural population consisted of only 429 colonists.

The system of subsidies presented many problems. One was sheer cost. Another was the opportunity for the concessioners to speculate. Finally, the subsidies did not lead to the development of independent colonist families. The concessioner's interest was to accept the subsidy as a reward for importing colonist families—and then to exploit the families in the same way that Libyan labor was exploited.

In short, Balbo concluded, the colonization programs "were a financial burden on the state, unsuitable to the needs of the concessioners and sterile with regard to the regime's basic goals. . . . There was nothing for me to do except change course decisively," he explained in an address to the prestigious Accademia dei Georgofili in 1939.[28] Latifundia had to give way to a colonization that would base itself "primarily on social goals," a system that would direct the government's financial sacrifices to "the true workers of the land."

Thus, Balbo opted for increasing state direction at the expense of the private sector. His institutional tools were the parastatal organization devoted to land settlement in Cyrenaica, the Ente per la Colonizzazione della Cirenaica (ECC), and a social welfare organization, the Istituto Nazionale Fascista per la Previdenza Sociale (INFPS). These types of organizations, with their mission of resettling the unemployed, were familiar institutions in Europe and the United States of the Depression era. With the financial backing of the government, of social welfare organizations, and of some private capital, these companies chose colonists from depressed areas and relocated them to reclamation projects. The companies provided the colonists with all the necessities for reclaiming their new farms: tools, seeds, houses, livestock, credit, technical advice and direction. The colonist and his family contributed only their labor. Gradually, as the farm became productive, the colonist was expected to repay his debts. At the end of twenty or thirty years, he would be independent.

By the time Balbo took office, the ECC had completed two villages in Cyrenaica and settled 150 families. Balbo extended the authority of the ECC to include Tripolitania and in 1935 changed the institutional name to Ente per la Colonizzazione della Libia (ECL) to reflect its new mandate. He invited the INFPS to participate in the colonization. In addition, Balbo tightened the conditions for contributions to the concessioners, intensified the search for artesian wells, encouraged reforestation projects and planting of windbreaks along the coastal dunes, and founded agricultural experiment stations for the development of livestock and crops.

Despite these efforts, the agricultural census of 1937 showed very modest results, as Balbo himself admitted.[29] Only one-fifteenth of the land under concession was devoted to small farms. All the rest was still in the form of latifundia. Nor had there been much success in attracting colonists. Out of 1,299 colonist families, 760 were distributed over 116,000 hectares, for an average of one family per 152 hectares. This was not the density that Balbo had hoped for. The crops that were being planted created more problems. The major ones such as vineyards, almonds, and olives were labor intensive. Without enough colonist families, the crops could be worked only by hiring more salaried labor. But this was contrary to the social goals of the colonization.

Another problem was the curious behavior of the colonization companies. Balbo favored them at the expense of private investment. Yet the Ente Cirenaica, for example, had behaved suspiciously like a private concessioner, he noted in a report to the ministry of colonies on May 22, 1936.[30] The company directed its operations with unconcealed "entrepreneurial criteria"; these included squeezing the colonist families by underpaying them or paying them in kind; dividing the harvest unfairly; failing to furnish livestock and machinery as promised; and ignoring many "verbal promises" which were common practice in the company-colonist relationship. Balbo also knew that under the Ente system, the colonists might live only for their subsidies and lose interest in developing their farms. To a visitor who raised the question in 1938, Balbo replied evasively that the Ente system was like a "big cooperative" from which every type of speculation was excluded. The loans that the state gave to the colonists had to be returned. "In reality, even with the new colonization, the peasant acquires his land by the sweat of his brow," he declared.[31]

Balbo did not waver in his direction; he redoubled his efforts. In May, 1938, he announced that the ECL and the INFPS would undertake a long-term program of "intensive demographic colonization" on behalf of the state. Twenty thousand colonists were to be settled annually for five years in succession. This was the first step toward realizing a population of 500,000 Italians in Libya by mid-century, he declared.

In the meantime, Balbo received friends, old comrades, and casual visitors in grand style. "What magnificence! What splendor! . . . only princes are received this way, not we modest *Alpini* accustomed to simple ways," an old comrade and veteran of the *Alpini* wrote to Balbo after he had hosted the sixteenth reunion of the 10th *Alpini* in Tripoli on March 20–21, 1935.[32] In the midst of all the "luxury and the pomp" of the various receptions, Balbo presided over the scene. "Your spirit and your personality shone with a bright light" and with "fraternal and model spontaneity," concluded the writer. Balbo in "exile" was not Balbo in isolation. If he could not be at the center, then as often as possible the center must come to him. His restless and gregarious temperament demanded a constant stream of friends, visiting dignitaries, and admirers. In 1938, for example, Balbo hosted two major scholarly gatherings, the Volta Congress with four hundred delegates, and a conference on tropical and subtropical agriculture with one hundred visitors; the annual Tripoli trade fair and an international convention of hotel-keepers; two major sporting events, the fourth annual Saharan air rally and the Tripoli Gran Prix auto race; a mass immigration of 20,000 colonists; and a war college exercise. The list of personalities ranged from the king and the prince of Piedmont to marshals Badoglio and Graziani and assorted Nazi luminaries.

Balbo's interest in attracting distinguished guests and tourists was based on more than satisfying his personal vanity. Visitors were integral to his plan for ensuring that Libya reached a level of civilization worthy of a "fourth shore"; tourists made a contribution to the colony's modest economy. To increase the flow of visitors, he called upon his talents and tastes as a host, promoter, and patron of the arts.

Attracting tourists to Libya posed a major challenge. The colony's potential for tourism was very modest. Of all the regions of North Africa, Libya was the poorest and most backward—no competition for well-established centers like Egypt with Cairo and the Pyramids, or French North Africa with the *souk*s of Tunis and Algiers. The folklore, customs, and handicraft did not compare with Marrakech and Kairouan, sniffed a French visitor.[33] Moreover, the facilities were no better than the attractions. Tripoli and Benghazi offered only modest hotels. If a traveller ventured into the interior oases, he had to stay in military outposts. The Italian Touring Club Guide of 1929 explained that Libya still retained its "original, primitive, Oriental fascination."[34] Moreover, the tourist could thrill before the Roman ruins being unearthed and the new farming communities wresting life and civilization from the sand. Despite the colony's minimal attractions and lack of facilities, during the five years before Balbo's arrival the number of tourists had quadrupled, from 7,209 in 1929 to 28,304 in 1933.[35] Balbo set about accelerating this trend.

One of his first acts was to place the tourist industry under state control. In May, 1935, he created the Ente Turistico ed Alberghiero della Libia (ETAL) to organize, supervise, and promote all tourist activities. This included building and operating a chain of hotels throughout the colony. Two major new hotels were completed in Tripoli in 1934–1935, the Albergo Casino-Uaddan, the "Waldorf Astoria" of Tripoli, in the words of an American journalist, and the more modest Mehari.[36] With luxurious rooms, a movie theater that seated five hundred, a gambling casino, a Turkish bath (renamed a Roman bath by a scandalized fascist party official) the Uaddan was a self-contained resort. In all of North Africa there was nothing like it, according to Italian claims—and, in 1939, all for three dollars a day per person.

Comfort and luxury could also be found on a more modest scale seven hundred kilometers inland, Balbo liked to brag. In remote oases like Jefren, Nalut, and Ghadames, the ETAL operated a chain of inns. To what end? a French visitor pondered. Only a few intellectuals seeking the solitude of the desert or perhaps a handful of curious artists and scholars would trek to such oases—and they would have been content with far more modest accommodations.[37]

The development of archeological sites was another of Balbo's pet projects.[38] Libya contained some of the grandest ruins of the classical world, from the great cities of Leptis Magna and Sabratha in Tripolitania to the Greek settlements of Cyrene, Tolemaide, and Tocra in Cyrenaica. Almost from the moment of the Italian occupation in 1911, archeologists began to excavate these sites. Because of the colony's unsettled political conditions, however, the work had proceeded erratically. Under Balbo, there was no interruption.

The list of major archeological projects completed or initiated by the time of Balbo's death was impressive: at Leptis Magna, a complete excavation of the Basilica and of the theater; at Sabratha, restoration of the theater; in Tripoli, consolidation of the Arch of Marcus Aurelius and restoration of the Turkish fortress; at Cyrene, major restorations and the complete exploration of the Temple of Jove. An outstanding achievement, a French journalist noted acidly—particularly when the basic needs of the colony, for example, for hospitals and schools, were still unfulfilled.[39]

Balbo took a personal interest in the excavations. Visitors to his office in the old Turkish fortress—one of Tripoli's major restoration projects—found prize bits of sculpture, pottery, and mosaics from the excavations on display. He had his own ideas about restorations and shared them with the archeologists. In general, he opposed complete restorations. With the Roman theater at Sabratha, begun at the end of 1936, he limited the restoration to the amount of original material that could be recovered. He also directed that the sites were not merely to be looked at; when possible, they were to be used. At Sabratha he established an annual festival of classical drama. The opening performance came in 1937, in time for Mussolini's visit. Balbo chose Sophocles' *Oedipus the King*, with a musical accompaniment of the works of the Baroque composer Andrea Gabrieli; the following year, Euripides' *Iphigenia in Aulis* was produced.

Balbo also promoted sporting events. His prestige in the aviation world and his love of flying led him to initiate an annual series of air rallies beginning in 1935. Typical was the ten-day Third Sahara Rally in February, 1938, which attracted about one hundred aviators divided into twenty-five teams. The circuit displayed the vastness of Libya, for it included stops in the major interior oases (Ghadames, Brak, Cufra). The participants came to appreciate the "grandeur of the work accomplished by the Italians in such a brief period with such limited means." The visiting airmen also got to know Balbo himself, "the most unforgettable souvenir of our trip. . . . What a man! What a leader!"[40]

Balbo contributed more than a ceremonial presence. When things went wrong, he took the lead in righting them. In 1938, an Italian participant in the rally, Count Franco Mazzotti, and his comrades went down between Brak and Cufra. Balbo not only organized the search; on the third day, he found the lost aviators himself.[41] Two years earlier, in 1936, a Belgian aviator, Guy Hansez, was lost for four days seventy kilometers northwest of Ghat. Balbo organized the rescue effort and participated in it, searching for six to eight hours at a stretch in temperatures that sometimes reached 43 degrees Centigrade.

In auto racing, Balbo promoted the Tripoli Grand Prix, first held in 1925, into a major event.[42] From nine cars racing over a 213-kilometer circuit to thirty racers from five nations competing

over a 524-kilometer circuit—that was the story of the Grand Prix
at the end of its first decade, Balbo told Italian-Americans in a
1935 radio message. He was especially enthusiastic about the
vastly improved technical services and the new facilities for spectators. A magnificent new stand capable of accommodating
30,000—practically the entire European population of Tripoli—
had been built. The course now permitted speeds of more than
220 kilometers per hour, almost the equal of the most modern
tracks of the day. The purse of 1.2 million lire was billed as "the
richest auto race in the world." A lottery held in conjunction with
the race financed the improvements. One sign of the race's popularity came in 1934 when the influx of visitors led to a temporary
crisis in accommodations. With all the hotels filled, Balbo had to
improvise quickly: he directed Tripoli residents to offer rooms in
private homes when possible; he found additional space aboard a
visiting cruise ship; finally, he directed the military to erect a
temporary tent city and open it to homeless tourists.

Like any host who loves to entertain, Balbo took great pains to
make his home and capital city attractive. "Tripoli was a jewel
personally carved by Italo Balbo. . . . He had built nearly everything in it and built well," the English journalist G. L. Steer
wrote of his visit to Libya in 1938.[43] Others described it as the
"Cannes of North Africa," or as resembling a city in Florida or
southern California, or as "better than the French Riviera."[44]

Balbo could claim much of the credit for this metamorphosis.
Of the major cities of North Africa, Tripoli was the smallest and
the last to be transformed into a European city.[45] When the Italians first occupied Tripoli in 1911, it was a sleepy, dusty Turkish
fishing village, while Tunis and Algiers were great cities. The
Italians initiated urban improvements: paved streets, lighting,
water supply, harbor developments. An Italian-style city began to
emerge south and east of the old city, which was surrounded on
three sides by palm groves. The new city, however, was "a mediocre eyesore, a European city of thirty years ago," a city where
too often surveyors and military engineers were given license to
act as architects, claimed one of Balbo's aides.[46]

Almost from the moment of his arrival, Balbo attacked the
city's problems.[47] He established a set of aesthetic standards and
building codes. In February, 1934, he created a commission to

rule not only on the aesthetics of Tripoli, but on the countryside as a whole. The newspapers were directed to publicize the government's aesthetic and urban concerns. Public works administrators were ordered to employ architects in compiling construction projects. A building commission ruled on any new project, public or private, to be built in the interior cities or on military bases. Acceptable models of colonist houses were to be furnished to interested parties. Between 1934 and 1937, Balbo completed many public works projects in both the old city and the new. These included sewage and drainage systems, paved streets, and lighting. An aqueduct that piped water from a well near Porta Ain Zara increased the city's water supply. Recreational, sports, and convention facilities boomed. The autodrome at Mellaha, the fairgrounds for the annual trade fair, and a host of new parks were developed or improved. Public housing projects went up at Sciara Ben Asciur and Zaviet Dahmani.

Balbo's interest in these projects is evident from his correspondence. He favored a simple, functional style that blended with the surroundings and also made for rapid construction and low costs. He vetoed designs that appeared too monumental or too imposing. In a frank letter in June of 1935 to the prominent architect Armando Brasini, Balbo told him why his project for the headquarters of the Tripoli Savings Bank had been rejected. The plan called for far too much marble in the interior. It might appear "very strange and contradictory" for a customer to see the bank refuse him a loan for a thousand lire when he could see all about him the marble on which the institution had spent millions, Balbo explained.[48]

The burst of building activity led to many changes. Between 1933 and 1936 the number of automobiles increased from 1,475 vehicles to 2,373; taxis, from 290 to 400; trucks, from 800 to 1,300.[49] Another major change was the influx of Libyans to the cities.[50] Already in 1896 an Italian traveller had remarked that Tripoli was the "heart" of the region, and "bidonvilles" or shantytowns had begun to develop in the 1920s. By 1935, Balbo felt that the shantytowns had gotten out of hand. He ordered that a "bedouin camp" be constructed outside Bab Tagiura. The development consisted of five hundred stone huts, and the community facilities included shops, a café, a marketplace, a mosque, and medical facilities. Other projects were completed for the benefit of the Libyans: a quarantine hospital at Forte Gargaresc, a restoration of the mosque of Sidi Scensian in the city center, and a reconstruction of the Suk el Muscir into a center for handicrafts.

By 1938, Balbo's Tripoli had taken on the air of a modern European city, as "spick and span" and "clear and efficient" as any of the new cities or urban development projects that Mussolini had undertaken in Italy.[51] To many visitors, Tripoli gave the same impression: "The great straight streets, the tall white architecture, the awesome public buildings, headquarters for Fascist youth organizations or for the Aeronautica or the Tripoli Savings bank, each with the 'badge of state' branded on it in the form of Roman numerals signifying the year of construction."[52] The streets swarmed with troops and men in party uniforms. Tripoli was "button hole land": in the lapel of nearly every male in view was the red, white, and green fascist insignia of the bundles of lictors' rods and the axes. The functional brusqueness of the buildings gave an air of speed and efficiency. This was reinforced literally during auto racing season, when Alfa Romeos and Mercedeses, preparing for the Grand Prix races, careened about the streets. Even the formal gardens along the seashore were pruned, disciplined, organized in the shape of fasces.

Yet even the most sympathetic visitors felt uneasy. The atmosphere of speed, efficiency, discipline, the rigid, monumental sobriety of the buildings did not ring quite true.[53] Like most of the other colonial capitals, Balbo's Tripoli was like a movie set, an exotic background against which the Europeans could play out their self-appointed roles as heroes, conquerors, and civilizers. "The Arab seems to understand that this is not his town," remarked an English journalist. The old city, while it was protected as a tourist attraction, was lost "behind the great brown Castello that flew the Italian flag and Balbo's ensign," he added.[54]

In contrast to the casbah and *souk*s of Tunis, which swarmed with Arab life, in Tripoli the Arabs seemed to be lost and self-effacing. This was remarkable, considering that out of a total population in the city of 104,000 in 1937, nearly two-thirds were indigenous peoples, most of them Arab-Berbers.

In the spring of 1937, Mussolini paid a ten-day visit to Libya. The occasion was the inauguration of the newly completed Litora-

nea. The trip had three purposes.[55] First, with the conquest of
Ethiopia nominally complete, Mussolini wanted to declare to the
great powers his peaceful intentions. Italy was now a "satisfied
power," eager to develop its empire and devoid of any further
expansionist designs. Second, Mussolini wanted to make a gesture toward the Libyans. He proclaimed himself as the "protector
of Islam" and thanked the Libyans for their loyalty and support
during the Ethiopian campaign. Not only had the colony remained quiet, many Libyans had fought in the Italian ranks and
contributed to the victory. Finally, Mussolini intended to pay
tribute to Balbo. For three years he had worked in comparative
obscurity. His "exile," some thought, was backfiring on the Duce,
winning Balbo support for the development of an anti-Mussolini
fronde.

Balbo greeted Mussolini with pride and joy—although an English diplomat had the impression that Balbo was bored by all the
preparations.[56] He wanted his triumph for Mussolini to match the
one he had enjoyed under the Arch of Constantine on his return
from the flight to Chicago. As early as the summer of 1936, Balbo
collected linguists among his staff to act as interpreters for the
foreign visitors; he rounded up nomads from the interior so that
they would arrive at the coast in time to stand by the Litoranea
and cheer the Duce when he drove by; he launched a slum
clearance program in Tripoli.[57] The Libyans seemed to catch the
spirit of the occasion. Balbo told a delegation of civic notables
who came to ask him how Tripoli should be decorated for the
great occasion, "I do not want to know anything about your plans
for decorating Tripoli. I only want to be astounded."[58] The president of the Tripoli Savings Bank reported that an unprecedented
number of Libyans had been bringing in their valuables as security for loans. When bank officials inquired into the reasons for
this vastly increased traffic, the answer was, "Duce come, buy
new baracano"—a new robe.[59]

For a host in a backward and thinly populated land, Balbo
found an amazing number of events to occupy his guest. There
were inaugural ceremonies, military spectacles, theater performances, banquets, horseback rides, and inspection tours of everything from the newly excavated archeological sites to the colonist
villages. The Duce's first ceremonial chore after his arrival on

March 12 in Cyrenaica was to inaugurate the Litoranea. On March 15, as Mussolini motored along the road toward Tripoli, Balbo prepared one of his "pièces de résistance": the inauguration of the Arae Philenorum, the triumphal arch that marked the boundary between Cyrenaica and Tripolitania.[60] There, in the midst of the Sirte Desert, 320 dusty miles from Benghazi, stood a huge triumphal arch made of Travertine marble, brought piece by piece from quarries near Rome. The monument commemorated the classical story of the Filene who preferred to be buried alive rather than to betray their country. Balbo arranged for a Hollywood-style premiere. As dusk fell over the desert, searchlights lit up the great arch like an altar. Flaming tripods encircled the surrounding piazza. Aircraft rumbled overhead. Honor guards of *zaptie* on camels and a battalion of Libyan soldiers lined the road. Their drumming and piping heralded the arrival of the column of automobiles bearing the Duce and his entourage. To the applause of the Italian and Libyan work crews, the Duce descended from his automobile. "With his long and sure stride that seems to take possession of whatever land it touches," Mussolini surveyed the arch. "Be proud to have left this sign of fascist power in the desert," he pronounced.

The dinner in the middle of the desert proved to be a memorable affair. Waiters in white gloves served the seven-course spectacular to the nearly three hundred guests. The diners savored caviar, goose liver, broth, bass, capon, and ice cream, according to the elegant menu which featured a drawing of a mounted *spahi* on the cover. Most impressive of all to the guests were the trays of fresh raw vegetables: radishes, leeks, celery, artichokes, and fennel from the colonists' gardens. "It was like finding a bunch of roses at the North Pole," a stunned French journalist remarked to a beaming Balbo. "If an Italian has reached the North Pole, you'll find roses there," he assured her.

More spectacles followed—this time for the benefit of the Libyans. The following day, March 16, Mussolini made a grand entry into Tripoli.[61] Just outside the city walls, his motorcade stopped. Mussolini mounted a horse and entered the city leading two thousand Libyan horsemen. Two Libyans bearing huge papier-mâché fasces preceded him like lictors. He inaugurated the Tripoli trade fair and gave a major speech promising peace and justice to the

Libyans and praising Balbo's "tireless, genial, and tenacious" activity as governor. On March 18 came the crowning ceremony: Mussolini received a gleaming "sword of Islam" (actually the work of Florentine craftsmen), as a symbol of his role as a "protector of Islam" and successor to the caliph. Anti-fascists and scholars of Islamic affairs snickered at the spectacle and at Mussolini's pretensions. The Libyans did not seem to mind. "The Oriental dearly loves a show and this was the pomp and splendor of Imperial Rome recaptured for his delectation"; with the Moslems of Tripoli, Mussolini's visit was an "undoubted" success, wrote an English correspondent.[62]

A flood of letters to Balbo assured him that the Duce's triumph was also his. "The nation in this, your triumph, admires and appreciates most of all your dignified calm," wrote a friend from Ferrara. An old soldier who had fought in Libya in 1911 thanked Balbo for completing the road. "How much walking," he recalled of the original campaign of conquest. "We needed the Litoranea."[63]

Personal triumph, return to the limelight: for Balbo, Mussolini's visit was all that, but it also marked a turning point in his plans for the colony's future. With the conquest of Ethiopia, Libya had become a bastion of empire, a center for radiating Italian power and influence throughout the Mediterranean. Mussolini's trip was a signal for Balbo to realize his grandiose plans for intensive colonization and to carry out the final legal steps that would create the "fourth shore."

Chapter Fourteen

Governor General of Libya:
Creator of the Fourth Shore

"Who does not remember the thousands of colonists Balbo led there [to Libya]?" asked a nationalist historian proudly.[1] "The most unique and valuable fruit of his work as governor," Federzoni concluded.[2] In the popular memory today, Balbo's name evokes two associations: his transatlantic flights and his direction of the Ventimila, the 20,000 colonists whom he escorted to Libya in a single mass convoy in October, 1938. The two events bear his unmistakable stamp: mass movements, under his own direction, executed with a military precision and a theatrical flair that impressed even his harshest critics.

The mass migrations were a logical culmination of Balbo's colonization policies. During his first three years as governor, he realized that drastic measures would be necessary if Libya was to be settled rapidly. Private enterprise, he concluded, had no real interest in attracting and settling large numbers of colonists. The government should choose, transport, and settle hundreds of families on prepared farms—all, of course, at public expense. Such a policy harmonized well with fascism's ideals of a beneficent totalitarian state bringing order, discipline, and well-being into the lives of even its humblest citizens. The scheme for intensive colonization in Libya also fitted in well with the government's domestic resettlement programs. In an effort to eliminate pockets of intense poverty and unemployment in the Po Valley and the Veneto, the government moved hundreds of families to projects such as the Pontine Marshes. Libya provided one more such outlet. The colonization also suited Balbo's style as governor: military, authoritarian, with a large dose of benevolent paternalism.[3]

On May 17, 1938, shortly after Mussolini's visit to Libya, Balbo announced his long-term program for intensive colonization. The first sailing was planned for the following October 28, the sixteenth anniversary of the March on Rome. That made for a frantic schedule of preparations. Balbo followed the progress minutely, even when he was temporarily absent from the colony.[4] In a little under six months, the colonization companies had to be ready for an immigration that would more than triple the number of colonist families under their care. From about 700 at the time of the 1937 agricultural census, the number of families would swell to 2,500 at the end of 1938. The colonization companies and the government provided for all of the colonists' initial needs. Roads, aqueducts, houses, and villages were built; fields were laid out; seeds, tools, and livestock were stockpiled. When the colonist families arrived, they found everything they needed to start their new lives, down to matches on the mantelpiece to light the fire. The labor needed to build the colonization projects provided temporary jobs for 5,000 men who emigrated from Italy and another 4,650 Italians who were hired in Libya. As usual, however, the bulk of the 33,000-man labor force was Libyan.

In Italy, a committee composed of representatives of the colonization companies, fascist party officials and representatives of the colonial government travelled throughout the country interviewing prospective families. According to Balbo's directives, politics played only a minor role in choosing the colonists. Far more significant were the size, the composition, and the health of the family. Their background and experience, their attitudes and social behavior were carefully investigated. Balbo wanted the families to be "well chosen and not from among those who think that they will be able to earn with little effort" or "be maintained by the government."[5] Malcontents and troublemakers, perhaps highly recommended by local police officials eager to get rid of them, had to be eliminated.

There was no dearth of applicants. The selection committee examined some 6,000 families and selected 1,800, or just under one in four. The committee ignored the old sentimental dream of Italian colonialists and patriots who preached that Africa, and Libya in particular, could become a great outlet for the Southern Italian peasantry. In 1938, nearly 80 percent of the families came from Northern Italy. The Veneto, especially the areas around Padova, Venice, Rovigo, and Treviso, furnished the largest numbers. Balbo's own Ferrara contributed the fourth largest contingent, 135 families.

"An army of rural infantry," Balbo called the colonists and, like the good showman that he was, proclaimed that his program was a "historical novelty." Unlike the masses of peasants who emigrated freely but haphazardly at the end of the nineteenth century, "the rural masses today move in compact formations, perfectly organized, to take on the grand work of colonization," he declared.[6] The general in him planned, organized, directed, and personally led his "rural infantry" in the same way that he had led his Blackshirts across the Romagna or his squadrons across the Atlantic. Special trains had to be arranged, supplies of food, medicine, and clothes for the needy had to be gathered. Scores of wicker cradles were ordered, for it was anticipated that many would be filled during the voyage. A huge bureaucracy, so numerous that at times it seemed as if "the shepherds would be almost as numerous as the flocks," supported him in these tasks.[7] The operation was planned minutely. Every man, woman, and child was color-coded with a cardboard label sewn to their clothing. The code signified the family's destination in Libya. The colonists knew day by day, sometimes hour by hour, what they would be doing from the moment they left their doorsteps in Italy until they stepped across the thresholds of their new homes in the colony.

On October 27, the eve of the anniversary of the March on Rome, the "rural army" began its march. From the mountain villages of the Veneto to the dusty hamlets around Rovigo, Ferrara, and Padova, the families converged on the nearest rail stations to board special trains. The colonists and their families and friends feasted, sang patriotic songs, and cheered lustily when the local *federale* harangued them. Late in the afternoon of October 27, the families boarded their trains. Streamers and banners proclaimed, "We are the Duce's countryfolk," and "We fascist peasants will always march wherever the Duce orders us to go." To snatches of the fascist anthem "Giovinezza," cries of babies, tearful farewells, and benedictions by the local priests, the trains headed for Genoa and the fleet of nine ships that would transport the colonists to Libya.

Balbo whirled in perpetual motion. On October 26, he flew from Tripoli to Naples; there he directed the preparation of six ships to transport the southern contingent of colonists. From Naples he flew to Ferrara and then to Genoa to supervise the 1,430 families scheduled to embark there. He had planned a round of patriotic and religious ceremonies and then a grand parade. An autumnal rain began to fall as the first of the seventeen trains bearing the colonists pulled into the station. The Genoese enthusiastically volunteered taxis, buses, and private cars; a triumphal motorcade replaced the triumphal parade on foot. Between 9 A.M. and noon on October 28, a total of more than a thousand vehicles transported the colonists from the trains to the docks—a sign of "the high spirit of Genoese fascism," Balbo telegraphed to Mussolini.[8] At the head of the procession, like the grand marshal in a parade, rode Balbo, not in a staid and pompous official vehicle but in a "frivolous little blue sports car."

On October 30 at noon, the convoy sailed from Genoa to rendezvous with the six ships in Naples. Balbo, aboard the luxury liner *Vulcania*, the flagship of the fleet, fairly exploded with energy, enthusiasm, good humor. At coffee on the promenade deck, at the second-class bar, from a table in the tourist lounge, he held an endless series of conferences and discussions with anyone who happened to crowd around him. Before he had been at sea twenty-four hours, every journalist felt he had secured a personal interview; every official was certain that the marshal had given him direct orders; and each colonist family was convinced that they were the governor's favorites.[9] Three babies were born before the convoy set sail. Once at sea, Balbo presided over the christenings. The first baby was a boy. In an effusion of patriotism, he was christened Italo Vittorio Benito, in honor of Balbo, the king, and Mussolini. (The order of the names provided gossip during the voyage.)

In a final salute to Duce and country, Mussolini, at Balbo's prodding, reviewed the entire convoy before it sailed for Tripoli.

With a showman's instincts and an eye on the morning's headlines, Balbo proposed two alternatives: an inspection at anchor off
the coast of Gaeta, or one in motion. "The inspection in motion of
a fleet of colonists represents a naval event without precedent,"
Balbo informed Mussolini, and the Duce, predictably, favored
that plan.[10] With the sea calm and the sun shining faintly, Mussolini, aboard the cruiser *Trieste*, escorted by four destroyers,
steamed down the long line of ships bearing the colonists, a line
that stretched for nearly eleven miles. The *Trieste* passed close
enough to their ships that the colonists could see the Duce's
stocky figure on the bridge, his arm outstretched in the "Roman"
salute. The colonists replied with roars of "Duce, Duce," and
saluted in return. Balbo, always anxious that his productions
should please his major critic, telegraphed Teruzzi, "Please let
me know how the review went and if the Duce was satisfied."[11]
That evening, one last ship, carrying 130 families from Syracuse,
joined the convoy. Two days later the fleet reached Tripoli.

Balbo and his army of aides were there to lead the colonists
into the promised land. Along the broad, palm-fringed, ocean-
front promenade they marched to the Piazza del Castello, in front
of the Governor's Palace, where they gathered for a welcoming
ceremony. It took two hours to assemble them all, a gathering
"more impressive than the oft-repeated gatherings in the Piazza
Venezia," remarked one foreign journalist.[12] A gigantic black,
steel-helmeted head, a thousand times life-size, painted on the
white wall of the largest building in the square made everyone
feel the Duce's presence. So did the banners and slogans that
declared "Mussolini redeems the earth and establishes cities" and
urged the new arrivals to "Begin your new life by vowing that you
will be worthy of Mussolini" and "Let every colonist be a soldier
under the command of Mussolini."

In contrast to the belligerent warrior's head and the fascist-
style martial slogans, Balbo's welcoming ceremony was "strangely
humble." The bands stopped playing. The crowd knelt in prayer.
A Franciscan gave the blessing. Then, according to Balbo's
wishes—and at his mother's suggestion—the crowd recited the
Lord's Prayer.[13] "We were all crying," Balbo later told his
friends.[14]

Thousands of Arabs in sand-colored robes had flocked into the piazza to watch the proceedings. Balbo did not neglect them. The prayer finished, he mounted a rostrum set beneath the wall of the Turkish fortress. All eyes turned to a shrouded monument at his side. When he pulled a cord, the drapery fell away, revealing a bronze equestrian statue of Mussolini. In its right hand the figure brandished the "Sword of Islam" that Mussolini had received during his visit in 1937; in the left the figure clutched a scroll, a symbol of Mussolini's pledge to protect the Libyans. Balbo's speech was brief and pointed: "People of Libya, old and new," he began, "a new era begins today for Libya."[15] He urged the colonists to work "with passion, with intelligence," as they had at home, to develop their farms and their new homelands. They also had to develop themselves mentally and spiritually, he told them. In their villages, they would find obligatory evening schools. Within three years illiteracy among the colonists would disappear, he declared. He reassured the Libyans that, as the equestrian statue indicated, their rights would be respected and defended.

For the rest of the day, the colonists enjoyed the run of the city and free food, drink, and entertainment. Tripoli became the site of a "colossal picnic."[16] In his passion for organization and detail— for totalitarian control, some might have remarked—Balbo ordered all the girls of Tripoli to attend the public dances in honor of the colonist families and to act as hostesses to the young men. Balbo himself drove about the city checking to see that all was well with "his people." The reactions of the colonists to this reception are not surprising: "Tripoli is a very beautiful city—I wouldn't have believed it," admitted one skeptical colonist; another marvelled at the "extraordinary things, not to be believed if we had not seen them."[17]

On November 4 the families, loaded into long convoys of army trucks, headed for their new homes. Balbo was often waiting in person, even in the remotest village, to greet the first arrivals. Jingling a great bunch of keys, he would walk down the column of trucks, calling out names and numbers.

"Bertelli, farm number 119."
"Here, Excellency."
"Where are you from?"
"Emilia, Excellency."

Fig. 22. Governor Balbo greets Italian colonists arriving in Libya during the mass emigration of October, 1938 (*Libia,* May–August, 1940)

"Ah, you'll find more room here. It's good land, but it needs hard work. Here's your key and good luck to you. We shan't forget you. I shall be around again soon and you must tell me if you have any difficulties."

"Yes, Excellency. Thank you, Excellency."[18]

In addition to directing and starring in his production, Balbo was his own best press agent. Correspondents from Germany, England, the United States, France, Poland, Switzerland, and even war-torn Spain covered the story. From his first press conference in Genoa to the landing in Tripoli, Balbo made himself accessible to the newsmen. So packed with journalists was the *Vulcania* during the emigration that there was room for only eighty colonist families, perhaps a quarter of the contingent on the other vessels. In Libya, Balbo did not arrange official tours and functions for the journalists; he left them free to wander as they pleased. However, he provided a guide-interpreter for every two journalists. Such an arrangement in a police state might have raised suspicions about the real nature of such escorts. Nevertheless, foreign newsmen, including those from the skeptical Anglo-Saxon countries, showed no doubts in this case. They were thoroughly conscious of Balbo's talents as "a master of the subtle art of . . . public relations,"[19] but they succumbed to his charm.[20] He was "thorough, disdains flattery, shows inexhaustible energy and a talent for giving and receiving friendships," one remarked. Moreover, some thought that the Balbian talents rubbed off on his subordinates. "He has imbued all his officials with something of his own character. I was astonished when I saw the colonial efficiency of the Italians in Libya." As for the colonization itself, an English journalist remarked, "I believe that short of a world war it will succeed, for it is carried through with the determination of the State and the personal enthusiasm of Marshal Balbo."

Balbo minimized the "two or three discordant and off-key" remarks. French journalists raised questions about the costs of the colonization and argued that free enterprise could have done the job just as well.[21] Agricultural experts who visited the settlements while attending an international congress in Tripoli also raised numerous questions.[22] What if the government withheld its subsidies? What of the Libyans who had been displaced from their grazing lands and farmlands and now appeared "sullen and restive and only submissive because forced to be so"? Still others raised questions about the salt content of the irrigation water, about the eventual shortage of good land, about the efficacy of the marketing system controlled by the colonization companies.

These doubters made little impression. Waves of enthusiasm and patriotic euphoria swept over Italy. "At last people are beginning to 'believe' in Libya: but most of all there is faith in your extraordinary organizational talents," wrote Ardito Desio, an internationally known geologist and professor at the University of Milan. "The emigration of the 20,000 has stirred even those who were asleep."[23] Another favorite theme, echoed over and over in public statements and private letters to Balbo, was the sentimental satisfaction that at last Italy's emigrants had found a home. "The tragic ghosts of the vessels that once transported millions of our countrymen overseas are now only a sad memory. Our people can now find shelter, work, prosperity in the shadow of our flag, in close union . . . with the Mother Country," wrote one Italian diplomat.[24] Such a good press irritated Mussolini. Officially, the Duce congratulated Balbo for "being the spirit and organizer of this enterprise that is worthy of the regime." Privately, according to Ciano's diary, "The Duce was annoyed at the trumpeting made by Balbo over the sending of the colonists to Libya."[25] In the future, he wanted them to leave in small detachments.

Balbo's "trumpeting" and the carnival-like atmosphere of the emigration had international repercussions.[26] What new direction would Mussolini take—toward Egypt or toward Tunisia? diplomats wondered. The Moslem populations of North Africa and the Middle East protested. In Baghdad, there were demonstrations against Italy's threat to Arab predominance in the Mediterranean; the French aired anti-Italian radio broadcasts in their colonies in North Africa and Syria. In 1939, the French resident general in Tunisia noted with satisfaction that "Moslems of Tunis now are complaining of the fate of their co-religionists in Tripolitania who were under Italian rule."[27]

The pampering and celebrations that characterized the emigration tended to spoil the colonist families. Balbo's carnival atmosphere "encouraged a Bengodi mentality in sharp contrast to the hard and serious tasks which lay ahead," a technical expert who worked with the families remarked in 1945. "It certainly has not been easy to lead these people back to reality; only in the last two years has this damaging mentality finally been overcome."[28]

The costs of the programs presented another difficulty. During the thirty-year Italian occupation of Libya, Italian investment has been estimated at 1.8 billion lire.[29] Nearly half of this investment, 960 million lire, occurred during the years 1937–1942. The colonization projects and the development of agriculture absorbed about 654 million lire, or roughly two-thirds of the expenditures during this period of intensive investment. The chief investor in Libyan agriculture was always the state, which in the form of subsidies, prizes, and direct contributions provided up to 75 percent of the funds. The costs of colonization climbed steadily. In part this was due to the crash nature of Balbo's program and in part to the enormous initial investments necessary in a country that had no infrastructure and a minimal tradition of settled agriculture. But the costs also climbed because the colonists were in no hurry to cut themselves off from their subsidies. In addition, critics raised questions about possible competition of Libyan agricultural produce, including wine, with that of Italy.

Balbo's advisers urged him to ignore the economic issues. Publicly, he should stress the social and political benefits of the colonization over mere economic calculus, they told him. In the event that government funds for the colonization dried up, he was prepared to appeal directly to the public for contributions. So confident was he of his prestige and of the popularity of the programs that he was certain he could raise whatever funds he needed. Many of his advisers concurred.

In October, 1939, Balbo plunged ahead with the second of the five planned annual mass migrations.[30] The scale was considerably smaller: a total of 1,359 families, about 10,000 colonists, made the trip. Once again families from Northern Italy dominated the emigration and once again Balbo supervised the operation. There was much less fanfare this time and no elaborate welcome in Tripoli. The colonists did not complain. They still sent home glowing reports of being "treated like royalty."

In his concern for the colonists Balbo did not ignore his other constituency, the 700,000 indigenous Libyans. "Peoples of Libya, old and new!" he had begun his welcoming address in Piazza del Castello in November, 1938, to the huge crowd that had gathered to greet the first installment of 20,000 colonists to Libya. Before the influx of colonists, Libyans had outnumbered the Italians 10 to 1. Balbo's policies toward the Libyans surprised many observers. "Within the limits of his typical totalitarian theory that the white man must be supreme in Libya, Marshal Balbo both likes and knows how to be liberal," an English journalist claimed in 1939.[31] "Wise, humane and—according to fascist ideals—beneficent," concluded another.[32] Even the eminent Islamicist Francesco Gabrieli concurred: "Pizzo di Ferro" was no great humanitarian, but Balbo was capable of combining "a ferocious scowl with a smile, a corporal's good humor and cordiality, sometimes even good sense and justice."[33] His "hardline" predecessors, De Bono and Graziani, grumbled in disbelief at Balbo's policies and wrote him angry letters.[34]

Compared to De Bono and Graziani, who were concerned with pacifying the colony, Balbo's directives were undoubtedly liberal and conciliatory. Yet, as Gabrieli warned, Balbo was not a true humanitarian. Like most European colonial governors, he was strict in quelling insubordination and in dealing with questions of "racial prestige."[35] Only three death sentences against Libyans were carried out during Balbo's half-dozen years as governor. The sentences resulted from the mutiny of twenty-three Tuareg soldiers who murdered their Italian commanding officer in order to gather weapons and turn to banditry. Balbo ordered virtually the entire colonial military establishment out to hunt down the fugitives. When three were eventually recaptured, Balbo ordered them executed on the spot where the crime had been committed. He himself presided, and he ordered all local chiefs and military units to be present. He was also very strict when matters of European "prestige" were at stake. Two Libyans, accused of having "touched" an Italian woman in the street, were sentenced to eight years in prison for having "violated racial prestige."[36] Foreign journalists remarked on the excessive formal respect the Italians demanded from Libyans. An English traveller commented, "The natives are browbeaten as nowhere else in North Africa," and noted the "embarrassing obsequiousness" of the Libyans.[37] Even in the most remote oases, they "snap and quiver to attention" as soon as a European appears. In Tripoli, bootblacks gave the fascist salute and bellowed "Evviva il Re-Imperatore, evviva Mussolini, evviva l'Italia," before they grabbed a customer's shoes.

Yet European visitors also remarked that under Balbo, Italians in some ways treated Libyans with a surprising informality and ease that was not typical of European colonial regimes.[38] Italians thought nothing of working side by side in the fields with Libyans; Italian officials greeted Libyan notables with great cordiality and friendliness. There was little discrimination in the use of public facilities. Libyans could stay in any hotel and could travel first class on public transport whenever they could afford it. A paternalistic and Arabophobe Frenchman, travelling in Libya in 1938, remarked that the Libyans were no less well cared for than Europeans. In Libya, at least, he remarked, he did not feel the need for a "thorough cleaning up" of the Arab population as he did in Tunisia.[39]

These apparent contrasts in policy reflected Balbo's personality and his ideals. He wanted to maintain Italian "prestige," but he also wanted to be genuinely popular with the Libyans and to carry out Europe's "civilizing mission," to share the best of fascism and European culture with a people that he perceived as being backward and steeped in misery. Balbo was also "liberal" and "conciliatory" because, as the English anthropologist E. E. Evans-Pritchard pointed out, he had little choice.[40] What Balbo feared most was the emergence of an indigenous nationalist movement. To forestall such a development, he concluded, that policy was best which stirred the Libyans least.

One of Balbo's first goals as governor was to eradicate all memory of the period of Italian repression. Italian military sovereignty over all of Libya had been secured only three years before he came to power. The tribes of Cyrenaica in particular, under the banner of the Sanusi religious order and the leadership of Omar el Mukhtar, had put up a fierce resistance. The Italians replied in kind with a ruthless campaign of summary executions, decimation of flocks, and mass internments of the nomadic populations of the Gebel. According to official Italian figures, the Cyrenaican population dropped from 225,000 in 1928 to 142,000 in 1931.[41]

When he arrived in the colony, Balbo knew very little about the indigenous peoples. He relied heavily on Giuseppe Daodiace, who had had long experience as a colonial bureaucrat in Cyrenaica. "If I learned to govern the Arabs, I owe it in large part to his experience," Balbo wrote to Teruzzi in December, 1937.[42] "Dao" suggested readings on colonial policy; Dao "formed" him through long conversations and discussions; Dao was his "trusted collaborator" in executing the policies that led to the "bright realities of today," declared Balbo. When he became governor, he found nearly all the Cyrenaican Arabs "in the concentration camps"; by 1937 they had been freed, boasted Balbo. Daodiace espoused no great theories or principles. He had always based his work as an administrator on "justice and equity" and a defense of the "moral and material elevation of the native," he wrote to Balbo in April, 1938. This general attitude of collaboration and accommodation enraged the hard-liner Graziani, who referred to him as an exponent of the "old demagogic-Masonic" regime.[43] Dao studied French models and he translated sections of French colonial manuals for Balbo to read. Such reading served more as solace than as a source of guiding principles, he decided, for he wrote to Balbo at the end of 1937, "the conclusion is that the world is all the same and that the experience of others isn't very helpful."[44]

To this background Balbo added his own temperament and experience. He developed a romantic admiration for the coastal Arab-Berbers and took his mission as representative of a civilizing nation quite seriously. "I love these Africans of the North, intelligent and virile, whose word alone is worth as much as any written document," he told a French journalist in 1935.[45] "Of his mixed motives for dealing with the natives, Balbo's own personal liking for the people is probably strongest," concluded a British newspaperman.[46]

Balbo's sympathy is evident in his public pronouncements. He tried to dispel the popular stereotype of the Arab as sleepy and indolent or as a violent xenophobe. On the contrary, according to Balbo, the Arab was by nature "sober and enduring, with a profound sense of respect and obedience toward the governing and religious authorities."[47] He had a sense of honor and made an excellent soldier, as the Libyan battalions who fought in the Ethiopian war had demonstrated. Such rhetoric merely substituted for a negative stereotype one more reassuring and more in keeping with fascist values of order, respect for authority, and military virtue. Balbo was also highly selective in his sympathies. He favored those Libyans whom he thought best fitted into the Italian scheme of things. The peoples of the coastal regions he admired because he regarded them as "superior races influenced by Mediterranean civilization" and capable of absorbing the new fascist values and institutions.[48] The Negroid peoples of the Fezzan, he concluded, were not at that level and must be left to their own devices under military rule. Balbo was also implacable with the nomads. They posed a threat to the colonization programs; their way of life had to be severely controlled and eventually eliminated. Nor did Balbo have any illusions about the long-term fidelity of the Libyans toward their Italian masters. All about him he sensed the paradox of colonial rule: the example of Italian civilization and the material improvements the Italians brought would awaken in the Libyans the "consciousness and dignity of a Mediterranean people." Toward the end of his term, Balbo watched the tide of Arab nationalism washing along the entire North African coast. He could only hope that by the time it reached Libya, the Italians would be sufficiently rooted to resist it.

Finding policies that would accommodate the Libyans was not easy, for they varied widely in their backgrounds and life styles.[49] When the Italians referred to their "faithful Libyan subjects," they quite naturally thought of the Arabs or Arab-Berbers who made up the vast majority of the indigenous population. They were descendants of the aboriginal Berbers and the Arab invaders of the eleventh century. Moslem in their religion, Arab in their language, these peoples engaged primarily in agricultural and pastoral occupations in the coastal areas, especially in centers such as Tripoli, Misurata, Benghazi, and Derna. More than half the population clustered in Tripoli province. Benghazi-Derna in 1936 claimed only a third of the population of Tripolitania. The huge expanse of the Libyan Sahara remained virtually empty, with a population of only 48,376. Even within the Arab-Berber majority, there were a wide variety of occupations, life styles, and customs. The nomadic shepherds of Cyrenaica's Gebel had little in common with the city-dwelling Tripolitanians, who were craftsmen and petty tradesmen, or small farmers who cultivated oasis gardens or modest dry and semi-irrigated plots.

Libya's minorities, in 1936, included 35,000 Cologhlas, the descendants of invading Turkish janissaries of the seventeenth century and the local women; 30,000 Negroes, descendants of the slave traffic in the Sudan; and 28,500 Jews whose ancestors had been expelled from Spain. All three groups spoke Arabic. The Cologhlas and Negroes generally adopted the dress and religion of the Arab-Berbers and mixed freely with them. The Jews, for the most part, were concentrated in their own quarter in Tripoli, where they worked as craftsmen and tradesmen.

Like most colonial officials, Balbo was wary of breaking down the traditional indigenous social order, for fear of what would follow. Throughout their North African colonies, the French had tried without success to assimilate their colonial subjects, to turn them into good Frenchmen. Balbo rejected such policies for Libya. Instead, he aimed at strengthening the traditionalist element in the Arab community. In harmony with Italian foreign policy and Mussolini's stance as "protector of Islam," Balbo collaborated scrupulously with the local notables, the established political and religious leaders of the Arab-Berber majority. They were superficially integrated into the Italian scheme of organizations and institutions. But fundamentally, as an English journalist observed, Balbo wanted to "petrify the Arab community in the past."[50] He promoted modest economic, social, and cultural reforms. In the realm of political rights, he took his boldest initiative: he proposed to grant full citizenship to the Libyans.

In the economic sphere, under Balbo's governorship, "Libya reached the highest standard of living it had ever known," concluded a Libyan writer in 1962. The Italians built the Litoranea, improved the harbors, and erected modern buildings in Tripoli and Benghazi. In addition, "All her fertile land was transformed into agricultural villages dotted with modern houses inhabited by the Italian farmers, who had brought their cattle and agricultural machinery with them."[51] The Italian farms flourished, of course, at the expense of the Libyans and their traditional forms of agriculture.[52] For his colonization schemes, Balbo claimed the best land for the Italians. The effect on the Libyans was twofold. In some cases, especially in Cyrenaica's Gebel Akhdar, the Libyans were displaced from their traditional grazing lands. In Tripolitania, the colonist farms disrupted the tightly integrated system of oasis gardens, dry farming, and pastoral enterprises that made up the traditional forms of agriculture in the area. Once their traditional life styles were disturbed, the Libyans became increasingly attracted to the alternatives that the Italians unwittingly provided: wage labor, and the glamor and excitement of the cities.

To Balbo this development looked ominous. He sought to provide alternatives to traditional forms of Libyan agriculture, and he was determined to stamp out the nomadic way of life where it interfered with Italian colonization schemes. Yet he wanted to forestall a rush to the cities, where the unemployed could only be sources of trouble and would compete with Italian labor. He offered a number of compensatory programs and incentives. Libyan entrepreneurs became eligible for land subsidies and tax advantages identical to those offered Italians. Libyan families who wished to take up sedentary farming but lacked financial resources could join Italian-designed "demographic villages" that paralleled those for the Italian colonists. Finally, Libyans were expected to benefit from the jobs that would develop in the agricultural sector as the Italian colonization schemes developed.

These programs were in operation too short a time to judge their effectiveness beyond their obvious propaganda value. For Libyans with financial means, land from the public domain became available only in April, 1937; by 1939, only twenty requests for concessions had been granted. For Libyan families without means—the analogue of the colonist families—Balbo offered settlement projects similar to those for metropolitan families. Balbo publicized these schemes well. During a diplomatic mission to Cairo in May, 1939, he displayed photographs of the villages to King Farouk, who showed great interest in them. Most of the villages, however, had not progressed beyond the blueprint stage when the war broke out. During their brief existence, the completed projects displayed the same technical, administrative, and morale problems as their Italian counterparts. The Libyan families milked the government for subsidies and showed little interest in establishing themselves as farmers. The Italian agricultural experts assigned to these villages privately considered them a farce, and the Cyrenaican bedouins described the local villages as "throwing dust in our eyes."

Far more important and attractive to the Libyans than the Italian agricultural schemes were the vast building programs. The Litoranea, the construction of the colonization villages, and the new buildings in the urban areas provided thousands of jobs for Libyans. Despite the popular belief in Italy that Italians would build the "fourth shore," in practice Libyans did, for their labor was far cheaper and more convenient than metropolitan labor. During peak construction on the Litoranea in August, 1936, for instance, the number of workers employed averaged 12,997; of these, 934 were Italians, a little under the 10 percent specified by the contracts. In the construction of the agricultural villages of Bianchi, Giordani, Oliveti, and Tarhuna during 1938, Libyans supplied almost two-thirds of the 3.3 million man-hours expended.

The enormous demand for Libyan labor produced a number of effects that alarmed the Italians. A free labor market operated— up to a point. There is no evidence of forced labor or impressment. The upward spiral of wages, however, provoked government intervention, as in the case of the Litoranea, when Balbo fixed Libyan wages at a level one-third below that of Italians. Still, these wages proved highly attractive to the Libyans. They preferred a salary to the risks of farming and favored the excitement of the cities to their traditional rural existence.

Balbo's modest provisions for education were a vast improvement over the situation he had found.[53] The cultural standard of the Libyan Arabs was lower than that of any other country in North Africa. Until the Italian pacification program was completed in 1931, there were virtually no schools outside Tripoli. On the elementary level, the only instruction available was in the *kuttab*, in which the students learned to recite memorized verses from the Koran. The Italians added a program of bilingual instruction. Despite the difficulties of finding qualified Libyan instructors, by 1938 or 1939 most villages had schools, with Libyan and Italian teachers working together.

In the realm of higher education, in May of 1935 Balbo realized a project that had been discussed for decades: the creation of a college of Islamic culture. The issue of such a project had first been raised in 1914, but the site always remained a problem. Was it to be located in Italy or in Libya? If in Libya, then in Tripoli or at Tagiura, where a tradition of learning existed? Balbo decided on Tripoli. The purpose of such an institution was frankly political: "Italy can thus more easily mold her *cadis*, her Libyan government officials and her Mohammedan teachers to her own ideals without recourse to Islamic universities in Cairo or in Tunis."[54] The program of legal and religious studies lasted anywhere from three to seven years. Thus, before Balbo's plan to produce graduates for the colony's civil service was realized, Italian rule in Libya had come to an end.

The elementary schools and the Islamic college followed a traditional Moslem pattern of education for males. With the reluctant assent of the Moslem leadership, Balbo took the innovative step of introducing schools for women. To please the Libyan notables, however, these institutions had to appear in a noneducational guise, as Feminine Schools of Instruction and Work. In 1936, Balbo founded a convent-school in Tripoli to train nurse's aides. Beginning with 16 students, the school expanded to 25 the following year. Other training centers were established in the interior; by 1940 there were 14 schools, with 1,163 pupils.

In addition to the schools, Balbo created in August, 1936, the Gioventù Araba del Littorio (GAL), a counterpart to the fascist youth organizations in Italy. No parade or festival in Libya was complete without a contingent of GAL. There is little evidence, however, that GAL succeeded in its chief aim: to transform its members into fervent young fascists.

Balbo worked to improve medical facilities and health services.[55] In a population that was highly mobile and whose attitude toward disease was generally fatalistic, it was difficult to introduce extensive public-health measures. The Italians established mobile medical units equipped with an operating table, an X-ray machine, and a laboratory to make regular trips into the desert. In the larger towns, hospitals with separate departments for Arab patients were created. In the smaller towns the Italians installed resident doctors. Annually, the government distributed fixed amounts of free medicines and dressings to the Libyans. To combat infant mortality, Italian nurses were paid a bonus to seek out unwilling patients, and laws were passed that prevented child marriages. These measures appear modest; however, to a population periodically ravaged by plague, cholera, smallpox, and a high rate of infant mortality, these efforts were a vast improvement over their previous situation.

Balbo's measures to improve the economic, social, and educational status of the Libyans proved to be tentative, cautious, modest. His policy of working in harmony with the Arab notables limited his attempts at innovation. Budget considerations also played a role. Huge sums went into building the colony's infrastructure and developing the colonization—projects designed to benefit primarily the Italians and to attract them to Libya. What meager funds were left over went to pacify and benefit the Libyans.

In the area of legal status Balbo took his boldest step. In October, 1938, he proposed that full citizenship be extended to all Libyans.[56] A number of factors prompted him to attempt such a radical stroke. First, the measure fulfilled a promise. During Mussolini's 1937 visit, he had declared he would "reward" the Libyans for their support during the Ethiopian campaign. Balbo also calculated that the measure would help combat stirrings of

Libyan nationalism. If the initiative was approved, fascist Italy would rank among the most enlightened of the European colonial powers.

Second, the measure harmonized with the goal of making the "fourth shore" a legal reality. With the influx of the 20,000 colonists in 1938, Libya was socially well on its way to becoming an extension of Italy. Mussolini wanted legal recognition of this fact. In November, 1939, he proposed to the Grand Council that the four coastal provinces of Libya, Tripoli, Misurata, Benghazi, and Derna, be integrated into the Italian kingdom. The Fezzan was to remain a military territory. The corporative system was to be extended to the colony. Some of the most experienced colonial administrators grumbled that Libya was not yet ready for full administrative integration and that granting citizenship would only create a class of "privileged Arabs," rather than a cadre of leaders.[57] Nevertheless, a decree of January 9, 1939, declared that Libya's four coastal provinces were now a part of metropolitan Italy. Just as France had turned Algeria into a province, so Italy had absorbed Libya's Mediterranean shore. Balbo had lost a bit of his glamor as governor of an exotic colonial territory, but he had fulfilled his goal of creating the "fourth shore."

Balbo's full citizenship measure for the Libyans came in the context of Libya's changed legal status. However, his proposal encountered another obstacle: Mussolini's newly initiated racial campaign. To discriminate against the Jews but not against the Libyans made no sense to the fascist hierarchy. The measure was quickly interpreted as one of Balbo's many protests against Mussolini's racist policies. "It is easy to recognize here a flat contradiction in our racial policy," Ciano noted in his diary. "The real party men, like Farinacci, Starace, and Alfieri, do not hesitate to oppose the proposal. Nor do I. The project has been shelved and will be presented again in very different garb."[58]

Balbo had to be satisfied with what came to be known as the *piccola cittadinanza* or "little citizenship"—a far cry from his original proposal. The "little citizenship" amounted to a token reward to Moslem Libyans who had served in Ethiopia. The measure was also intended to create an elite favorable to the Italians. Qualified Libyans could now acquire certain rights and privileges—mainly that of joining fascist organizations for Libyans—without losing

Fig. 23. Governor Balbo presents Libyan notable with certificate of citizenship in April, 1940 (Caproni Museum Archive)

their family and inheritance rights under Moslem law. Under the "little citizenship" Libyans could pursue a military career in Libyan units; serve as *podestà* (mayor) of an Arab community—but not a mixed one; serve in public office within the corporative system; and join the Associazione Musulmana del Littorio, the party organization for Libyans. But in return for this "special citizenship," a Libyan had to renounce his right to apply for metropolitan citizenship. Moreover, the "special citizenship" was valid only in Libya. This guaranteed that there would be no "immission of Arab elements into the peninsula," noted the *Padano*.[59]

Publicly, Balbo made the best of his defeat. In May, 1939, in an interview with *Al Ahram* while on a visit to Cairo, he declared that of all the European powers, Italy had found the best formula for allowing Moslems to become citizens of a Christian state without "in the least" losing their personal rights according to the laws of the Koran.[60] The government had received many thousands of requests for special citizenship, and Balbo himself had proudly distributed the first certificates, he declared. In practice, the "many thousands" of applications boiled down to about 2,500—most of them government employees who assumed tacitly that the special citizenship was a condition for retaining their jobs, much as membership in the fascist party was a condition for government employment in metropolitan Italy.

How the Libyans felt about Balbo is difficult to judge because the evidence is so scant. The director of the Oriental Institute in Naples, based on his experience at a professional congress in Tripoli where he and his colleagues mixed with Libyan notables, claimed in 1936 that Libyans now felt "a sincere love for Italy."[61] That seems unlikely. Balbo's relatively benevolent policies, after Graziani's repressions, probably won him a certain amount of good will among the Libyans. Perhaps they admired his lavish spectacles and his manly image, his sense of honor and chivalry. They repaid him in kind. A number of times when Balbo on some aerial or automobile excursion found himself isolated and defenseless in the desert, local nomads helped him. In at least one case they knew with whom they were dealing.[62] Undoubtedly the Libyans were grateful for gestures such as saving the Tripolitanian flocks during the terrible 1935–1936 drought. At that time, Balbo detailed fifty ships to transport 300,000 animals from Tripolitania to the Cyrenaican highlands. The flocks were then gradually driven back to Tripolitania after Balbo arranged for huge quantities of water to be available along the path of the migration.[63]

The notables—the various *cadis* and chiefs whom Balbo consulted before issuing any major legislation—supported him because he supported them. Much of their authority rested on religious tradition, and Balbo was always careful to encourage their religious liberty. He rebuilt mosques, many of which Graziani had destroyed; he supported religious education in the Koranic elementary schools and the Institute for Islamic Culture; he forbade the sale of alcoholic beverages during Ramadan. When he introduced measures that were likely to arouse opposition—prohibition of child marriages, of fakiristic practices, of usury—he did so only after consulting with the notables.[64] A letter an important Arab leader wrote to Daodiace in 1938 reflects the attitudes of the notables: "We hope that his excellency Balbo will always remain our governor. We feel that we love him because we are certain that under his rule we Arabs will be properly respected."[65] In March, 1940, the *New York Times* concluded—as most foreign journalists did—that the Italians were not very popular in Libya; nevertheless, Balbo's strict control maintained "absolute quiet" among the Libyans and there was no sign of resistance.[66] Ironically, after Libya's independence—but before Qaddafi's revolution of 1969—Balbo still enjoyed a good press among the Libyans. A brief popular history published for the tenth anniversary of Libya's independence praised the material improvements the Italians had introduced, "particularly under the governorship of Marshal Balbo."[67]

With the influx of the 30,000 colonist families and his attempts, however flawed, to integrate the Libyans into the Italian scheme of things, Balbo brought the "fourth shore" from patriotic vision to concrete reality. At its height, before the war broke out, his Libya was a reflection—as he wanted it to be—of fascist Italy. The swarms of military and militia uniforms, the monumental architecture, the statues of the Duce, and the new colonization projects were all faithful mirrors of the mother country. Balbo ruled over Libya as a benevolent tyrant. Totalitarian political theory harmonized with his natural impulses, his drive to be everywhere, to do and control everything. He put his stamp on everything from the editorials in the Tripoli newspapers to the decoration of the chapels in the colonist villages. Like Ferrara, Libya was his fief.

Without the war, what would have happened to the "fourth shore"? Some have argued that Balbo's programs could have worked. Given time and money, the colonists would have rooted themselves, the Libyans would have been integrated, the colony would have prospered. Such a rosy scenario ignores both the realities of Balbo's day and the post-war history of decolonization. Time was the one factor that was in short supply. Italian Libya was a creature of fascist Italy. Ironically, just as Libya reached the peak of its development as a colony, Mussolini plunged into World War II. Many of the agricultural settlements, especially those in Cyrenaica, were destroyed when the Axis and the Allies chased each other back and forth across Libya and Egypt in three successive campaigns during 1941 and 1942. The government evacuated the bulk of the colonists to Italy at the end of 1942. A rump remained in Tripolitania, even after Libya achieved her independence in 1951. In 1970, shortly after he seized power, Qaddafi ignominiously expelled the last colonists. For a few fleeting years, Balbo had transformed the dream of a "fourth shore" into a reality. Without him, and especially without the financial support of Mussolini's Italy, the "fourth shore" quickly foundered and disappeared.

Chapter Fifteen

Frondeur: The Germanophobe

During his six years as governor general of Libya, Balbo flourished; so did the colony and the mother country—at least outwardly. Mussolini, riding one of the crests of his popularity, led his regime to imperial glory with the Ethiopian war. Alarming signs followed: the Spanish civil war and worse—alliance with Germany. Fascism assumed a totalitarian and Germanophile cast; the Duce surrounded himself more and more with incompetent yes-men; the party, under Starace, became a laughingstock. From the Governor's Palace in Tripoli, Balbo, frustrated and helpless, blustered and fulminated to whoever would listen.[1] "A brief talk with Balbo. Sour and hostile to everthing. He spoke ill of the Germans, defended the Jews, attacked Starace, criticized *voi* and the business of the Roman salute," gloated Galeazzo Ciano in June, 1938.[2] Nor was Mussolini spared. Before the Grand Council and in private meetings, Balbo warned the Duce again and again that his policies would lead Italy to disaster.

Balbo also joined such "loyal opposition" as there was. By 1937 a *"fronde"* had formed within the Grand Council. The group included two of Balbo's closest personal friends, Federzoni and Bottai, as well as two of his fellow *quadrumvirs*, De Vecchi and De Bono. Dino Grandi, Balbo's old comrade from his days as a *squadrista*, and Alberto De Stefani, the economist and former finance minister, completed the group.

This *fronde*, however, turned out to be a pale imitation of the French model. The original *frondeurs*—comprised mostly of recalcitrant nobility—mounted a legal opposition and, eventually, an armed revolt against royal power during the minority of Louis XIV. Nothing of the sort happened in Mussolini's Italy. The Duce met no serious legal opposition—much less an armed one—until the Grand Council deposed him peacefully on July 25, 1943. The *frondeurs* whom Balbo joined argued with Mussolini, coaxed and cajoled him, tried to convince him to moderate his stands. Yet they never seriously risked their positions. In the end, they accomplished very little.

Balbo differed more in style than in substance from his fellow *frondeurs*. He spoke out loudly and clearly against the mounting list of Mussolini's follies. Yet he stopped well short of resigning his powers and privileges—and he carefully hedged his bets. As enemies of his such as Farinacci protested, what was an old republican and Freemason doing hosting members of the royal family and a eucharistic congress in Libya? Such actions suggested "a real and authentic air of *fronde*."[3]

This was little more than palace rumors and backbiting. In perspective, Balbo's reputation as a *frondeur*—like his earlier reputation as an intransigent—appears overblown. How he developed his image as a *frondeur*, however, is not difficult to explain. First, Balbo was not one to bury his light under a bushel. "Bluff, yet suave, fearless and supple, he was not the type to pass unnoticed anywhere," the *New York Times* recalled in his obituary notice.[4] Moreover, Balbo seemed to be in political perpetual motion. "He knew how to live only in terms of factions, always on the alert, at the highest pitch, all polemical waves, always ready to defend and to attack," Bottai summed him up.[5] In his head Balbo carried an account book in which he perpetually assessed friends and enemies, "transferring names from one column to another."[6]

The exact direction of Balbo's political motion did not always matter, nor was it always consistent. Sometimes he staked out a position only because it stood diametrically opposed to that of an enemy—or even to that of Mussolini. Farinacci, among others, did the same. The more his "hated rival" Balbo wraps himself in his "equivocal" republicanism, the more Farinacci "as an instinctive antithesis" supports the right, Federzoni remarked in his diary.[7]

Naturally, enemies, including Ciano and Farinacci, nourished

Balbo's *frondeur* image in the late 1930s. Police reports and anonymous letters, such as one dated November 10, 1937, reported
Balbo as head of "a real sectarian organization with branches
everywhere."[8] De Bono often complained in his diary in 1937 and
1938 about Balbo's "plotting," and commented, "Balbo is certainly
collecting the malcontents, whose numbers are not so small."[9]
Balbo, Bottai, and Lessona, minister of Italian Africa, were reported to be preparing a coup d'état to eliminate Mussolini, with
the help of the Colonial Police Force (PAI).[10] Farinacci, in February, 1940, warned Mussolini of the "*fronde* of the *quadrumvirs*"
that might develop out of a meeting of De Bono, De Vecchi, and
Balbo at Rhodes.[11]

Foreign journalists contributed to Balbo's image as a *frondeur*.
In the late 1930s, especially, as relations between Italy and the
United States became strained over the Ethiopian war and the
Axis, American magazines portrayed Balbo as a dissident, as a
malcontent, as a possible successor to Mussolini. At the time of
the Ethiopian war, a popular magazine, *Collier's*, pictured Balbo
and Badoglio "each as anxious to get his knife into Mussolini's
neck as a hunter is to get the fox's brush."[12] *Esquire,* another
popular American periodical, in February, 1938, published an
anonymous article that pondered, "Wondering how long Balbo,
that once-proud hero of Fascism, will serve il Duce by standing
and waiting in Libya?"[13] The opening line cast Balbo as "Brutus to
Mussolini's Caesar." The *New York Times*, however, doubted that
Balbo posed much of a threat to Mussolini. Balbo did rank high
on the list of potential successors, with Grandi, Costanzo and
Galeazzo Ciano, and Starace. "Some of these men have strong
followings, but none has the mettle of Mussolini," cautioned the
Times.[14]

Balbo protested the *frondeur* stories vigorously. In a long, angry letter to *Esquire's* editor, Balbo declared that he was loyal
both to Mussolini and to the monarchy. The stress, however, was
plainly on his relationship with Mussolini, which had lasted
twenty-four years. "From the loveliest days of my youth, I have
loved Mussolini" and admired him for the way in which in a few
short years he had elevated the Italian people "to an exceptional
level of dignity and worth," protested Balbo. As to the question of
succession, no Italian with "good sense" raised the issue. Musso-

lini, fortunately, enjoyed excellent health and could live another fifty years, "as I wish him with all my heart." To be a worthy successor to Mussolini, it would be necessary to have "the genius, the strength, and the prestige . . . of the great Chief—qualities that I certainly do not possess," Balbo declared. Anyway, in Libya, he was "very well, happy and content."

Mussolini received a copy of the letter with a handwritten note in which Balbo asked the Duce to send him to America on the first favorable occasion to speak on "A Fascist's View of Mussolini." Balbo certainly wrote the letter to the editor to cover himself, but there is an authentic ring to his protest. He did not take nearly a quarter of a century of political battles at Mussolini's side lightly. Nor, as a patriot, did he welcome the criticism of outsiders. His basic loyalty to Mussolini and the regime was genuine and proved far stronger than his doubts.

Like many of the other *gerarchi*, during fascism's first decade Balbo was often critical of Mussolini's domestic policies. He questioned the value of the corporative state, the Lateran Pacts, and Mussolini's dyarchy. Where Balbo stood out was in his opposition to the dictator's foreign policy, especially during the last years when he concluded the alliance with Germany. Here again, Balbo was not alone except in his candor and his directness. To his credit, however, Balbo showed signs of disillusion somewhat earlier than most Italians, who supported their Duce at least through the Ethiopian war.

Until early 1934, Balbo backed Mussolini's foreign policies enthusiastically. This was easy enough. Since Mussolini was chiefly preoccupied with stabilizing and securing his dictatorship, he had paid relatively little attention to foreign affairs and had followed along the lines of his Liberal predecessors. He sought to expand in Italy's traditional areas of interest: the Adriatic, the Eastern Mediterranean, the Balkans, North and East Africa. In his alliances, he maintained good relations with the British while looking for expansionist opportunities in the Mediterranean and Middle East. With the French he cultivated a spiteful rivalry in the Mediterranean, the Balkans, and the Middle East. He dismissed the League of Nations with cynical contempt.

Such policies suited Balbo. Two major influences shaped his thinking on foreign affairs: his patriotism, and his career ambi-

tions as a military man. As a good nationalist, Balbo believed in
Italy's status as a great power and he wanted her to be treated as
such. As a patriot and military man, he believed in *Realpolitik*.
Pacifism, disarmament, the League, to Balbo were both unfascist
and unworkable. On this point, he had not changed his position
from his *tesina orale* during his university days.

As air minister Balbo used both his office and his fame as an
aviator to further Mussolini's foreign policies. Often he worked
quite directly with the Duce, coordinating trips, appearances,
and speeches with shifts in foreign policy line. In 1927, Mussolini
was busily cultivating the British alliance. On a trip to London,
Balbo and Sir Samuel Hoare exchanged toasts about the inaltera-
ble and enduring nature of Italian-English friendship. With
France, Balbo helped stir up rivalry with Italy's "Latin sister." In
coordination with Mussolini's visit to Libya in April, 1926, Balbo
created a furor during his four-day tour of Tunisia. Again in an
anti-French vein, in March, 1930, in Genoa, Balbo announced
that Italy's "years of vassalage had gone forever. We do not want
to be second to anyone."[15] In July, 1932, he carried out Mussolini's directives to torpedo the Geneva disarmament conference—
including Grandi. In the spring of that year, Balbo and Mussolini
intrigued with Spanish anti-republican rebels to support a coup
that aborted.

His disenchantment with Mussolini's foreign policy began in
1933, during his last year with the Aeronautica. "He sees the
international situation as black, and us without a clear line,
against everyone, suspected by everyone," Ojetti remarked in
February of 1934.[16] Disappointment over his transfer to Libya
undoubtedly colored Balbo's judgment, but there was more: Mussolini had changed his policies. With Hitler's rise to power, the
Duce knew that he could play on British and French fears of a
resurgent Germany, and he embarked on a far more ambitious
and adventurous policy. First came a challenge to the British with
the "Mediterranean crisis" in the summer of 1935; then the
Ethiopian conflict and the Spanish civil war; and finally, with the
Rome-Berlin Axis, the beginnings of the German alliance.

Balbo's criticisms of the new line were not always consistent.
Sometimes his common sense appeared to war with his love of

adventure and his ambition. He knew about Italy's military weaknesses firsthand and dreaded the prospect of war, "any war," claimed Federzoni.[17] Yet in the summer, 1935, "Mediterranean crisis," for example, Balbo reportedly was ready to gamble far more recklessly than Mussolini. Imperial rivalries in the Mediterranean and Anglo-French fears of Mussolini's designs on Ethiopia prompted the crisis. The British responded by assembling their Mediterranean fleet in July; the Italians countered by sending two divisions and seven hundred aircraft to Libya during the first days of September, and a third division followed a week later. The British, acutely aware of how ill prepared their Mediterranean forces were, summoned the Home Fleet. The "crisis" disappeared in the shadow of Mussolini's attack on Ethiopia in October.[18]

According to De Bono, Balbo, as governor of Libya and supreme commander of Italy's forces in North Africa, was the one to call for reinforcements in Libya. Badoglio opposed sending the troops; "it was Balbo who insisted, but it was a stupidity."[19] Balbo was also ready to attack the Home Fleet when it entered the Mediterranean, according to police reports. "Mussolini, however, did not dare and it was later learned that [the English] had no ammunition, so that the stroke would have succeeded completely and by humiliating London the history of Italy and of the world would have been changed."[20] For that error Italy would pay dearly, Balbo predicted. When England rearmed within two years, she would want her revenge "and we will have a much harder bone than Abyssinia to deal with," he warned. Rumors circulated that Balbo was also ready to head an expeditionary force that would strike out across Egypt and march on Alexandria and the Suez Canal. In a letter written three years after the crisis, Balbo referred to such an operation "according to my plan."[21]

Whether Balbo was really ready to attack the Home Fleet and march on the Canal is difficult to say. Police reports dated six months after the fact, rumors in diaries, and Balbo's own boastful reference are not the best evidence. Yet such proposals sound typical of him. In October, 1922, he had been ready to march on Rome; in the fall of 1935, he might well have been ready to march on Suez—even on information obtained from tourist guidebooks, as his enemies jeered.[22] Such a coup, if successful, would have once again transformed him into a national hero and repositioned him on political center stage.

Yet, as always, Balbo's enthusiasms were subject to sudden changes. Five months after he urged Mussolini to take on the Home Fleet, Balbo was dubious about Italy's chances against Ethiopia. Under De Bono's command, Mussolini's invasion had bogged down in January, 1936, and Italy faced League of Nations sanctions. In a remarkable display of indiscretion that embarrassed his listener, Balbo poured out his frustrations and fears to the German consul in Naples, Hermann Immelen.[23]

"We are sitting in a circle of fire," Balbo told the consul. Rarely had such an enterprise on such a scale been undertaken with such lack of competence and such frivolous ingenuity, he asserted. In every respect—diplomatic, political, financial, and military— Mussolini had failed in his preparations. In his diplomacy, the Duce had placed far too much importance on the process of negotiation with Laval and not enough on the substance; in his defiance of the League of Nations Mussolini had badly miscalculated. Balbo himself had no respect for the organization, he said, but no country in the world could survive long against the pressures of fifty-two nations. Even Germany in the First World War, although far more powerful and better prepared than Italy was now, had succumbed to the dozens of nations allied against her. The Grand Council, Balbo claimed, had not anticipated that matters would go so far, that Italy would go to war over Ethiopia. Mussolini had simply presented the council with a *fait accompli*. As for Italy's military failures in Ethiopia, these were no surprise, said Balbo, for the operations had been entrusted to that old and worn-out general, De Bono, who simply was not up to the task. Balbo did not see any quick solution. In the best of cases, with no international complications, he anticipated several years before a tolerable situation would be reached. In the meantime, he worried about the costs of the campaign. "We are spending as if Father had already died," he observed tartly.

At the heart of Italy's dilemma was the problem of Mussolini. "The Chief," as Balbo referred to him, perhaps with a touch of sarcasm, was living in isolation within his four walls, neither seeing nor hearing reality. Flatterers surrounded him and told him only what he wanted to hear. "If someone hears a hundred times a day that he is a genius, he will begin to believe in his own infallibility," concluded Balbo.

To some extent, sour grapes motivated such comments. Balbo had hoped to command the military operations and was disappointed when De Bono was chosen. But even earlier he had shown himself cool to Mussolini's projects in Ethiopia. In March, 1935, he had objected strenuously to sending either Libyan troops or laborers to Ethiopia, and in the end sent one Libyan division in place of the 25,000 troops originally requested.[24]

Corridors buzzed with Balbo's reputed anti-war attitudes. A month after the conversation with Immelen, Dino Alfieri of the fascist ministry of propaganda questioned Balbo: Why was he so passive before foreign press reports that he was against the war? In his reply, March 6, 1936, Balbo failed to disclaim his criticisms, "if a higher sense of responsibility toward the Chief and the nation can be called criticism."[25] Shortly afterwards, however, in an interview with a French paper, Balbo assumed a positive and patriotic tone. It was better to settle the matter of Ethiopia in 1935 than in 1940, he declared; by then, the League of Nations would have armed the emperor and enabled him to defend his rights, including—Balbo added sarcastically—the right to maintain slavery. As for the financial sacrifice, Balbo stated, if it proved necessary "for us and for our children" to "eat bread and onions" for ten years to pay for such a venture, he was ready to do so.

Such declarations, of course, did not scotch the rumors, the police reports, the accusations: Balbo was sour on the war because he was not in command of it; Balbo was benefiting from the war because the troops called up for the war and stationed in Libya had taken a liking to him; Balbo had not shown enough enthusiasm in Tripoli in celebrating the capture of Addis Ababa.[26] The last charge, from Attilio Teruzzi, minister of Italian Africa, especially infuriated Balbo—though perhaps he suspected that this was another of Mussolini's jabs to keep him on the defensive. How could he, supreme commander of the Italian forces in North Africa, who had been ready to march on Alexandria and liberate the Suez Canal, fail to rejoice in the Italian victory? So Balbo fulminated in a letter of March 28, 1938.

Balbo's opposition to the Ethiopian war was a quarrel over means, not ends. The patriot in him certainly rejoiced in the triumph; so did the imperialist. Overpopulated countries like Italy needed colonies, he told the *New York Times*. "The world simply must recognize the problem and do something about it"; otherwise, as history had demonstrated, "the only way to get what you want is to go after it."[27] Yet Balbo was undoubtedly dismayed, as he told Immelen, at the Duce's clumsy methods—and he was not alone. Many of his friends, such as Ojetti and Federzoni, were also disturbed. Federzoni, with Marshals Badoglio and Enrico Caviglia and prominent senators, in September, 1935, had gone to see the king about Mussolini's provocative and belligerent diplomacy.[28]

Barely two months after the fall of Addis Ababa in May, 1936, the Spanish civil war erupted. Mussolini, drunk with his African victory, intervened massively. "Crazy," was Balbo's reaction—or so Farinacci claimed.[29] Even Federzoni admitted that Balbo was "lukewarm" at best.[30] Yet the civil war was not Balbo's first acquaintance with Spanish politics.[31] Between 1932 and 1934, with Mussolini, Balbo was involved in at least two anti-republican plots. In April of 1932 he received Juan Ansaldo, a Spanish aviator and monarchist who had been sent to Italy to win support for an insurrection to be headed by General Sanjurjo. Balbo promised arms and ammunition as soon as the uprising, scheduled for August 10, occurred. It failed, and the following year in the autumn Ansaldo returned, this time with the monarchist Calvo Sotelo. The Spaniards met with Balbo and Mussolini again. Most likely, they only wanted to find out if the Duce would be willing to back them again. A few months later, in March, 1934, shortly after Balbo had assumed his post in Libya, four anti-Liberal monarchists came to Rome seeking help. Balbo signed a written agreement promising that Italy would grant diplomatic recognition to the new regime as soon as feasible. Mussolini verbally promised guns and money. He then left the room and the Spaniards continued their discussions with Balbo alone. He laid particular stress on Italy's main diplomatic concern: maintaining the status quo in the Mediterranean. Mussolini feared that the Iberian peninsula might become a bridge or transit station for French colonial troops making their way to the continent.

Balbo served as more than simply a go-between in these intrigues. In 1931, he had suggested to Mussolini that Italy should take advantage of the crisis in Spain to claim Melilla in Spanish Morocco as a military base.[32] In addition to arranging, in the meetings of 1934, for arms and ammunition for the insurgents, Balbo also planned to train about twenty insurrectionists in Libya.[33] All these negotiations were handled as a private affair among Balbo, Mussolini, and the Spaniards. The Italian foreign ministry, the ministry of war, the intelligence service (SIM) were all kept in the dark or told after the fact.

Against this background, Balbo's lack of support for the civil war appears surprising, but the contradiction is only apparent, for the two affairs are quite different. As veteran diplomat Raffaele Guariglia noted in his memoirs, the anti-republican plots were bits of extramural diplomacy normally left to intelligence services.[34] They were low-risk enterprises that involved no major official commitments or diplomatic shifts. Even the arms were to be delivered *after* the insurrections had broken out. Mussolini found these intrigues useful to keep the foreign ministry on its toes and remind them who was boss. Balbo was probably attracted to the intrigues because they appealed to his "Don Quixote spirit," as Guariglia called it. The Spanish civil war was something else: a massive commitment for which Italy was no better prepared than she had been for Ethiopia; a war with ideological overtones that challenged traditional diplomatic alignments and that tied Italy closer to Germany. Like Ethiopia, Spain offered no opportunities for Balbo. Finally, and most disturbing, the Spanish adventure confirmed what Balbo had sensed at least since the beginnings of the Ethiopian war: Mussolini had changed.

Balbo had described the transformation quite accurately in his conversation with the German consul in January, 1936. Isolated and surrounded by adulators, "he saw and felt nothing of reality."[35] Many others confirmed this judgment. They commented on Mussolini's terrifying solitude, his lack of contact with ordinary mankind, his habit of speaking in private as if he were addressing large crowds, his refusal or his inability to listen to criticism.

Unfortunately, after Ethiopia, the Duce's prestige and charisma were unassailable. Within the fascist hierarchy, public or official dissent vanished. "If you attended the meeting of the Council of Ministers, which lasts at most an hour because no one else speaks besides him, you'd feel even more humiliated than here [in the Foreign Office]," Ciano told Bastianini in 1939.[36] Nevertheless, the *gerarchi* did little more than grumble and murmur. When asked why he did not resign, Ciano replied, "I'd be ready to do it if the others would also, but everyone complains and no one tells him with the necessary firmness that things can't go on like this."[37] "I can't find myself anymore because so many things are going smash," complained De Bono. "Talk to the Boss about it? Never. Mine would be a solitary voice. Everyone or nearly everyone thinks like me, but who has the courage to speak up?"[38] For those who worked closely with Mussolini, tyrannicide, of course, was always an option. "Should Brutus' dagger be raised against him?" Bastianini wondered, and then added, "but little spaces are not always easy to traverse." What made this particular "little space" difficult to cross were a residual loyalty to the man, a sense of patriotism, and a faint hope that somehow in the end, the Duce's "genius" would save Italy from disaster. "We love him with that love that nourishes itself on admiration and suffering. We stand beside him and do our duty as Italians," wrote Bastianini and so summed up the choice that virtually every major *gerarca*—including Balbo—made.[39] In the name of loyalty, patriotism, and duty, Italy went down to disaster.

Balbo made his choice. Within his fiefdoms, Libya and Ferrara, he could do pretty much as he pleased. In the Grand Council, he could speak up and he still had the authority and prestige to confront the Duce directly. But as he sensed, like the other *gerarchi*, he was on a tether. Unless he broke with the regime, there was little he could do to stop Mussolini. Should he give up his position, resign his many offices? Should he risk more, perhaps even his life, by organizing a revolt? Beyond his immediate coterie of faithful, who would have followed him? The other *gerarchi*, suspicious, mistrustful, jealous, perhaps ready to betray him for the sake of their own advantage? The timid king and the army, who feared civil war? Even if he succeeded in ousting Mussolini, would he have been capable of filling the Duce's shoes, of living up to the larger-than-life image that Mussolini and the fascist propaganda machine had conjured up? Other moral questions of military discipline, of patriotic duty, of loyalty and friendship assailed him. In 1929, he claimed that he had given up politics for the Aeronautica; similarly, in 1936, perhaps to comfort himself, he told the German consul that he was out of politics. He had a job to do in Libya and was determined to do it in the most "brilliant" way possible.[40] From 1936 to 1940, fascism was a slowly sinking ship. Balbo chose to stay aboard, bail, and from time to time shout advice to a deaf captain.

"He says that he doesn't trust the Germans. That one day they will let us down. That they may well turn against us," Ciano noted in his diary in 1937.[41] And three years later: "Balbo does not discuss the Germans. He hates them. And it is this incurable hatred which guides his reasoning."[42] One of the chief sources of Balbo's reputation as a *frondeur* was his Germanophobia. With his patriotic background, his admiration for the Risorgimento, and his experiences as a war veteran, his hostility toward the Germans is not surprising. Nevertheless, his Germanophobia was neither fixed nor implacable. He despised the Nazi regime; he had nothing but contempt for its racist policies, and he opposed Mussolini courageously when the dictator introduced similar policies into Italy. Yet Balbo's attitude toward the Germans was full of quirks and inconsistencies. On the one hand, he spoke out against any rapprochement with the Nazis. He resisted both the Axis and the Pact of Steel. Yet he maintained correct, even cordial, relations with top Nazis, especially those such as Goering, Milch, and Udet, whom he had met as air minister. For a reputed Germanophobe, Balbo found an odd confidant when he poured out his frustrations to the German consul in January, 1936. That conversation contained no hint of hostility toward Germany. On the contrary, Balbo claimed that Italian-German relations were a subject "close to his heart" and he regretted that the first Mussolini-Hitler meeting in Venice in 1934 had not gone more smoothly. In August, 1938, Balbo visited Germany. In Libya, he consistently hosted visiting Nazi dignitaries: Hess came in 1936, and Himmler the following year. In January, 1939, he went hunting with Udet, and in April he hosted Goering. Balbo did so even when he must have understood that such actions could only support the very policies that he opposed. Like the *Padano,* within the limits of dissent allowed by the regime Balbo spoke out—but only within those limits. From his friend Bottai Balbo demanded "I don't know what sort of heroic opposition."[43] But in dealing with the Nazis, Balbo himself, mercurial, temperamental, susceptible to Mussolini's assurances, did not always show the stuff of heroes.

Balbo was clearest and at his best in opposing Mussolini's racial policies. Mussolini proclaimed them officially for the first time with the "Manifesto della Razza" published on July 14, 1938. As usual, however, Mussolini had launched a trial anti-Semitic campaign in the newspapers during the spring and Balbo had sensed what was coming. He told the king, during a royal visit to Libya in May, "I'm here in Africa, but I'm hearing certain news about the Jews. Surely we're not going to imitate the Germans!"[44]

But Mussolini, more out of political and propagandistic motives than conviction, did decide to imitate the Germans. Mussolini's anti-Semitic policies were totally alien to Balbo. Far more gregarious and, thanks to his travels as an aviator, far more worldly, Balbo shared none of Mussolini's personal mistrust of Jews. Balbo had learned his politics in Ferrara, where Jews had reached positions of prominence and power. The city's prosperous Jewish community numbered about seven hundred. Most of them were middle class, engaged in business, the professions, and education. They were, according to a 1936 police report prompted by a rare anti-Semitic incident, industrious and hard-working, totally loyal to the fascist regime and to Italy.[45] The incident was attributed to students who had failed their university examinations. Balbo was perfectly sincere when he proclaimed publicly in Tripoli in October, 1937, "I do not differentiate between Catholic Italians and Jewish Italians. We are all Italians."[46] Since his adolescence, he added, he had had only three "true and sincere" friends. "And do you want to know who these friends were?" he continued theatrically. "Well, all three were Jews."[47]

Mussolini's anti-Semitic campaign, then, violated Balbo's personal code of friendship and struck at his political arrangements in Ferrara. In addition, to him such policies had nothing to do with Italy or with fascism. The *Padano* had made this abundantly clear four years before the Manifesto on Race was published. In 1934, the paper had engaged in a brief but violent polemic against the anti-Semitic *Il Tevere*, published in Rome. The exchange was significant, for the Roman paper was known as a stalking-horse for Mussolini.

The polemic began over a book review, a scholarly study on the origins of the Jews. *Il Tevere* declared itself alarmed at the book's conclusion—that no Jewish "race" existed. The *Padano* replied furiously, "A 'Jewish question' does not exist in Italy. *Il Tevere* is trying to create one."[48] Furthermore, the Ferrarese paper charged, *Il Tevere* was the "official organ" of national socialism in Italy and a servant of Hitler. Such doctrines as the Nazis espoused, in which politics is reduced to "biology, if not to the zoology of racism . . . is not made for Italy. In fact, it is not made for a civilized people." Ironically, the *Padano* ended the polemic by invoking the authority of the Duce: in 1932, Mussolini himself had warned the Germans against racism, the paper concluded.[49]

Balbo's policies toward the Jews in Libya provide odd but unmistakable confirmation of his opposition to Mussolini's racial policies.[50] When Balbo first arrived in the colony, the Jewish community there, which numbered nearly 30,000, welcomed him enthusiastically, for he had a reputation for being sympathetic to Jewish problems. His first few weeks in office, for instance, coincided with the *Padano* polemic against *Il Tevere*.

The Jewish community that Balbo found in Libya, however, was profoundly different from the middle-class professionals he was accustomed to in Ferrara. In the colony, the Jews lived on the same level as the Arabs and the other indigenous Libyan peoples and suffered from the same problems of poverty, illiteracy, high unemployment, and high birthrate. More than 22,000—about two-thirds of the entire Jewish community—clustered in Tripoli, where, for the most part, they worked as artisans and petty tradesmen. In all of Libya, there were only fourteen Jews who were professionals, and two who were artists.

The "backward" state of the Libyan Jewish community disturbed Balbo and he was determined to change it. Like most European colonial administrators of his day, Balbo believed in his nation's "civilizing mission." "Backward" peoples could and should be raised to the level of European civilization—meaning the standards of the mother country. His determination and his occasionally forceful methods—not unusual in a colonial context—embroiled him in conflict with the Libyan Jewish community between 1935 and 1937 and led to charges that he was anti-Semitic.

At issue were questions of observing the Sabbath and a child marriage that Balbo considered improper. Since the Sabbath was the traditional day of rest, Jews kept their stores closed on Saturday in Tripoli. Balbo wanted the shops to remain open so that both the shopkeepers and the colony as a whole could benefit from the weekend tourist trade. Balbo's methods of enforcing his policies appeared shocking, especially in the case of the shopkeepers. He was particularly harsh on the ringleaders. Two were given ten lashes in public with a kurbash. A third, excused from the public flogging for medical reasons, served a three-month jail sentence. These incidents impressed the Jewish press abroad and some papers speculated on whether this was the beginning of an anti-Semitic campaign in Italy. The Italian Jewish press, however, did not protest the incidents; nor, significantly, did the anti-Semitic Italian papers play up the events.

Balbo was certainly guilty of meddling in the life of the Libyan Jewish community, of trying to force it to conform to the Italian colonial regime. In his mind, a better-integrated community would benefit Jew and Gentile alike. He did not consider his policies to be anti-Semitic. A speech he gave in October of 1937 to a reunion of Blackshirts at the Teatro Miramare in Tripoli makes the point. In a traditional October review of fascist accomplishments during the year, Balbo raised the "Jewish question."[51] When the crowd began yelling "Death to the Jews" and "Jews get out of our country," Balbo angrily demanded silence. He then declared that he once again wanted to pay tribute to the "industriousness, the discipline, and the loyalty" of the Libyan Jewish community to the regime. He also apologized for enforcing the law on keeping the shops open on the Sabbath, but argued that the policy was good both for the Jewish community and the city. Then, with his usual theatrical flair, he called on a Jewish member of the audience to stand. "Raise your arm," Balbo commanded. The man raised his arm. "Now raise the other," Balbo ordered. The man replied, "Excellency, it's missing." Balbo then drove home his little homily. "Look, comrades: this Jew sacrificed his arm during the Great War, fighting like a good Italian."

Balbo's application of the 1938 racial laws in Libya confirms his opposition to them. He avoided ideological arguments, knowing that outright confrontation would only arouse Mussolini's intransigence. Instead, Balbo concentrated on ways to lessen the bite of the legislation. In a letter of January 19, 1939, he assured Mussolini that the laws were being applied in the colony. Jewish government employees had been dismissed and Jewish students were barred from secondary schools. A blanket application of the provisions, however, would lead to serious disruptions in the local economy, he pointed out. He gave examples of special cases that should be exempted: women employees of cigarette factories, nurses in certain hospitals, government interpreters. "I cannot be accused of weakness, if, as everyone remembers, two years ago I did not hesitate to order the flogging of Jews in the public marketplace," Balbo wrote.[52] Only at the conclusion of the letter did Balbo hint at his dissent with the regime's policies. "The Jews are already dead; it is not necessary to rage against them," Balbo wrote, especially since their plight was now arousing the compassion of their traditional enemies, the Arabs.

Mussolini agreed to Balbo's request that the laws be applied "in the manner suggested by the highly particular local situation." The Duce, however, could not restrain himself from a parting shot: "reminding you that the Jews appear to be but are never definitively dead." Thanks to Balbo's intervention, Libyan Jews remained virtually undisturbed until after his death.

In his battle against the racial laws, Balbo knew that what he did in Libya mattered relatively little compared to the struggle in Italy. When the Manifesto on Race was published, Balbo immediately spoke out against it. "Balbo is indignant and will speak at the Grand Council," noted De Bono in his diary for September 7, 1938.[53] When his close friend Bottai, as minister of education, proposed legislation excluding Jewish children from public schools, Balbo was "scandalized"—but still susceptible to being soothed and reassured by Mussolini.[54]

On October 6, the Grand Council met to discuss the racial laws. Of the four who spoke out against the policies, Federzoni, De Bono, Balbo, and Giacomo Acerbo, Balbo was the most vociferous—up to a point. Mussolini, as always, came well prepared. The Manifesto "could have been avoided," he claimed hypocritically several years later.[55] Yet, at the meeting, he made it clear that he had virtually dictated the document himself, and he came ready to blackmail or embarrass any recalcitrant council members into conformity.

In Balbo's case, the Duce seized on an article that Nello Quilici had published two weeks before the meeting in the prestigious journal of political and cultural affairs edited by Federzoni, *Nuova Antologia*.[56] Entitled "Defense of the Race," the article was a shabby, incoherent defense of the regime's policies. In an unnamed "provincial city" of 100,000 (Ferrara), where the author lived, the article began, the Jewish community of 750 people had achieved a remarkable degree of power—and Quilici listed the positions of authority that Jews held. How had they managed it? Invoking the crudest forms of stereotyping, Quilici "explained" how the Jews played on the good will and innocence of their Italian and Christian neighbors. The Jews extended their influence over the community like a "spiderweb" and won their positions through favoritism, "for the ability of Jewish communities to ensnare, their instinct to support their own, is well known." This favoritism was easy to carry out, for "the Jew recognizes a fellow Jew by sight, by voice, by smell," the article declared.

Such gutter racism seemed totally incongruous coming from a sophisticated journalist like Quilici. The article appeared to walk a tightrope between conformity and parody of the regime's policies. Germanic or "scientific" racism was condemned as too fantastic, arbitrary, or materialistic, but Italians were reassured that they belonged among the "oldest and most select of the northern dolichocephalic races of the continent." Perhaps for those who could read between the lines, the article was a clever balancing act between conformity and parody of the regime's policies.[57] Balbo, however, could not disavow the piece without looking ridiculous himself and perhaps harming his friend Quilici. At the Grand Council meeting, Mussolini used his advantage ruthlessly. Waving pages from the article as he spoke, the Duce announced caustically, "Listen to what has happened in a city of the Po Valley." Bottai observed, "The 'blow' strikes directly at Balbo, who tries to appear grave."[58]

When it was Balbo's turn to speak at the meeting, he did not raise Federzoni's legal-constitutional objections, nor philosophical and consitutional arguments like Acerbo's. Instead, like De Bono,

Balbo sought to mitigate the effects of the laws. Balbo recalled how many Jews had backed the fascist revolution and had been entrusted with positions within the hierarchy. He specifically urged broader "exemptions" for war veterans. According to some accounts, he proposed that soldiers who had been awarded the war cross should be exempt. When Mussolini refused on the grounds that the award was too common, Balbo shot back, "Then if you were Jewish, you would not be exempt."[59]

Mussolini, with Buffarini-Guidi, Farinacci, and Bottai supporting him, fought against any deviation from a hard line. Nevertheless, in the long meeting Balbo and the rest of the *fronde* scored a partial victory. Mussolini wavered, "wanting to soften a bit." The specific provisions for discrimination or exclusion did not matter, he concluded. The important point was to raise the problem. "Now anti-Semitism has been injected into the Italian blood. It will continue to circulate and develop by itself."[60]

Balbo carried on the fight two weeks later, at another meeting of the Grand Council. On this occasion he defended his proposal for full citizenship for the Arabs in Libya. In large part because the proposal contradicted the racial laws, Balbo in the end had to be content with the far more limited "little citizenship."

Personally, then, Balbo spoke out with great courage and integrity against the racial laws. Even Mussolini paid him tribute— well after Balbo's death. "He defended them with great courage. No one was able to touch a hair of Commendatore Ravenna," commented Mussolini. Nevertheless, Balbo's opposition stopped well short of the "heroic gestures" he had suggested for Bottai. Nor did his entourage over which he had such ascendancy, including Quilici and the *Padano,* show much of the *frondeur* spirit.

During the summer and fall of 1938, the *Padano* exhibited little opposition to the regime's official line. As Nello Quilici had done in his *Nuova Antologia* article, the paper differentiated Italian fascist "spiritual" racism from the "scientific" or "physical" concepts of the Nazis. The eccentric but often influential writer-philosopher and artist Giulio Evola echoed these themes in the paper's columns.[61] Yet the paper did its best to justify and defend the regime's policies. Quilici, using a line similar to the one in his *Nuova Antologia* piece, presented a populist defense of Mussolini's policies. The real meaning of the regime's policies, he explained in an article entitled "To the Source," was that they cleared away the overlay of values that suffocated the true "popular soul."[62] With an unusual nod of approval toward the German example, Quilici praised the great party gatherings at Nuremberg as an outpouring of the popular will. Italy's policies, too, would free the people suffocated by the Jewish-Freemason bourgeoisie, would liberate the "popular soul" from its subservience to "the middle class, ossified in its intellectual rigidities, chained to its predatory instincts, and basically indifferent to any high ideals."

Such ingenuous nonsense must have embarrassed Quilici as well as Balbo. The articles often appear defensive, as if the writer were conscientiously trying to make the best of a bad lot. The editorial that followed the October 6 Grand Council meeting, for example, defended what had been done.[63] So many exemptions and exclusions were available that, by Quilici's calculations, at least a third of the Italian Jewish community would be exempt from the provisions, he wrote. Compared to the policies in Germany and Hungary, Italy's provisions were mild and proved that fascism was not interested in "vendettas"—only in preserving "the integrity of Italians of pure Italian race." Yet, as if ashamed and alarmed at how all-consuming the racial issue had become, Quilici tried to minimize it. More significant problems such as the empire and the new order in Europe needed to be dealt with, he concluded.

The nagging question remains: why did the *Padano* not take a stronger stand? Why did it not reflect more clearly Balbo's personal convictions and the position he took in the Grand Council or in Libya? Why did Balbo, who was ultimately responsible, not make the paper reflect his voice? There are more possible explanations than there is evidence. The *Padano* was Balbo's paper, but it was more than his mouthpiece. Although he followed the paper quite closely, he was off in Libya and absorbed in other matters. Moreover, Quilici had a mind and career of his own. Despite their close friendship, they often saw each other only in passing—a "radar friendship," Quilici's widow recalled.[64] Hence, the paper and Balbo were not perfectly synchronized. A second argument reflects the role of newspapers under the regime. Balbo's speeches in the Grand Council or his conversations with friends would have spread by means of the grapevine. Nevertheless, they were relatively innocuous, unlikely to raise much public clamor. Public opposition in a newspaper was something else again—something that Mussolini the journalist, always concerned with the morning's headlines, was not prepared to tolerate.

How could Quilici, a sophisticated journalist, write articles like the one in *Nuova Antologia* or the embarrassed defenses of racism in the *Padano?* His wife's explanation was the familiar one of the collaborator: he went along to prevent what might have been worse. In particular, concerning the *Nuova Antologia* article, she claimed that Renzo Ravenna, a close friend of Balbo's, *podestà* of Ferrara and a prominent member of the city's Jewish community, asked Quilici to write it rather than having some unknown do the dirty work. Critics have pointed out that the article and the *Padano*'s stand were no worse than others of the period and contained as much implied criticism as was feasible at the time. Perhaps that is the case. Nevertheless, there is something shabby and shameful about such talents and intelligence wasted on such apparent cunning, such *furberia*. The Duce's secret was to entangle his collaborators in compromises that left them with a series of illusions: that they could collaborate and still maintain their self-respect; that somehow these unpleasant episodes, such as the Axis and the racial laws, would come to an end; that the Duce would somehow turn out to be other than what he was. If he was a master at fostering these illusions, his collaborators created their own self-delusions. Understandably, they preferred their delusions, preferred the easier path of going along with Mussolini to facing alternatives without or against him.

These considerations help to explain the quirks and inconsistencies in Balbo's Germanophobia at this time. Despite Balbo's well-publicized antipathy toward the Nazis, when Goering invited him to Germany for a visit Balbo accepted. Perhaps his much-publicized friendship with Goering made the prospect of the visit somewhat more palatable. How much that friendship was official—the comradeship of aviators and air ministers of allied countries—and how much was genuine is difficult to tell. The two men did share a passion for aviation, for hunting, and for living in the grand manner. By 1938, they had known each other for six years. Even before the Nazis came to power, Balbo had advised Goering on the future development of the Luftwaffe and had been Goering's guest. Balbo "makes an excellent impression. Friendly greetings were exchanged," Goebbels recorded in his diary for December 10, 1932. Goering certainly worked to develop the relationship. When a German edition of the *Diario 1922* was published in 1933, Goering wrote the preface; when in July of that year a German newspaper claimed that Balbo was a baptized Jew, Goering ordered the paper to suspend publication for three months.[65]

Balbo's visit to Germany, August 9–13, 1938, came about a month after the publication of the Manifesto on Race. The German motive for the visit was clear. With the possibility of a formal alliance between the two regimes in the air, the Nazis wanted to highlight Italian-German cooperation and specifically the military comradeship between Balbo and Goering. Goering and Milch had their own motives: to show off the Luftwaffe. Ever since the Olympic Games of 1936, Goering had been inviting the top authorities and personalities of the aviation world. Balbo was one more in the parade.

Mussolini wanted Balbo to make the trip in order to flatter him and to dampen his hostility toward the Germans. "As Balbo seems to be worrying about the hidden reasons for his mission, the Duce authorized me to tell him that he wanted to have him as the most competent—'which is not true,' he immediately added—observer of German air power now that things are moving toward a showdown," Ciano wrote.[66]

From Mussolini's point of view the trip proved to be a great success. Balbo was favorably impressed with the warmth of his reception in Germany. From the moment he crossed the German border and, in the air, exchanged telegrams of greetings and welcome with Hitler, the Germans turned out to pay him tribute. The Italian embassy in Berlin concluded that the Nazis were saluting him for his achievements as a pioneering aviator and thanking him for his help during early phases of the Luftwaffe's reconstruction. That was the main theme of Goering's luncheon toast to Balbo at Karinhall on the first day of the trip. Balbo was a man whose friendship for Germany "did not wait until Germany had found her place in the sun," declared Goering, and recalled Balbo's visit to Germany in December, 1932, on the eve of the Nazi ascent to power. Balbo replied as if he were a fanatic supporter of the Axis: "Germany and Italy will remain invincible if, guided by Benito Mussolini and Adolf Hitler, they continue to follow a common policy."

Between the ceremonial wreath layings at Unter den Linden in Berlin on the first day, and the exhibitions of Luftwaffe prowess on the third and fourth days at Zingst in Pomerania and at the experimental center at Rechlin on the Baltic came the usual round of parties and receptions. There Balbo met top Nazis such as Hess and von Ribbentrop. The highlight of the final day was a visit to Berchtesgaden, where Hitler honored his guest by coming to the door to greet him. He then hosted Balbo for afternoon tea. Many of Hitler's entourage, some of whom were notorious Italophobes, distrusted Balbo. They suspected him of being an Anglophile, gossiped about his Jewish origins and his associations with the Masons, and speculated about his opposition to Mussolini.[67] Hitler disagreed—although there is some dispute about this. According to his "table talk" in 1942, he regarded Balbo as the only worthy successor to Mussolini, as a man who was a true popular *condottiero* both within the armed forces and in the ranks of the fascist party.[68] But Hitler also described Balbo as having a "Jewish face."[69]

A photograph of the Berchtesgaden meeting shows Balbo in uniform, dripping with sashes, gold braid, medals, and ribbons, looking a bit like a general in a musical comedy. He manages a smile, but he appears overwhelmed. Hitler, austere in a tunic, unadorned except for a swastika armband, also manages a smile. His arms are folded across his chest, as if to emphasize his lack of rapport with his guest. Apparently there was very little. Hitler, according to his interpreter, launched into a long harangue about Italian-German friendship, the power of the German army, and the political and moral weakness of the British. Balbo agreed that the German army would tip the balance in the Mediterranean in favor of the Axis, but he disagreed with Hitler's assessment of the British. From his trips to England, Balbo said, he knew that Englishmen were not all playboy types like "Mister Eden." In the Mediterranean, Gibraltar, Malta, Cyprus, and Egypt were manned by English of the Rudyard Kipling school who still believed in the great traditions of the British empire. Furthermore, Balbo added, he knew all too well the capabilities and limits of

Fig. 24. Balbo reviews Nazi troops during his visit to Germany in August, 1938 (Caproni Museum Archive)

Italy's air force. Hitler, annoyed, changed the subject, and Balbo later boasted that he had spoken bluntly.[70]

The visit had no particular diplomatic consequences, but Balbo "was enchanted with the visit, the Germans, their aeroplanes, everything. Now that his vanity has been flattered, he talks like the most convinced supporter of the Axis," Ciano snickered. Balbo gave no sign of having understood Mussolini's ulterior motives for the trip. "One is always happy when one does not understand," Ciano quoted Mussolini as remarking. Others, too, noted Balbo's momentary enthusiasm for Germany. He had company; the king was reported to have said that now it was time to establish the alliance with Berlin, since "with these others [Britain and France] there was nothing to be done."[71]

Yet, like most of Balbo's enthusiasms, this one faded quickly. He reverted to his Germanophobia and to his opposition to any diplomatic rapprochement with the Nazis. When the Axis was announced in 1936, he reportedly confronted Mussolini "with a

Fig. 25. Adolf Hitler and Balbo during Balbo's visit to Germany in August, 1938 (G. Bucciante, ed., *Vita di Balbo*)

pistol on the table."[72] When the Anschluss came up for discussion before the Grand Council, Balbo was the only member who opposed Mussolini's decision to accept the annexation. "Balbo fears for Trieste and criticizes the proceedings of the Germans," Ciano remarked, and added maliciously, "naturally, he does this behind the scenes and in whispers."[73] Like the majority of Italians, Balbo greeted the Munich crisis of September, 1938, with an enormous sense of relief. At the request of the British and French, Mussolini helped mediate the crisis. For one last moment he appeared to live up to the image of the great statesman and "good European." By Christmas, however, he was tilting toward a formal link with Germany.

The prospect of a formal alliance with the Nazis appalled Balbo, and shortly before a Grand Council meeting of this period he told

Federzoni, "You'll see, I'll put that lunatic on his guard against the blunder he is about to commit."[74] He then spoke, according to Federzoni, with a "freedom of judgment" never before used in matters of foreign policy in the halls of Palazzo Venezia. The two revolutions, Nazi and fascist, had nothing in common, neither in their origins nor in their content, Balbo declared. Italians cared nothing for the analogies between the two systems. In fact, he said, the more they knew, the more they would oppose the Nazis. No alliance could be more unpopular. Italian hatred for the Germans was both justified and insuperable. He invoked memories of the Risorgimento, including the five days of Milan; he invoked the glories of World War I, including the intervention crisis and Vittorio Veneto. "For the sake of the nation—or for the salvation of the regime—Italy should never have tied herself to Germany," he claimed. Mussolini, his eyes bright with anger, blustered and puffed until at last he turned to Ciano to provide a reply. Balbo's peroration made little difference. Mussolini had his own frustrations with the Germans. Nevertheless, at the Grand Council meeting of March 21, in a speech that Ciano described as "argumentative, logical, cold, and heroic," the Duce called for "uncompromising loyalty to the Axis." De Bono and Balbo jeered, and Balbo retorted, "You are licking Germany's boots."[75]

Yet three weeks later, April 9–12, Balbo was hosting Goering in Libya. The visit reciprocated Balbo's visit to Germany of the previous summer. Once again in squiring his portly guest, often resplendent in his white *Reichsmarschall* uniform, to see the sights of the colony, Balbo was promoting the Axis—at least officially. Unofficially, in a series of calculated incidents, he delighted in embarrassing and humiliating his guest.[76] As he often did, Balbo invited a dozen middle-class Jews to a dinner at the Governor's Palace. Since the occasion was in his honor, Goering could scarcely miss the point. In a second insult, Balbo included a visit to the Jewish quarter and to the synagogue as part of a tour of Tripoli. Goering contracted a "diplomatic illness." Balbo's personal physician found nothing wrong and claimed that outdoor exposure to the African climate would be particularly beneficial to the visitor's "ailment." Balbo contrived one final prank on Goering the art collector. While touring Sabratha, Goering admired a statuette of a bacchante and asked to buy it. Balbo promised it as

Fig. 26. Air Marshal Balbo and Reichsmarschall Hermann Goering, the two flying air ministers (Caproni Museum Archive)

a gift, but claimed that first he needed permission from the ministry of antiquities. Instead, he sent a replica—made, on Balbo's orders, by a Jewish artisan. The replica adorned Goering's living room at Karinhall; the original graced the antechamber of the governor's office in Tripoli.

Such tricks undoubtedly vented some of Balbo's anxieties and frustrations. They did nothing to prevent Italy's slide toward disaster. On May 22, 1939, Mussolini signed what he dubbed the Pact of Steel. Nine days earlier, during the negotiations, Ciano had remarked, "I have never read such a pact. It contains some real dynamite."[77] Among its peculiarities, the pact did not contain the usual "defensive" formula: that only if one partner was first attacked by an aggressor was the second partner bound to provide help. Under the circumstances, the Germans were likely to launch a war first. The Pact of Steel bound the Italians to follow them.

The *Padano*, like the rest of the Italian press, greeted this "new style" diplomacy with enthusiasm. Among the advantages of the pact, Quilici explained, was that it did away with such subtleties as defining who the aggressor was; it eliminated the possibility of one side or the other "defecting" under the hypocritical formula of "neutrality"; it cut out the shameful Italian tendency to swing back and forth between diplomatic blocs, "the swing of the daily blackmail," as Quilici phrased it. Balbo's comment to Grandi and De Bono as they sat at a café on Via Veneto was less sanguine: "May God help us."[78]

Worse was yet to come, much worse. First there was the astounding Nazi-Soviet Nonaggression Pact of August 23, 1939. Nine days later, Hitler attacked Poland, and World War II began. For Balbo, as for many of the other *gerarchi*, the Nazi-Soviet Pact seemed particularly infamous—a betrayal of everything that fascism stood for. According to one report, upon hearing of the pact Balbo flew to Rome and demanded, unsuccessfully, a convocation of the Grand Council with the goal of reexamining the alliance with Germany.[79] "I have never heard such criticism of fascism and of its internal and foreign policy as now; and from *gerarchi*," Ojetti exclaimed at the end of October. He had been present at a gathering of some of Balbo's cronies, including Bottai, Bastianini, and Vittorio Cini, at the Hotel Excelsior, one of Balbo's favorite haunts when he was in Rome.[80] That evening at a dinner party, Balbo was particularly indignant: "Balbo, soldier, was more loyal toward Mussolini; but his wrath against the Germans and the Russians is just as fierce. He repeated Bastianini's charge: an Italian, a fascist, a Catholic finds himself, thanks to Adolf Hitler, side by side with the Soviets. Every ideal has been betrayed," Ojetti observed. Then, to the amusement of the other guests, Balbo let his imagination run free: the pope should excommunicate Hitler. Three cardinals, followed by a large escort, should bear the bull of excommunication. "Picturesque; but Balbo himself admits that it would be difficult to find three cardinals capable of going there and then to prison with their heads held high," concluded Ojetti.

The Nazi-Soviet Pact, with its betrayal of both the Pact of Steel and the very anti-bolshevik cornerstone of fascist ideology, outraged Balbo and Quilici. Most Italian papers, in conformity with the new line, softened their anti-communist stand. The *Padano* did just the opposite. The paper launched an anti-bolshevik campaign so violent that it was easily interpreted as anti-German. Balbo, who had made one of his frequent trips to Ferrara during this period, may well have had a direct hand in planning the articles. The German ambassador, Hans Georg von Mackensen, in an October 12 telegram, demanded an end to the campaign, and Mussolini was furious.[81] Their annoyance increased when a number of English, French, Scandinavian, American, and Canadian newspapers reprinted the article.

"Sfasatura" (Out of Phase), the article that annoyed Mackensen, appeared in the *Padano* on October 8. In it Quilici savagely attacked a profile, published in a Roman paper, of the Soviet minister K. E. Voroshilov. The old bolshevik, an intimate of Stalin's, sounded like a tame Garibaldi instead of a gangster who raided the Imperial Bank at Tiflis, Quilici fumed. In unusually crude language, he declared that Voroshilov and his comrades, "like all the swine of bolshevik Russia, naturally do not interest us worth a damn." Whether they praise each other or knife each other, it is their business. At best there might be fewer thugs in the world. "We were born anti-communists and we want to remain that way. To the bolsheviks, not one gram of esteem or one ounce of sympathy. For us they are, and will be, tragic clowns, professional liars, models of the crudest bestiality, monsters," living at the service of one of the maddest, crudest, and most inhumane regimes in the history of the world.

Quilici followed up two days later with "Sic vos non vobis," in which he took to task those commentators who wanted to treat the Soviet Union as if it were an ordinary great power. Such an attitude totally ignored the Soviet Union as a center for the spread of communism, Quilici argued. Once again, the ministry of popular culture chastised him. Quilici admitted that perhaps his language had been intemperate, but claimed he saw nothing wrong with an anti-bolshevik line. Nevertheless, he promised not to take up the subject of the Soviets again.

Throughout the fall, however, though in more moderate language, he continued the campaign.[82] In addition to being reprinted abroad, his articles attracted a flood of Italian sympathy. Many old Blackshirts privately wrote him letters of support and complained about the betrayal of fascism's ideals. When the December 7 article appeared, Mussolini snarled, "[Balbo] thinks . . . that he can fish in troubled waters at home but he should remember that I am in a position to put everyone without exception to the wall."[83] He need not have blustered so. At this point, Balbo was not about to betray the fascist cause. He saw no alternative but to do what he considered his patriotic duty.

Chapter Sixteen

Fascist: The Model Fascist's Fascism

"It is impossible to know what he wants," Roberto Farinacci complained about his archenemy Balbo in a long, polemical letter to Mussolini in January, 1940.[1] Although Balbo could not have benefited more from the regime, he always played the *Bastian contrario*, the "contrary Joe," charged Farinacci. "We go into Africa; he declares himself against the enterprise. We go into Spain; he describes our intervention as crazy. We begin the battle against the Jews; he immediately takes a common stand with the honorary Jews, Federzoni, De Vecchi, De Bono," Farinacci grumbled. But "the most scandalous gesture" was Balbo's recent visit to the pope, and nearly as outrageous was the inaugural session at the Chamber of Deputies. There was Balbo, "the ferocious republican," together with De Bono and De Vecchi, "screaming at the top of his lungs . . . 'Long live the King.' "

Factious and self-serving as the letter was, Farinacci had a point. By 1940, Balbo had served nearly fourteen years in high government positions ranging from minister to colonial viceroy. Outwardly, he appeared little changed from his Blackshirt days: still the musketeer, still fiery and proud, with an unlimited faith in friendship, according to his friend Federzoni.[2] Beneath that appearance, however, as Balbo matured, his attitude toward politics had changed from his "youthful chimeras." "A habit of reflection was developing, a deeper sense of duty and of the seriousness of

life." He had "converted sincerely to the principles of order and he
favored a constitutional restoration." In short, according to Federzoni, Balbo had embraced those very principles—dear to the
Nationalists—that he had once rejected so contemptuously. By
early 1940, what was Balbo, the model fascist, like? And what did
fascism finally mean to him in his maturity?

He was nearly forty-four, in the prime of his life. Deeply tanned
from the African sun, his famous goatee a bit wider and more
pointed than in the past, he was "always the proud Balbo, awake and
full of vitality," remarked an American correspondent.[3] When he
was not wearing his air marshal's uniform, he appeared smaller and
his stocky figure showed signs of girth. To shed the extra pounds, he
wrapped himself in blankets and lay in the sun. He also swam,
sparred with a boxing coach, rode horseback, flew off on hunting
expeditions. His energy flowed inexhaustibly—and so did his talk. A
"self-ejecting, self-diffusing, even self-universalizing entity," art
critic Bernard Berenson concluded after a dinner at the Governor's
Palace.[4] Balbo's rush of conversational topics—pet theories about
history, about art, about politics—left no time to do any of them
justice, complained Berenson. Balbo's frenetic activity and flow of
words were a cover, for "he feared the empty spaces, the pauses,
time stopped," observed the writer Leo Longanesi in a wicked
sketch.[5] Balbo needed to be admired constantly, to be the center of
attention, even if his audience was only a servant girl pausing in the
midst of her household chores. To work off his energy, his impatience, his recurrent periods of boredom, he sometimes went to the
harbor in Tripoli and hunted seagulls. "Rifle shots are healthy, they
chase away boredom," he assured Longanesi after a session of
slaughter.

Romance provided another cure for boredom.[6] From 1936 until
his death, Balbo carried on an affair with the actress Laura Adani,
whom he met when she came to do a series of shows in Libya. A
slender, blond woman with a pointed face dominated by a large
nose, she was famous more for her charm than for her beauty.
Balbo fell deeply in love with her—partly, perhaps, because she
was seventeen years younger than he. Since she was often travelling with her company, Balbo from time to time followed her
about Italy, naively thinking that his indiscretions remained un-
observed. The police followed his movements with malicious de-

Fig. 27. Balbo and family in 1940 (l. to r., Valeria, Paolo, Donna Manù, Giuliana) (G. Fanciulli, *L'eroica vita di Balbo*)

light, and the gossips jeered that in his Claretta Petacci Mussolini had at least chosen a pretty mistress.

Spoiled and self-indulgent though he was, Balbo—unlike Mussolini and some of the other *gerarchi*—knew how to laugh at himself. When people remarked on his penchant for perpetual motion, he liked to tell the story of the Arab whom he once met in the remote southern oasis of Ghadames. "It takes me only a few hours to fly here from Tripoli," Balbo boasted to the Arab. "It takes me twenty-eight days to make the trip," replied the Arab; "how do you manage to put in the twenty-seven days that I spend in travelling?"[7]

Maturity tempered Balbo's ambitions a bit. He had been happiest leading the air force. From time to time, Mussolini still dangled a high military position before him. In August, 1939, the Duce told him, "Soon you'll return to Italy. I've thought of a position for you." When Balbo replied, "I know, at the party or on the general staff," Mussolini replied, "The party? Never. Get that out of your head."[8] For awhile, in 1936, Balbo aspired to succeed Graziani and the Duca d'Aosta as viceroy in Ethiopia.[9] Foreign newspapers continued to speculate about his posting to Ethiopia.[10] By 1938, however, Balbo had changed his mind about the attractions of East Africa. To Daodiace, who kept him informed about the rumors in Addis Ababa, Balbo wrote on June 27, 1938, "I believe that I have succeeded in thwarting the danger of my being sent to Ethiopia . . . or, to put it better, I have thwarted the danger of . . . the transfer so loudly acclaimed in Italy by the usual voices." Advise the Duca d'Aosta well, Balbo urged his friend, both for the sake of the country "and also for the undersigned who finds Addis Ababa too far from heavenly Italy."[11]

By 1938, domestic politics in Italy disgusted him. A few days before writing his letter to Daodiace, Balbo told Ciano, "There no longer exists a taste for sincerity in Italy."[12] Libya had its advantages. He was outside the domestic political brawl, but not too far; he enjoyed a free hand over his own kingdom—a freedom he would lose if he took a position such as minister of Italian Africa, another post for which he was mentioned.[13] "Balbo thinks of staying in Libya, as he realizes that that is still the best solution," Ciano observed in his diary on June 23, 1938.[14] Things had changed very little by the spring of 1940. De Bono, looking for a position himself, concluded that Libya "will remain Balbo's fiefdom for quite awhile."[15] And after his African experience? In a whimsical mood before a group of English journalists whom he had been briefing about the colonization schemes, he commented, "Who knows, once this African experience is over, whether I'm destined to teach political economy in an English university?"[16]

Another factor serving to temper Balbo's ambitions was his powerlessness. He had no other real options. Rome was only an aerial hop across the Mediterranean; nevertheless, it was difficult to intrigue from Tripoli. Even if he had put his mind to ousting Mussolini, Balbo's allies were not as powerful as his enemies.[17] In the late 1930s, Grandi, Farinacci, Ciano, and Starace were all hostile to him. His friends—Federzoni, Giovanni Giuriati, Vittorio Cini, Giuseppe Volpi, Alessandro Lessona—were either conservatives or big businessmen, "men of order" who would think twice about conspiracies, no matter how justified. Balbo's other close friend—the only one with a faith in fascism as an ideology— was Bottai, who remained deeply committed to Mussolini. In sending Balbo into "exile," Mussolini had triumphed.

As the international situation deteriorated and the regime declined, Balbo vented his frustrations and his fears about the future in caustic remarks, savage humor, and emotional confrontations. After the conquest of Ethiopia, he sometimes appeared for an appointment at Palazzo Venezia with the request, "May I speak with the Founder of the Empire?" As the Axis solidified and the prospects of war loomed, in Balbo's lexicon Mussolini became "that madman" and "a product of syphilis." Earlier, when Bottai commented, "We have a Duce but not always a chief," Balbo shot back, "He's no chief, he's a rag."[18] Finally, before his last trip back to Libya, Balbo declared angrily, "We're ten years younger than *he*, time is on our side."[19] As war approached, he blew off steam with childish threats or comments such as "one of these days I'll make a little sortie over Palazzo Venezia with a couple of little bombs."[20]

Thus, Balbo pinned his hopes—if he had any—of succeeding Mussolini on the age gap, on simply waiting until the Duce resigned or expired. In the eternal speculation on the succession, Balbo ranked very high. Mussolini preferred to avoid the question or to blackmail the monarchy with a "list" of successors, drawn up by the Grand Council, that may well have been fictitious.[21] When the issue came up before the Grand Council in

March, 1939, the members generally agreed that a triumvirate
should succeed Mussolini. Balbo and Grandi won the council's
approval. The third candidate, Galeazzo Ciano, ran into serious
opposition from De Bono and De Vecchi, and thus the matter was
left unresolved.[22] In reality, such were the animosities between
them that even a succession of Balbo and Grandi would not have
lasted.

In the meantime, Balbo strengthened his ties with the two
"principles of order," as Federzoni pointed out: the church and
the monarchy. Balbo's audience with the pope on December 8,
1939—the audience that so infuriated Farinacci—was not the
result of any personal religious change, although some claim that
he was genuinely moved and fell to his knees before the pontiff.[23]
"I do not believe that he, *quadrumvir* of the Revolution, kneeling
before the pope meant to be forgiven his long membership in the
Masonry and the murder of Don Minzoni," jeered Farinacci, who
added that Balbo had always been a "devourer of priests, an
unrepentant blasphemer and, if not more than I, an unlimited
libertine as far as women are concerned."[24] Farinacci was probably right. When Balbo was in Ferrara, he went to mass to please
his mother, and he took care to see that his children were instructed in the church.[25] Although he was a believer, according to
his wife, he was not observant.

More important to him was the church as an institution and
symbol of political power and order. In 1929, he had opposed the
Lateran Pacts, but he now saw the church as one of the keys to
transforming Libya from a colonial society to a "fourth shore."
Accordingly, he encouraged and facilitated the church's presence.
In November, 1937, he hosted a eucharistic congress; in April,
1939, the Grand Master of the Sovereign Order of the Knights of
Malta visited Tripoli.[26] Moreover, most Sundays when he was in
Tripoli, Balbo promoted the church, and himself, at the High
Mass. For that occasion, he and his family rode to the cathedral in
a horse-drawn carriage, escorted by Libyan *zaptiè* on horseback.
In the cathedral, they sat to the side of the altar, on a raised
platform. "It was not a throne, but it took on the importance and
significance of one, and in those moments, Balbo truly assumed
the august solemnity of a viceroy."[27]

Balbo's audience with Pius XII, then, was in keeping with his gradual rapprochement with the church. Two more immediate factors explained the audience. First, Balbo had more than a passing acquaintance with the new pope. As Cardinal Pacelli, Pius XII had shown great interest in the Eucharistic Congress of 1937 and had met with Balbo afterwards. Second, in the fall of 1939, with Italy in a state of "nonbelligerence" and poised on the brink of war, though Mussolini jeered, many of the top figures of the Italian establishment hastened to forge links with the church. Balbo's meeting preceded by two weeks the king's audience with the pope; and by three, the pope's unprecedented return visit to the king on December 28.[28]

Long before 1940, Balbo, the republican, had embraced another principle of order: the monarchy. In the past, his relations with the king and with the royal family had been checkered. "Balbo seems to me to be very little loved at court," Ojetti jotted in his notebook in 1927 at the time of the Schneider Cup disaster.[29] In view of Balbo's reputation as a plotter, a republican, and a Blackshirt hothead, such royal suspicion was not surprising. Yet by 1931, at the time of Balbo's aerial triumphs, relations had changed. "Balbo is also happy with the king, who told him that the whole country is grateful to him," noted Ojetti.[30] When Balbo left for Libya in 1933, the king encouraged him with the thought that the new position would prepare him for more important posts later.

As he did with the church, Balbo favored royal visits to the colony as a sign that Libya was indeed an extension of the mother country. Balbo basked in reflected glory during these occasions. Little wonder, then, that from time to time he cultivated and encouraged such visits. A charming, gallant, and enthusiastic note of February 7, 1935, to the prince and princess of Piedmont, the heirs to the throne, accompanied a gift of spring strawberries and almond flowers and reminded the couple of "the *promised* trip to Libya." The messenger also bore a possible itinerary for the visit. "I would propose at least another hundred and come to Naples myself to present them, if Your Majesties so desire, in hopes of having at least one accepted," Balbo wrote.[31] His suit was successful. The visit took place in the spring. Balbo, resourceful host and master showman, arranged for the exotic Thousand and One Nights dinners and receptions that he knew how to stage so well in the gardens of the Governor's Palace and in remote desert oases such as Ghadames. Star of these occasions, of course, was the princess, her slim, elegant figure wrapped in a blue burnoose.[32] In May, 1938, the king attended the military maneuvers in the colony. The following year, the crown prince was present. Balbo personally piloted the prince from Italy to Tripoli and back.

Balbo's sympathy for the monarchy was on a par with his rapprochement with the church. Like Ciano and others, Balbo used his monarchist sentiments primarily to strike *frondista* poses against Mussolini. This was certainly the case in 1939 at the ceremonial opening of the newly created Chamber of Fasces and Corporations with which Mussolini had replaced the old parliament—the incident Farinacci had complained about in his letter to Mussolini. To minimize the royal presence on such a "fascist" occasion, Starace, the party secretary, ordered senators and deputies not to wear their royal decorations. To enforce compliance he stationed loyal Blackshirts at the entrances. De Bono protested and jeered; Bottai refused to remove his; Balbo physically attacked and threatened to banish a fellow *Ferrarese* who allowed his medals to be removed.[33] Such signs of pro-monarchist sympathies offered an opportunity for Balbo's enemies to taunt him. "You, so monarchist," Costanzo Ciano needled him in April of 1939 as he prepared to sign an oath of loyalty to the new royal chamber. Farinacci, who had overheard, prepared to join in, but Balbo stopped him cold: "Dear Roberto, remember that I took my first oath of allegiance to the king at eighteen as a volunteer second lieutenant in the *Alpini*."[34]

By 1940, there was a more compelling reason for rapprochement with the monarchy. The House of Savoy offered one of the few alternatives to Mussolini's warmongering and totalitarian madness. Early in April, 1940, at the invitation of Maria José, the princess of Piedmont, Balbo met with her and the Duca d'Aosta in Rome in a futile effort to turn Mussolini against the war.[35]

Over the years, then, Balbo's fascism had evolved. The violent, anti-socialist fury of the Blackshirt had long since dissipated. From a radical republican, he had become a princely dissident. Mussolini's appeal, when he declared war in June, 1940, to "Italy, proletarian and fascist," was meaningless to Balbo. He was accustomed to living in viceregal splendor and consorting with king and pope. He obeyed Mussolini out of a sense of duty and patriotism, but a fascist party report of a decade earlier summarized his position.[36] Fascism had failed, the report on fascism in the provinces concluded: failed to capture the masses, and failed to achieve its revolutionary goals. The regime followed a day-to-day policy and survived purely on the prestige of the Duce. If he were to die, the way had to be prepared for a "return to the monarchist normality." What was good and just in fascism must be saved and directed toward a royal restoration, urged the report.

Balbo's fascism of 1940, then, had little to do with Mussolini's, with alliances that linked Italy to German racist and totalitarian nightmares. For Balbo, fascism was first and foremost an Italian phenomenon. He might have enjoyed a classic anecdote of the period in which the Duce reportedly offered a three-word definition of fascism. Annoyed at his sons for interrupting his meal with the question, "What is fascism?" Mussolini replied with model fascist brevity, "Eat and shut up" (*Mangia e taci*). The Duce's flip and cynical dinner-table "definition," with its overtones of corruption and repression, would undoubtedly have appealed to Balbo's caustic sense of humor. Once he had finished laughing, however, in his energetic, staccato voice with the unmistakable lisp, he would have demanded, *"Az-colta, az-colta"* (Listen, listen), *"Mangia e taci"* was the spirit of the decadent Liberal regimes. Fascism was a revolution just *because* it had saved the country from such a mentality. Fascism and Mussolini's inspired leadership—at least in the early years—had rejuvenated Italy and united her. The world looked on her with new respect. That, for him, was the essence of fascism. He would have agreed with his friend Federzoni, who saw fascism as a restorative political force, a reviver of national values, the matrix of a new class of political leaders. That was the way fascism was born and matured "before the dictatorship killed it," Federzoni wrote.[37] In a speech delivered July 4, 1926, commemorating the Risorgimento hero Carlo Pisacane, Balbo echoed the theme of fascism as a restorative and patriotic force.[38] Fascism, he declared, was a continuation both of the Risorgimento and of "the spirit of the trenches" during the Great War. Unlike the Risorgimento, however, Balbo continued, fascism's spirit of revival permeated all classes.

How to capture this spirit in the form of institutions? Balbo was far too authoritarian by temperament to favor any truly democratic system. He needed to be leader and to have ultimate authority. At the same time, he included within his circle a wide variety of individualists and eccentrics. As long as his primacy remained unchallenged, he tolerated, even enjoyed, dissent as much as he enjoyed dissenting. By extension, then, in his political views Balbo favored strong leadership of the sort that Mussolini had provided for the first ten years of his rule. However, Balbo vigorously opposed the totalitarian system that Mussolini imposed for his second decade. In January, 1940, Balbo had a long conversation with the British ambassador, Sir Percy Loraine. In his eagerness to find common ground for Italy and Britain to work together, the diplomat argued that too much stress had been laid on the antithesis between fascism and democracy. Fascism and democracy, Loraine asserted—and Balbo agreed—were similar, in that the state was to be the servant of the people, and not vice versa as in Nazism and communism.[39] And how were the people to express their views? Balbo favored some form of popular consultation, but never universal suffrage as Mazzini preached. As early as 1922, Balbo made clear that the vote should be restricted to those who are qualified by education.[40] In 1937, he declared, "I am against investitures from on high. The Chief knows it."[41] Like Bottai, Balbo felt that limited elections or referendums were necessary as a sort of "thermometer" to take the temperature of the public mood. In its political form, Balbo's fascism amounted to a Caesarian democracy, a dictator, or perhaps a strong prime minister, who directed the country in response to limited elections or plebiscites. Nineteenth-century models come to mind: Crispi's parliamentary dictatorships, Napoleon III's authoritarian state. For Balbo the model fascist, twentieth-century totalitarian states of the Nazi variety held no appeal.

Particularly galling to him, as his sarcastic gibes indicated, was the transformation of his old friend and fellow revolutionary, Benito Mussolini, into the mythical "Duce." This imperial Mussolini of the uniforms, the mass parades, and choreographed rallies "in which no one believes" was no longer the Mussolini that "old fascists" obeyed. So declared Grandi at the July 25, 1943, meeting of the Grand Council. Balbo would have agreed. He would have supported Grandi's rhetorical plea: free Italy from all the military tunics and the caps with the imperial eagles and "leave us only with our old black shirts."[42]

Paradoxically, Balbo, the great mobilizer and organizer of the masses, was never really a populist. In his days as a *squadrista*, he expressed vague hopes of a populist element in fascism. Unlike Mussolini, however, by 1940 Balbo clearly preferred an Italy that was fascist but not proletarian. As a Mazzinian, socialist "demagogy" had always repelled him. The interests of the nation must always come before those of class. As a fascist, he found that the middle class—enriched by bright young men like himself—still served the interests of the nation best. Social justice need not mean social revolution. The paternalist charity and patronage he had learned as a child, augmented by more government welfare programs, could serve just as well. The paternalistic, highly structured colonization programs were as close as Balbo got to social experiment. He worked not to create a new egalitarian utopia but to build a traditional colonial society, a "fourth shore" that mirrored the mother country. In that society, his role was to rule in princely splendor.

In perspective, then, Balbo's fascism amounted to old-fashioned, middle-class, flag-and-country patriotism. It was more a spirit than a systematic ideology or a set of institutions. This is not surprising. He was a soldier, not an ideologue; an activist, not a theorist. To fascism he contributed his organizing skills and his own example. His history showed that a good fascist might begin as a thug with a *manganello,* but he need not remain that way. A good fascist could display loyalty without servility, discipline without pedantry, authority without violence. He could speak out against racist and totalitarian madness and still survive. In a crisis like that of 1940, however, patriotic spirit and personal rectitude provided very little guide for action. Certainly, experience and maturity deepened Balbo's political vision, as Federzoni pointed out. Balbo had seen the advantages of the "principles of order." Why not? By 1940, he had succeeded in becoming a part of it. Unfortunately, that order was inextricably linked with Mussolini and fascism. When the Duce's regime went sour, Balbo could not find any real alternative. Perhaps at the famous Grand Council meeting of July 25, 1943, Balbo the *frondeur* finally had his day. A large number of his fellow *Ferraresi* voted against the Duce, and some said that his spirit permeated the session.[43] By that time, however, he had been dead a little more than three years. In 1940, Balbo, alive and appalled at the course of events, blustered and did what he considered his duty.

Chapter Seventeen

Soldier: North African Commander

During the fall of 1939 and the spring of 1940, for the second time in a generation Italy faced an intervention crisis. The Pact of Steel bound the Italians to support the Germans even if they initiated a war. Nevertheless, the Nazis attacked Poland on September 1 without warning their ally. They had also signed a nonaggression pact with the Soviets a few days before—an agreement which the Italians felt went beyond the spirit of the Axis. These were grounds enough for Mussolini to assert Italy's "nonbelligerence"—a status that had no basis in international law but sounded more virile than "neutrality."

Italians greeted the decision with a sigh of relief. As Grandi noted rather tardily at the Grand Council meeting of July 25, 1943, unlike World War I, when a consensus developed, this time the Italian people saw neither a just cause nor the necessity for intervention.[1] When Mussolini finally declared war, the people followed "not with the faith of an army, but with the patient resignation of a herd."[2]

In general, the leadership behaved shamefully. A few pro-Nazi fanatics were centered on Farinacci and *Il Tevere*, but the king, the major *gerarchi*, the heads of the industrial and financial world, the military leadership, and the church all balked at going to war. Most of them knew that Italy's military preparation was bluff. They despised the Axis and they lacked faith in Mussolini. They were not even convinced that the war, as Mussolini predicted, would be quick and easy. Like Mussolini, however, they were, for the most part, timid, petty, and opportunistic, and the prospect of new personal honors and glories at bargain prices proved irresistible. When the Nazis, apparently invincible, overran Western Europe in the spring of 1940, to many of the *gerarchi* it seemed foolish not to share in the booty. After the war was lost, many claimed that they had opposed it; in the spring of 1940, however, going with the tide of German victories, they clamored for intervention. For the most part, the fascist hierarchy and the nation's leadership, timid and passive, grumbled among themselves but were subject to fits of bellicose enthusiasm. From time to time, when the situation looked too risky, they tried without success to dissuade Mussolini. Not a single major figure—not one—resigned in protest.

Balbo did not resign, but neither did he have illusions about the war. It would be a repeat of 1918 and the Germans would lose, he predicted. "I'll bet my head on it," he declared in November, 1939, and added, in a jab at Mussolini, "You have to be an elementary schoolteacher and never have been to America not to understand these things."[3] The war would prove to be a disaster not only for the Germans but for fascism, for Italy, for all of Europe. For the *gerarchi* personally, Balbo predicted a grim future. In mid-November of 1939, in an image that he was to repeat frequently throughout the winter and spring, he told a friend, pointing to the street lamps on Via Veneto, "You'll see us all hanging from those lampposts."[4]

Despite this gloomy and accurate assessment, Balbo did not despair. "To the last," he opposed the war, Ciano conceded.[5] Short of replacing Mussolini, Balbo explored all avenues against the war. In the fall of 1939, the *Padano* conducted its violent anti-German campaign disguised as anti-bolshevism. In December, Balbo met with the pope and also shored up his relations with the monarchy. On December 7, the day before his audience with the pope, Balbo spoke before the Grand Council. Without arousing protests from anyone, he hinted at possible diplomatic and perhaps even military support of the British and French. Farinacci's insistent arguments for intervention on the side of the Germans found no backing, and Ciano once again reaffirmed Italy's "nonbelligerent" status. The anti-German mood of the meeting buoyed Balbo's spirits. Reassured, Balbo told Federzoni that the reaffirmation of nonbelligerence meant Italy's definitive renunciation of entering the war.[6]

At the end of January, 1940, in another maneuver against intervention, Balbo met with De Bono and De Vecchi on the island of Rhodes. Farinacci, recognizing that with their prestige the three *quadrumvirs* constituted an important anti-war force in the Grand Council, warned Mussolini of a "plot." Yet nothing overt came of the encounter at Rhodes beyond mutual commiseration and fretting about the war. Balbo, acutely aware of his vulnerable military position in Libya, complained that the colony was considered a secondary theater and he had nothing to fight with. "They are hypnotized by German power. . . . They talk of German tanks, airplanes, and guns as if for us it is enough to talk about someone else's power!"[7] Indirectly, however, the meeting may have affected Mussolini. Because he did not want to face the opposition of the *quadrumvirs* and of Balbo in particular, before declaring war, he did not convoke the Grand Council.[8] In February, Balbo briefly explored the possibility of having himself named ambassador to Washington in hopes of bringing American pressure to bear on Mussolini.[9]

Balbo took care to publicize his anti-war views. With urgency and passion he talked to friends, to diplomats, to reporters. With an American correspondent, at Christmas, 1939, he was "very cordial . . . but also he appeared to me very thoughtful, worried and uneasy."[10] He hoped that Italy would stay out of the present conflict, and if she stayed out of the war, she could help "anyone in Europe." Yet he clearly had his doubts about Italy's present status. "With very emotional words he repeated that Italy was not neutral and could not pretend to be so."[11] To Sir Percy Loraine, at a dinner-party on January 19, 1940, he sounded like an Anglophile. He ridiculed the idea of the Germans winning the war and dismissed the notion that the Italians might join the German side as "just rubbish."[12]

Finally, in his campaign against the war Balbo confronted Mussolini directly. One encounter took place during the winter. Balbo, determined to impress Mussolini with the low morale of the troops in Libya, collected a file of soldiers' letters home that had been intercepted by the censors. When Mussolini refused to look at the letters, Balbo read some aloud: "We are forming a battery here, but there aren't any cannons"; "that swine in Rome" (Mussolini) is sending soldiers to the slaughter. "That's the spirit of the soldiers with whom you want to make war," Balbo told Mussolini. At the end of April, according to Grandi, Balbo pleaded with Mussolini for military reinforcements for the colony. Mussolini, unsure about whether to intervene until a few weeks before he actually declared war on June 10, reassured Balbo, "There won't be any war. Think about your colonists, your wells, your olives."[13] By the end of May, Mussolini had decided on war. Most likely it was at this time that Balbo, waiting in an antechamber with Badoglio to see Mussolini, met the aviator Arturo Ferrarin. "You're going in before us," Balbo said. "You tell him too that to drag us into a war would be a crime. For heaven's sake, tell him." And when Ferrarin emerged, frustrated, Balbo whispered anxiously, "Did you talk to him? What did he say?"[14] Shortly before war was declared, Balbo met with Mussolini twice. The first time was an afternoon meeting together with Badoglio on May 31.[15] On that occasion, with war decided, Balbo, like Badoglio, argued for postponement. He wanted hostilities to begin at the end of June so that he could stockpile more supplies in Libya. By June 2—the second meeting—postponement was out of the question. Mussolini had already informed Hitler that Italy would intervene on June 10.

From these last meetings with Mussolini, Balbo emerged enraged but resigned. Everything was at stake: fascism, Italy, his career, his very life—and the odds were hopeless. "It's all over, here, because the madman wants to make war," he told Annio Bignardi. Italy would last six months; he would die a soldier's death in the war. "As for the rest of you, there won't be enough lampposts in Piazza Venezia to hang you all," he declared.[16] To add to his burdens, Balbo knew that many of his friends—and perhaps a good segment of the nation, as well—looked to him for leadership and inspiration. "More than ever these days I think of you, as chief and *condottiero,* and look to you with great faith, with certain hope," wrote Ambassador Scola Camerini, head of Balbo's cabinet in Libya for six years.[17] Elisabeth Cerruti, wife of the veteran diplomat, noted that "there were many of us who put our faith in him," but Balbo was not encouraging. Nothing more was to be done, he replied bluntly. He had tried in vain to dissuade Mussolini. The decision was made. "As for me, he wants my life and he'll have it," he told her.[18] The intervention crisis also softened Balbo's attitudes toward old feuds and rivalries. "A good half-day passed with Balbo," De Bono recorded on May 14, after visiting with him at the inauguration of the Overseas Fair in Naples.[19] Ciano "speaks to me with less hatred toward Balbo," Bottai noted at the beginning of August, 1939.[20]

Outwardly, Balbo behaved with his usual gusto. On the evening of June 1, Bottai remembered him surrounded by friends, including Francesco Pricolo, Felice Porro, Nello Quilici, Umberto Klinger. With an audience before him, he became expansive, "counting his airplanes, his tanks, his cannons, his divisions, explaining his plans, in a game like some great bearded child."[21] From time to time he studied his reflection in a mirror and stroked his goatee, perhaps fantasizing about a woman. But the reflection, "alert and sad," sobered him. Bottai, sensing his interior struggle, during a private moment asked him what he was thinking. "It's going to be tough," he replied softly, as if afraid that the others would overhear. "It's going to be very tough." And he deplored the lack of preparation, blaming Mussolini, "his eternal sacrificial goat."

Except for these outbursts, he behaved like a loyal soldier. At the end of May, he spent some days at his villa at Punta Ala, because, as he remarked, "Who knows when we'll be back?"[22] The Spanish broom was in blossom. When friends returned with huge golden armfuls, he greeted them joyfully. About the war he said very little, referring to it only if the conversation turned upon it. Nevertheless, he spent some sleepless nights mulling over preparations for the conflict. After a long talk with him on June 2, Ciano noted, "He is preparing to return to Libya. He has made up his mind to do the best he can, but he does not believe that the war will be quick and easy. . . . He is a soldier and he will fight with energy and determination."[23]

"Practically hopeless," caught between the British in Egypt and the French in Tunisia "like a slice of ham in a sandwich":[24] so Balbo—colorful, theatrical, and blunt, as usual—described the military situation in Libya if Italy entered the war against the British and French. No one doubted that Balbo, commander in chief of Italian forces in North Africa, would give a good account of himself personally, but he alone could not make up for demoralized troops and an absurd lack of matériel. De Bono commented in his diary for August 16, 1939, "I wouldn't like to be him—the first to be attacked, and a first French success against us would be deleterious."[25]

Balbo had good reason for his widely proclaimed pessimism. Morale among his troops was indeed low. Although his officers were adequate, the rank and file appeared "resigned and, all in all, not very solid in spirit," he noted in September, 1939.[26] Lax discipline, he claimed, had much to do with the current state, and he favored restoring an older, harsher rule, at least for the current crisis. His blistering memorandum to the commanders of the outposts in the Libyan Sahara, following an inspection tour of their outposts in the winter of 1940, indicated his concern over shoddy discipline. At the end of a long list of criticisms ranging from slovenly uniforms, mess halls, and latrines to inadequate medical supervision of local prostitutes, Balbo concluded, "In what is our racial superiority supposed to consist if not in a high standard of living, of civilization and prestige?"[27] A German military observer in May, 1940, confirmed Balbo's assessment of morale: "Everywhere the gloom of an impending war was only too apparent—a war that the people did not desire and for which it saw no reason."[28]

The shortages of matériel were equally worrisome to Balbo. Tanks, armored cars, anti-aircraft batteries, anti-tank weapons, trucks, modern aircraft—he lacked them all. His repeated requests for them during the previous fall and winter had had no results. Furious, bitter, he harangued fascist party and military officials at the Teatro Miramare in Tripoli a few days before the declaration of war. Rome, "ignoring or pretending to ignore the situation," answered his requests by declaring "that they did not have any [equipment] and that if they had, they would have sent it elsewhere," Balbo fumed. He had poured all his available funds into the colony's defenses. With what he had left, "I will be able to buy you some sticks. If you think they will be of help, use them."[29]

His defensive fortifications were in a dismal state. When the war broke out, the structures to defend the Tunisian frontier were in their earliest stages. In 1939, out of about a hundred planned emplacements, seven had been completed and thirteen were under construction.[30] All the rest—gun emplacements, observation posts, communications centers—remained nothing more than plans. On the Egyptian frontier, the series of extant small fortresses, effective in putting down the Sanusi, were useless against a modern army. The famous "Graziani wall," a barbed-wire fence that stretched from the coast southward for about a hundred kilometers, was equally useless. An enemy tank could break through it or nose it aside. The outer line of fortifications at Bardia were still in the planning stage. Only Tobruk was a real stronghold.

Balbo's pessimism was well grounded, then—but he also protested too much. If he was being "left in the lurch," as he told a German military observer in May, 1940, he too was responsible.[31] Commanders seldom see their ideals of men and matériel embodied. The General Staff did have to consider the nation's defense needs other than those of Libya.[32] Balbo's dilemma also reflected both his own shortcomings as a military leader and the confused state of Italy's military preparedness at the outbreak of the war. That lack of preparedness, in turn, reflected the nature of the fascist regime, which all too often substituted bluff for concrete policies and actions. For twenty years Balbo had served as one of the pillars of this regime. What he had sown for two decades, he was now reaping.

One major source of Balbo's troubles lay in the nature of the war he was asked to fight in June, 1940. Mussolini wanted "to declare war, in order not to fight it," General Quirino Armellini, Badoglio's assistant, noted in his diary.[33] The Duce undoubtedly sought a real war, with real battles and real casualties; he needed a "few thousand dead" so that he could secure a seat at the imminent peace conference, he told Badoglio. But Mussolini also wanted a war that would be short, victorious, cheap—one that entailed minimal risks. His General Staff, under Badoglio, for the most part preferred to avoid war completely. They followed orders, but they, too, were eager to make war as little as possible.

Balbo knew that a quick, easy war was a fantasy. He had warned anyone who would listen during the intervention crisis, and he never ceased hammering at this theme once the war began. Libya's situation, in particular, in case of a Mediterranean conflict would be perilous. The colony would immediately be cut off from the mother country. Isolated, impoverished, still in the first phase of her economic development, Libya would be unable to support either the troops or the rapidly expanding civilian population. There was only one solution, Balbo explained to Graziani in a letter of January 13, 1940: *"We will have to conquer our means of subsistence* and there is no other solution except to fix on Egypt."[34] For some years, he wrote, he had been elaborating a scheme to parry the French threat from Tunisia and then concentrate his forces to the East and drive "with a very determined spirit on Alexandria and the Delta. . . . The operation is less difficult than it appears, and at the right time I will draw up a plan."[35] For about three years, until October, 1939, Balbo had the support of General Alberto Pariani, the army chief of staff and undersecretary of war. At the end of October, 1938, Balbo did present a plan along these lines.[36] For the offensive against Egypt, his scheme envisioned seven motorized divisions with the capability of off-road movement. Pariani supported him, favoring even stronger forces—twelve motorized divisions. Budget limitations, however, meant that the buildup would have to be gradual—so Pariani wrote to Balbo on January 7, 1939.

Bold projects for an invasion of Egypt, however, clashed with Badoglio's cautious outlook. He sniffed at the display of armor that he saw on a visit to Germany in 1937 and ridiculed the idea of motorized divisions. He believed the war in Libya would be fought the way he knew it from his days as governor. Movement and maneuver depended on the abilities of native troops to fight in the heat.[37] Furthermore, during the fall of 1939, the period of nonbelligerence, Badoglio wanted to avoid stirring up Mussolini, who was already highly excitable. The mere existence of war plans might set him off, Badoglio feared, and therefore he did his best to avoid making any.

Balbo, however, was determined to push for his invasion scheme. In a letter to Pariani on September 10, 1939, Balbo insisted that he "did not want to renounce" his project. Pariani's staff drew up a detailed plan and presented it to Badoglio. Commenting that in his judgment the plan "did not correspond to reality," Badoglio rejected it on November 15 and asked that it be resubmitted. In the meantime, Pariani was forced to resign. His successor, Graziani, ruled that Balbo's plan was not feasible. Balbo persisted. To give him some measure of satisfaction, the General Staff discussed the plan again at the end of the month. Balbo received permission to study a plan which would become operational "if exceptionally favorable circumstances should develop." The "exceptionally favorable circumstances," as the General Staff intended them, probably never would have developed. For Mussolini, fearful that the war would end suddenly and find him empty-handed, those circumstances arrived abruptly on June 20. He gave the order to invade Egypt—but Balbo died before he had time to launch the project.

In perspective, it seems doubtful that Balbo's march on the Canal would have proved successful by any conventional standard. Doubt exists even about whether he had drawn up a detailed plan. Graziani claimed that when he succeeded Balbo in July, 1940, he found no such plan.[38] General Felice Porro, commander of the Italian air force in Libya, claims that during the second half of May, 1940, he was shown a complete study in relief. Attached were Badoglio's initials and a note that there "will never be an attack on this front."[39] Badoglio had a point. The logistics of such an operation were stupendous. From Tripoli to the Nile Delta was a distance of about 2,000 kilometers, most of it through waterless desert. Balbo badly lacked transport. At the time of the English offensive in the fall of 1940, a few months after Balbo's death, the entire motor pool in Libya consisted of fewer than 2,000 vehicles of all kinds.[40] A single motorized German division had more. Such considerations probably would not have stopped Balbo. When he spoke of a march into Egypt, he probably meant it almost literally. He had led Blackshirt legions across the dusty roads of Emilia and Romagna; perhaps he imagined that he could carry out a similar feat across the Western Desert. To discourage anyone who thought of retreat, he talked of filling in the waterholes behind him. Even if he lost half his troops on the way, a hundred thousand would have reached the heart of Egypt, he claimed.[41] His plan suggested heroism and poetry—and headlines—but not much military sense.

The plan proved to be purely academic. Throughout the spring, Balbo pleaded frantically for more men and, especially, for more equipment. He even talked of making another visit to Germany "to visit my friend Goering"; as head of German armament, he was "the only person in a position to give me adequate and speedy aid."[42] At the beginning of May, Rome promised Balbo an additional 80,000 men. Then the French and English forces would only outnumber him three to one, Balbo declared, grossly overestimating—as Badoglio did—the real enemy strength. The number really did not matter as much as the equipment, Balbo noted. Without adequate artillery, anti-aircraft and anti-tank weapons, such reinforcements had little meaning. As he wrote on May 11, "The finest of Caesar's legions would collapse if faced with a machine gun platoon."[43] But the nature of his requests indicate that, like the rest of the military establishment, he had only a rudimentary grasp of the elements of desert warfare. Not until June 2 did he request an armored division. Perhaps there was also some attempt to "cover himself" against any future catastrophes by demanding far more matériel than was available. For example, he requested 880,000 anti-tank shells; Italy's monthly production at the time was only 40,000. He wanted fifteen mobile anti-aircraft batteries; there were twenty-four in all of Italy.[44]

If Balbo was covering himself, his requests also revealed clearly how Mussolini planned to substitute bravura for bullets in fighting his war. In any case, as Balbo told the crowd at the Teatro Miramare at the beginning of the war, his demands largely went unanswered. The needs of other battle theaters also had to be met, he was told, and he was admonished for violating the chain of command and going directly to Mussolini. When hostilities began on June 11, Mussolini's orders for Libya remained: maintain the defensive, on both the Tunisian and the Egyptian front.

A quarter of a century almost to the month after joining the armed forces in the First World War, Balbo began to fight in the Second. This time, he was not a reserve officer of the *Alpini* in charge of a platoon; he was a marshal in charge of nearly 200,000 men, all the Italian forces in North Africa. The land where he fought was also different. In place of the shell-pocked, limestone plateau of the Grappa, he faced the heat and sandy wastes of Libya. The trench warfare he had learned in the earlier conflict was useless. And the ideals for which he struggled had changed. In his youth, in the name of Italy he had taken up arms against the Hapsburg tyrant and Prussian militarism. This time, still in the name of Italy, he fought for a man and a regime that had promised to rejuvenate Italy and make her great. His faith in Mussolini and fascism had virtually evaporated. Nevertheless, for Balbo, the patriot and soldier, no honorable alternative to fighting existed.

How Balbo fought the war did not change much. He was a marshal, a commander in chief, but he led as if he were still a lieutenant in charge of a platoon or a company. Almost immediately after hostilities began, to be near the front Balbo transferred his headquarters from Tripoli to Cyrene, a beautiful little town in the Gebel Akhdar, beloved by tourists for its Greek ruins. From the nearby airport at Derna he made daily flights to the most advanced positions. In pith helmet, bush jacket, khaki shorts, and Sam Brown belt, binoculars dangling at his waist, he inspected frontier outposts along the Egyptian border. At the most advanced air fields, at El Adem and Tobruk's T-2, he appeared a bit more formally. In saucer cap and tunic, breeches, and leggings, a cigarette dangling from his lips, he talked over the latest reconnaissance data with his helmeted pilots.

He was in the best of spirits. Whatever conflicts had tormented him during the intervention crisis disappeared. He was intent on doing the best job possible and setting the best example he could for everyone, from his men to his family and friends. "Italo magnificent in form, serene, calm, cheerful, strong, very affectionate. I'm very glad I came," Quilici wrote to his sister the day of his arrival in Libya, June 12.[45] "Italo . . . could not be more extraordinary in his loving attention, despite his important . . . responsibilities and preoccupations," Quilici scribbled in a note to his wife two days later.[46] On June 23, he wrote, "Italo is in perfect form. . . . He does marvelous things and is a real lion."[47] The day before the fatal crash that claimed him as well as Balbo, he noted, "It's incredible how Balbo is calm, good, kind. His presence on the front is miraculous because the situation is uneven so far as means; the desert units have a very hard life."[48] And Balbo's nephew Lino wrote on the same day, "I've never seen Uncle as serene as now."[49]

Balbo's pace was frantic and left his friends and collaborators gasping, but his example inspired them. Quilici, who acted as Balbo's "flying secretary" and complained of twenty-two-hour

days, wrote to his wife on June 14, "If I'd had to go through a day
like this in Italy I'd be dead from fatigue. Instead, I'm very well.
A good bath revived me."[50] The schedule for the previous day to
visit Tobruk had included a four-and-a-half-hour flight from Tripoli to Derna and then a 350-kilometer automobile ride. Quilici
had been up from 3:30 in the morning to 2:00 the following
morning. He confessed on June 16, "Today I asked for mercy
because I was exhausted, and permission was granted for me to
stay here and write. But tomorrow we'll start all over."[51]

The risks involved in these inspections were considerable. The
danger came not only from enemy fire but also from Balbo's own
poorly trained and badly armed troops. Disorganization and confusion—states not peculiar to the Italian armed forces—were ram-
pant during these first days of the war. Horror stories abounded:
crews arrived without equipment; equipment arrived without
crews—or with crews that were untrained.[52] Balbo complained to
Badoglio of SM.79 bombers arriving unarmed and with the wrong
bomb racks and that he could "go on like this for three pages."[53]
The possibilities for accidents, for cases of mistaken identity under
these circumstances were very high. Quilici noted at least two such
cases in his diary, including an incident on June 15 in which Italian
aircraft mistakenly strafed one of their own columns.[54] During this
period Balbo returned home one evening in a rage because he had
mistakenly been fired on from the ground. "I'll have to paint it
red," he said, referring to his plane.[55]

During these first days, the action was "more guerrilla than
war," as Quilici observed.[56] When hostilities began on June 11,
Balbo's military position turned out to be the reverse of what he
had anticipated. No massive French North African army swept in
from Tunisia. Apart from a few clashes between border patrols
and a rare air raid on Tripoli which caused little damage, there
was little activity. Within two weeks, on June 25, the French
signed an armistice. Such threat to Libya as there was came from
Egypt. There, a tiny British force of 36,000 and a much larger but
uncertain Egyptian army stood in the way of the Canal. Although
the British force was small, it was comparatively well equipped,
with 360 tanks and armored cars for desert warfare. Air raids on
Tobruk and on other airfields occurred almost daily, and British

armored cars swept across the frontier and surrounded or captured a string of Italian outposts.

These early British successes meant very little from a strategic point of view. Bardia, the last major settlement before the Egyptian frontier, amounted to a small village with one street of clean white houses for officers and government officials, a church, a mosque, some depots, and primitive barracks.[57] Ridotta Capuzzo, located a few kilometers to the east of Bardia at the end of the Balbia, marked the frontier line. Visitors found a series of crumbling brick structures dating to the Turkish period. The buildings had been somewhat enlarged and embellished to present a more imposing picture at the border. Outposts like Bir el-Gobi and Sidi Omar were even less substantial. They were manned by twenty to forty Libyan colonial troops led by an Italian officer or two; their armament consisted of nothing more than a machine gun or perhaps a small cannon. The British made little effort to hold their prizes. When the Italians reoccupied Ridotta Capuzzo on June 15, they found it abandoned.

Insignificant as the British raids were militarily, they proved devastating for morale. Despite their vast advantage in manpower, the Italians had nothing—no armored cars, no reliable tanks, not even enough trucks—to oppose the British armor, except rifles and machine guns. "We will not give up and we will perform miracles," Balbo assured Badoglio, but added, "if I were the English commander, I would already be in Tobruk."[58] Balbo concentrated on propaganda and raising the morale of his troops. "We cannot give the impression that we will not react to their attacks," he told a staff meeting.[59] He planned an aero-naval attack on the British bases at Sidi Barrani and Sollum. The operation came to nothing, because the enemy had disappeared. He directed a D'Annunzio-style propaganda raid on June 24, showering Cairo with leaflets. The most irritating problem was the "infernal armored cars." Balbo's concern with them led to one of his last adventures and undoubtedly contributed to the incident that ended his life.

The "infernal armored cars, which run over all types of ground and move at fifty kilometers per hour," had been making life miserable for the Italians.[60] The cars had played a major role in overrunning the frontier outposts and in attacking a truck convoy along the Litoranea on June 16 and 17. The troops, especially the Libyan colonials, "were convinced that nothing could stop" the machines. "It is time to discredit the legend," Balbo declared.[61] On June 17, he ordered his men "to seek combat" with the armored units. Ground troops working with aircraft were to lay a trap for the enemy vehicles. A small unit of fighters or dive bombers was to fly from Tobruk to frontier outposts such as Bir el-Gobi, Sidi Azeiz, or Amseat. From these positions, a few trucks would be sent out as bait to attract the armored cars. When the enemy appeared, the Italians would be ready for them with infantry, artillery, and aircraft. "In short, we have to give it to them," declared Balbo.[62]

Four days later, he directed the capture of the first car and its crew of four. Like any good war story, this one became embellished as it made the rounds. An Italian version has Balbo sighting the enemy from the air, landing, and alerting a nearby garrison. Impatient at their reluctance, he took off again, landed near the vehicle, leaped from the cockpit, "and with a few of his crewmen armed with rifles" attacked the car with guns blazing.[63] A British version turned the incident into a humanitarian gesture and combined the capture of the armored car with the story of Balbo's death. Thanks to Balbo's "impulsive and generous nature," he rescued the crew that was "lost and dying of thirst and starvation"; while he was rushing them to a hospital in his aircraft, he was shot down over Tobruk.[64]

The most authentic version is only a shade less dramatic than the more fanciful ones.[65] Following his normal routine during that period, Balbo flew to an outpost, Bir el-Gobi, on an inspection tour. With him was a typical entourage: his nephew Lino, a German journalist, an Italian army photographer, and a movie operator. Around 12:30 P.M., while circling over the camp and waiting for a car to meet him at the landing strip, Balbo surveyed a favorite haunt of the armored cars, the region between the camp and the air field, a distance of about six kilometers. Sure enough, "with the intuition of the hunter," he spotted one. It was poorly camouflaged beneath a few stalks of hay—in a region where there was no hay—but sufficiently well hidden that Frailich, the co-pilot, did not see it, even when Balbo flew low and pointed it out.

Fig. 28. Balbo, supreme commander of Italian forces in North Africa, inspires his troops in June, 1940 (G. Bucciante, *Vita di Balbo*)

Frailich landed just long enough for Balbo and Lino to disembark; then he took off again to watch over the prize while Balbo and his nephew went to the camp for help. With considerable reluctance, for Balbo's subordinates feared that the armored car

Fig. 29. Balbo and the captured British armored car (G. Bucciante, *Vita di Balbo*)

might call in its own reinforcements, a small contingent of Italian tanks rumbled to the site and surrounded the enemy vehicle. The car's crew, fearful of the bomber circling overhead and immobilized by their vehicle's flat tire, surrendered without a fight. During the actual capture, Balbo remained at the camp, haranguing the assembled Libyan troops. When the prisoners were brought in, he took charge of them, loading them into his plane; with Lino guarding them, he flew back to Tobruk. To the senior British man, worried about being short of money for his minor personal expenses, Balbo handed a thousand lire of his own, saying, "You can return it when the war is over." The captured car was displayed to the Italian troops at Bardia, Derna, and Tobruk, so that they could study the vehicle's vulnerable points—the tires, the thin armor plate in the rear, and the open canopy.

In the meantime, on June 20, exciting orders from Rome: authorization from Badoglio to invade Egypt. Balbo replied requesting trucks, cistern trucks, and medium tanks. On June 25, Badoglio excluded an immediate invasion but urged Balbo to make plans for one. "Always proceed by degrees: first be sure to secure the front door, then consider going ahead," he wrote.[66] The very next day brought an abrupt reversal. In an astonishing letter apparently motivated by nothing more than rumors of a German invasion of England, Badoglio advised Balbo, "We may be forced to strike toward the East as soon as possible if we do not want to remain empty-handed at the conclusion of the peace." The seventy "magnificent" tanks that Balbo had requested would arrive in Benghazi on July 5 or 6, and Balbo could have all the aircraft he needed. "Put wings on everyone's feet," Badoglio urged, and predicted victory because the enemy, unlike the Italians, were not accustomed to the heat of the desert. "I wrote to you above as I did because the Duce is quivering and I think very soon he will give the 'go' sign." A June 28 telegram set July 15 as the date of the offensive. Balbo never read it. It arrived after he had made his last flight.

Chapter Eighteen

Soldier: Death of a Hero

"On the day of June 28, flying over Tobruk, during an enemy bombing action, the aircraft piloted by Italo Balbo crashed in flames. Italo Balbo and the members of his crew perished."[1] So read the stark official announcement of Balbo's death. The crash, barely a week after the capture of the armored car, also claimed the lives of eight of Balbo's closest aides, friends, and members of his family.

The peculiar circumstances of the incident and the identities of its victims inspired many rumors. Stories still circulate today about plots and assassination attempts. Although some details remain obscure, the general outlines of Balbo's death are indisputable. I-MANU and its crew were accidental victims of Italian anti-aircraft batteries. Confusion, disorder, and lack of training brought Balbo down—not conspiracies, machinations, and intrigues.

To these factors must be added Balbo's own contradictory personality. The manner of his death mirrored his way of life: courageous, generous, romantic, but also reckless, despotic, impulsive. Always one to lead from the front, to set the example, he took off on a self-appointed morale-building mission that exposed him to considerable personal danger. Nevertheless, as his aides protested, the mission was appropriate for Balbo the lieutenant in the *Alpini* or the Blackshirt leader, but not for the air marshal, the governor general of Libya, the commander of Italian forces in North Africa. Moreover, in the past Balbo had shown himself to be a firm believer in military regulations and a careful planner. He had chastised subordinates in Saharan outposts for minor in-

Fig. 30. Mussolini's *Il Popolo d'Italia* announces Balbo's "heroic death" on June 28, 1940 (Caproni Museum Archive)

fractions of military discipline and had plotted his transatlantic cruises in meticulous detail. Yet he embarked on his last flight with remarkable casualness and an impatient disregard for military procedures. Over Tobruk, against his own announced plans and against common sense, impulsively he flung himself—and those who accompanied him—into a perilous situation. Once again, he dared—this time, too much.

The precise motivations behind Balbo's last flight will never be known. Official versions state that the accident occurred while Balbo was on an inspection and morale-building expedition. He planned to visit troops of the Second Libyan Division at the frontier outpost of Sidi Azeis, which had recently been recaptured, and at Ridotta Capuzzo. Balbo's goal was to "greet the troops and to reaffirm solemnly, with the reoccupation of the territory, our superiority over the enemy."[2] Other sources claim that the inspection was only a cover; Balbo's real mission was to hunt more armored cars.

General Felice Porro, head of the Aeronautica in Libya, in a separate aircraft, had accompanied Balbo on his last flight. According to Porro, Balbo had been disappointed at the results of his first expedition. His example had not led to the destruction of more enemy vehicles, so he planned a second expedition.[3] His technique remained much the same as on the first attempt: a number of aircraft were to land at Sidi Azeis to act as bait for the enemy cars in the Sollum area. Once the cars had been attracted, a high-flying aircraft would signal for circling Italian fighters and for a column from nearby Ridotta Capuzzo to close the trap. For security reasons, according to Porro, Balbo maintained the official story of the inspection mission. Other sources are not explicit about the "hunting expedition" story, but they do give some supportive evidence.[4] Balbo ordered a rendezvous over Tobruk with an escort of fighters—either three or five; accounts disagree—to accompany him. The fighters might have been simply for protection, since he was venturing into an advanced area. They might also have been useful in his hunting operation.

Perhaps Balbo had both missions in mind, for the two are certainly not mutually exclusive. A morale-building visit and inspection of the front-line areas fitted his normal pattern of activities. If he also captured more armored cars, that could only enhance the success of his visit. The mission was originally scheduled for June 26. However, a *ghibli*, a violent desert sandstorm, made flying impossible for two days. Bablo also received a report that an enemy attack had temporarily closed the airfield at Sidi Azeis.[5] Those on his staff who knew of his intentions ahead of time, especially Porro and General Giuseppe Tellera, Balbo's chief of staff, tried to dissuade him.[6] For an officer of his rank to direct such an operation was totally inappropriate, they argued. Balbo retorted that the question of the armored cars was an important one, and he rationalized his participation as a matter of morale.

For two days, while the *ghibli* blew, Balbo seemed content to let the matter rest. On the morning of June 28, however, the weather cleared. Around noon Porro, who had made a reconnaissance flight during the morning, reported to Balbo at Derna.

"How is the weather?" Balbo asked him.

"Magnificent," Porro replied, and he exulted over the photographs he had taken in the morning under such excellent conditions.

"Then today is the day we'll go to Sidi Azeis. Do you want to go too?" Balbo asked.

"I'd love to," Porro replied.

"Good. Be at the field at 1500 hours."[7]

Up to this point, there is no evidence that Balbo had plans to hunt armored cars. Sometime between noon and two o'clock, however, he received word that enemy vehicles had been sighted near Sidi Azeis and that the field was now clear for landing. He then ordered one of his staff, Lieutenant Ernesto Romagna-Manoja, with the commander of the colony's air forces in the Eastern Sector, General Silvestri, to precede the main party to Sidi Azeis. Romagna-Manoja's orders were to fly from Derna to the T-2 airfield at Tobruk. There he was to pick up an escort of CR.42 fighters and proceed to Sidi Azeis. They were to clear the airfield and await the marshal's arrival. Around 3:30 P.M. Romagna-Manoja left Tobruk in a small observation plane with General Silvestri and the escort of CR.42's. Over Sidi Azeis they discovered three armored cars, one of which was on the airstrip, no more than a hundred meters from the fort. The Italians attacked. However, the fighters' guns were jammed from the sandstorm and never fired, and Romagna-Manoja's Ghibli was not armed for such an operation. The armored cars scattered into the desert.

About the same time that Romagna-Manoja and the fighters were skirmishing with the armored cars over Sidi Azeis, Balbo assembled his party at Derna. The number and composition of that party prompted many questions after Balbo's death. Why were nine people aboard I-MANU, a standard trimotor SM.79 bomber whose normal complement was five? Why did the party include so many high-ranking officers and so many of Balbo's closest aides, friends, and family?

Such questions were natural; yet anyone familiar with Balbo's habits knew that he loved turning such an expedition into "a sort of family outing," as one writer later described it.[8] The previous week's mission had been similar. On that one, in addition to his normal crew of co-pilot, flight engineer, and radioman, Balbo took along his nephew, a German journalist, a photographer, and a cameraman. Lino and the journalists had had to squeeze into the aircraft and then had to stand. Nevertheless, Quilici remarked: "Unfortunately, Caretti and I have to stay on the ground."[9] Later it was explained that the presence of so many high-ranking officers on such a mission to the front lines was good for morale.[10] The entire party, which eventually totaled eighteen, squeezed into two SM.79's.

With Balbo aboard I-MANU on this last flight, there were no strangers, only trusted friends and comrades, *atlantici, Ferraresi,* and family. The basic crew consisted of Balbo as pilot, Major Ottavio Frailich as co-pilot, Captain Gino Cappannini as flight engineer, and Sergeant-Major Giuseppe Berti as radioman. Frailich, Cappannini, and Berti had all been flying with Balbo since the days of the *crociere*. Originally Balbo had taken aboard General Tellera, his chief of staff, and Lieutenant Colonel Rosario Sorrentino, who was in the operations office, and Quilici. Either at noon or as the party was boarding, Balbo ordered Tellera and Sorrentino to fly with Porro. "You, Tellera, you're too fat," he jibed.[11] The switch made room for two members of his immediate family, his nephew Lino and Cino Florio, his brother-in-law. There were now seven aboard, and the engines were turning over. From the cockpit Balbo looked out and spotted two old friends on the runway seeing him off, Enrico Caretti and Claudio Brunelli. Caretti, a physician, was a Ferrarese, an old friend from Balbo's Blackshirt days and currently the *federale* of Tripoli. Brunelli was a war veteran and *squadrista* who had held various party positions before Balbo called him to Libya to direct the organization for hotels and tourism. Always a bit of a tyrant, Balbo motioned them aboard.

The second aircraft carried several of Balbo's top aides. Porro was the pilot; Captain Leardi, the co-pilot. The passengers included, in addition to Sorrentino and Tellera who had been shifted from Balbo's plane, General Egisto Perino, who had arrived just that day from the air ministry in Rome to observe the Libyan situation firsthand. A photographer who had flown on the first armored-car trip, Captain Goldoni, completed the party. To make room for the others, Porro tried to shift Goldoni to Balbo's plane. Balbo, who wanted him to take photographs of I-MANU, ordered him back.

About 5:00 P.M., I-MANU, with Balbo at the controls, rumbled down the dusty runway at El Feteyat and took off into the brilliant blue desert sky. Balbo's first checkpoint was the Tobruk-2 (T-2) airfield, about 160 kilometers away. The fighters with which he was scheduled to rendezvous for Sidi Azeis were based there. In the SM.79 trimotor, which had a cruising speed of about 370 km/hr., flying time from Derna to T-2 was twenty to twenty-five minutes. Balbo's plane took the lead. Porro followed behind and to the left to watch for enemy aircraft. The route from Derna lay in a southeasterly direction, paralleling the Litoranea as it cut through the rugged limestone massif of the Marmarica. Off to the left, the Gulf of Bomba's blue waters shimmered in the summer sun.

Before the takeoff, Derna advised T-2 of Balbo's anticipated appearance. The Tobruk airfield received the message; the command post of the naval batteries in the harbor, however, did not. The error was an important one, because command over the anti-aircraft defenses was divided between the navy and the air force. Nor were the naval batteries alerted visually. About two-thirds of the way along Balbo's route lay Ain el-Gazala, the advance-warning outpost for the naval batteries. According to regulations, friendly aircraft were required to make a 360-degree turn over the point at an altitude of no more than 300 meters. During those first days of the war, however, the rules were often violated, sometimes through ignorance, sometimes for reasons of inter-service rivalry. The air force, for instance, protested to the navy that for a formation of aircraft to make a full circle was cumbersome and time-consuming. Whether from impatience with these formalities or from eagerness to make up for lost time, Balbo ignored the regulations. He flew at 700 meters—more than double the prescribed altitude—and failed to make a complete circle. Porro, in order to keep up with Balbo, also violated the rules.

About 60 kilometers from Tobruk, or about seven minutes' flying time, with excellent visibility, Porro discerned trouble ahead: "black clouds of smoke, which I understood to be from bomb explosions at the T-2 airport."[12] Almost simultaneously he saw, as did the other occupants of his aircraft, "close to our aircraft the trail of tracer bullets from our anti-aircraft guns."[13] No one, however, could sight the enemy.[14]

Porro immediately tried to warn Balbo. He flew very close—

there was no voice radio equipment aboard—to Balbo's plane "to signal to him to fly to the south in order to avoid flying over the field. . . . But despite the signals that both my co-pilot and I made, he saw nothing because his eyes were fixed on the bombed airfield."[15]

What Porro and his flying companions observed—and Balbo must have also—were traces of a British air raid. At Tobruk these were almost daily affairs. On this occasion, beginning at about 5:10 P.M., nine twin-engine Bristol Blenheims, attacking in three waves of three, swooped in suddenly at a low level from the northeast and made a diagonal bombing run over the T-2 airfield. The damage was not very extensive. Most of the bombs fell on the edges of the runway, setting fire to a few of the parked aircraft and a fuel dump. The latter was the source of the black smoke Porro and the others had observed. What unnerved and infuriated the Italian defenders on the ground were the surprise and the speed of the attack. The first three bombers made their pass before the alarm cannon boomed and disappeared before the Italian batteries got off a shot. The gunners anticipated that this group, which had flown to the southwest, toward the sun, might return for a second pass. By the time the second and third group of Blenheims attacked, the Italian gunners had recovered enough to fire a few shots, but the enemy bombers veered off unscathed to the southeast, toward the airfield at El Adem.

By about 5:30, when I-MANU and Porro's bomber approached the air space over Tobruk at an altitude of about 1,000 meters, the enemy raid had ended. The anti-aircraft batteries were silent. Porro, however, sensed danger. Moreover, he had understood that on the way to Sidi Azeis, Tobruk was to be only a checkpoint. Yet, to his surprise, Balbo began to descend and Porro "understood that he wanted to land."[16] Obediently, Porro intended to throttle his motors and follow Balbo. His young and relatively inexperienced co-pilot, however, instinctively grabbed the stick and gunned the motors to gain altitude. Porro's aircraft climbed well above Balbo's and veered off to the left. His co-pilot's action, Porro reflected afterward, probably saved the lives of everyone on board.

From the ground, eyewitnesses recall seeing the two SM.79's approaching from the west—from the direction and at roughly the altitude at which the first wave of Blenheims disappeared. Since it was daylight-saving time, the sun was still quite high. "We saw in the west two aircraft low like the English . . . even if against the sun their silhouettes appeared confusing, we were convinced that they were two of the three Blenheims from the first wave, coming back for a second pass," an eyewitness recalled.[17] The tension of the moment and the particular direction—against the sun—from which Balbo's plane was approaching help explain the uncertainty. The poor training of the anti-aircraft crews and their lack of equipment—many, for instance, lacked binoculars—compounded the confusion. Under normal circumstances, the silhouettes of the two aircraft were quite distinctive. The trimotor SM.79 with its "humped" fuselage and a ventral gondola earned it the unofficial nickname of *Gobbo Maledetto* or "Damned Hunchback." The British had no trimotors and the twin-engine Blenheim had very different lines. Moreover, Balbo's plane was approaching from the direction of Derna, not from Sollum or Bardia, the normal enemy routes. On the ground, confusion reigned: some swore the British were back; others shouted that the intruders were friendly. The airman in charge of communications at T-2 tried frantically to contact the naval batteries in the harbor and relay the message from Derna that Balbo was expected. He got no answer. During the air raid, his counterparts had abandoned their posts.

The confusion incited one nervous machine gunner, located near the airport, to fire off four or five rounds. He realized his error and ceased fire immediately. The first volley, however, set off the entire Italian anti-aircraft network: "Everyone was firing: from land, from the cruiser *San Giorgio*, from submarines, from the ships; a real inferno was unleashed around the two aircraft," a ground observer remembered. From the ground, an eyewitness noted that Balbo, seeing that he was being fired upon, tried to land as quickly as possible.[18] He dove more sharply, at the same time turning to the left. The maneuver merely exposed him better as a target. At an altitude of 200 to 250 meters, with his landing gear down, he was an easy mark. Popular wisdom attributes the fatal shot to a shell from the *San Giorgio*, an old cruiser that had been sunk and heavily ballasted to command the entrance to the harbor. More likely a 20 mm incendiary shell from a naval battery located between the harbor and the airfield struck

I-MANU's fuel tanks. The big bomber, now in flames, slid over onto its left side, crashed on the bank overlooking the harbor, and exploded. Convinced that they had brought down an enemy at last, a raucous cheer went up from some of the anti-aircraft crews.

Porro, unaware of what had happened and concerned about the safety of his own aircraft, dove sharply for the hulk of the *San Giorgio* to give the impression that he too had been hit. In fact, a few bullets and shell fragments had punctured holes in the fuselage without causing serious damage. By flying low, he assumed that the anti-aircraft defenses would recognize him. He cleared the harbor, then a low range of hills on the other side, and flew over the ocean at wave top until he was out of range. Still intending to follow Balbo and land at T-2, he swung back for a second pass. At this point, he and his passengers observed "a great column of black smoke" in the vicinity of T-2 where the marshal's plane should have been and suspected "the horrible truth."[19] Despite his low altitude, which should have made his aircraft easily recognizable, the batteries continued to fire at him. Porro flew back to Ain el-Gazala, landed, then sped by car to the scene of the crash.

The wrecked I-MANU burned fiercely for several hours. Rescue teams reached the scene almost immediately, but the heat, the flames, and periodic explosions of the ammunition made their efforts useless. Recovery and identification of the bodies began late at night and continued into the early morning hours. Almost immediately, the legends began. Some claimed that Balbo's remains were easily recognizable. His jacket had been burned but the epaulettes were unmarked and among the personal effects recovered was a gold cigarette case inscribed "Italo from Philip— January 1940"—a New Year's memento from Philip Sassoon, the RAF undersecretary from 1924 to 1935.[20] More likely, since the wreck had burned all night, only dental evidence remained to identify Balbo. Two journalists, eager to bolster the image of Balbo's heroic death, invented the discovery of a partially charred scrap of paper with his typewritten political testament, "The person who doesn't know how to die for the Fatherland isn't worthy of enjoying the sun of Italy." The story was repeated on Rome radio and in the foreign press, but eventually the journalists, unable to produce the original for Italian authorities, admitted their patriotic hoax.[21]

For five days, from June 29 to July 4, Italians and Libyans in the colony officially mourned Balbo and those who had fallen with him. On June 30, a cortège of five military trucks with police escort bore the remains over the long winding road through the Gebel Akhdar to Benghazi. Despite a fierce *ghibli* that blinded the drivers and slowed the convoy, all along the Litoranea, through raw-looking, white-walled villages and towns, colonist families greeted the procession with flowers. On July 1, Benghazi paid official tribute and the following morning the bodies were flown to Tripoli. For two days the coffins lay in state in Balbo's office at the governor's palace. On July 4, following a requiem mass at the cathedral of San Francesco, the coffins, mounted on a gun-carriage, were borne through the streets of Tripoli. At Mussolini's own suggestion, as long as it did not conflict with the wishes of the widow Balbo's temporary resting place was to be the Monument to the Fallen, a massive, squat rotunda overlooking the ocean.[22] At war's end, the body was to be returned to Italy with full honors.

Condolences and tributes poured in. From Italy, expressions of grief came from the royal family, Mussolini, representatives of the Vatican, the various ranks of the party. From abroad, friend and foe, enemy and ally alike offered sympathy and praise. The Sudan *Herald* published the announcement of Balbo's death in black borders. In Madrid, the newspapers published a message of sympathy from Franco to Mussolini—the first public communication from Franco to one of the Axis powers in months. In Germany, the announcement of Balbo's death "provoked real consternation" despite his reputed Germanophobia, recalled an Italian diplomat, for Balbo was widely admired in the army and the air force.[23] In a telegram to Mussolini, Hitler said that "the German people mourn beside the Italian people" and that Balbo's action "on behalf of the young Roman empire will never be forgotten by us." Goering expressed condolences directly to the widow and attended a solemn mass in Berlin arranged by the Italian embassy. Shortly afterwards he called General Pricolo, commander of the Aeronautica, to request a souvenir from the I-MANU's wreckage.

In October, 1940, Pricolo sent him part of the burnt and twisted remains of the flying column.[24] One of the most unusual tributes came from the RAF. In a gesture that recalled the chivalry and brotherhood among airmen during World War I, a British aircraft flew over Italian lines in Libya the day after Balbo's death and dropped a box tied with tricolored ribbons. The box contained the following message:

> The British Royal Air Force expresses its sympathy in the death of General Balbo—a great leader and gallant aviator, personally known to me, whom fate has placed on the other side. [signed] Arthur Longmore, Air Officer Commanding-in-Chief, British Royal Air Force, Middle East[25]

A rush of posthumous recognition followed. In Libya, where Graziani succeeded him as governor and commander of the Italian armed forces, Balbo's photograph continued to be displayed in all government offices. A mania for naming public works projects after him developed: streets, working-class housing developments in the major towns, a Libyan agricultural village, the Via Litoranea, quays and wharfs all came to bear his name. When a radio station was also proposed, Graziani protested that Balbo's memory would soon lose all dignity.[26] In Rome, the major boulevard in front of the air ministry was named Viale Italo Balbo. (In 1944, with the change of political climate, it was given the name it bears today, Viale Pretoriano.)[27] In Ferrara, little memorial shrines were set up in many working-class homes. Photographs of Balbo, Lino, and Mussolini, bordered in tricolor, recalled the patriotic shrines to Garibaldi and Victor Emmanuel II that adorned peasant homes of an earlier generation.[28]

Among posthumous medals, Balbo received Italy's highest military decoration, the gold medal for military valor. Those who died with him were awarded the silver medal. The presentation was made on December 10, 1940, the feast day of the Madonna di Loreto, the patron saint of airmen. A few murmurs and some private grumbling could be heard among the professional military. Normally the medal was awarded for actions committed in combat with the enemy. Since there were no enemy aircraft in sight when Balbo crashed, to some it appeared that the criteria for the award were being stretched a bit. But most agreed that the medal was an appropriate way of honoring Balbo's many services to his country.

"What a stupid thing death is . . . except for its sheer weight, it means nothing," Balbo once commented.[29] In his own case, he misjudged, for Balbo dead was not Balbo gone. His deeds, his reputation, his personality cast a long shadow throughout the remaining years of the fascist regime.

Under the best of conditions, the death of such a public and controversial figure would have generated gossip and rumors. Balbo's sudden and violent end under such apparently mysterious circumstances accentuated these tendencies. Mussolini, to dispel the gossip and contradictory stories, made it plain that Balbo's death was an accident and that the naval batteries at Tobruk were to blame. However, perhaps to perpetuate Balbo's heroic image for propaganda purposes, he noted that the "all clear" after the air raid had not been sounded when Balbo appeared; therefore, he died "while he was carrying out a mission in combat."[30] The first official news, a report by the *carabinieri*, was accurate.[31] Among the *gerarchi* and high-ranking ministers there were no mysteries about what had happened. "A tragic mistake has brought his end," Ciano recorded, and De Bono noted that Balbo's plane "was brought down by our guns" who mistook it for an enemy straggler.[32]

Nevertheless, the end came so suddenly and so senselessly that even his friends were left without any satisfying or meaningful explanation.[33] Meanwhile, the irresponsible and the imaginative, who wanted to see plots, did not lack material for their fantasies. Motives for an assassination attempt were plentiful: Balbo's opposition to the war, his feuds with Ciano and other members of the hierarchy, his ambivalence toward Mussolini, his extramarital affairs, even his continual pestering for more equipment for Libya—all seemed plausible.[34] On the other hand, as Balbo's widow pointed out, for Mussolini to be the prime mover of the "plot" made no sense. The Duce had a war to fight. What was the point of doing in one of his best soldiers? Nor, to those who knew Mussolini, did such a "conspiracy" seem typical of his methods. When he wished to eliminate top rivals, the Duce usually resorted to a "changing of the guard."

Yet circumstances continued to favor the conspiracy theory.

One factor was the potential embarrassment to the war effort and
to the Italian armed forces if the full truth were known. Balbo,
one of the regime's few authentic heroes, had to die like one. For
these reasons the official communiqué was limited to two sentences and the newspapers and radio insisted that Balbo died in
combat. Nor, for obvious reasons, did the armed services show
much interest in investigating the incident. On June 30, Porro
pressed General Tellera for a thorough inquiry and General Pi-
tassi Mannella was assigned the task. Despite Porro's repeated
requests to be interrogated, he was never called. No one, so far as
is known, was ever punished or even reprimanded. Porro's investigation was on his own initiative. He passed it on to the General
Staff with the following preface: "To avoid attributing, as usual, to
grievous fatality what is due to lack of skill, lack of preparedness,
and disorganization, I declare the following: . . ."[35]

For purposes of propaganda, the Allies too favored the conspiracy theory. The British disputed the official Italian story that
Balbo died in combat. "No British aircraft was concerned in the
crash of Balbo's machine and there is thus no truth in the statement that he fell in battle," the Foreign Office News Department
declared.[36] Up to this point, the British were literally correct. By
the time I-MANU reached Tobruk the British raid was over and
Porro's party never even sighted them. But then the British in-
dulged in speculation of their own. Balbo's case, hinted the Foreign Office, paralleled that of General Werner von Fritsch, an
opponent of Hitler's domestic and foreign policies, who had died
"in an unexplained airplane disaster" in Warsaw the previous
September.[37]

Finally, the questions over Balbo's death persisted because
many could not resist the temptation to adorn what was banal,
pedestrian, and embarrassing. As Italian newspapers developed
the story, they left plenty of ambiguity. Others printed purely
fanciful versions that stressed Balbo's heroism. The *New York
Times,* for instance, included a report from the *Popolo di Roma*
which told a wild story of Balbo arriving over Tobruk in the midst
of "a violent air battle." "Desiring to take part in the battle, the
plane threw itself against an important enemy formation," but "a
burst of enemy machine-gun fire" brought it down, declared the
paper.[38] Some could not resist the temptation to shine at cocktail

parties. Scarcely a week after the incident over Tobruk, Ciano was visiting in Berlin. Eager to make an impression on a beautiful woman at a diplomatic reception, he readily admitted that Italian guns were responsible for Balbo's death. "And maybe," he added with a wink, "it wasn't an accident."[39]

Those who thought beyond the circumstances of the fatal crash wondered what effect the death of "this man with guts . . . one of the most genuine of the regime"—as the writer Giuseppe Prezzolini put it—would have on fascism.[40] "He was one of the few *real* men, courageously free, of fascism, who observed the discipline, but never pedantically or with servility. . . . Everyone mourns him, everyone senses the great void that he leaves," wrote painter and literary figure Ardengo Soffici, an old friend of both Balbo's and Quilici's.[41]

Mussolini reacted coldly. He gave no commemorative speech and signed none of the rush of journalistic tributes and biographies of Balbo that appeared immediately after his death. Mussolini's family claimed that he was deeply moved by Balbo's death, but that for political reasons, as the "invincible Duce" leading his nation in war, he could not express his grief. Balbo's friends, naturally, saw matters differently. "The order is *not to speak of him any more*," De Bono noted furiously as he prepared to leave for Ferrara and the requiem mass a month after Balbo's death.[42] Like Bottai, he was outraged that Mussolini refused to receive Donna Manù.[43] The story of the RAF tribute was suppressed in the newspapers. Rumors surfaced of the "fabulous riches" Balbo had accumulated through his associations with the *agraria* in Ferrara and his friendships with major financiers such as Volpi and Cini. Mussolini appointed Ciano as chairman of a committee to investigate the matter. They found that Balbo's wealth consisted of his apartment on Via del Colle Oppio, the villa at Punta Ala (Grosseto), and the antiquated printing presses of the *Corriere Padano*, which was operating at a deficit.[44]

These attacks on Balbo's reputation apparently stirred what little conscience Mussolini had. In Ferrara, friends, including some high party officials, gathered privately from 1941 to 1943 to commemorate Balbo's memory. Moreover, about a year after Balbo's death the journalist Yvon de Begnac published a commemorative article. For this he was attacked by the same elements who had pushed for an investigation into Balbo's alleged riches. Mussolini, however, praised Begnac for defending Balbo's memory and ordered that a memorial ceremony be held at an airfield.[45] Bottai noted on November 12, 1941, while visiting Mussolini about a proposal to name the University of Ferrara after Balbo, that the Duce had a "fleeting moment of emotion"; Balbo was an "honest and brave man," even if "we didn't always get along."[46] The high point of Balbo's persistent influence came with the Grand Council meeting of July 25, 1943. "It was said that Balbo's shadow weighed on that assembly," Acerbo commented afterward.[47] De Vecchi, in speaking against the war at that session, specifically recalled Balbo's position at the previous council meeting, nearly four years earlier.[48] When the votes were counted in that last fateful meeting that precipitated the end of fascism, the majority went against Mussolini nineteen to seven. *Ferraresi* cast five of the majority votes. Outside the room, a sixth, Renzo Chierici, head of the police, had also gone over to the opposition.

With the fall of the regime he had once symbolized, in Italy Balbo's name went into eclipse. The plan to return his body with full military honors evaporated, and in the flood of anti-fascist sentiment his story was buried. In Chicago a major thoroughfare through Grant Park still bore the name of Balbo Drive, but Italy named no street after him—not even in Ferrara.[49] Busts of the once-acclaimed aerial conqueror of oceans and continents and portraits of the African colonizer who ruled with imperial Roman grandeur disappeared from public display.[50] The post-war Aeronautica, trying to live down its reputation as the most fascist of the armed services, made grotesque efforts to deny its paternity. Foreigners, who remembered the gallant airman more than the fascist, proved more charitable. *Life* described him as "the best type of Italian adventurer."[51] For awhile his name literally remained part of the flying vocabulary and it can still be found in technical dictionaries of aviation. Crossword-puzzle fans sometimes encounter him as a five-letter word for "transatlantic aviator," and mystery writers and popular novelists, creating a background of fascist Italy, recall him as a colorful and influential figure of the era who advised "never to lead from the back."[52]

In Italy, time muffled some of the shrillness of post-war anti-fascism. For three decades Balbo's remains rested in Libya. In 1970, in a wave of xenophobic nationalism, the Libyan government threatened to disinter the Italian cemeteries in Tripoli. Balbo's family arranged privately to have the body returned to Italy. For a final resting-place they chose a site at Orbetello, near the old seaplane base from which he had launched his great flight of 1933. Balbo now rests there with all the companions of his last flight except Nello Quilici, who was buried in Tuscany. In recent years, several *atlantici* have been buried beside Balbo. Others have requested that when their time comes, they too would like to rest beside their chief and their comrades.

Balbo's gravestone has no epitaph. Ironically, Ciano, his old rival, provided a possible one. In an outburst of genuine grief, scribbled in his diary the day after Balbo's death, he offered a summation that Balbo himself might have agreed with. Yet in his final tribute to a man who had spent the majority of his career publicly praising fascism and whom the regime had exalted as the epitome of fascism, Ciano never once used the term *fascism*. Exuberant and restless, Balbo "loved life in all its manifestations," Ciano wrote. "He had more dash than talent, more vivacity than acumen. He was a decent fellow, and even in political clashes, in which his partisan temperament delighted, he never descended to dishonorable and questionable expedients. Balbo's memory will linger long among Italians because he was, above all, a true Italian, with the great faults and great virtues of our race."[53]

Abbreviations

AB	Archivio Balbo (Rome)
ACS	Archivio Centrale dello Stato (Rome)
AP	Atti Parlamentari
APCD	Atti Parlamentari, Camera dei Deputati
ASMAI	Archivio Storico Ministero Africa Italiana
CP	*Corriere Padano*
ORIGA	United States National Archives, Official Records of Italian Government Agencies (1922–1944), Washington, D.C.
USE	Ufficio Storico Esercito

Notes

1. Journalist: The Young Mazzinian

1. Giuseppe Prezzolini, *Diario 1939–1945* (Milan, 1962), p. 226.

2. Balbo celebrated his birthday on June 6 and that is the day usually listed. His birth certificate records June 5.

3. R. Forti and G. Ghedini, *L'avvento del fascismo: Cronache ferraresi* (Ferrara, 1923), 135.

4. G. Ward Price, *I Know These Dictators* (Port Washington, N.Y., 1970; orig. pub. 1937), 225.

5. G. Titta Rosa, *Vita di Balbo* (Rome, 1941), 3–4; "La morte del Prof. Camillo Balbo," CP, July 17, 1931, 4; July 18, 1931, 5.

6. CP, July 17, 1931, 4.

7. Italo Balbo, *Diario 1922* (Milan, 1932), 150.

8. Ibid., 137.

9. Interview with Egle Balbo Orsi, Ferrara, March 18, 1974.

10. Giuseppe Fanciulli, *L'eroica vita di Italo Balbo narrata ai giovani* (Turin, 1940), 3.

11. For the following see Titta Rosa, *Vita di Balbo*, 5.

12. Sergio Panunzio, *Italo Balbo* (Milan, 1923), 14.

13. Titta Rosa, *Vita di Balbo*, 5–6.

14. Balbo, *Diario 1922*, 6.

15. Alberto Brizio, "Fausto Balbo, un poeta ferrarese," *Corriere Emiliano*, June 13, 1931, 3.

16. Fausto Balbo, *Canti lirici 1903–1905* (Bologna, 1905).

17. Nello Quilici, "L'interventismo ferrarese," *Rivista di Ferrara* (1935), 11.

18. Luigi Lotti, *I repubblicani in Romagna dal 1894 al 1915* (Faenza, 1957), 185–86; Museo Centrale del Risorgimento, "Fondo Albani," busta provvisoria 956.

19. Fanciulli, *Eroica vita*, 28.

20. Ibid.

21. Panunzio, *Italo Balbo*, 8.

22. Ibid., 9.

23. Titta Rosa, *Vita di Balbo*, 8; interview with Francesco De Rubeis, Ferrara, March 19, 1974.

24. "Condannati" and "La monarchia è salva," *La Raffica*, April 13, 1913, 3.

25. Titta Rosa, *Vita di Balbo*, p. 8; Fanciulli, *Eroica vita*, 29.

26. Fanciulli, *Eroica vita*, 30.

27. Italo Balbo, "Roberto Fabbri, il più giovane aviatore del mondo: ricordi e note raccolte dall'amico Italo Balbo" (Ferrara, 1913).

28. *Il Popolo d'Italia*, April 19, 1915.

29. *Il Popolo d'Italia*, December 20, 1914, 1. The article is unsigned and amateurish.

30. Italo Balbo, "La guerra nelle elezioni," *L'Alpino*, October 5, 1919, 1.

31. Renato Sitti and Lucilla Previati, *Ferrara, il regime fascista* (Milan, 1976), 19–20.

32. Panunzio, *Italo Balbo*, 14.

33. Paul Corner, *Fascism in Ferrara, 1915–1925* (London, 1975), p. 40.

34. Italo Balbo, "La guerra nelle elezioni," *L'Alpino*, October 5, 1919, 1.

35. Corner, *Fascism in Ferrara*, 27.

2. Soldier: Hero of the *Alpini*

1. G. Fanciulli, *L'eroica vita di Italo Balbo narrata ai giovani* (Turin, 1940), 54.

2. Ufficio Storico dell'Aeronautica, Libretto Personale, "Balbo, Italo," contains the official record of assignments and evaluations by Balbo's superiors.

3. Giorgio Rochat, *Italo Balbo aviatore e ministro dell'aeronautica. 1926–1933* (Ferrara, 1979), 173.

4. Italo Balbo, "Bandiere al Vento," *L'Alpino*, October 24–November 4, 1919.

5. Ufficio Storico dell'Aeronautica, Libretto Personale.

6. G. Titta Rosa, *Vita di Italo Balbo* (Rome, 1941), 11.

7. Rochat, *Italo Balbo aviatore*, 174; Titta Rosa, *Vita di Balbo*, 12.

8. Ufficio Storico dell'Aeronautica, Libretto Personale.

9. Rochat, *Italo Balbo aviatore*, 175 n. 5.

10. Ufficio Storico dell'Aeronautica, Libretto Personale.

11. Ibid.

12. Balbo, "I nostri eroi: Franco Michelini-Tucci," *L'Alpino*, October 24–November 4, 1919, 3.

13. E. Faldella, ed., *Storia delle Truppe Alpine* (Milan, 1972), II, 964–67.

14. For the following account see Balbo, "I nostri eroi."

15. AB, "Scritti e discorsi," I.

16. Rochat, *Italo Balbo aviatore*, 172.

17. Fanciulli, *Eroica vita*, 64.

18. Paolo Orano, *Balbo* (Rome, 1940), 42–43.

19. AB, "Scritti e discorsi," I.

20. Ufficio Storico dell'Aeronautica, Libretto Personale.

21. N. Rodolico, "Ricordo di Italo Balbo," *Gli annali dell'università italiana* I, no. 4 (1940), 527–28.

22. Italo Balbo, *Diario 1922* (Milan, 1932), 7.

23. Archivio Facoltà di Scienze Politiche, Università di Firenze, Filza n. 873, Inserto 22709.

24. Alessandro Roveri, *Le origini del fascismo a Ferrara, 1918–1921* (Milan, 1974), 132 n. 51. The story apparently originated in Carlo Rosselli's *Giustizia e Libertà*, August 9, 1935.

25. Rodolico, "Ricordo di Balbo," 529.

26. For the following see Giordano Bruno Guerri, *Italo Balbo* (Milan, 1984), 53–54, and the report of the Examining Commission in the "Cesare Alfieri" Archives.

27. The following is based on interviews with the late Donna Emanuella Balbo.

28. Sergio Panunzio, *Italo Balbo* (Milan, 1923), 17; Italo Balbo, *Diario 1922* (Milan, 1932), 7.

29. *L'Alpino*, September 14, 1919, 1.

30. "La guerra nelle elezioni," *L'Alpino*, October 5, 1919, 1.

31. Balbo, *Diario 1922*, 6; "L'Inchiesta di Caporetto e la speculazione degli imboscati," *L'Alpino*, September 4, 1919, 1.

32. Balbo, *Diario 1922*, 7.

33. "L'ora storica," *L'Alpino*, September 28, 1919, 1.

34. "I nostri eroi," 3–4.

35. Italo Balbo, *Diario 1922*, 5.

36. Roveri, *Origini*, 11–24; Paul Corner, *Fascism in Ferrara, 1915–1925* (London, 1975), 48–49.

37. R. Gilardi, "L'altro uomo, Italo Balbo," *Visto*, November 23, 1957, 17–18.

38. Corner, *Fascism in Ferrara*, 81.

39. R. Forti and G. Ghedini, *L'avvento del fascismo: Cronache ferraresi* (Ferrara, 1923), 13–14.

40. Ibid., 14.

41. Forti and Ghedini, *Avvento del fascismo*, 26–32.

42. Quoted in Guerri, *Italo Balbo*, 62.

43. Ibid., 61.

44. Roveri, *Origini del fascismo*, 71.

45. Corner, *Fascism in Ferrara*, 37.

46. Balbo, *Diario 1922*, 8.

47. Roveri, *Origini del fascismo*, 46–53; Corner, *Fascism in Ferrara*, 67–68.

48. For the following see Corner, *Fascism in Ferrara*, 106–7.

49. Manlio Cancogni, *Storia dello squadrismo* (Milan, 1959), 74–83; CP, April 12, 1939, 5.

50. Forti and Ghedini, *Avvento del fascismo*, 220–23.

51. Roveri, *Origini del fascismo*, 91–92.

52. Ibid., 94.

53. Balbo, *Diario 1922*, 8.

54. Corner, *Fascism in Ferrara*, 129–36.

55. Gilardi, "Altro uomo," 17–18.

56. *La Voce Repubblicana*, November 29, 1924, 1; quoted in Roveri, *Origini del fascismo*, 132.

57. Guido Torti, letter in *La Voce Repubblicana*, November 27, 1924.

58. Guerri, *Italo Balbo*, 64.

59. See *La Voce Repubblicana*, December 2 and 5, 1924.

60. ACS, busta 102, Mostra della Rivoluzione Fascista, Carteggio del Comitato Centrale dei Fasci.

61. *La Voce Repubblicana*, December 2, 1924, 4.

62. Interview with author, March, 1973.

63. Tamaro, *Venti anni*, I, 122–23.

64. The text is in *La Voce Repubblicana*, December 4, 1924, 4.

65. Corner, *Fascism in Ferrara*, 8 n. 2, 124–28; Alessandro Roveri, *Dal sindacalismo rivoluzionario al fascismo* (Florence, 1972), 350; Giorgio Rochat, *Italo Balbo* (Turin, 1986), 35–39.

66. ACS, SPD, CR, busta 98 X/R, sotto fasc. 8.

67. Roveri, *Origini del fascismo*, 118–19.

68. Ibid., 120.

69. *Il Balilla*, I, no. 3 (February 6, 1921), 2.

70. Roveri, *Origini del fascismo*, 136.

71. Ibid., 140–41.

3. *Squadrista:* Campaigns 1921

1. Attilio Tamaro, *Venti anni di storia* (Rome, 1953), I, 125; Adrian Lyttelton, *The Seizure of Power: Fascism in Italy 1919–1929* (London, 1973), 54–55.

2. Paul Corner, *Fascism in Ferrara, 1915–1925* (London, 1975), x.

3. Italo Balbo, *Diario 1922* (Milan, 1932), 11.

4. Ibid., 9–10.

5. For the following see Alessandro Roveri, *Le origini del fascismo a Ferrara, 1918–1921* (Milan, 1974), 89–133.

6. Lyttelton, *Seizure of Power*, 52–53; Christopher Seton-Watson, *Italy from Liberalism to Fascism* (London, 1967), 571.

7. W. B. Courtney, "Mussolini's Unhappy Warrior," *Collier's*, April 11, 1936, 13.

8. Leo Longanesi, "La lezione di Sorel," in *Il meglio di Leo Longanesi* (Milan, 1958), 79–91.

9. Balbo, *Diario 1922*, 10–11.

10. Tamaro, *Venti anni*, I, 127.

11. Ibid., 148.

12. Curzio Malaparte and Enrico Falqui, *Vita di Pizzo di Ferro* (Rome, 1931), 48–49.

13. Balbo, *Diario 1922*, 10.

14. Tamaro, *Venti anni*, I, 154.

15. Interview with Augusto Maran, Gualtiero Finzi, and Francesco De Rubeis, Ferrara, March, 1974.

16. Interview with Augusto Maran, Ferrara, March 20, 1974.

17. Tamaro, *Venti anni*, I, 154; Sergio Panunzio, *Italo Balbo* (Milan, 1923), 40–41.

18. Roveri, *Origini del fascismo*, 136–99 passim.

19. Renato Sitti and Lucilla Previati, *Ferrara, il regime fascista* (Milan, 1976), 61.

20. Luigi Salvatorelli and Giovanni Mira, *Storia d'Italia nel periodo fascista* (Turin, 1964), 179.

21. R. Forti and G. Ghedini, *L'avvento del fascismo: Cronache ferraresi* (Ferrara, 1923), 130–31.

22. Ibid., 238–43.

23. Giordano Bruno Guerri, *Italo Balbo* (Milan, 1984), 80–81.

24. Roveri, *Origini del fascismo*, 195–96.

25. Ibid., 211.

26. Panunzio, *Italo Balbo*, 37.

27. Giuseppe Fanciulli, *L'eroica vita di Italo Balbo narrata ai giovani* (Turin, 1940), 87; interview with Egle Balbo Orsi, Ferrara, March, 1974.

28. AB, "Scritti e discorsi," f. "Da mettere la data" (discorso Dino Gardini, June 29, 1941).

29. Fanciulli, *Eroica vita*, 88.

30. AB, "Scritti e discorsi," I.

31. Panunzio, *Italo Balbo*, 35–37.

32. Corner, *Fascism in Ferrara*, 177; Roveri, *Origini del fascismo*, 177–82.

33. Roveri, *Origini del fascismo*, 181.

34. Renzo De Felice, *Mussolini il fascista: La conquista del potere (1921–25)* (Turin, 1966), 36–39.

35. A. Rossi, *The Rise of Italian Fascism*, trans. Peter Wait and Dorothy Wait (New York, 1966), 121–22.

36. "Dalla primavera del 1921 alla primavera del 1925, impressioni e ricordi," CP, May 28, 1925, 1.

37. Roveri, *Origini del fascismo*, 200.

38. De Felice, *Mussolini il fascista*, 46–47.

39. ACS, MI, 77B; Alessandro Roveri, *L'affermazione dello squadrismo fascista nelle campagne ferraresi, 1921–1922* (Ferrara, 1979), 6.

40. Corner, *Fascism in Ferrara*, 186.

41. Roveri, *Affermazione*, 6.

42. Ibid., chap. 2.

43. Ibid., 20.

44. Ibid., 21; De Felice, *Mussolini il fascista*, 151 n. 3.

45. De Felice, *Mussolini il fascista*, 157 n. 1.

46. A. Roveri, *Affermazione*, 21.

47. Balbo, *Diario 1922*, 11–13; Tamaro, *Venti anni*, I, 187.

48. Balbo, *Diario 1922*, 12.

49. Tamaro, *Venti anni*, I, 187; G. A. Chiurco, *Storia della rivoluzione fascista* (Rome, 1973), I, 395.

50. AB, "Scritti e discorsi," I.

51. ACS, Mostra Rivoluzione Fascista, busta 102.

52. Roveri, *Affermazione*, 25–26.

53. Ibid, 74–77, for the text.

54. Ibid., 27–35; Corner, *Fascism in Ferrara*, 197–98.

55. Roveri, *Affermazione*, 89.

56. Ibid.

57. Ibid., 30.

58. Ibid., 29.

59. Corner, *Fascism in Ferrara*, 198–200; Rossi, *Rise of Italian Fascism*, 166; Roveri, *Affermazione*, 93–95.

60. Chiurco, *Storia della rivoluzione fascista*, I, 441, 442; Tamaro, *Venti anni*, I, 203.

61. Roveri, *Affermazione*, 93–95.

62. *Il Resto del Carlino*, November 29, 1921, 1; AB, "Scritti e discorsi," I.

63. AB, 1921–1922, Marcia su Roma alfabetico, f. "Gino Baroncini."

64. Balbo, *Diario 1922*, 18.

65. Tamaro, *Venti anni*, I, 206; Lyttelton, *Seizure of Power*, 66–67.

66. AB, 1921–1922, Marcia su Roma, f. "Norme sulla organizzazione della squadre."

67. AB, 1921, Marcia su Roma, f. "Lettere di Capi del PNF."

68. AB, 1921–1922, Alfabetico, f. "Dino Perrone Compagni."

69. Balbo, *Diario 1922*, 140.

70. Ibid., 143.

71. Ibid., 13.

4. *Squadrista*: Campaigns 1922

1. Italo Balbo, *Diario 1922* (Milan, 1932), 20.

2. Ibid., 3.

3. Duilio Susmel, "La verità su Balbo," *Domenica del Corriere*, June 13, 1967, 13.

4. For the following see Giordano Bruno Guerri, *Italo Balbo* (Milan, 1984), 104–6.

5. *Diario 1922*, 4.

6. A. Répaci, *La marcia su Roma, mito e realtà* (Rome, 1963), I, 13.

7. Balbo, *Diario 1922*, 19.

8. Ibid., 18.

9. Ibid., 19.

10. Ibid., 17–18.

11. Ibid., 90.

12. Ibid., 30.

13. Ibid., 29.

14. Ibid., 21.

15. Ibid., 46.

16. Ibid., 45.

17. Ibid., 22.

18. Ibid., 64–65, 137, 149, 192.

19. Ibid., 20.

20. Ibid., 31.

21. AB, 1921–1922, Marcia su Roma, f. "Fiume."

22. Balbo, *Diario 1922*, 38.

23. Ibid., 40.

24. Ibid., 63.

25. Renzo De Felice, *Mussolini il fascista: La conquista del potere (1921–25)* (Turin, 1966), 253, 299; F. Cordova, "Le origini dei sindacati fascisti," *Storia Contemporanea* I, n. 4 (December 1970), 1006.

26. Cordova, "Origini dei sindacati fascisti," 1002.

27. Balbo, *Diario 1922*, 51.

28. Ibid., 52.

29. Ibid., 54, 61.

30. Ibid., 56.

31. Guerri, *Italo Balbo*, 110.

32. Balbo, *Diario 1922*, 63.

33. For the following see ibid., 65–70.

34. Ibid., 69.

35. For the following see Cordova, "Origini dei sindacati fascisti," 1004–5.

36. Balbo, *Diario 1922*, 74.

37. Ibid., 74–75.

38. For the following, ibid., 77–81.

39. Guerri, *Italo Balbo*, 115.

40. Balbo, *Diario 1922*, 88.

41. Ibid., 89.

42. Ibid., 91.

43. Ibid.

44. Ibid., 95.

45. Ibid., 96–107.

46. Ibid., 103.

47. Ibid.

48. Ibid., 104; AB, 1921–1922, Marcia su Roma, f. "Varie."

49. Balbo, *Diario 1922*, 95.

50. Ibid., 104.

51. Ibid., 109.

52. Ibid., 110.

53. Ibid., 119.

54. Guerri, *Italo Balbo*, 122.

55. Ibid., 121; Balbo, *Diario 1922*, 147.

56. Balbo, *Diario 1922*, 136.

57. AB, 1921–1922, Marcia su Roma, f. "Varie."

58. Guerri, *Italo Balbo*, 122.

59. Balbo, *Diario 1922*, 111.

5. *Quadrumvir*: The March on Rome

1. C. J. Sprigge, "When Mussolini Led the March on Rome,"in J. Weiss, ed., *Nazis and Fascists in Europe* (Chicago, 1969), 32–33.

2. Giordano Bruno Guerri, *Italo Balbo* (Milan, 1984), 122.

3. Christopher Seton-Watson, *Italy from Liberalism to Fascism* (London, 1967), 629.

4. Renzo De Felice, *Mussolini il fascista: La conquista del potere (1921–25)* (Turin, 1966), 307.

5. Ibid., 296 n. 1.

6. Italo Balbo, *Diario 1922* (Milan, 1932), 4.

7. Balbo, *Diario 1922*, 189.

8. Guerri, *Italo Balbo*, 132.

9. Seton-Watson, *Italy from Liberalism to Fascism*, 617; A. Rossi, *The Rise of Italian Fascism*, trans. Peter Wait and Dorothy Wait (New York, 1966), 262–64.

10. A. Rossi, *Rise of Italian Fascism*, 266.

11. Balbo, *Diario 1922*, 144.

12. Ibid.

13. Dino Grandi, "Il diario della Marcia su Roma," *Epoca*, September 15, 1972, 70.

14. Balbo, *Diario 1922*, 168, frontispiece.

15. Ibid., 163.

16. Ibid., 164.

17. Ibid., 192; Rossi, *Rise of Italian Fascism*, 276.

18. Balbo, *Diario 1922*, 168.

19. Ibid., 139–40.

20. Guerri, *Italo Balbo*, 125.

21. Ibid., 143.

22. Ibid.

23. De Felice, *Mussolini il fascista*, 316–18.

24. A. Répaci, *La marcia su Roma, mito e realtà* (Rome, 1963), II, 291.

25. Cesare Rossi, *Trentatre vicende mussoliniane* (Milan, 1958), 122.

26. Balbo, *Diario 1922*, 167.

27. Ibid., 169–73.

28. AB, 1921–1922, Marcia su Roma, f. "Azioni su Parma."

29. Balbo, *Diario 1922*, 173.

30. AB, Marcia su Roma, Lettere di Capi del PNF, "Parma."

31. Copies are in ibid.

32. De Felice, *Mussolini il fascista*, 343.

33. Répaci, *Marcia su Roma*, I, 431.

34. For the following, see Balbo, *Diario 1922*, 177–82.

35. Ibid., 185.

36. C. Rossi, *Trentatre vicende mussoliniane*, 132–33.

37. Balbo, *Diario 1922*, 185.

38. Ibid.

39. Ibid., 148.
40. Ibid., 186.
41. Ibid., 187.
42. Ibid., 192.
43. Ibid., 193.
44. Ibid.
45. Ibid., 194.
46. Ibid., 195.
47. Ibid.
48. Ibid.
49. Ibid., 196–97.
50. Ibid., 198.
51. Répaci, *Marcia su Roma*, I, 447–48.
52. Balbo, *Diario 1922*, 200.
53. Ibid., 199.
54. Italo Balbo, "Da Perugia a Roma," *Gerarchia* VII, 10 (October, 1927), 957–58.
55. For the following see Grandi, "Diario della Marcia su Roma," 76.
56. De Felice, *Mussolini il fascista*, 324; Seton-Watson, *Italy from Liberalism to Fascism*, 625–26.
57. A. Rossi, *Rise of Italian Fascism*, 308–12; Seton-Watson, *Italy from Liberalism to Fascism*, 626–29.
58. Répaci, *Marcia su Roma*, I, 449.
59. Balbo, *Diario 1922*, 198.
60. Ibid., 199.
61. Ibid., 200.
62. Ibid., 201.
63. Ibid, 204–5.
64. Ibid., 204.
65. Ibid., 205.
66. For the following, see ibid., 207–8.
67. Guerri, *Italo Balbo*, 136.
68. Ibid., 139.
69. Ibid., 140.
70. Balbo, *Diario 1922*, 209–10.
71. Guerri, *Italo Balbo*, 141–42.
72. Balbo, *Diario 1922*, 212.
73. Ibid., 213.
74. Ibid., 213–14; between October 27 and 31 fascist casualties totaled 31: De Felice, *Mussolini il fascista*, 358.
75. Balbo, *Diario 1922*, 214.

6. *Ras* of Ferrara: The Intransigent

1. Giordano Bruno Guerri, *Italo Balbo* (Milan, 1984), 145.

2. ACS, Carte Bianchi, busta 1, fasc. 6, 12.

3. Adrian Lyttelton, "Fascism in Italy: The Second Wave," *Journal of Contemporary History* I, 1 (1966), 78.

4. Christopher Seton-Watson, *Italy from Liberalism to Fascism* (London, 1967), 641.

5. Paul Corner, *Fascism in Ferrara* (London, 1974), 251, 276; Giorgio Rochat, *Italo Balbo aviatore e ministro dell'aeronautica 1926–1933* (Ferrara, 1979), 7.

6. Seton-Watson, *Italy from Liberalism to Fascism*, 634.

7. Ibid.

8. Adrian Lyttelton, *The Seizure of Power: Fascism in Italy 1919–1929* (London, 1973), 246.

9. Guerri, *Italo Balbo*, 148–54; Rochat, *Italo Balbo aviatore*, 6–7.

10. Italo Balbo, "Lavoro e milizia per la nuova Italia" (Rome, 1923).

11. Corner, *Fascism in Ferrara*, 226.

12. AB, 1921–1922, Marcia su Roma, Lettere di Capi del PNF, "Parma."

13. Balbo, *Diario 1922* (Milan, 1932), 140.

14. Corner, *Fascism in Ferrara*, 228–29; A. Répaci, *La marcia su Roma, mito e realtà* (Rome, 1963), II, 273–75.

15. Balbo, *Diario 1922*, 149.

16. Corner, *Fascism in Ferrara*, 226–31; Répaci, *Marcia su Roma*, II, 273–75; ACS, Carte De Bono, busta 1 (1922), nn. 18, 21, 23, 24, 26.

17. ORIGA, T-586 (1118), 073794.

18. Corner, *Fascism in Ferrara*, 237–47.

19. Ibid., 243.

20. ACS, Carte De Bono, busta 1 (1922), n. 24.

21. ORIGA, T-586 (1118), 073792–93.

22. ACS, Carte Michele Bianchi, busta 3, fasc. 53.

23. *Il Mondo*, December 6, 1924, 4.

24. Corner, *Fascism in Ferrara*, 248 n. 5; Guerri, *Italo Balbo*, 163.

25. Giorgio Rochat, *Italo Balbo* (Turin, 1986), 188–89.

26. G. Titta Rosa, "Italo Balbo e gli artisti," CP, June 28, 1941, 5.

27. Italo Balbo, *Il volo d'Astolfo* (Ferrara, 1928).

28. Renato Sitti and Lucilla Previati, *Ferrara, il regime fascista* (Milan, 1976), 93–95; Guerri, *Italo Balbo*, 112–13; Corner, *Fascism in Ferrara*, 282–85; Giorgio Rochat, *Italo Balbo* (Turin, 1986), 151–166.

29. Sitti and Previati, *Ferrara*, 93.

30. Ibid., 95.

31. Corte di Assise di Ferrara, Sentenza (20 giugno 1947), 13–14.

32. Ibid.; "In memoria di Don Giovanni Minzoni Arciprete di San Nicolò di Argenta" (Ravenna, 1923), 14–16; Lorenzo Bedeschi, *Don Minzoni* (Milan, 1973), 11–16.

33. Corte di Assise de Ferrara, Sentenza, 92–95.

34. "La speculazione," *Il Balilla*, September 29, 1923, 3.

35. R. Gilardi, "L'altro uomo, Italo Balbo," *Visto*, December 21, 1957, 18.

36. Quoted in Guerri, *Italo Balbo*, 170.

37. Corte di Assise di Ferrara, Sentenza, 44–47, 87–88.

38. "Documenti del costume politico sotto il regime fascista," *Il Mondo*, December 6, 1924, 3.

39. Corte di Assise di Ferrara, Sentenza, 97–98.

40. "Documenti del costume politico."

41. *La Voce Repubblicana*, November 27, 1924.

42. Text in Attilio Tamaro, *Venti anni di storia* (Rome, 1953), II, 35.

43. *La Voce Repubblicana*, November 29, 1924.

44. George Seldes, *Sawdust Caesar* (New York, 1935), 217.

45. George Seldes, "Hero Balbo," *The Nation*, August 2, 1933, 131.

46. For the following see Lyttelton, *Seizure of Power*, 248–50.

47. Ibid., 261.

48. Lyttelton, "Fascism in Italy," 84–85; Lyttelton, *Seizure of Power*, 262–64.

49. Lyttelton, "Fascism in Italy," 86–87; Luigi Salvatorelli and Giovanni Mira, *Storia d'Italia nel periodo fascista* (Turin, 1964), 351–52.

50. Renzo De Felice, *Mussolini il fascista: La conquista del potere (1921–25)* (Turin, 1966), 711, claims Balbo stayed out of the conspiracy.

51. Carlo Silvestri, *Matteotti, Mussolini e il dramma italiano* (Milan, 1981), xx.

52. Anna Folli, *Vent'anni di cultura ferrarese, 1925–1945: Antologia del Corriere Padano* (Bologna, 1978), i, xv, xvi; Guerri, *Italo Balbo*, 183–90.

53. Alberto Aquarone, "Nello Quilici e il suo 'Diario di Guerra,'" *Storia Contemporanea* VI, 2 (1975); Guerri, *Italo Balbo*, 184–88.

54. *La Conquista dello Stato*, April 5, 1925.

55. CP, November 15, 1925, 6.

56. Folli, *Vent'anni di cultura ferrarese*, I.

57. CP, April 25, 1925, 1.

58. CP, May 5, 15, 1925; ORIGA, T-586 (468), 035755.

59. Ruggero Zangrandi, *Il lungo viaggio attraverso il fascismo* (Milan, 1962), 456–59.

60. Guerri, *Italo Balbo*, 188.

61. Luciano Bergonzini, ed., "Testimonianza di Paolo Fortunati," in *La resistenza a Bologna: Testimonianze e documenti* (Bologna, 1967), I, 320–22.

62. Folli, *Vent'anni di cultura ferrarese*, i, xvii.

63. Corner, *Fascism in Ferrara*, 277, 280.

64. Lyttelton, *Seizure of Power*, 283.

65. Guerri, *Italo Balbo*, 146–48; A. Mola, *Storia della Massoneria italiana dall'Unità alla Repubblica* (Milan, 1976), 450, 550.

66. Galeazzo Ciano, *Ciano's Diary 1939–43*, ed. Malcolm Muggeridge (London, 1947), 53.

67. Tamaro, *Venti anni*, II, 111.

68. Ibid.

69. CP, October 18, 1925.

70. CP, September 12, 1925, 1.

71. AB, Ministero Economia Nazionale, f. "Regio Corpo delle Foreste."

72. Rochat, *Italo Balbo aviatore*, 9.

73. AB, Ministero Economia Nazionale, f. "ENIT" and "Commissione Interministeriale Controllo Importazioni."

74. CP, April 9, 1926, 1.

75. Salvatorelli and Mira, *Storia d'Italia*, 707–8.

7. Undersecretary: Douhet's "Disciple"

1. Quoted in Giordano Bruno Guerri, *Italo Balbo* (Turin, 1984), 287, 289.

2. Air University (U.S.), Aerospace Studies Institute, *The United States Air Force Dictionary* (New York, 1956), 69.

3. Ufficio Documentazione e Propaganda dello Stato Maggiore Aeronautica, "Breve storia dell'Aeronautica Militare Italiana" (Rome, 1973).

4. Luigi Federzoni, *Italia di ieri per la storia di domani* (Milan, 1967), 152.

5. Rochat, *Italo Balbo aviatore*, 69–71, 168–69; Giuliano Colliva, *Uomini e aerei* (Milan, 1973), 90; S. Licheri, *L'arma aerea italiana nella seconda guerra mondiale* (Milan, 1976), 29; Macgregor Knox, *Mussolini Unleashed, 1939–1941* (New York, 1982), 22.

6. Guerri, *Italo Balbo*, 201.

7. Ibid., 202.

8. CP, May 21, 1926, 5.

9. CP, June 19, 1926, 5.

10. *Interavia*, June 19, 1933, 3.

11. AB, Min. Aeronautica Riservato I, f. "Aeronautica: Relazioni di S.E. Balbo a S.E. Mussolini."

12. Rochat, *Italo Balbo aviatore*, 45.

13. *Aviation*, April 4, 1927, 661.

14. *New York Times*, January 25, 1927, 4.

15. AB, Min. Aeronautica Riservato I, f. "Aeronautica: Relazioni di S.E. Balbo a S.E. Mussolini."

16. Guerri, *Italo Balbo*, 205.

17. AB, Min. Aeronautica Riservato I, f. "Aeronautica: Relazioni di S.E. Balbo a S.E. Mussolini."

18. AB, Min. Aeronautica I, f. "Condizioni aeronautica nel giugno 1926—Ten. Armando Preziosi."

19. E. Canevari, *Graziani mi ha detto* (Rome, 1947), 307.

20. Giuseppe D'Avanzo, *Ali e poltrone* (Rome, 1976), 98.

21. For the following see Claudio G. Segrè, "Douhet in Italy: Prophet without Honor?" *Aerospace Historian* (June, 1979), 69–80.

22. G. Douhet, *La guerra integrale*, preface by Italo Balbo (Rome, 1936), viii.

23. D. Irving, *The Rise and Fall of the Luftwaffe* (Boston, 1973), 31.

24. Italo Balbo, *Sette anni di politica aeronautica (1927–1933)* (Milan, 1935), 249–50.

25. For the following see General Balbo, "Italy's Air Force," in AB, "Scritti e discorsi," n. 1, f. "Articoli dopo il 1922."

26. Ibid.

27. For the following, see Italo Balbo, "Arte della guerra aerea," *Enciclopedia Italiana*, App. I (Rome, 1938), 699–701.

28. A. F. Hurley, *Billy Mitchell: Crusader for Air Power* (New York, 1964), 114.

29. R. Abate, *Storia dell'aeronautica italiana* (Milan, 1974), 177–78.

30. Rochat, *Italo Balbo aviatore*, 85 n. 6.

31. Balbo, *Sette anni*, 248.

32. Ibid., 166.

33. Ibid., 240.

34. Ibid., 252.

35. ORIGA, T-586 (468), 035699; AB, Ministero Aeronautica Riservato I, f. "Relazioni di S.E. Balbo a S.E. Mussolini."

36. Guerri, *Italo Balbo*, 208.

37. Ibid.

38. Balbo, *Sette anni*, 79.

39. APCD, Legis. XXVIII, 1a Sessione, *Discussioni*, May 28, 1930, 2881.

40. Balbo, *Sette anni*, 79–81.

41. Ibid., 166–68.

42. Ibid., 234.

43. Ibid., 16; B. H. Liddell Hart, *Europe in Arms* (London, 1937), 113.

44. Ibid., 166.

45. Cf. table in D'Avanzo, *Ali e poltrone*, 858; AP-Senato, Legis. XXVIII, 1a sessione, *Discussioni*, May 20, 1932, 5206–10.

46. Balbo, *Sette anni*, 167.

47. APCD, Legis. XVIII, 1a Sessione, *Discussioni*, March 12, 1930, 1788.

48. "Military and Naval," *Aviation* 31, 3 (March, 1932), 131–39, has some excellent comparative tables of air force budgets and the difficulties of evaluating the figures.

49. Colliva, *Uomini e aerei*, 83.

50. Balbo, *Sette anni*, 136–37. I have taken 300,000 lire as an average. The lira was calculated at about 5 cents to the dollar.

51. "Military and Naval," 134.

52. Archivio Federzoni, "Diario 1927," III, March 29, 1927, 82–83.

53. Balbo, *Sette anni*, 166–68.

54. "The dryness of the figures and the precision of the material data transform themselves before the imagination's eyes into a vision of power, skill, and courage that moves and exalts," commented the *Corriere della Sera*, April 30, 1931, about Balbo's budget speech.

55. Attilio Tamaro, *Venti anni di storia* (Rome, 1953), II, 410.

56. Knox, *Mussolini Unleashed*, 293; D'Avanzo, *Ali e poltrone*, 858.

57. Text is reprinted in Rochat, *Italo Balbo*, 188–207.

58. Colliva, *Uomini e aerei*, 91–92.

59. Christopher Chant, *Aviation: An Illustrated History* (London, 1978), 191.

60. Rochat, *Italo Balbo*, 128.

61. Colliva, *Uomini e aerei*, 93.

62. Giuseppe Santoro, *L'aeronautica italiana nella seconda guerra mondiale* (Milan-Rome, 1966), I, 39.

63. For the following see Jonathan Thompson, *Italian Civil and Military Aircraft 1930–1945* (Fallbrook, 1963); Piero Vergnano, *The Fiat Fighters 1930–1945* (Genoa, 1969); Rochat, *Italo Balbo*, 125–26.

64. Edward Homze, *Arming the Luftwaffe* (Lincoln, 1976), 128–29.

65. Balbo, *Sette anni*, 160–62.

66. Rochat, *Italo Balbo*, 127–28.

67. Thompson, *Italian Civil and Military Aircraft*, 251.

68. Rochat, *Italo Balbo*, 121.

69. Balbo, *Sette anni*, 112.

70. Santoro, *Aeronautica italiana*, I, 17–18.

71. Ibid., 19.

72. D'Avanzo, *Ali e poltrone*, 726–27.

73. Rodolfo Gentile, *Storia dell'aeronautica dalle origini ai nostri giorni* (Rome, 1958), 281–82; Santoro, *Aeronautica italiana*, II, 480–81.

74. Abate, *Storia dell'aeronautica italiana*, 136, 137.

75. AB, Aeronautica Alfabetico III, f. "Industria aeronautica," contains some reports marked "top secret" which Verduzio prepared for Balbo; Balbo, *Sette anni*, 84–85.

76. For the following see AB, Ministero dell'Aeronautica, "Bilancio di Previsioni, 1932–33."

77. "Military and Naval," 139.

78. Balbo, *Sette anni*, 39–41, 43, 84, 86; Santoro, *Aeronautica italiana*, I, 15, 39.

79. AB, Aeronautica Alfabetico, 3, f. Guidoni, "Memorandum, n. 33, March 14, 1928."

80. AB, Ministero Aeronautica, "Bilancio di Previsione, 1932–33"; Homze, *Arming the Luftwaffe*, 74.

81. Ugo Ojetti, *I Taccuini 1914–1943* (Florence, 1954), 247.

82. Balbo, *Sette anni*, 44–45, 50–51; AB, Aeronautica Alfabetico III, f. "Industria aeronautica."

83. Ibid., 181.

84. AB, Ministero Aeronautica Riservato I, f. "Verbali rapporti 1926."

85. D'Avanzo, *Ali e poltrone*, 131–34.

86. Ibid.

87. For the MF 5 and DO X affairs: "Guidi" files in the Museo Caproni, Rome; AB, Ministero Aeronautica, Varie I, f. "Consorzio aeronautico italiano"; P. Boni Fellini, *Fatti e retroscena di vita aeronautica* (Rome, 1946), 182–83.

88. Abate, *Storia dell'aeronautica italiana*, 198–200; R. E. G. Davies, *A History of the World's Airlines* (London, 1964), 9–10, 38, 62; Balbo, *Sette anni*, 180; "Foreign Activities," *Aviation* 30, 3 (March, 1931), 175.

89. G. Mattioli, *Mussolini aviatore* (Rome, 1939), 264; ACS, *Diario De Bono*, v. 32, October 3, 1928.

90. For the following, see AB, Ministero Aeronautica Riservato II, f. "Aviazione civile 1927–28"; Balbo, *Sette anni*, 143.

91. AB, Aeronautica Alfabetico I, f. "Ala Littoria—Linee atlantiche 1939"; Ministero Aeronautica Riservato II, f. "Aviazione civile."

92. Balbo, *Sette anni*, 180.

93. AB, Aeronautica Alfabetico R–Z, f. "Tedeschini Lalli."

94. Balbo, *Sette anni*, 180.

95. Balbo, *Sette anni*, 143–44; Aeronautical Chamber of Commerce, Inc., *Aeronautical Yearbook 1928* (New York, 1928), 217–18, 223.

96. Balbo, *Sette anni*, 180.

97. Fondazione Einaudi, Archivio "Thaon di Revel," 28.4.

8. Minister: Father of the *Aeronautica*

1. Italo Balbo, *Sette anni di politica aeronautica (1927–1933)* (Milan, 1935), 172.

2. Ibid., 59–63, 101.

3. AB, Memoriale Anonimo, f. "Comandante Nemo."

4. Balbo, *Sette anni*, 226.

5. For the following, see Giorgio Rochat, *Italo Balbo aviatore e ministro dell'aeronautica (1926–1933)* (Ferrara, 1979), 70, 134–35; Balbo, *Sette anni*, 172.

6. Balbo, *Sette anni*, 64.

7. Rochat, *Italo Balbo*, 136.

8. Balbo, *Sette anni*, 226–27.

9. ORIGA, T-586 (468), 035658.

10. For the following see ACS, Segreteria Particolare del Duce, Corrispondenza Riservata, b. 51, 278/R.

11. Giordano Bruno Guerri, *Italo Balbo* (Milan, 1984), 226.

12. Ibid., 227: "Tu hai il mal dell'agnello." "????" "Ti cresce la pancia e ti cala l'uccello."

13. Ibid.

14. AB, Alfabetico I, f. "Stefano Cagna."

15. Balbo, *Sette anni*, 144–45; "Nel primo decennale della R. Aeronautica," *L'Aerotecnica* XIII, 4 (1933), 335–36.

16. Cmdr. Silvio Scaroni, "The Equipment of Air Forces," *Aviation* 32, 12 (December, 1933), 375.

17. Manlio Bendoni, *L'epopea del reparto alta velocità* (Asola, 1973); Giuseppe D'Avanzo, *Ali e poltrone* (Rome, 1976), 99–101.

18. For the following see Rochat, *Italo Balbo aviatore*, 136–37; "Military and Naval," *Aviation* 31, 3 (March, 1932), 131; Balbo, *Sette anni*, 256.

19. *Almanacco aeronautico 1931*, II (Milan, 1931), 104–7.

20. AB, Aeronautica Alfabetico, n. 2, f. "Convegno internazionale Aviatori Transoceanici."

21. Giuseppe Valle, *I miei trent'anni di volo* (Milan, 1939), 255–56; Giuliano Colliva, *Uomini e aerei* (Milan, 1973), 89–91.

22. Christopher Chant, *Aviation: An Illustrated History* (London,

1978), 131–50; Henry R. Palmer, Jr., *This Was Air Travel* (New York, 1962), 183–200.

23. Ugo Ojetti, *I Taccuini 1914–1943* (Florence, 1954), 260.

24. P. Boni Fellini, *Fatti e retroscena di vita aeronautica* (Rome, 1946), 180.

25. ORIGA, T-586 (468), 035702; AB, Aeronautica Alfabetico E–F, f. "A. Ferrarin"; Aeronautica Alfabetico III, f. "Capt. Guazzetti."

26. AB, Aeronautica Alfabetico 3, f. "Guidoni."

27. Balbo, *Sette anni*, 199–202.

28. Valfredo Fradeani, *Storia di un primato* (Milan, 1976), 124–28.

29. Balbo, *Sette anni*, 218–20; Valle, *I miei trent'anni di volo*, 239–41; Guerri, *Italo Balbo*, 229–31.

30. Balbo, *Sette anni*, 218–19.

31. Major Al Williams, *Airpower* (New York, 1940), 37–39.

32. AB, Aeronautica Alfabetico R–Z, f. "Riccardi."

33. Guerri, *Italo Balbo*, 231.

34. For the following see Rochat, *Italo Balbo*, 90–99; Colliva, *Uomini e aerei*, 83–85.

35. Guerri, *Italo Balbo*, 210.

36. Rochat, *Italo Balbo*, 110; Balbo, *Sette anni*, 194–96.

37. Balbo, *Sette anni*, 194.

38. Rochat, *Italo Balbo*, 98.

39. ORIGA, T-586 (468), 035649–53.

40. Romeo Bernotti, *Cinquant'anni nella marina militare* (Milan, 1971), 202; Francesco Pricolo, *La regia aeronautica nella seconda guerra mondiale* (Milan, 1971), 237.

9. Aviator: The Mediterranean Cruises

1. Christopher Chant, *Aviation: An Illustrated History* (London, 1978), 151–63; David Mondy, ed., *The International Encyclopedia of Aviation* (New York, 1977), 428–32.

2. "Italy's Achievement," *Aviation* XXV, 3 (July 16, 1928), 175.

3. Italo Balbo, *Sette anni di politica aeronautica (1927–1933)* (Milan, 1935), 145.

4. Ibid.

5. Ibid., 113.

6. Ranieri Cupini, *Cieli e mari* (Milan, 1973), 30.

7. E. Colston Shepherd, *Great Flights* (London, 1939), 70–75.

8. Giordano Bruno Guerri, *Italo Balbo* (Milan, 1984), 242–43.

9. Cupini, *Cieli e mari*, 27–55.

10. *Passeggiate aeree sul Mediterraneo* (Milan, 1929), 25–26.

11. AB, Aeronautica Alfabetico n. 2, f. "Crociera Mediterranea Occidentale 1928."

12. ORIGA, T-586 (682), 050605.

13. ORIGA, T-586 (682), 053062–63.

14. ORIGA, T-586 (468), 035715–16; Duilio Susmel, "La verità su Balbo," *Domenica del Corriere*, June 13, 1967, 36–37.

15. Susmel, "Verità su Balbo," 36.

16. Nobile tells his side in Umberto Nobile, *La tenda rossa* (Milan, 1969), and *Ali sul polo* (Milan, 1975). Wilbur Cross, *Ghost Ship of the Pole* (New York, 1960), is naively pro-Nobile.

17. ORIGA T-586 (682), 050546–97.

18. Quoted in Guerri, *Italo Balbo*, 219.

19. For the following, see ORIGA, T-586 (686), 053099–100.

20. Luigi Mancini, ed., *Grande enciclopedia aeronautica* (Milan, 1936), 203; "Dodici velivoli italiani a Londra," *Aeronautica* (July, 1928), 578–79; interview, General Alberto Briganti, Rome, July 7, 1976.

21. AB, Viaggi e voli, f. "Volo Roma-Londra-Berlino-Roma luglio 1928."

22. Giuseppe Fanciulli, *L'eroica vita di Italo Balbo narrata ai giovani* (Turin, 1940), 128–29.

23. AB, "Scritti e discorsi," I.

24. Italo Balbo, "Contributo dell'Italia alla navigazione aerea" (Rome, 1928), 16–17.

25. U.S. National Archives, RG38, ONI General Corr., 39–42, Box 42, A2–14/EF36/EN1–11, vol. 1.

26. Balbo, "Contributo dell'Italia," 9.

27. Ibid., 10.

28. CP, January 9, 1929, 4.

29. U.S. National Archives, RG 38, ONI Gen. Corr., 29–42, A2–14/EF36.

30. *New York Times*, January 4, 1929, 14.

31. CP, January 18, 1929, 1–2.

32. ORIGA, T-586 (468), 035720–22, 035723–33; CP, January 5, 1929, 1; January 18, 1929, 1; *New York Times*, January 4, 1929, 14.

33. CP, January 18, 1929, 1.

34. ORIGA, T-586 (468), 035733.

35. Italo Balbo, *Stormi in volo sull'oceano* (Milan, 1931), 13–14.

36. Ibid.

37. Italo Balbo, *La centuria alata* (Milan, 1934), 11.

38. Italo Balbo, *Da Roma a Odessa* (Milan, 1929); Cupini, *Cieli e mari*, 55–105.

39. *New York Times*, June 9, 1929, 6; June 10, 8; June 11, 12; June 14, 13; Balbo, *Da Roma a Odessa*, 94.

40. Balbo, *Da Roma a Odessa*, 102–3.

41. Renzo De Felice, *Mussolini il fascista: L'organizzazione dello stato fascista, 1925–1929* (Turin, 1968), 26; Giuseppe D'Avanzo, *Ali e poltrone* (Rome, 1976), 102.

42. Balbo, *Da Roma a Odessa*, 105.

43. Ibid., 149–50.

44. Ibid., 150.

45. Ibid., 138–39.

46. Ibid., 117.

47. Ibid., 156.

48. Ibid., 128.

49. Ibid., 99.

50. Ibid., 165.

51. Paolo Monelli, *Italo Balbo* (Rome, 1941), 56–57.

52. Balbo, *Da Roma a Odessa*, 159–60.

53. D'Avanzo, *Ali e poltrone*, 120.

54. On the Balbo–De Pinedo rivalry: Giorgio Rochat, *Italo Balbo aviatore e ministro dell'aeronautica 1926–1933* (Ferrara, 1979), 76–81; Arturo De Pinedo with Mario Conti, "Vita ardente di Francesco De Pinedo," *Il Mattino*, January 30, 1951, and February 4, 1951; De Pinedo and Conti, "Ardimentosa vita di Francesco De Pinedo," *Il Giornale di Sicilia*, February 3 and 4, 1951; D'Avanzo, *Ali e poltrone*, 111–15.

55. Duilio Susmel, "Verità su Balbo," *Domenica del Corriere*, June 13, 1967, 37–40, contains extensive excerpts from the letter.

56. Rochat, *Italo Balbo aviatore*, 188–207, reprints the memorandum and the report.

57. Quoted in Guerri, *Italo Balbo*, 221.

58. ACS, "De Pinedo," busta 51 278/R, sotto fasc. 4; Rochat, *Italo Balbo aviatore*, 80–81.

59. John P. V. Heinmuller (*Man's Fight to Fly* [New York, 1944], 38–43) was a personal friend of De Pinedo's and witnessed the final crash.

60. Arturo De Pinedo, "Francesco De Pinedo: Dal Trionfo al Rogo," *Il Momento*, February 4, 1951.

61. "Turkey Buys Italian Planes," *United States Naval Institute Proceedings* 57, 345 (November, 1931), 1583.

62. Romeo Bernotti, *Cinquant'anni nella marina militare* (Milan, 1971), 203–6.

63. "A Sea-Air Fleet," *United States Naval Institute Proceedings* 55, 9 (September, 1929), 810.

64. Franco Fucci, *Ali contro Mussolini* (Milan, 1978).

10. Aviator: The First Atlantic Cruise

1. Italo Balbo, *Stormi in volo sull'oceano* (Milan, 1931), 14–15.

2. Ranieri Cupini, *Cieli e mari* (Milan, 1973), 106–7.

3. Balbo, *Stormi in volo*, 18–19.

4. *Almanacco Aeronautico* II (Milan, 1931), 181–82.

5. Archivio del Vittoriale, f. "Balbo."

6. Cupini, *Cieli e mari*, 112–13.

7. Ibid., 117–18; Balbo, *Stormi in volo*, 55–56; Italo Balbo, *Sette anni di politica aeronautica (1927–1933)* (Milan, 1935), 204.

8. M. Cervi, *L'aviatore* (Florence, 1962), 7–9.

9. Balbo, *Stormi in volo*, 28.

10. Cupini, *Cieli e mari*, 114.

11. Balbo, *Stormi in volo*, 30.

12. Ibid., 32–35; Giordano Bruno Guerri, *Italo Balbo* (Milan, 1984), 277.

13. Italo Balbo, *La centuria alata* (Milan, 1934), 194.

14. *Daily Express*, December 15, 1930.

15. Cupini, *Cieli e mari*, 129–30; Balbo, *Stormi in volo*, 100.

16. Balbo, *Stormi in volo*, 108–14.

17. Cupini, *Cieli e mari*, 131–33.

18. Ibid., 140–41.

19. Ibid., 142–45.

20. Balbo, *Stormi in volo*, 184–85.

21. Ibid., 187.

22. For the accidents at Bolama see Cupini, *Cieli e mari*, 146–47; Balbo, *Stormi in volo*, 189, 194, 217.

23. Ibid., 196.

24. Ibid., 205–6.

25. Ibid., 219.

26. Ibid., 251.

27. Elisabeth Cerruti, *Je les ai bien connus: Souvenirs d'ambassades* (Paris, 1950), 134–35.

28. Ibid.

29. Balbo, *Stormi in volo*, 255.

30. The pun on *conti* can be translated as "the accounts don't balance" and "he didn't come back a count."

31. ACS, *Diario De Bono* 36, February 21, 1931, 47.

32. AB, "Crociera aerea transatlantica Italia-Brasile, Documentazione Britannica"; also testimonials collected by General Piccio, the Italian air attaché in Paris.

33. London *Morning Post*, January 7, 1931; London *Daily Mirror*, January 7, 1931.

34. *London Times*, January 9, 1931; *Daily Telegraph*, January 9, 1931; for Balbo's reaction, Balbo, *Stormi in volo*, 283.

11. Aviator: The Second Atlantic Cruise

1. Italo Balbo, *Stormi in volo sull'oceano* (Milan, 1931), 15.
2. Italo Balbo, *La centuria alata* (Milan, 1934), 271–72.
3. Christopher Chant, *Aviation: An Illustrated History* (London, 1978), 158.
4. ACS, "Diario De Bono," vol. 38, 32.
5. Gianfranco Bianchi, *Rivelazioni sul conflitto Italo-Etiopico* (Milan, 1967), 14.
6. Paolo Monelli, *Italo Balbo* (Rome, 1941), 64.
7. Balbo, *Centuria alata*, 16.
8. Attilio Tamaro, *Venti anni di storia* (Rome, 1953) III, 29.
9. For the following, see Ranieri Cupini, *Cieli e mari* (Milan, 1973), 179–81; Balbo, *Centuria alata*, 34–62.
10. Interview, General Ranieri Cupini, Rome, November 17, 1973.
11. Cupini, *Cieli e mari*, 233–34.
12. AB, Aeronautica Alfabetico, n. 2, f. "Convegno Internazionale Aviatori Transoceanici."
13. "Balbo Shows the Way," *U.S. Air Services* (August, 1933), 13.
14. David Darrah, *Hail Caesar* (Boston, 1936), 231.
15. Ibid., 232–33.
16. Balbo, *Centuria alata*, 93.
17. Cupini, *Cieli e mari*, 216.
18. Balbo, *Centuria alata*, 92.
19. Ibid., 79–80, 83.
20. Darrah, *Hail Caesar*, 230.
21. For the following see ibid., 234–35.
22. Cupini, *Cieli e mari*, 207–11.
23. Balbo's version of the crossing is in *Centuria alata*, 94–235. For an English translation see Italo Balbo, *My Air Armada*, trans. Gerald Griffin (London, 1934), which uses the flight over the Alps on the dust jacket. See also Cupini, *Cieli e mari*, 218–38.
24. *Columbus: The Magazine of Italo-American Relations* XIX (December, 1933), 54.
25. Balbo, *Centuria alata*, 152.
26. For the following see ibid., 191–96.
27. Ibid., 205.
28. Cupini, *Cieli e mari*, 233.
29. For the following see *Time*, July 24, 1933, 22.
30. Balbo, *Centuria alata*, 259.

31. Ibid., 262–63.

32. Ibid., 275.

33. Ibid., 280.

34. Ibid., 276–78.

35. Ibid., 284.

36. Henrietta Nesbitt, *White House Diary* (New York, 1949), 91–92.

37. Balbo, *Centuria alata*, 289.

38. Ibid., 300; *New York Times*, July 24, 1933, 2.

39. Balbo, *Centuria alata*, 300.

40. Balbo reproduces the final version of the speech in *Centuria alata*, 297–98. For earlier versions see AB, "Scritti e discorsi" II, f. "Discorsi di S.E. Balbo."

41. Balbo, *Centuria alata*, 301.

42. Ibid., 303; *Chicago Tribune*, July 24, 1933, 1.

43. For the following see Giordano Bruno Guerri, *Italo Balbo* (Milan, 1984), 260–63.

44. *New York Times*, July 15, 1933, 3.

45. AB, "Scritti e discorsi" II, "Discorsi di S.E. Balbo."

46. *New York Times*, July 16, 1933; personal correspondence, Egidio Clemente, November 21, 1975.

47. *Chicago Tribune*, July 16, 1933, part I, 2; *Daily Worker*, July 17, 1933, 11.

48. George Seldes, "Hero Balbo," *The Nation*, August 2, 1933, 131.

49. Edmund Wilson, *The Thirties: From Notebooks and Diaries of the Period*, ed. Leon Edel (New York, 1980), 374–75.

50. Balbo, *Centuria alata*, 300.

51. Balbo, *My Air Armada*, 184.

52. J. Diggins, *Mussolini and Fascism: The View from America* (Princeton, 1972), 146.

53. *San Francisco Chronicle*, July 17, 1933, 1.

54. For a collection, see *Columbus* XIX (December, 1933).

55. *Christian Century*, August 2, 1933, 973, favored the flight as a gesture of Italian-American friendship, but added that there was "no reason to think more highly of fascism than before."

56. "General Mitchell on Balbo Flight," *U.S. Air Services* XVIII, 8 (August, 1933), 41.

57. "Italy's Great Achievements: Past and To Come," *U.S. Air Services* XVIII, 6 (June, 1933), 23.

58. *Columbus* (December, 1933), 55–58, 99.

59. *Literary Digest*, August 12, 1933, 4.

60. For the return flight see Balbo, *Centuria alata*, 305–69; Cupini, *Cieli e mari*, 254–71.

61. Guerri, *Italo Balbo*, 264.

62. Quoted in Edward R. Tannenbaum, *The Fascist Experience* (New York, 1972), 227, and translated by him.

63. Balbo, *Centuria alata*, 372.

64. Ibid., 378.

65. Darrah, *Hail Caesar*, 235–36.

66. Balbo, *Centuria alata*, 381.

67. Ibid., 383.

68. For the following see AB, "Considerazioni dopo la seconda crociera atlantica."

69. Italo Balbo, *Sette anni di politica aeronautica (1927–1933)* (Milan, 1935), 207–10.

70. G. Rochat, *Italo Balbo aviatore e ministro dell'aeronautica 1926–1933* (Ferrara, 1979), 68.

71. "Navy Makes Longest Oversea Formation Flight," *U.S. Air Services* (October, 1933), 7. For the French Expedition: *Time*, August 14, 1933, 26; Balbo, "La crociera nera," CP, December 24, 1933, 1.

72. Balbo, *Centuria alata*, 354.

73. R. E. G. Davies, *A History of the World's Airlines* (London, 1964), chaps. 14, 15.

74. Guerri, *Italo Balbo*, 265.

75. Ibid.; Cupini, *Cieli e mari*, 279.

76. AB, Aeronautica Alfabetico E–F, "Francobolli commemorativi crociere"; personal correspondence, Aldo Alonge, Milano.

77. Giuseppe D'Avanzo, *Ali e poltrone* (Rome, 1976), 858. These figures exclude "special" appropriations for the Ethiopian war and the Spanish civil war.

78. "Background of the American Aeronautical Corporation," *U.S. Air Services* XIV, 9 (September, 1929), 64.

79. Guerri, *Italo Balbo*, 259.

80. *Columbus*, XIX (December, 1933), 83, 98.

81. Guerri, *Italo Balbo*, 256.

82. AB, "Scritti e discorsi" n. 2, f. "Discorsi di Balbo."

83. *Il Tempo*, August 9, 1953.

84. G. Pillon, "Ritorno a Balbo Avenue," *Il Borghese*, October 28, 1973.

12. Air Marshal: The Road to Exile

1. Ugo Ojetti, *I Taccuini 1914–1943* (Florence, 1954), 393.

2. Giordano Bruno Guerri, *Italo Balbo* (Milan, 1984), 272–73.

3. Ojetti, *I Taccuini*, 326.

4. Italo Balbo, *Diario 1922* (Milan, 1932), 6.

5. David Roberts, *The Syndicalist Tradition and Italian Fascism* (Chapel Hill, 1979), 211.

6. Renzo De Felice, *Mussolini il fascista: L'organizzazione dello stato fascista, 1925–1929* (Turin, 1968), 319–20.

7. "L'abito fa il monaco," CP, October 10, 1927.

8. Ministero delle Corporazioni, *Atti del secondo convegno di studi sindacali e corporativi (Ferrara 5–8 maggio, 1932)*, Rome, 1932, vol. III, 19.

9. Ibid., 53–54.

10. Alberto Aquarone, *L'organizzazione dello stato totalitario* (Turin, 1965), 200; Guerri, *Italo Balbo*, 191.

11. ORIGA, T-586 (468), 035467–68.

12. Guerri, *Italo Balbo*, 190–91.

13. Ojetti, *I Taccuini*, 373.

14. ACS, "Diario De Bono," vol. 33, February 16, 1929.

15. CP, March 16, 1929, 1.

16. Guerri, *Italo Balbo*, 273–74; De Felice, *Organizzazione*, 198 n. 2.

17. De Felice, *Organizzazione*, 151.

18. Guerri, *Italo Balbo*, 274.

19. Ibid.

20. Giuseppe D'Avanzo, *Ali e poltrone* (Rome, 1976), 212–13.

21. Italo Balbo, *Lavoro e milizia per la nuova Italia* (Rome, 1923), 18–20, 37–44.

22. Guerri, *Italo Balbo*, 274.

23. Alexander J. De Grand, *The Italian Nationalist Association and the Rise of Fascism in Italy* (Lincoln, 1978), 178–79.

24. Giuseppe Bottai, *Diario 1935–1944*, ed. G. B. Guerri (Milan, 1982), 206–7.

25. Ugo Alfassio Grimaldi and Gherardo Bozzetti, *Farinacci: Il più fascista* (Milan, 1972), 242.

26. G. Invernizzi, "Italo Balbo: Da un caffè di provincia al governatorato della Libia," *Historia* (August, 1967), 27.

27. P. Badoglio, *Italy in the Second World War*, trans. Muriel Currey (London, 1948), 23.

28. Bottai, *Diario*, 212.

29. Giuseppe Bottai, *Vent'anni e un giorno* (Milan, 1949), 213. In Bottai's diary, however, under the same date, November 12, 1941, Mussolini merely complained that if Balbo rather than Graziani had commanded Italian forces in Libya, the Italians would have been victorious.

30. Giorgio Rochat, *Italo Balbo aviatore e ministro dell'aeronautica (1926–1933)* (Ferrara, 1979), 53–54.

31. Ugo Guspini, *L'orecchio del regime* (Milan, 1973), 81.

32. ORIGA, T-586 (468), 035559–65.

33. ORIGA, T-586 (468), 035571–76.

34. ORIGA, T-586 (468), 035566–67.

35. Archivio Federzoni, "Diario 1927," I, 1–6; Federzoni, "Ricatto al Re," *L'Indipendente* II, 149 (June 28, 1946).

36. ACS, "Diario De Bono," February 27, 1931, May 18, 1931.

37. For the following see Renzo De Felice, *Mussolini il Duce: Lo stato totalitario, 1936–1940* (Turin, 1981), 6; and especially Guerri, *Italo Balbo*, 278–81.

38. ORIGA T-586 (1294), 111678.

39. Guerri, *Italo Balbo*, 282–83.

40. Luigi Salvatorelli and Giovanni Mira, *Storia d'Italia nel periodo fascista* (Turin, 1964), 750.

41. Charles S. H. Londonderry, The Marquess of Londonderry, *Wings of Destiny* (London, 1943), 68.

42. AB, Stampa Ventimila, f. "Stampa estera"; interview Witold Korab-Laskowski, 1938.

43. Guerri, *Italo Balbo*, 283; A. J. Toynbee, *Survey of International Affairs 1932* (London, 1933), 260–61.

44. For the text, see De Felice, *Mussolini il Duce: Gli anni del consenso, 1929–1936* (Turin, 1974), 404–5.

45. Ojetti, *I Taccuini*, 400.

46. E. Canevari, *Graziani mi ha detto* (Rome, 1947), 151–53, 307; Canevari, *La guerra italiana* (Rome, 1948), I, 220–21; Piero Pieri and Giorgio Rochat, *Pietro Badoglio* (Turin, 1974), 636–37.

47. De Felice, *Mussolini il Duce: 1929–1936*, 284.

48. Guerri, *Italo Balbo*, 285–86.

49. Ojetti, *I Taccuini*, 400.

50. Ibid.

51. For the following see ACS, SPD, CR busta 61; or Duilio Susmel, "La verità su Balbo," *Domenica del Corriere*, June 20, 1967, 20.

52. For the following, see Guspini, *Orecchio del regime*, 117–18.

53. ACS, SPD, CR busta 57, 362/R sottofasc. 7.

54. ACS, *Diario De Bono*, vol. 38, November 28, 1933.

55. Canevari, *Guerra italiana*, I, 221 n. 1.

56. AB, Aeronautica Alfabetico, III, "Douhet."

57. AB, Aeronautica Alfabetico M–O, "Erhard Milch."

58. For the following, see ACS, SPD, CR, busta 57, 362/R, sottofasc. 7.

59. Ibid. For the following, see ACS, SPD, CR, busta 61; also in Guerri, *Italo Balbo*, 287–88.

60. Ojetti, *I Taccuini*, 400.

61. Ibid., 417.

62. CP, December 20, 1933, 1.

63. CP, December 21, 1933; AB, "Scritti e discorsi" II, "Discorsi di S.E. Balbo," for a handwritten draft.

64. For the following, see ORIGA, T-568 (486), 035632–38.

65. Ojetti, *I Taccuini*, 430.

66. Guerri, *Italo Balbo*, 292–93; Gianfranco Bianchi, *Rivelazioni sul conflitto Italo-Etiopico* (Milan, 1967), 26–28.

67. Bianchi, *Rivelazioni sul conflitto*, 28–30.

68. Ibid., 132.

69. CP, January 17, 1934, 1.

70. Giovanni De Luna, *Badoglio: Un militare al potere* (Milan, 1974), 129.

71. ACS, "Diario De Bono," vol. 38, 48–49, 51.

13. Governor General of Libya: Builder and Colonizer

1. Claudio G. Segrè, *Fourth Shore: The Italian Colonization of Libya* (Chicago, 1974), 35–41.

2. Ardito Desio, "Short History of the Geological, Mining and Oil Exploration in Libya," Istituto di Geologia dell'Università degli Studi di Milano, ser. G, n. 250.

3. Segrè, *Fourth Shore*, 20–25.

4. J. L. Miège, *L'impérialisme colonial italien de 1870 à nos jours* (Paris, 1968), 186–87.

5. Spectator Libycus, "Due anni di governo del Maresciallo Balbo in Libia" (Tripoli, 1936), 3.

6. CP, January 16, 1934, 1.

7. G. Bucciante, *Vita breve di Italo Balbo* (Rome, 1941), 30.

8. R. Gilardi, "L'altro uomo, Italo Balbo," *Visto*, February 1, 1958, 18.

9. C. Eylan, "Choses vues en Italie et en Libye," *Revue des Deux Mondes*, March 1, 1936, 136–37.

10. ACS, Carte Graziani, sc. 6, fasc. 11.

11. Spectator Libycus, "Due anni," 4–7.

12. For the following, see ACS, "Diario De Bono," vol. 39, April 21, June 12, August 10, 1934.

13. Ibid., August 10, 1934.

14. Ibid., October 13, 1934.

15. AB, Libia Alfabetico N–Z, "Gen. Giuseppe Valle."

16. CP, February 23, 1934, 2.

17. Spectator Libycus, "Due anni," 32.

18. Italo Balbo, "La Litoranea Libica," *Nuova Antologia*, March 1, 1937, 5.

19. *La strada Litoranea della Libia* (Verona, 1937), 16–21.

20. Ibid., 9, 35; Spectator Libycus, "Due anni," 36.

21. *La strada Litoranea della Libia*, 43–45.

22. Ibid., 59.

23. Ibid., 46–51.

24. Ibid., 45.

25. ORIGA, T-586 (468), 035469–70 (1202), 088910.

26. AB, Alfabetico F–M, f. "Lazzari, Tommaso."

27. Segrè, *Fourth Shore*, 35–79.

28. Italo Balbo, "La colonizzazione in Libia," *L'Agricoltura Coloniale*, XXXIII, 8 (August, 1939), 464.

29. Ibid., 463.

30. Istituto Agronomico per l'Oltremare, Osservatore Rurale n. 2067, Italo Balbo, "La situazione dei coloni dell'Ente in Libia Orientale," 2–3.

31. AB, Libia Alfabetico A–D, "Dompieri."

32. AB, Congressi Raduni n. 3, f. "XVI Adunata del 10° Alpini in Tripoli."

33. J. A. Ducrot, "Que se passe-t-il en Libye?" *L'Illustration*, March 26, 1938, 328.

34. L. V. Bertarelli, *Guida d'Italia del Touring Club Italiano: Possedimenti e colonie* (Milan, 1929), 269.

35. Eros Vicari, "Ente turistico ed Alberghiero della Libia," *Gli annali dell'Africa Italiana* V, 4 (December, 1942), 958.

36. Hamilton Wright, Jr., "Tripoli Rejuvenated," *Atlantica* XX, 1 (January, 1939), 80.

37. Ducrot, "Que se passe-t-il en Libye?" 328.

38. Giacomo Caputo, "I grandi monumenti della romanità risuscitati da Balbo," *Libia* IV, 5–8 (May–August, 1940), 44; Renato Simoni, "I teatri di Sabratha e Leptis," ibid., 48–49.

39. Ducrot, "Que se passe-t-il en Libye?" 349.

40. A. Tapproge, "Impressions du III Ralley Saharien de Tripolitaine," *L'Aviation Belge*, March 12, 1938.

41. AB, Libia: Congressi, Raduni, Manifestazioni, I, "Press Clippings."

42. AB, Libia, Raduni, Manifestazioni, II, "IX Gran Premio"; G.L. Steer, *A Date in the Desert* (London, 1939), 146–49.

43. Steer, *Date in the Desert*, 131.

44. Wright, "Tripoli Rejuvenated," 77; Marquess of Donegall, "Almost in Confidence," *Sunday Despatch*, November 6, 1938.

45. R. S. Harrison, "Migrants in the City of Tripoli, Libya," *Geographical Review* LVII, 3 (July, 1967), 399, 410.

46. Giuseppe Bucciante, "Lo sviluppo edilizio della Libia," *Note ad uso dei Giornalisti* (Tripoli, 1937), 3.

47. Spectator Libycus, "Due anni," 37–41; A. Giovannangeli, "Cenni sull'attività Municipale di Tripoli," *Note ad uso dei Giornalisti*.

48. AB, Libia Alfabetico A–D, "Brasini."

49. Giovannangeli, "Cenni sull'attività Municipale di Tripoli."

50. Harrison, "Migrants," 397–423.

51. Alan Houghton Broderick, *North Africa* (London, 1943), 27.

52. For the following, see Steer, *Date in the Desert*, 134.

53. Broderick, *North Africa*, 27.

54. Steer, *Date in the Desert*, 132–33.

55. Attilio Tamaro, *Venti anni di storia* (Rome, 1953), III, 242.

56. Charles Mott-Radclyffe, *Foreign Body in the Eye: Memoir of the Foreign Service, Old and New* (London, 1975), 33.

57. E. D. O'Brien, "With the Duce in Libya," *English Review* 64 (May, 1937), 550–51.

58. Mott-Radclyffe, *Foreign Body in the Eye*, 33.

59. AB, Libia Varie II, f. "Telegrammi e lettere dopo visita del Duce 1937."

60. The following description is based on Ugo Ojetti, "L'Arco sulla Litoranea," *Cose Viste* (Florence, 1960), 1459–60.

61. Tamaro, *Venti anni*, III, 242.

62. O'Brien, "With the Duce in Libya," 554.

63. AB, Libia Varie II, f. "Telegrammi e lettere pervenute dopo la visita del Duce 1937."

14. Governor General of Libya: Creator of the Fourth Shore

1. G. Volpe, *L'Italia che fu* (Milan, 1961), 123–24.

2. Luigi Federzoni, *Italia di ieri per la storia di domani* (Milan, 1967), 154.

3. Claudio G. Segrè, *Fourth Shore: The Italian Colonization of Libya* (Chicago, 1974), 102–31.

4. AB, Viaggi e Voli, f. "Viaggio in Africa Orientale, aprile-maggio 1938."

5. Giovanni Comisso, "Italo Balbo nei miei ricordi," *Libia* IV, 5–8 (May–August 1940), 28.

6. Italo Balbo, "Coloni in Libia," *Nuova Antologia*, November 1, 1938, 3.

7. Martin Moore, *Fourth Shore* (London, 1940), 34–35.

8. AB, Libia, I Ventimila e gli Undicimila, f. "Telegrammi al Duce da Genova e in navigazione."

9. Moore, *Fourth Shore*, 50.

10. AB, Libia, I Ventimila e gli Undicimila, f. "Telegrammi al Duce da Genova e in navigazione."

11. Ibid. The file contains no reply.

12. Moore, *Fourth Shore*, 117.

13. Giuseppe Fanciulli, *L'eroica vita di Italo Balbo narrata ai giovani* (Turin, 1940), 240; Cornelio di Marzio, "Ritratto di Balbo," CP, September 8, 1940, 3.

14. L. Federzoni, *Italia di ieri per la storia di domani* (Milan, 1967), 155.

15. AB, Scritti e discorsi, f. "Da mettere la data."

16. Vincent de Pasca in *Evening Standard*, November 7, 1938.

17. "I coloni scrivono," *L'Azione Coloniale*, January 5, 1939, 8.

18. Moore, *Fourth Shore*, 121.

19. *Ibid.*, 115.

20. For press reaction, see Segrè, *Fourth Shore*, 108–9.

21. AB, Libia, I Ventimila e gli Undicimila, f. "Colonizzazione demografica, anno XVIII."

22. Segrè, *Fourth Shore*, 110–11.

23. AB, Libia Alfabetico A–D, "Desio."

24. AB, Libia, I Ventimila e gli Undicimila, f. "Lettere e telegrammi in occasione dei 20,00" (Tommaso Bertele).

25. Galeazzo Ciano, *Ciano's Hidden Diary* (1937–38), trans. Andreas Mayor (New York, 1953), 191.

26. Segrè, *Fourth Shore*, 110–11.

27. ORIGA, T-586 (410), 003888.

28. Osservatorio Rurale, Istituto Agronomico Oltremare, Florence, f. 2252, A. Tucci, "Considerazioni sui cessionari" (30 September 1945).

29. Segré, *Fourth Shore*, 164–66.

30. Ibid., 111.

31. G. L. Steer, *A Date in the Desert* (London, 1939), 163.

32. Moore, *Fourth Shore*, 168.

33. Francesco Gabrieli, "La spada dell'Islam," *Il Ponte* VIII, 10 (October, 1952), 1453–54.

34. ACS, *Diario De Bono*, vol. 42, March 2 and 19, 1937, 43–45, 48; ACS, Carte Graziani, sc. 6, fasc. 10.

35. C. Eylan, "Choses vues en Italie et en Libye," *Revue des Deux Mondes*, March 1, 1936, 142–43.

36. Giordano Bruno Guerri, *Italo Balbo* (Milan, 1984), 338.

37. Alan Houghton Broderick, *North Africa* (London, 1943), 28.

38. Steer, *Date in the Desert*, 163–65; Eylan, "Choses vues en Libye," 141; E. W. Polson-Newman, "The Italians in Libya," *English Review* 58 (April, 1934), 447–48.

39. J. A. Ducrot, "Que se passe-t-il en Libye?" *L'Illustration*, April 16, 1938, 426.

40. *The Sanusi of Cyrenaica* (Oxford, 1949), 209.

41. G. Rochat, "La repressione della resistenza araba in Cirenaica nel 1930–31," in *Il movimento di liberazione in Italia* (n.p., 1973), n. 110, 3–39; Segrè, *Fourth Shore*, 151.

42. For the following, see AB, Libia Alfabetico A–D, f. "Daodiace."

43. ACS, Carte Graziani, sc. 6, fasc. 10.

44. AB, Libia Alfabetico A–D, "Daodiace."

45. Eylan, "Choses vues en Italie et en Libye," 136.

46. Moore, *Fourth Shore*, 169.

47. Gaspare Ambrosini, "La politica islamica," *Libia* IV, 5–8 (May–August, 1940), 30.

48. Segrè, *Fourth Shore*, 88; D. H. Weir, "Italian Colonization," in *Handbook on Cyrenaica*, pt. XI (British Military Administration, Cairo, 1944–1947), 12.

49. Moore, *Fourth Shore*, 171–72; Chia-Lin Pan, "The Population of Libya," *Population Studies* III, 1 (June, 1949).

50. Steer, *Date in the Desert*, 165.

51. Mohamed ben Massaud Fusharka, *A Short History of Libya from Remotest Times up to Date* (Tripoli, 1962), 58.

52. For the following see Segrè, *Fourth Shore*, 144–61.

53. For the following see Viaggio del Duce in Libia, "Note ad uso dei giornalisti" (Le istituzioni scolastiche, Tripoli, 1937); Spectator Libycus, "Due anni di governo del Maresciallo Balbo in Libia" (Tripoli, 1936); Moore, *Fourth Shore*, 179; Ducrot, "Que se passe-t-il en Libye?" 425.

54. Anon., "Italy and the Mohammedans of Italian Africa" (Rome, 1940), 52.

55. Moore, *Fourth Shore*, 182–83; Ducrot, "Que se passe-t-il?" 426.

56. Segrè, *Fourth Shore*, 104–5.

57. ASMAI, "Materiale recuperato dal Nord," cart. 7, fasc. 46, 118–20; ACS, *Diario De Bono*, vol. 44, 33.

58. *Ciano's Hidden Diary*, 138.

59. "Roma apre alla Libia le sue grandi braccia," CP, October 27, 1938, 1.

60. CP, May 16, 1939, 5.

61. AB, Congressi Raduni I, f. "Congresso della Società per il Progresso delle Scienze."

62. Guerri, *Italo Balbo*, 338.

63. Moore, *Fourth Shore*, 174.

64. Moore, *Fourth Shore*, 178–79; Eylan, "Choses vues en Italie et en Libye," 138–39.

65. AB, Libia Alfabetico A–D, "Daodiace."

66. *New York Times*, March 18, 1940, 3: 8.

67. Mohammed ben Massaud Fusharka, *A Short History of Libya*, 58–60.

15. *Frondeur:* The Germanophobe

1. Luigi Federzoni, *Italia di ieri per la storia di domani* (Milan, 1967), 156.

2. Galeazzo Ciano, *Ciano's Hidden Diary* (1937–38), trans. Andreas Mayor (New York, 1953), 128.

3. Meir Michaelis, "Il Maresciallo dell'aria Italo Balbo e la politica mussoliniana," *Storia Contemporanea* XIV, 2 (April, 1983), 335.

4. *New York Times*, July 1, 1940, 18.

5. Giuseppe Bottai, *Vent'anni e un giorno* (Milan, 1949), 179–80.

6. Ibid., 180.

7. Archivio Federzoni, "Diario 1927," I, 6.

8. ORIGA, T-586 (468), 035604.

9. ACS, *Diario De Bono*, vol. 42, 95.

10. Alberto Sbacchi, *Il colonialismo italiano in Etiopia* (Milan, 1980), 49.

11. Michaelis, "Il Maresciallo," 334–35.

12. W. B. Courtney, "Mussolini's Unhappy Warrior," *Collier's*, April 11, 1936, 13.

13. Anonymous, "The Beard of Iron," *Esquire* (February, 1938), 35.

14. Arnaldo Cortesi, "After the Dictators—What?" *New York Times Magazine*, May 31, 1936. For the following, see ORIGA, T-586 (468), 035502–3.

15. Quoted in Luigi Salvatorelli and Giovanni Mira, *Storia d'Italia nel periodo fascista* (Turin, 1964), 737.

16. Ugo Ojetti, *I Taccuini 1914–1943* (Florence, 1954), 431.

17. Federzoni, *Italia di ieri*, 162.

18. Rosaria Quartararo, "L'altra faccia della crisi mediterranea (1935–36)," *Storia Contemporanea* XIII, 4–5 (October, 1982), 759–820.

19. ACS, *Diario De Bono*, vol. 41, 34.

20. ORIGA, T-586 (468), 035493.

21. ORIGA, T-586 (468), 035612; ACS, *Diario De Bono*, vol. 40, 88 (August 29, 1935).

22. G. Rochat, *Militari e politici nella preparazione della campagna d'Etiopia* (Milan, 1971), 229 n. 35.

23. For excerpts see Michaelis, "Il Maresciallo," 337–38; for full text see *Documents on German Foreign Policy, 1918–1945*, ser. C, vols. 1– 5, ed. Margaret Lambert et al. (London, 1957–1966), IV, doc. 352, 1072.

24. Giordano Bruno Guerri, *Italo Balbo* (Milan, 1984), 318.

25. Renzo De Felice, *Mussolini il Duce: Gli anni del consenso, 1929– 1936* (Turin, 1974), 721 n. 3.

26. Michaelis, "Il Maresciallo," 344; ORIGA T-586 (468), 035602–3.

27. *New York Times*, October 27, 1935, 8: 7.

28. S. Casmirri, "Luigi Federzoni," in F. Cordova, ed., *Uomini e volti del fascismo* (Rome, 1980), 295–96.

29. Michaelis. "Il Maresciallo," 335.

30. Federzoni, *Italia di ieri*, 162.

31. John F. Coverdale, *Italian Intervention in the Spanish Civil War* (Princeton, 1975), 41–42, 51–54.

32. ORIGA, T-586 (1295), 112744–45.

33. M. Mazzetti, "I contatti del governo italiano con i cospiratori militari spagnoli prima del luglio 1936," *Storia Contemporanea* X, 6 (November–December, 1979), 1181.

34. Raffaele Guariglia, *Ricordi 1922–46* (Naples, 1949), 189–90.

35. Michaelis, "Il Maresciallo," 337; Renzo De Felice, *Mussolini il Duce: Lo stato totalitario, 1936–1940* (Turin, 1981), 254–58.

36. De Felice, *Mussolini il Duce: 1936–1940*, 255 n. 1.

37. Ibid.

38. Ibid.

39. Ibid.

40. Michaelis, "Il Maresciallo," 337.

41. Ciano, *Ciano's Hidden Diary*, 43–44.

42. Galeazzo Ciano, *Ciano's Diary 1939–43*, ed. Malcolm Muggeridge (London, 1947), 260.

43. Giuseppe Bottai, *Diario 1935–1944*, ed. G. B. Guerri (Milan, 1982), 133.

44. Nino D'Aroma, *Vent'anni insieme: Vittorio Emanuele e Mussolini* (Bologna, 1957), 266–67.

45. Renzo De Felice, *Storia degli ebrei italiani sotto il fascismo* (Turin, 1961), 209–10.

46. Renzo De Felice, *Ebrei in un paese arabo* (Bologna, 1978), 262.

47. Ibid.

48. "Risposta al Tevere," CP, March 2, 1934, 1.

49. "Ultima replica al Tevere," CP, March 4, 1934, 1.

50. For the following see Renzo De Felice, *Ebrei in un paese arabo*, chaps. 5, 6.

51. For the following see ibid., 262–63.

52. Ibid., 264–65.

53. ACS, *Diario De Bono*, vol. 43, 26–27.

54. Bottai, *Diario 1935–1944*, 133, 135.

55. De Felice, *Storia*, 250.

56. Nello Quilici, "La difesa della razza," *Nuova Antologia*, September 16, 1938, 133–39.

57. Michaelis, "Il Maresciallo," 351.

58. De Felice, *Mussolini il Duce: 1936–1940*, 496.

59. The story appears in a number of places. Cf. Michaelis, "Il Maresciallo," 353.

60. De Felice, *Storia*, 296.

61. "Precisazione del problema della razza," CP, September 1, 1938, 1.

62. "Alla Sorgente," CP, September 7, 1938, 1.

63. "Equità," CP, October 6, 1938, 1.

64. Interview, Mimì Quilici Buzzacchi, Rome, August 12, 1974.

65. *London Times*, July 18, 1933, 14e.

66. Ciano, *Ciano's Hidden Diary*, 143. For the following, see CP, August 11, 1938, 1.

67. U.S. Army, European Command, Historical Division, "Foreign Military Studies, 1945–54," D217, 5.

68. *Hitler's Table Talk, 1941–1944*, ed. H. R. Trevor-Roper (London, 1953), 614.

69. Michaelis, "Il Maresciallo," 352.

70. Guerri, *Italo Balbo*, 366.

71. Ciano, *Ciano's Hidden Diary*, 43–44. Nino d'Arona, *Vent'anni insieme: Vittorio Emanuele e Mussolini* (Rocca San Casciano, 1957), 269.

72. Ruggero Zangrandi, *Il lungo viaggio attraverso il fascismo* (Milan, 1962), 286–87.

73. Ciano, *Ciano's Hidden Diary*, 87.

74. For the following see Federzoni, *Italia di ieri*, 162–63.

75. Ciano, *Ciano's Diary, 1939–43*, 53.

76. Vincenzo Poli, "La controrivoluzione di Balbo," *Il Pomeriggio*, February 3, 1948, 1.

77. Ciano, *Ciano's Diary, 1939–43*, 87.

78. Leo Longanesi, "Il grande anno," in *Il meglio di Leo Longanesi* (Milan, 1958), 183.

79. Poli, "Controrivoluzione di Balbo," 2.

80. Ojetti, *I Taccuini*, 540.

81. For the following, see Alberto Aquarone, "Nello Quilici e il suo 'Diario di Guerra,'" *Storia Contemporanea* VI, 2, 1975, 305–58.

82. See, for example, October 14, "Imbecillità integrale"; November 8, "Una riconferma superflua"; December 7, "Snobismo filo-bolscevico."

83. Ciano, *Ciano's Diary 1939–43*, 182.

16. Fascist: The Model Fascist's Fascism

1. Meir Michaelis, "Il Maresciallo dell'aria Italo Balbo e la politica mussoliniana," *Storia Contemporanea* XIV, 2 (April, 1983), 335.

2. For the following see Luigi Federzoni, *Italia di ieri per la storia di domani* (Milan, 1967), 154.

3. AB, Libia Alfabetico W, "K. H. V. Wiegand."

4. Mary Berenson, *A Vicarious Trip to the Barbary Coast* (London, 1938), 12.

5. Leo Longanesi, *Un morto fra noi* (Milan, 1932), 82.

6. Giordano Bruno Guerri, *Italo Balbo* (Milan, 1984), 360–61.

7. Berenson, *Vicarious Trip*, 12.

8. Giuseppe Bottai, *Diario 1935–1944*, ed. G. B. Guerri (Milan, 1982), 151.

9. ORIGA, T-586 (468), 035473–76.

10. *New York Times*, May 4, 1937; *London Times*, June 15, 1938.

11. AB, Libia Alfabetico A–D, "Daodiace."

12. Galeazzo Ciano, *Ciano's Hidden Diary*, trans. Andreas Mayor (New York, 1953), 128.

13. *New York Times*, October 27, 1938, 16: 5.

14. Ciano, *Ciano's Hidden Diary*, 128.

15. ACS, *Diario De Bono*, vol. 44, April 27, 1940, 7.

16. P. Fortunati, "Italo Balbo," *Supplemento Statistico ai Nuovi Problemi* VI, 1 (1940), 5.

17. Guerri, *Italo Balbo*, 347–48.

18. Giordano Bruno Guerri, *Giuseppe Bottai, un fascista critico* (Milan, 1976), 207.

19. Ibid.

20. Giordano Bruno Guerri, *Galeazzo Ciano: Una vita 1903/1944* (Milan, 1979), 480.

21. Denis Mack Smith, *Mussolini* (New York, 1982), 169; Federzoni, *Italia di ieri*, 226.

22. Attilio Tamaro, *Venti anni di storia* (Rome, 1953), III, 365.

23. Leo Nunzio, *Italo Balbo* (Bologna, 1940), 140–41.

24. Michaelis, "Il Maresciallo," 335.

25. Giuseppe Fanciulli, *L'eroica vita di Italo Balbo narrata ai giovani* (Turin, 1940), 273.

26. AB, Libia Alfabetico N–Z, "Sovrano Ordine di Malta."

27. G. A. Facchini, "Gio: Vita con Italo," unpublished manuscript, 490.

28. Galeazzo Ciano, *Ciano's Diary 1939–43*, ed. Malcolm Muggeridge (London, 1947), 186–89.

29. Ugo Ojetti, *I Taccuini 1914–1943* (Florence, 1954), 260.

30. Ibid., 373.

31. AB, Libia Varie, n. 1, f. "Visita dei principi di Piemonte in Libia."

32. Dino Alfieri, *Due dittatori di fronte* (Milan, 1948), 56.

33. Tamaro, *Venti anni*, III, 352.

34. Bottai, *Diario*, 146.

35. R. Trionfera, "Incontri con Maria José nel castello di Merlinge," *Il Giornale*, August 19, 1978, 5.

36. Renzo De Felice, *Mussolini il Duce: Gli anni del consenso, 1929–1936* (Turin, 1974), 8.

37. Federzoni, *Italia di ieri*, 287.

38. AB, Scritti e discorsi, I, f. "Carlo Pisacane."

39. Public Record Office, London, FO 371/24949 R1507/60/22; G. Waterfield, *Professional Diplomat: Sir Percy Loraine of Kirkhale, 1880–1961* (London, 1973), 257–58.

40. Guerri, *Italo Balbo*, 109.

41. ORIGA, T-586 (468), 035467–68.

42. Federzoni, *Italia di ieri*, 288–89.

43. Acerbo notes the existence of a *Ferrarese* clique on the Grand Council (Albini, Rossoni, Pareschi, Balella, Bignardi): G. Acerbo, *Fra due plotoni di esecuzione* (Rocca San Casciano, 1968), 499.

17. Soldier: North African Commander

1. Luigi Federzoni, *Italia di ieri per la storia di domani* (Milan, 1967), 284–85.

2. Ibid., 285.

3. Giuseppe D'Avanzo, *Ali e poltrone* (Rome, 1976), 159; Vincenzo Poli, "La controrivoluzione di Italo Balbo," *Il Pomeriggio*, February 3, 1948, 1.

4. Interview, Michele Intaglietta, Rome, October 22, 1973.

5. Galeazzo Ciano, *Ciano's Diary 1939–43*, ed. Malcolm Muggeridge (London, 1947), 272.

6. Federzoni, *Italia di ieri*, 164.

7. U. A. Grimaldi and G. Bozzetti, *Farinacci—il più fascista* (Milan, 1972), 188–89.

8. Renzo De Felice, *Mussolini il Duce: Lo stato totalitario 1936–1940* (Turin, 1981), 720–21.

9. Ibid., 721.

10. AB, Libia Alfabetico W, f. "Wiegand to Hay."

11. Ibid.

12. Public Record Office, London, FO 371/24949 R 1507/60/22.

13. De Felice, *Mussolini il Duce 1936–1940*, 793.

14. Federzoni, *Italia di ieri*, 164.

15. De Felice, *Mussolini il Duce: 1936–1940*, 823, 835.

16. Interview, Annio Bignardi, Ferrara, March 18, 1974.

17. AB, Libia Alfabetico N–Z, f. "Scola Camerini."

18. Elisabeth Cerruti, *Je les ai bien connus: Souvenirs d'ambassades* (Paris, 1950), 299.

19. ACS, *Diario De Bono*, vol. 44, 10.

20. Giuseppe Bottai, *Diario 1935–1944*, ed. G. B. Guerri (Milan, 1982), 150.

21. For the following see ibid., 207.

22. G. Bucciante, ed., *Vita di Balbo* (Novara, 1940), 28.

23. Ciano, *Ciano's Diary 1939–43*, 260.

24. U.S. Army, European Command, Historical Division, Foreign Military Studies (1945–1954), D217, 13; Renzo Trionfera, "Incontri con Maria José nel Castello di Merlinge," *Il Giornale*, August 19, 1978, 5.

25. ACS, *Diario De Bono*, vol. 43, 67.

26. ACS, Carte Graziani, busta 41, all. 1.

27. AB, Militari, f. Varie, I.

28. U.S. Army, European Command, Foreign Military Studies, D217, 12.

29. Igino Mencarelli, "Italo Balbo," Ufficio Storico Aeronautica Militare (Rome, 1969), 16–17.

30. USE, *In Africa Settentrionale: La preparazione del conflitto* (Rome, 1955), 54 n. 2.

31. U.S. Army, European Command, Historical Division, Foreign Military Studies (1945–54), 12.

32. USE, *In Africa Settentrionale*, 174.

33. Quoted in Macgregor Knox, *Mussolini Unleashed, 1939–1941* (New York, 1982), 121.

34. ACS, Carte Graziani, busta 41, all. 7.

35. Ibid.

36. Emilio Faldella, *L'Italia e la seconda guerra mondiale* (Rocca di San Casciano, 1967), 68–69.

37. Piero Pieri and Giorgio Rochat, *Pietro Badoglio* (Turin, 1974), 755.

38. Faldella, *Italia*, 117–18; R. Graziani, *Africa Settentrionale 1940–41* (Rome, 1948), 47.

39. Private correspondence with Porro-E. Quadrone, June 25, 1954.

40. Attilio Tamaro, *Venti anni di storia* (Rome, 1953), III, 418.

41. Ibid.

42. U.S. Army, European Command, Historical Division, Foreign Military Studies (1945–52), 14.

43. USE, *In Africa Settentrionale*, 172.

44. Ibid., 174, 175.

45. Nello Quilici, "Ultime lettere di Nello dal fronte" (printed privately, Verona, 1944), 11.

46. Ibid., 12–13.

47. Ibid., 28.

48. Ibid., 34.

49. Giuseppe Fanciulli, *L'eroica vita di Italo Balbo narrata ai giovani* (Turin, 1940), 273.

50. Quilici, "Ultime lettere di Nello dal fronte," 12–13.

51. Ibid., 17.

52. USE, *In Africa Settentrionale*, 114 n. 1.

53. Ibid., 200.

54. Alberto Aquarone, "Nello Quilici e il suo 'Diario di guerra,'" *Storia Contemporanea* VI, 2 (1975), 338.

55. Interview, Paolo Balbo, Palo Alto, October 15, 1978.

56. Nello Quilici, "Ultime lettere dal fronte," 20.

57. The following descriptions are based on US Army, European Command, Historical Division, Foreign Military Studies, 19–20.

58. USE, *In Africa Settentrionale*, 200.

59. Aquarone, "Nello Quilici," 344.

60. AB, Militari, f. "Lettere a Mussolini." Also occurs in telegram to Badoglio, June 16–17.

61. Igino Mencarelli, "Italo Balbo," Ufficio Storico Aeronautica Militare (Rome, 1969), 17–18.

62. Aquarone, "Nello Quilici," 348.

63. Bottai, *Diario*, 212.

64. *Toronto Daily Star*, November 4, 1941, 21; *Time* 38 (November 17, 1941), 26.

65. Aquarone, "Nello Quilici," 354–55.

66. For the following see Faldella, *L'Italia*, 119.

18. Soldier: Death of a Hero

1. CP, June 30, 1940.

2. ORIGA, T-586 (464), 035768–69, "Tellera report."

3. Felice Porro, "Come fu abbattuto l'aeroplano di Balbo," *Quaderni aeronautici*, 340, S (1948), 1.

4. Franco Pagliano, "La morte di Balbo," in *Aviatori italiani* (Milan, 1964), 16–17; Pagliano, "L'ultimo volo di Balbo," *Storia illustrata* IX, 6 (June, 1965), 781.

5. Igino Mencarelli, "Italo Balbo," *Ufficio Storico Aeronautica Militare* (Rome, 1969), 18–19.

6. Porro, "Come fu abbattuto l'aeroplano di Balbo," 1.

7. Ibid.

8. Giuseppe Prezzolini, *Diario 1939–45* (Milan, 1962), 226.

9. Alberto Aquarone, "Nello Quilici e il suo 'Diario di guerra,'" *Storia Contemporanea* VI, 2 (1975), 354.

10. Pio Gardenghi, "Il testamento di Balbo," *Libia* IV, 5–8 (May–August, 1940), 4.

11. Pagliano, "Ultimo volo di Balbo," 781.

12. Porro, "Come fu abbattuto l'aeroplano di Balbo," 1–2.

13. ORIGA, T-586 (464), 035768–69, "Tellera report."

14. ORIGA T-586 (468), 035771–75, "Incidente di volo del Maresciallo Balbo—Relazione," July 1, 1940.

15. Porro, "Come fu abbattuto l'aeroplano di Balbo," 2.

16. Ibid.

17. For the following, see Pagliano, "Morte di Balbo," 12.

18. Ministero della Difesa, Aeronautica, "Morte di Balbo."

19. ORIGA, T-586 (464); 035768–69.

20. Pagliano, "Morte di Balbo," 20.

21. Ernesto Quadrone, "La verità sulla morte di Italo Balbo," *Tempo*, April 22, 1954; *New York Times*, July 2, 1940, 7: 2; Giordano Bruno Guerri, *Italo Balbo* (Milan, 1984), 392.

22. ACS, Carte Graziani, busta 47, Teruzzi to Graziani, July 3, 1940.

23. Leonardo Simoni, *Berlino ambasciata d'Italia, 1939–43* (Rome, 1946), 139.

24. F. Pricolo, *La regia aeronautica nella seconda guerra mondiale* (Milan, 1971), 212.

25. Duilio Susmel, "La verità su Balbo—il rogo di Tobruk," *Domenica del Corriere*, July 4, 1967, 34.

26. ACS, Carte Graziani, busta 47, Graziani to Bruni, July 12, 1940.

27. G. Valle, *Uomini nei cieli* (Rome, 1958), 151–52.

28. Renato Sitti and Lucilla Previati, *Ferrara: Il regime fascista* (Milan, 1976), 194.

29. Ugo Ojetti, *Cose viste* (Florence, 1960), 1624.

30. Giuseppe Bottai, *Diario 1935–1944*, ed. G. B. Guerri (Milan, 1982), 212.

31. ACS, SPD, CR, fasc. "Balbo/gerarca."

32. Galeazzo Ciano, *Ciano's Diaries 1939–43*, June 29, 1940; ACS, *Diario De Bono*, vol. 44, July 1, 1940, 21, 22; G. Gorla, *L'Italia nella seconda guerra mondiale: Memorie di un milanese, ministro del re nel governo di Mussolini* (Milan, 1959), 87.

33. Ardengo Soffici and Giuseppe Prezzolini, *Diari 1939–45* (Milan, 1962), 226.

34. Balbo's mother-in-law apparently insisted on this last motive, according to the prefect Testa to Bocchini, head of the police, in a letter of July 10, 1940. ACS, SPD, CR, fasc. "Balbo/gerarca."

35. Porro, "Come fu abbattuto l'aeroplano di Balbo," 2.

36. *New York Times*, June 30, 1940, 1: 5; July 1, 1940, 6: 1; *Newsweek* XVI (July 8, 1940), 31; *Time* XXXVI (July 8, 1940), 30.

37. The German press made the same parallel, but insisted that Fritsch had died heroically. Hence, the Germans claimed that Balbo died in the same spirit.

38. *New York Times*, July 2, 1940, 7: 2.

39. Duilio Susmel, *Vita sbagliata di Galeazzo Ciano* (Milan, 1962), 222.

40. Soffici and Prezzolini, *Diari*, 226.

41. Ibid., 76–77.

42. ACS, *Diario De Bono*, vol. 44, July 25, 1940, 28.

43. G. B. Guerri, *Giuseppe Bottai, un fascista critico* (Milan, 1976), 207.

44. Y. de Begnac, *Palazzo Venezia* (Rome, 1950), 16.

45. Ibid., 17.

46. Giuseppe Bottai, *Vent'anni e un giorno* (Milan, 1949), 213. In his *Diario* under the same date, Bottai comments on Mussolini's "emotional evocation of Balbo," but then the Duce went on to blame the Libyan defeat on Graziani.

47. G. Acerbo, *Fra due plotoni di esecuzione* (Rocca San Casciano, 1968), 499.

48. Luigi Federzoni, *Italia di ieri per la storia di domani* (Milan, 1967), 279.

49. East Balbo Avenue, formerly East Seventh Street, connects State

Street and South Michigan Avenue, then, as Balbo Drive, continues through Grant Park to South Lake Shore Drive.

50. Through the devoted efforts of Countess Maria Fede Caproni, much of this memorabilia has survived and is on display in Rome in her private museum.

51. *Life*, July 22, 1940, 24.

52. Anthony Price, *The October Men* (New York, 1974), 3.

53. Ciano, *Ciano's Diaries 1939–43*, 272.

Bibliographical Note

For those who wish to explore Balbo's life further, below I describe the major primary and secondary sources that I found helpful in this study. The discussion is intended as an orientation, not as a complete or exhaustive guide. The notes to each chapter provide more detailed references.

Primary Sources

Italo Balbo's personal papers are in the hands of the family in Rome. The archive is a relatively small one but rich in correspondence, reports, notes, and newspaper clippings, especially from Balbo's days as air minister and as governor of Libya. As one of the first scholars to use this material, I prepared an annotated guide (unpublished) for future researchers. The Caproni Museum in Rome, the private collection of Countess Maria Fede Caproni di Taliedo, contains a major store of documents and memorabilia from Balbo's flying days. Other indispensable archival sources in Rome include the Archivio Centrale dello Stato and the archive of the Ufficio Storico dell'Aeronautica. The Centro Storico Fiat, Turin, has an excellent collection of journals, clippings, and models that document the early history of Italian aviation. The Biblioteca Comunale Ariostea in Ferrara contains important collections of newspapers and journals that document Balbo's Blackshirt days.

Published Sources

For a man of action, by nature restless, impatient, always on the go, Balbo left an impressive body of writings—many of them undoubtedly produced with collaborators. I detail the major works below. Nor should the reader overlook the *Corriere Padano*, beginning in 1925. In addition to the

450

collection at the Biblioteca Ariostea in Ferrara, a microfilm copy of the newspaper is available at the Hoover Institution, Stanford, California.

The best short article on Balbo remains A. Berselli's "Italo Balbo" in the *Dizionario biografico degli italiani* (1960–), vol. 5. My own brief study appeared in Ferdinando Cordova, ed., *Uomini e volti del fascismo* (Rome, 1980). Among the best of the journalistic accounts that have been published since World War II are Duilio Susmel's "La verità su Balbo," *Domenica del Corriere*, June 13–July 4, 1967.

The most recent full-length biographies are Giorgio Rochat's scholarly and polemical *Italo Balbo* (Turin, 1986) and Giordano Bruno Guerri's more journalistic *Italo Balbo* (Milan, 1984). Balbo, concludes Rochat in his highly analytical study, was a great organizer and propagandist and one of fascist Italy's most capable and efficient leaders— who, nevertheless, lacked the gifts of a first-rate politician and statesman. Rochat's analysis, especially of Balbo's role as boss of Ferrara and his relations with the province's agricultural and banking powers, is often stimulating. Yet Rochat is so absorbed in elucidating his subject's significance and attacking earlier studies that a flesh-and-blood Balbo never emerges.

Guerri's gossipy and anecdotal portrait reveals Balbo the man far more clearly. Like Rochat, Guerri highlights Balbo's organizational talents and his ability to exploit the mass media. Even more than Rochat, Guerri treats Balbo's role as pioneering aviator and colonial governor in cursory fashion and focuses on the "revolutionary" phase of Balbo's career—Balbo the Blackshirt and leader of the March on Rome. Guerri concludes that Balbo was a revolutionary more in his violent technique than in his ideology. In addition to the book's lack of balance, Guerri is too eager, on the basis of slim and unpersuasive evidence, to picture Balbo as constantly plotting against Mussolini. Guerri's work is also riddled with factual errors and does not do justice to the new sources that the author uncovered. Both Guerri and Rochat, however, are a giant step forward over the adulatory and hagiographic studies that appeared during the fascist period. Of these, only Giovanni Titta Rosa's *Vita di Balbo* (Rome, 1941), and Giuseppe Fanciulli's *L'eroica vita di Italo Balbo narrata ai giovani* (Turin, 1940) based on interviews with the Balbo family, contain valuable nuggets of information, especially on Balbo's childhood. Both these studies appeared shortly after his death and stress his heroism, his patriotism, and his "exemplary life" as the "new Italian" that Mussolini created.

Balbo, of course, appears in the memoirs and diaries of the major fascist *gerarchi*. Luigi Federzoni and Giuseppe Bottai, two of Balbo's best friends, and Ciano, a bitter rival, provide the best insights. Federzoni's brief essay in *Italia di ieri per la storia di domani* (Milan, 1967) is patronizing but affectionate. Ciano's *Diario 1937–43* (Milan, 1971) is a mixed bag of jealousy, anxiety, and vindictiveness—then shock and genuine grief at Balbo's sudden death. Bottai, torn between admiration for Mussolini and friendship with Balbo, probably projected too much of his own admiration for Mussolini in his portrait of Balbo in *Diario 1935–1944*, edited by G. B. Guerri (Milan, 1982), and in the memoir *Vent'anni e un giorno* (Milan, 1949). The writer and art critic Ugo Ojetti's *I Taccuini 1914–1943* (Florence, 1954) contain many delightful vignettes. The entries become frankly adulatory by the time Balbo became governor of Libya.

For Balbo's career as a Blackshirt, Paul Corner's *Fascism in Ferrara, 1915–1925* (Oxford, 1975) and Alessandro Roveri's *Le origini del fascismo a Ferrara, 1918–1921* (Milan, 1974) are excellent, complementary guides to the development of fascism in Ferrara. Neither is sympathetic to Balbo. Roveri's continuation, *L'affermazione dello squadrismo fascista nelle campagne ferraresi, 1921–1922* (Ferrara, 1979), is disappointing in its analysis but helpful for the archival material that he cites. Sergio Panunzio's *Italo Balbo* (Milan, 1923) provides an indispensable portrait of Balbo and sharp insights into the psychology of the peasantry. Renato Sitti and Lucilla Previati's *Ferrara: Il regime fascista* (Milan, 1976) is useful as a collection of documents and excerpts from the period, although the identifying captions on the photographs are often incorrect. Balbo tells his version of the March on Rome in his *Diario 1922* (Milan, 1932). Despite suppressions and omissions, the work is an excellent guide to Balbo and his activities, moods, and attitudes during this period—and it makes exciting reading. It must be balanced by works such as Renzo De Felice's *Mussolini il fascista: La conquista del potere (1921–1925)* (Turin, 1966), and Antonino Répaci's *La marcia su Roma, mito e realtà* (Rome, 1963), 2 vols.

Balbo's theories of air power and his role in building the Aeronautica are surprisingly well documented in his *Sette anni di politica aeronautica (1927–1933)* (Milan, 1935), the collection of his annual messages to the Chamber of Deputies between 1927 and 1933. His conclusions about Douhet and aerial warfare are clearly outlined in his article "Guerra aerea" (a subsection of the longer "Guerra, arte della") in the *Enciclopedia italiana* XVIII (Rome, 1933). Despite its irritating tone of grudging admiration, Giorgio Rochat's *Italo Balbo aviatore e ministro dell'aeronautica, 1926–1933* (Ferrara, 1979) provides an excellent analysis of Balbo's procurement and personnel policies and of his relations with other armed services. The book also contains useful documents, including De Pinedo's critique of the Aeronautica in 1929. Gossipy and often unreliable, but useful for insights into the lore of the period, is Giuseppe D'Avanzo's *Ali e poltrone* (Rome, 1976). Jonathan Thompson's unique *Italian Civil and Military Aircraft 1930–1945* (Fallbrook, 1963) provides a mine of technical information and photographs of the aircraft.

For an account of Balbo's aerial cruises, his own *Da Roma a Odessa* (Milan, 1929), about his Eastern Mediterranean cruise, *Stormi in volo sull'oceano* (Milan, 1931), about his first Atlantic cruise to Brazil, and *La centuria alata* (Milan, 1934), about his second Atlantic cruise to Chicago, are indispensable starting points. Part adventure story and part travelogue, these volumes make exciting, upbeat reading and were popular in their day. Understandably, the books say little about the technical errors and the political backgrounds of the cruises. Ranieri Cupini, an admirer of both Balbo and De Pinedo and a participant in Balbo's second Atlantic cruise, provides a first-rate chronicle—including some critical observations on Balbo's leadership—in his *Cieli e mari: Le grandi crociere degli idrovolanti italiani 1925–1933* (Milan, 1973).

Balbo outlined his basic policies in Libya in a number of addresses that were widely reprinted or published in journals. These include "La politica sociale fascista verso gli arabi della Libia," an address before the Volta Congress in 1938, "La colonizzazione in Libia," presented before the Reale Academia dei Georgofili in 1939, and "La litoranea libica," *Nuova Antologia*, March 1, 1937. The anonymous "Spectator Libycus" in "Due anni di governo del Maresciallo Balbo in Libia" (Tripoli, 1936), and "Bozze di Stampa per i giornalisti" (Tripoli, 1939), a series of notes for journalists who accompanied the first mass colonization in October, 1938, contain much useful statistical information and many valuable insights into everything from urban renewal to school and medical programs. My own *Fourth Shore: The Italian Colonization of Libya* (Chicago, 1974) details Balbo's colonization programs and the mass emigrations of 1938 and 1939. Renzo De Felice's *Ebrei in un paese arabo* (Bologna, 1978), translated as *Jews in an Arab Land* (Austin, 1984), contains excellent sections on Balbo's attitudes toward the racial laws and the Jews in Libya. E. E. Evans-Pritchard's *The Sanusi of Cyrenaica* (Oxford, 1949) is an old but still valuable introduction to Balbo's governorship as seen by the Libyans.

Balbo's opposition to the war and his pessimism about its outcome can be followed in Ciano's and, especially, Bottai's diaries. Balbo's last days in Libya are well detailed in Alberto Aquarone's "Nello Quilici e il suo 'Diario di Guerra,'" *Storia Contemporanea* VI, 2 (1975). Franco Pagliano's "L'ultimo volo di Italo Balbo," *Storia Illustrata*, IX (June, 1965) presents the most balanced account of Balbo's last flight.

Index

Acerbo, Giacomo, 349, 350
Adani, Laura, 364
Aerial cruises: anti-fascist publicity and, 213–14; awards and promotions of Balbo, 197, 214, 228; Cruise of the European Capitals, 201–2; De Pinedo's role in, 194; fascist recruiting by Balbo during, 201; Maddalena's role in, 194; military value of, 213, 261–62; origins of, 192–93; purposes and goals of, 182, 193, 213, 231, 263. *See also* Eastern Mediterranean cruise; North Atlantic cruise; South Atlantic cruise; Western Mediterranean cruise
Aeronautica. *See also* Aerial cruises; Aviation and aviators; Schneider Cup competition
—aircraft carriers and, 189
—airpower: adequacy of aircraft, 161–62, 163; bombers, 164; compared to other countries, 151, 159; fighter planes of, 163–64; number and types of aircraft, 165; seaplanes of, 164–65
—Balbo's administration of: Balbo becomes undersecretary of, 141; criticism of, 146–47, 161–62, 211; denigration of, 146; doctrine for, 154; goals for, 152; statutes of 1931, 189
—Balbo's resignation from: his disappointment at, 282–83; his letters to De Bono afterward, 286–87; Mussolini requests, 277, 281; world reaction to, 283
—budget: compared to other armed services, 158, 161; compared to other countries, 157–59; consolidation of

army and navy air forces with, 188–89; limitations on, 156–57, 159–60
—De Pinedo's death and, 212
—DO X affair, 170–71, 211
—Douhet's influence on, 152–55
—fascist politics and, 177
—flying time of pilots, 180–81
—independence from other armed services, 154, 177, 188, 189
—MF 5 affair, 170
—Mussolini and: balances power with other armed forces, 160–61; disputes number of aircraft, after Balbo's resignation, 285–86; purges Balbian influences from, 286; reorganization, 150
—new building for, 185–86
—personnel: American-style work schedule for, 186–87; Balbo's code of behavior for, 177–78, 187; discipline and esprit de corps of, 179–80; number of pilots, 175; number of support personnel, 176; *prima donna* and *diva* attitudes of, Balbo's opposition to, 179; recruitment problems, 174–75; standards for, 176–77; training programs for, 180–81
—sections of, 188
—service and medical sections in, 175–76
—status of: after World War I, 149–50; when Balbo takes office, 151
—tactical air units of, 154
—Wing Days (Giornata dell'Ala), 181–82
Agello, Francesco (aviator), 146, 184; speed record of, 231
Agraria: alliance with the *fascio* at Ferrara, 42, 44–46, 115; control of Fer-

Agraria (continued)
rara, 121, 122, 124–25; land reform
plan of, 45–46, 67; socialism in Ferrara and, 35–36, 37; unemployed laborers and, 80–81
Agrarian fascism, 38, 44, 48
Agricultural laborers: dependence on fascists for jobs, 79
Air marshal: Balbo receives air marshal
baton, 258, 284–85
Air Ministry. *See* Aeronautica
Aircraft carriers: Balbo's opposition to,
189
Aircraft industry, Italian: Balbo's promotion of, 166–67; Balbo's relationship
with, 169–70; compared to other nations, 166–67, 168; development of,
167; production capacities of, 168; sales
of, 168–70; shortcomings of, 165–66.
See also Aviation and aviators
Airships. See *Italia* expedition
Albani, Felice, 12, 13
Alfieri, Dino, 294, 341
Alpine Regiment, 8th: Balbo's military
service with, 22–24
L'Alpino (newspaper): Balbo's editorship
of, 32–34
Anti-bolshevism: Quilici's articles on,
361–62
Anti-Semitism: Balbo's opposition to,
346; Balbo's treatment of Jews in Lib-
ya, 347–49; Grand Council on, Balbo
speaks out at, 349–51; Manifesto della
Razza, 346, 349; polemic of *Corriere
Padano* against *Il Tevere*, 346–47;
Quilici's articles on, 350, 351–53
Archeological sites in Libya: restoration
of, 303–4
Ariosto, Lodovico: *Orlando Furioso*, 125
Armed forces: Balbo attempts to become
head of, 279–81; Balbo's plans for mo-
dernizing and reforming, 279–81; cost
of modernization plan, 280–81; Musso-
lini rejects Balbo's plans, 281. *See also*
Aeronautica
Arpinati, Leandro, 75, 283
Articles by Balbo. *See* Publications of
Balbo
Artioli, Professor, 14
Associazione Arditi, 32
Associazione Nazionale dei Combattenti,
32
Aviation and aviators: Balbo obtains pilot
license, 149; Balbo's early interest in,
16–17, 148–49; Balbo's fame in, 146;

commercial, development of, 171–73,
259, 260–61; cost of airplane design
and development, 159; design and
production of military aircraft, 162;
designers, 165; fascism's relationship
with, 148, 149; monoplanes compared
to biplanes, 163–64; *prima donna* and
diva attitudes of, Balbo's opposition
to, 179, 192; public perception of,
after World War I, 191–92; records
set by Italians in, 162. *See also* Aerial
cruises; Aeronautica; Aircraft industry,
Italian; Schneider Cup competition;
and names of specific aviators
Avvenire d'Italia (newspaper): Minzoni
affair and, 129
Axis. *See* German-Italian Alliance

Badoglio, Pietro: Balbo attempts to replace as head of armed forces, 279–80;
criticism of military aviation and
Balbo's aerial maneuvers, 160, 182;
Egyptian invasion plan and, 382–83,
391; policies in Libya, 288, 292
Baistrocchi, Federico: appointment as
undersecretary of war ministry, 280;
army chief of staff, 157
Balbo, Camillo (father): career of, 5–6;
photograph, 8; political beliefs of, 6,
11
Balbo, Edmondo (brother): Balbo continues education with, 14; political beliefs of, 11
Balbo, Egle (sister): favorite playmate of
Balbo, 6; *squadrista* march on Dante's
tomb and, 62
Balbo, Fausto (brother): character of, 11;
death of, 12; influence on Balbo, 11–
12; Mazzinian beliefs of, 12; political
beliefs of, 11
Balbo, Fiorenza (niece): Balbo's devotion
to, 12
Balbo, Italo: charitable disposition of, 10;
early education, 8–9; early leadership
abilities, 10; energetic personality of,
364; grammar school education, 14–
15; high school education, 15, 17; personality quirks of, 178–79; photographs of, 7, 20, 55, 63–64, 112, 119,
195, 256, 258, 317, 356, 357, 359,
365, 389, 390; popularity, after aerial
cruises, 266; romantic affairs of, 364–
65; showmanship of, 56; university
education, 29–31. *See also* Death of
Balbo; Publications of Balbo

Balbo, Lino (nephew): accompanies Balbo on last flight, 396; Balbo's devotion to, 12; capture of armored car and, 388–89

Balbo, Malvina Zuffi (mother): family ties of, 6; photograph, 6

Baldini, Nullo, 86

Il Balilla (newspaper), 57; Balbo's attack on Mussolini, 46, 49; Balbo's defense of the *agrari* in, 68; editors of, 46; establishment of, 46, 49

Balkan wars: Balbo's attempt to join Garibaldi's expedition, 14; Ricciotti Garibaldi and, 13

Baracca, Francesco, 150

Baroncini, Gino: and dissident fascists, 71, 121, 122

Bastianini, Giuseppe, 103, 360

Battleships: Balbo's opposition to, 189

Begnac, Yvon de: commemorative article on Balbo by, 405–6

Belluzzo, Giuseppe: Minister of National Economy, 140

Beltrani, Tomaso: on Balbo's control over Ferrara, 123; Minzoni affair and, 128–30

Benni, Antonio, 141

Berenson, Bernard, 364

Bernotti, Romeo, 188

Berti, Giuseppe: radioman on Balbo's last flight, 396

Bianchi, Michele: Balbo meets, 15; as head of Fascio Rivoluzionario d'Azione Internazionalista, 19; supports the March on Rome, 99, 100; as syndicalist, 18, 267

Biennio rosso, 35

Bignardi, Annio, 378

Black shirts: as fascist uniform, 52

Blackshirts. See *Fascio* at Ferrara; Militia, fascist; *Squadristi*

Bladier, Gennaro, 82

Bogiankino, Edoardo, 68

Bologna, fascist siege of, 84–85

Bolzano, occupation of, 97

Bondanelli, Enrico, 127

Bonzani, Alberto, 150–51

Bottai, Giuseppe: attitude toward Fascist Party, 270; on Balbo's relationship with Mussolini, 272; as *frondeur*, 334; Futurist poet, 9; World War I experience of, 27

Brasini, Armando, 306

Breviglieri, Arturo: early fascist martyr, 38–39, 53

Brombin, Francesco: career, after expulsion from party, 124; member of *Celibanisti*, 39; resignation from *fascio* at Ferrara, 121–22

Brunelli, Claudio: accompanies Balbo on last flight, 396

Buozzi, Bruno, 15

Burzagli, Ernesto, 188

Caffè Milano: meeting place for Republicans, 12

Cagna, Stefano (aviator), 179; *Italia* expedition and, 199; role of, in aerial cruises, 194; South Atlantic aerial cruise and, 218

Capone, Al, 272

Caporetto, Italy: Austro-German offensive at, 23–24

Cappannini, Gino: flight engineer on Balbo's last flight, 396

Caproni, Giovanni, 165, 266, 276–77

Caretti, Enrico: accompanies Balbo on last flight, 396; resignation from *fascio* at Ferrara, 122

Castello Estense (Ferrara): socialist and fascist clash at, 40

Castoldi, Mario, 165

Catholic Church: Balbo's alliance with, 368–69

Cavazza, Filippo, 141

Ceccherini, Sante, 99

Cecconi, Fausto: long-distance flight of, 217

Celibanisti (fascio), 38–39

Charter of Carnaro, 70

Chavez, Geo, 16

Chicago. See North Atlantic cruise

Chiozzi, Giuseppe, 53

Ciano, Costanzo, 336, 370

Ciano, Galeazzo: enmity toward Balbo, 160, 334, 335; successor to Mussolini, 336, 368; tribute to Balbo at his death, 407

Cini, Vittorio: financier and member of Ministry of Economy committees, 124, 140, 266, 360; plan for economy of Ferrara, 126

Civil aviation. See Aviation and aviators

Codos, Paul: long-distance flight of, 253

Colamarino, Giulio, 138, 269

Collaboration of authorities with fascists, 57–58

"Column of fire" operation, 86–87, 135

Commercial aviation. See Aviation and aviators

La Conquista dello Stato (newspaper): on
appearance of *Corriere Padano*, 136;
intransigent newspaper, 132
Corporativism: Balbo's skepticism toward, 267, 269; definition, 267; military corporativism, 268–69; proprietary corporativism, 269
Corridoni, Filippo, 18, 19
Corriere Padano (newspaper): Balbo as
editor of, 9, 136; founded by Balbo,
135; growth of, 135–36; investors and
supporters, 136–37; left-wing social
theorist writers in, 269; Mussolini
and, 137, 138; nonconformist stance
of, 137–38; polemic against *Il Tevere*,
346–47; Quilici as editor of, 75, 136;
Quilici's anti-bolshevik articles in,
361–62; Quilici's anti-Semitic articles
in, 352–53; staff of, 138
Costanzi, Giulio, 169, 171
Crocco, Arturo, 169
Crociera del Decennale. *See* North Atlantic cruise
Crosio, Tullio: *Italia* expedition and, 199
Cupini, Ranieri, 287

Daily War Bulletin: report of Balbo in,
25
D'Annunzio, Gabriele: as aviator, 150;
Balbo and Mussolini pay homage to,
59; Balbo's admiration for, 69, 70; Fiume expedition of, 33; Interventionist
leader, 18; peace pact with socialists
and, 62
Daodiace, Giuseppe: educates Balbo
about Libyan colony, 322–23; Libyan
colonial administrator, 293, 366
d'Azeglio, Massimo, 51
De Bernardi, Mario (aviator), 179; wins
Schneider Cup, 183, 192
De Bono, Emilio: Balbo's campaign for
Libyan administrative reform and,
294; behavior, during March on
Rome, 110; criticism of Balbo's governorship of Libya, 320; first commanding general of MVSN, 117; as *frondeur*, 334; joint commander of fascist
militia, 96; Matteotti affair and, 132;
speaks out against anti-Semitism, 349;
verification of Balbo's *Diario 1922*, 76,
110
De Bosis, Lauro: anti-fascist propaganda
flights and, 213–14
De Pinedo, Francesco (aviator), 146;
Balbo ruins career of, 179; Balbo's

moral responsibility for death of, 212–
13; critique of Balbo's administration
of Aeronautica, 161–62, 211; death of,
212; deteriorating relationship with
Balbo, 209–10; flight to South America, 216; long-distance flights of, 192,
193, 211–12, 253; promotion in rank
and position, 197, 209; resignation
from Aeronautica, 210, 211; role of, in
aerial cruises, 194, 197; ties with monarchy, 209–10
De Stefani, Alberto: as *frondeur*, 334
De Vecchi, Cesare Maria: as *frondeur*,
334; account of March on Rome, 110–
11; appointed governor of Somalia,
117; investigates dissident fascists,
121; joint commander of fascist militia,
95–96; plans to avoid military clash
with government, 105; verification of
Balbo's *Diario 1922*, 76, 110
Death of Balbo: announcement of, 4,
393; Ciano's tribute, 407; commemorative article by Yvon de Begnac,
405–6; controversy over, 4, 400–401,
403–4; downing of his plane, 399–
400; Goering requests souvenir from
I-MANU, 401–2; international condolences, 401–2; messages informing Tobruk of Balbo's flight, 397; mistaken
identity of his aircraft, 3, 392, 399;
mourning of, 401; Mussolini's reaction
to, 405; passengers aboard Balbo's
plane, 395–96; passengers on Porro's
plane, 396; Porro attempts to warn
Balbo of danger, 397–98; Porro's personal investigation of, 404; posthumous recognition and awards, 402–3;
reasons for mission leading to, 393–
94; return of body to Italy, 407. *See
also* Libya: World War II in
Decennial Air Cruise. *See* North Atlantic
cruise
Del Prete, Carlo (aviator), 146; flight to
South America, 216; long-distance
flights of, 194, 217
Desenzano (Lake of Garda), 183, 184;
aircraft research and development fa-
cility, 180
Desio, Ardito, 318
Destree, Jules, 19
Diario 1922 (Balbo's memoir): Mussolini's editing of, 75; publication of,
74–75; Quilici as collaborator, 75
Diaz, Armando, 109
Dirigibles. *See Italia* expedition

Dissident fascists: Balbo censured by commission of inquiry, 121; Barbato Gattelli as leader of, 66–67, 118, 120–21; collapse of, 122; commission on inquiry investigation of, 121; expectation of support from Mussolini, 68; formation of autonomous *fascio*, 67; Olao Gaggioli and, 67; goals of, 118, 120; revolts against Balbo, 66–67; support of labor strike in Ferrara, 120–21

Distinguished Flying Cross: Balbo and Aldo Pellegrini receive, 263

Divisi, Giulio, 39

La Domenica dell'Operaio (newspaper): absorbed by *Corriere Padano*, 136

Donati, Giuseppe: Minzoni affair and, 129

Douhet, Giulio: influence on Balbo and aviation, 152–55

Eastern Mediterranean cruise: map of route, 205; route for, 204–5; Soviet Union and, 206–8

Economy, Ministry of. *See* Ministry of National Economy

Egypt: Badoglio orders Balbo to invade, 391; British forces in, 386–87; Italy plans to invade, 382–83

Eisenhower, Dwight: visits Balbo's family in 1950, 264

Ente per la Colonizzazione della Cirenaica (ECC), 300

Ente per la Colonizzazione della Libia (ECL), 300

Ente Turistico ed Alberghiero della Libia (ETAL), 303

Ethiopia: Balbo aspires to be viceroy of, 366; Balbo's opposition to invasion of, 340, 341–42

Evola, Giulio, 351

Fabbri, Roberto (aviator): Balbo's commemoration of, 16–17, 148

Facta, Luigi: prime minister, 79, 86, 88, 103

Fara, Gustavo, 99

Farinacci, Roberto: attitude toward Fascist Party, 270; political opposite of Balbo, 177, 335, 351, 363, 367, 375

Fasci d'Avanguardia: Balbo joins, 15

Fascio at Ferrara: alliance with the *agrari*, 42, 44–46; Balbo as political secretary of, 42–43, 47, 60; Balbo's policy on violence, 56; Balbo's power over and control of, 123–25; *Celiba-*

nisti, 38–39; dissidents form autonomous *fascio*, 67; early activities of, 39–40; funerals for martyrs staged by Balbo, 56–57; land reform plan of the *agrari*, 45–46, 67; triumph over socialists, 57–59. *See also* Fascism

Fascio at Florence: Balbo's purge of, 139

Fascio Rivoluzionario d'Azione Internazionalista, 19

Fascism: agrarian, 38; army's support of, 93; Balbo's attitude toward, during and after aerial cruises, 208, 267–68; Balbo's attitudes toward, before World War II, 370–73; Balbo's beliefs in, in his *Diario*, 77–78; Balbo's conversion to, 42–43; Balbo's criticism of, after Nazi-Soviet Nonaggression Pact, 360–61; bolshevism and, differences between, 207–8; defined, xi–xii; dissident movement of, 65–69, 71, 118, 119–22; first *fascio* in Ferrara, 38; founding of, 37; manpower, before March on Rome, 106; military organization of, 49; National Congress of 1921, 68–69; peace pact with socialists, 61–62, 69; recruitment for, during Balbo's aerial cruises, 201; Second Provincial Congress of 1921, Balbo's speech at, 69–71; urban, 38. *See also* Corporativism; *Fascio* at Ferrara; Intransigents; March on Rome; Militia, fascist

Fascist party: Balbo's attitude toward, 177, 270–71; Bottai's attitude toward, 270; Farinacci's attitude toward, 270; Mussolini's shaping of, 270

Federzoni, Luigi: as *frondeur*, 334; literary critic, 9; Minister of Colonies, 141; opinion of Balbo as head of Aeronautica, 146–47; speaks out against anti-Semitism, 349

Ferrara: birthplace of Balbo, 4–5; Castello Estense, socialist and fascist clash at, 40; cultural life under Balbo, 125; economic condition, after World War I, 35; economic condition, under Balbo, 126; fascist siege of, 80–83; first *fascio* constituted, 38; industrial program for, 126; socialism and, 35–37. See also *Fascio* at Ferrara

Ferrarin, Arturo (aviator), 146, 179; flight to South America, 216; long-distance flights of, 192, 217; opposes war, 378

Finzi, Gualtiero, 43

Fiume: expedition of, 33; fascist takeover
of, 79
Florence: Balbo assists insurrection at,
108–9; Balbo reviews military problems at, 101; recurrence of *squadrismo* at, 138
Florio, Cino: accompanies Balbo on last
flight, 396
Florio, Emanuella: courtship by Balbo,
31–32; marriage to Balbo, 32, 115
Flying. *See* Aviation and aviators
Ford, Henry, 203
Foreign policy of Mussolini: Balbo's co-
operation with, 338; early policies,
Balbo's agreement with, 337–38;
Ethiopian invasion, Balbo's opposition
to, 340, 341–42; German alliance,
Balbo's criticism of, 338–39; Mediter-
ranean crisis, 339; Spanish civil war
involvement, 342–43; Suez canal ex-
pedition, rumor of, 339–40. *See also*
German-Italian Alliance
Forest militia, 140
Forti, Raoul: implication in Minzoni af-
fair, 134
Four Power Pact of Mussolini, 233
Fourth Shore. *See* Libya
Fovel, Massimo, 138, 269
Frailich, Ottavio: co-pilot on Balbo's last
flight, 396
Fratti, Antonio: martyrdom of, 13
Frondeurs: Giuseppe Bottai, 334; Emilio
De Bono, 334; Alberto De Stefano,
334; Cesare Maria De Vecchi, 334;
Luigi Federzoni, 334; and foreign
journalists' view of Balbo, 336; Dino
Grandi, 334; image of Balbo as, 335–
36; loyalty to Mussolini, Balbo pro-
fesses, 336–37; Mussolini's foreign
policy and, 337–39. *See also* Foreign
policy of Mussolini
Funerals for fascist martyrs staged by
Balbo, 56–57

Gabrielli, Giuseppe, 165
Gaggioli, Olao: career, after quelling of
dissidents, 124; *Celibanisti* and, 38,
39; dissident fascists and, 67, 120; negotiator for Balbo's secretaryship of
fascio, 42
Gandolfo, Asclepia: candidate for joint
command of fascist militia, 96; and directives for fascist militia, 71–73; head
of fascist militia, 133
Gardenghi, Pio, 138

Garibaldi, Giuseppe, 13, 51, 402
Garibaldi, Peppino, 249
Garibaldi, Ricciotti: Balbo's attempt to
join expeditions of, 14, 19; Balkan
wars and, 13; leader of Partito Mazziniano, 12–13
Gattelli, Barbato: Balbo's assistance of,
124; expelled from Fascist Party, 121;
as leader of dissident fascists, 66–67,
118, 120–21; negotiator for Balbo's
secretaryship of the *fascio*, 42
Gazzera, Pietro, 280
Gazzetta Ferrarese (newspaper), 57; absorbed by *Corriere Padano*, 136;
Balbo's interventionist manifesto published in, 19; sympathy for dissident
cause, 123
Gazzettino Rosa (newspaper), 19
German-Italian Alliance: Balbo's criticism
of, 338–39, 356–58; German violation
of, 375; nonbelligerent status of Italy,
375–76; Pact of Steel signed by Mussolini, 359
Germany: Balbo's ambivalence toward,
345; and Balbo's hatred of Nazism,
345; Goering hosts Balbo's visit to,
353–54; Hitler meets with Balbo,
355–56
Ginnasio Ariosto: Balbo organizes student strike against, 14
Giolitti, Giovanni: fascist fear of, 94;
leader of Liberals, 18, 34
Giovani Esploratori Cattolici, 127
Gioventù Araba del Littorio (GAL), 328
La Giovine Italia (newspaper): Balbo's
contributions to, 15
Giuliani, Sandro, 18
Giunta, Francesco, 32, 79, 270
Giuriati, Giovanni, 101
Giusquiano, Antonio, 12–13
Gobetti, Pietro, 138
Goering, Hermann: cultivates friendship
with Balbo, 354, 384; hosts Balbo's
visit to Germany, 353–54; photo-
graph, 359; requests souvenir from I-
MANU, 401–2; visits Balbo in Libya,
358–59
Gramsci, Antonio, 138
Granata, Luigi, 122
Grandi, Dino: Balbo's attack on in news-
paper article, 279; Balbo's plots
against Mussolini and, 277; Balbo's replacement of at Geneva disarmament
conference, 278–79; dissident fascists
and, 67; march to Dante's tomb and,

65; as *frondeur*, 334; on need for insurrection, 94, 106; negotiates peace
pact after occupation of Ravenna, 86;
officer in World War I, 27; visit to
d'Annunzio, 62
The Grappa: military operations at, 25–
27
Graziani, Rodolfo: criticism of Balbo's
governorship of Libya, 320, 322; Litoranea Libica (highway) and, 296;
succeeds Balbo as governor of Libya,
383; vice governor of Cyrenaica, 293
Grosoli, Giovanni, 44
Guariglia, Raffaele, 343
Guarneri, Felice, 140

Hitler, Adolf: Balbo meets, 355–56; photograph, 357
Hoare, Sir Samuel, 201

Igliori, Ulisse, 71, 99
Immelen, Hermann, 340, 341
Insurrection, Balbo's belief in, 94. *See
also* March on Rome
International League of Aviators: awards
gold medal of honor to Balbo, 214,
228
Interventionism: Balbo's participation in,
17–21
Intransigents: activities, after March on
Rome, 115; Balbo as, 115–16, 132; intransigent fascism defined by Balbo,
139–40; pressure on Mussolini, 135
Irredentist causes: Balbo's participation
in, 15
Istituto Nazionale Fascista per la Previdenza Sociale (INFPS), 300
Istituto Superiore di Scienze Sociali
"Cesare Alfieri," 29–31
Italia expedition: Balbo's opposition to,
198; disastrous end of, 197; inquiry
afterward, 199–201; Nobile's accusations against Balbo, 198, 199; Nobile's
behavior in, 197; rescue of survivors,
199

Johnson, Amy, 191, 253

La Guardia, Fiorello, 150
Labor Alliance: fascist occupation of Ra-
venna and, 85
Labor unions, fascist, 79–80
Laborers, agricultural: dependence on
fascists for jobs, 79
Landowners. See *Agraria*

Lateran pacts of 1929, 269–70, 337
League of Nations: Balbo's attitude toward, 278–79
Lenin, Vladimir, 78
Libya. *See also* Libyans; Tripoli,
Libya
—Balbo's governorship of: administrative
tasks facing Balbo, 292; air rallies in,
304; appointment of Balbo, 277, 281–
83; archeological site restoration, 303–
4; Balbo's departure for Libya, 287;
coastal provinces integrated with Italian kingdom, 329; communication systems, improvement of, 295; Grand
Prix auto racing in Tripoli, 304–5; improvements under Italian rule, 325;
military rule over interior, 295; physical division of government before
Balbo, 293; union of Tripolitania and
Cyrenaica into one colony, 294–95
—colonists: Ente per la Colonizzazione
della Cirenaica (ECC) and, 300; Istituto Nazionale Fascista per la Previdenza Sociale (INFPS) and, 300; need
for, 299; problems in attracting, 300;
problems with concessioners, 301;
subsidies and bonuses for, 299
—first visit of Balbo, 141
—Litoranea Libica (highway): construction of, 295–98; inauguration of, by
Mussolini, 309; labor problems and,
297–98; water supply for laborers,
297
—mass colonization project: approval of,
318–19; arrival of colonists at Tripoli,
315–16; costs of, 319–20; criticism of,
318; international reaction to, 319;
Mussolini's review of ships, 314–15;
news coverage of, 317–18; second
mass migration, 320; selection of colonists, 312–13; transfer by train to
ships, 313–14; transfer from Tripoli to
new homes, 316–17
—Mussolini's visit: Balbo's preparations
for, 307; dinner in the desert, 309; entrance to Tripoli, 309–10; inauguration
of the Arae Philenorum, 309; purposes
of, 307
—tourism: Ente Turistico ed Alberghiero
della Libia (ETAL) established, 303;
hotels built in Tripoli, 303; number of
tourists before Balbo's arrival, 302–3
—visitors to: Balbo hosts, 301–2; Goering, 358–59; prince and princess of
Piedmont, 369–70

Libya (*continued*)
—World War II in: accidents from lack of training, 386; armored car, Balbo leads attack on, 388–90; Balbo prepares for, 379–80; Balbo requests more equipment and men, 383–84; British attacks, 386–87; fortifications for, 380–81; matériel shortages, 380; morale of troops, 380; plans for invasion of Egypt, 382–83, 391; Quilici's impressions of Balbo during, 385–86; transfer of headquarters to Cyrene, 385
Libyans: Arab-Berbers, Balbo's admiration for, 323; attitude toward Balbo, 331–32; attraction to urban living, 325; Balbo's policies toward, 320–22; differences among, 324; education and training for, 327–28; Fezzan Negroid peoples, Balbo's attitude toward, 323; health services for, 328; Italian citizenship for, 325, 328–31; Italian interactions with, 321; Jews, Balbo's attitude toward, 347–49; jobs provided by Italian building projects, 326–27; lack of discrimination against, 321; minority groups, 324; nomads, Balbo's subjugation of, 323, 325; placation of Cyrenaican tribes, 322; racial problems, 321; settlement projects for, 325–26; status quo, Balbo preserves, 324–25
Lindbergh, Charles A., 145, 191, 242
Litoranea Libica (highway): construction of, 295–98; inauguration, by Mussolini, 309; labor problems and, 297–98; water supply for laborers, 297
Locatelli, Antonio, 169
Longanesi, Leo, 50, 51, 266, 364
Loraine, Percy: British ambassador to Italy, 372, 377
Lyautey, Marshal: comparison of Balbo to, 293

Mackensen, Hans Georg von: German ambassador to Italy, 361
Maddalena, Umberto: commander for South Atlantic aerial cruise, 218, 223, 224; *Italia* expedition and, 199; long-distance flights of, 217; role of, in aerial cruises, 194
Malaparte, Curzio, 266, 275, 277
Mantovani, Vico: and election of May 15, 1921, 59; prominent agrarian fascist, 44–45, 80

Manù, Donna. *See* Florio, Emanuella
March on Rome: Balbo's belief in, 105–6; financing of, 108; government resistance and, 110; mobilization of, in Naples, 107; Mussolini and militia triumvirate plan for, 99–100, 103–4; Mussolini's hopes for, 94; necessity for, 93–94; Perugia as headquarters of, 102; political situation during, 111, 113; problems at Florence, 108–9; revolutionary nature of, according to Balbo, 92–93; secret bands of terrorists, 108; steadfastness of Balbo during, 111; victory of fascists, 113; weakness of plans for, 105
Marchetti, Alessandro, 165
Marinelli, Olinto, 29
Marinetti, F. T., 255
Marinoni, Ottavio, 47
Masons: Balbo's connection with, 139; Mussolini's opposition to, 139
Mass flights. *See* Aerial cruises
Matteotti, Giacomo: anti-fascist martyr, 132; murder of, 128
Matteotti affair: Mussolini mobilizes militia during, 132; Mussolini's government and, 132; resurgence of *squadrismo* and, 138; rumors of Balbo's plots against Mussolini and, 118
Mattern, James, 253
Mazzini, Giuseppe: Balbo's praise of in his *Diario*, 76; Balbo's university thesis on, 30–31
Mazzinianism: Balbo's definition of, 13, 44. *See also* Partito Mazziniano; Republicanism
Mecozzi, Amedeo, 154
Mediterranean crisis, 339
Milch, Erhard, 152, 283
Military aviation. *See* Aeronautica; Aviation and aviators
Military experience of Italo Balbo: Caporetto and, 23–24; commander of Pieve di Cadore battalion's assault platoon, 24–25; 8th Alpine Regiment and, 22–24; at The Grappa, 25–27; medals awarded, 25, 27; at Monte Valderoa, 27; 7th Alpine Regiment and, 24; training as officer, 22; transfer to Aeronautica, 23; Val Fella battalion and, 22–24; volunteer duty of, 22. *See also* Aeronautica; Libya: World War II in; Militia, fascist
Militia, fascist: advantages and disadvantages of, 116; code for, importance of,

97; directives for, prepared by Balbo, 71–72; disassociation of Balbo from, 271; Gandolfo becomes commander of, 134; mobilization, during Matteotti affair, 132; Mussolini and, after Matteotti affair, 133–35; reorganization by Balbo, 95–97; resignation of Balbo after Minzoni affair, 131, 133; resignation of De Bono after Matteotti affair, 133; revolt of consuls, 134–35; shortcomings of directives for, 73; triumvirate command of, 95–97; uniform of, 102. *See also* Milizia Volontaria per la Sicurezza Nazionale; *Squadristi*

Milizia Forestale, 140

Milizia Volontaria per la Sicurezza Nazionale: Balbo as commander of, 116–17; merging with regular army, 116; role of, after March on Rome, 117–18. *See also* Militia, fascist

Ministry of National Economy: Balbo appointed undersecretary to, 140; Balbo chairs committees of, 140–41

Minzoni, Don Giovanni: anti-fascist activities of, 126–28; murder of, 127

Minzoni affair: anti-fascist exploitation of, 128; Balbo's involvement in, 127–28, 368; Balbo's trial, 128–31; remembrance of, during North Atlantic cruise, 250; second trial of, 131

Mitchell, William (Billy), 155, 251

Mollison, James, 253

Monarchy, Italian: Balbo's alliance with, 369–70

Montanari, Alberto: Balbo's conversion to fascism and, 43; expelled from Fascist Party, 121; member of *Celibanisti*, 39

Monte Grappa, 25–27

Monte Valderoa, 27

Monterotondo, Italy: Balbo inspects during March on Rome, 111

Mori, Cesare, 84

Mussolini, Benito: aviation and, 148, 156; becomes prime minister, 93; *Celibanisti* member, 39; disrespect of Balbo for, 367; division among ministers, promoted by, 277–78, 353; doubts Balbo's leadership during South Atlantic cruise, 223; editor of *Popolo d'Italia*, 18; and election of May 15, 1921, 59; establishes dictatorship, 134, 135; fails to promote Balbo after South Atlantic aerial cruise, 228; fear of Balbo, 273; fears for success of

fascism, 48; forms government after March on Rome, 113, 114–15; Four Power Pact proposal, 233; government crisis after occupation of Bologna and, 85; intervention in World War II, Balbo and, 378; isolation from reality, 340–41, 343–44, 372; loyalty of Balbo for, 272, 336–37, 344–45, 371; March on Rome and, 97–100, 103–4; meets Balbo for first time, 18; ministers' failure to oppose, 344; North Atlantic aerial cruise and, 236, 248–49, 255, 257–58; peace pact with Socialist Party and, 61–62; personality of, compared to Balbo, 273; photograph, with Balbo, 256; praise of in Balbo's *Diario*, 76–77; relationship with Balbo, 94, 148, 160, 271–75; relationship with his lieutenants, 272; removal from office by Grand Council, 406; resignation from Fascist Party because of peace pact, 62; rewards Balbo with air marshal baton, 258; rumors of Balbo's plots against, 275–77; secretive nature of, 94–95; *squadristi*, importance to, 68–69; *squadristi* swear allegiance to, in Naples, 103; successor for, speculation about, 367–68; surveillance of Balbo, 274–75; totalitarianism of, Balbo's opposition to, 372; visit to Libya, 307, 309–10. *See also* Foreign policy of Mussolini

MVSN. *See* Milizia Volontaria per la Sicurezza Nazionale

Naples: Mussolini's speech at, before March on Rome, 103

Nasi, Guglielmo, 294

Nazism. *See* Germany

Nazi-Soviet Nonaggression Pact, 360, 361

Night at the Opera (film): parody of Balbo in, 146

Nitti, Francesco Saverio, 95

Nobile, Umberto (aviator), 146; accusations against Balbo, 198, 199; Balbo ruins career of, 179; behavior, in *Italia* expedition, 197; *Italia* inquiry and, 199–201

North Atlantic cruise: aircraft and instrumentation used, 235; American reaction to, 253; Amsterdam, arrival and celebration at, 237–38; anti-fascist demonstrations during, 250; Balbo and Aldo Pellegrini receive Distinguished

North Atlantic cruise (*continued*)
Flying Cross, 264; Balbo Avenue in Chicago, 244, 249, 264; Balbo in aviation gasoline advertisement, 252; Balbo initiated into Sioux tribe, 244, 245; Balbo's analysis of, 259–60; Balbo's inspiration for, 215; cartoon of Balbo, 251; cartoon of reception at Amsterdam, 240; celebrations on return to Italy, 255, 257–58; Chicago, arrival and celebrations at, 242–44; commemorative stamps of, 260, 262; comparison with Columbus's voyage, 242; costs of, 259–60, 262; criticisms of, 260, 261; departure, 237; doubts about, 231; Iceland leg of, 239–40; international assistance with, 234; Ireland, landing at, 239; Labrador leg of, 240–42; losses of aircraft and crew, 234, 237, 255, map of route, 232; military benefits of, 261–62; Minzoni affair recalled, 250; Mussolini and, 236, 248–49, 255, 257–58; New York, arrival and celebrations at, 244–47; Newfoundland leg of, 242; newspaper photograph of, 246; photograph of, over the Alps, 239; photograph of Mussolini greeting Balbo, 256; photograph of SM.55X, 238; planning and training for, 233–34; publicity for Italy from, 263; purposes of, 231, 263; return flight, 254–55; support from private corporations, 259; symbol of Italian-American friendship, 264–65; visitors, before flight, 236; weather information for, 234–35; White House luncheon for Balbo, 245–46

Nuova Antologia: Quilici's racist article in, 350, 353

Nuovi Problemi (journal): edited by Nello Quilici, 136

Oberdan, Guglielmo, 18
Ojetti, Ugo, 266, 267, 338, 342, 369
Olivetti, A. O., 18
Omar el-Mukhtar, 322
Orbetello, Italy, 180, 193, 194, 215, 219, 222, 229, 233–34, 236, 237, 259

Pact of Steel, 359–60, 375
Padano. See *Corriere Padano* (newspaper)
Palazzo d'Accursio (Bologna): socialist and fascist clash at, 40
Panunzio, Sergio, 13, 20, 267

Pariani, Alberto, 382
Parma: Balbo plans second occupation of, 98; fascist occupation of, 88–89
Partito Mazziniano: Antonio Giusquiano as leader of, 12–13; Balbo becomes member of, 13; Felice Albani as founder of, 12–13. *See also* Mazzinianism; Republicanism
Pedriali, Vittorio, 46
Pegna, Giovanni, 165
Pellegrini, Aldo, 263
Penzo, Pier Luigi, 199
Perrone Compagni, Dino, 71, 72, 73
Perugia: headquarters for March on Rome, 102; success of insurrection at, 109
Petacci, Claretta, 365
Philibert, Emmanuel, Duke of Aosta, 96
Pieve di Cadore battalion's assault platoon: Balbo as commander of, 24–25
Pinzano al Tagliamento, 28
Pischedda, Agostino, 286
Pius XII (pope), Balbo's audience with, 368–69
Poledrelli, Mario, 21; photograph, 20
Police cooperation with fascists, 57–58
Il Popolo (newspaper): Minzoni affair and, 129
Il Popolo d'Italia (newspaper): Balbo meets Mussolini at, 18; Mussolini as editor of, 18; Mussolini's call for discipline in, 67; Sandro Giuliani as editor of, 18
Porro, Felice, on Balbo's last flight: attempts to warn Balbo of danger, 397–98; explains Balbo's mission, 393–94; passengers with, 396; personal investigation of Balbo's death, 404
Post, Wiley: Balbo meets in New York, 247–48; "golden age" aviator, 145; round-the-world flight of, 253
Pricolo, Francesco, 379
Provincia di Ferrara (newspaper), 66, 67, 68
Publications of Balbo: "The Art of Aerial Warfare," in *Enciclopedia Italiana*, 154–55; attack on Mussolini in *Il Balilla*, 46; editor of *Il Balilla*, 46; *Diario 1922*, 74–76; "The Economic and Social Thought of Giuseppe Mazzini," 30–31; editor of *Corriere Padano*, 136; editor of *L'Alpino*, 33–34; "From the Trench of 1921," 137; in *Gazzetta Ferrarese*, 19; in *La Giovine Italia*,

15; "The Gospel of Fascism: Why We Aren't Socialists," 46–47; "Lavoro e milizia per la nuova Italia," 117–18; in *Popolo d'Italia* and *Corriere della Sera*, 279; in *La Raffica*, 15; "Roberto Fabbri, the Youngest Aviator in the World," 16; in *Vere Novo*, 15. *See also names of specific publications*
Pugliese, Samuele, 57
Punta Ala, Italy, 259, 379, 405

Queen Mother: Balbo and, 100–101; meeting with De Bono and De Vecchi, 100–101
Quilici, Mariula, 136
Quilici, Nello: accompanies Balbo on last flight, 396; anti-bolshevik articles of, 361–62; articles on anti-Semitism, 350, 351–53; collaborator on Balbo's *Diario 1922*, 75; editor of *Corriere Padano*, 136; editor of *Nuovi Problemi* (journal), 136; impressions of Balbo during World War II, 385–86; involvement in Matteotti affair, 136
Quilici Buzzacchi, Mimì, 136

Racism. *See* Libyans; Anti-Semitism
La Raffica: Balbo's article in, 15
Rapallo, Treaty of, 79
Ravegnani, Giuseppe, 15–16
Ravenna: fascist occupation of, 85–86; *squadrista* march on, 62, 65
Ravenna, Renzo, 353
Red biennium, 35
Red leagues: in Balbo's thesis, 30
Red-shirts: Balkan wars and, 13
Regia Aeronautica. *See* Aeronautica
Republican party: Balbo campaigns for, 41; Balbo resigns from, 44; involvement with Labor Alliance at Ravenna, 85–86
Republicanism: Balbo's early choice of, 11; Balbo's persistent faith in, 14, 28, 43–44. *See also* Mazzinianism; Partito Mazziniano
Resto del Carlino (newspaper), 136
Rocca, Massimo, 18
Rogers, Will, 250
Romagna-Manoja, Ernesto: Balbo's last flight and, 395
Roosevelt, Franklin Delano: luncheon with Balbo at White House, 245–46
Rosatelli, Celestino, 165
Rossi, Maurice: long-distance flight of, 253

Rossi, Romualdo: Balbo's article in defense of, 15
Royal Air Force (RAF): air display at Hendon, 181; tribute to Balbo at death, 402
Royalty, Italian. *See* Monarchy, Italian

Salandra, Antonio, 18
Salvemini, Gaetano, 40
San Marino, Italy: Balbo completes high school at, 15
Sarfatti, Margherita, 157
Sassoon, Philip, 400
Savoia Marchetti SM. 55, 164–65, 217, 235
Schneider, Jacques, 182
Schneider Cup competition: Britain wins trophy permanently, 184; costs of competing in, 184; importance of, 185; Italy's involvement in, 183–84; Mario De Bernardi wins, 183; origins of, 182
Scintilla (newspaper): Edmondo Balbo's articles in, 11
Il Selvaggio (newspaper), 132
Sibille, Luigi, 24–25
Slav Nationalism: *squadrista* action against, 49
Socialism and socialists: Balbo's views of, in his *Diario*, 77–78, *biennio rosso* in Ferrara, 35–37; defeat by Ferrarese *fascio*, 57–59; demonstrations against, 32, destruction of offices of, in Ferrara, 55–56; fascist peace pact with, 61–62, 69; Ferrara's *agrari* and, 35–36, 37; general strike, failure of, 92, 93; red leagues, in Balbo's thesis, 30; violence in Ferrara and, 36
Sonnino, Sidney, 18
South Atlantic cruise: aircraft used for, 217; Balbo's accident prior to, 220; fuel load required for, 218; instrumentation for aircraft, 217–18; loss of aircraft and crew, 225–26; map of route, 221; Mussolini's failure to promote Balbo after, 228; Natal, arrival at, 226–27; photograph of instrumentation, 219; planning for, 217; Rio de Janeiro, arrival at, 227–28; route for, 220, 222; storm at beginning of, 222–23; takeoff from Bolama, 223–25; training for, 218–20
Soviet Union: Balbo visits, during Eastern Mediterranean aerial cruise, 206–8; Balbo's impressions of, 207

Spanish civil war: Balbo's involvement with Spain before, 342–43; Mussolini and, 342–43

Spirito, Ugo, 269

Squadristi: activity after Matteotti affair, 138; attacks on Slavic groups in Venezia Giulia, 49; Balbo's early leadership of, 47; collaboration of local authorities with, 57–58; "column of fire" operation, 86–87; early raids, between January and April, 1921, 53–55; necessity of, to Fascist Party, 68–69; occupation of Ferrara, 81–83; occupation of Parma, 88–89; occupation of Ravenna, 85–86; overview of Balbo's role in, 50–52; siege of Bologna, 84–85. *See also* Militia, fascist

Squaglia, Enrico, 255

Squarzanti, Edmo, 53

Starace, Achille, 103

Sterle, Mario, 15, 18

Student strike against Ginnasio Ariosto, organized by Balbo, 14

Suffrage: Balbo's attitude toward, 372

Syndicalism: Balbo's participation in, 15–16; Balbo's support of, 70

Tamburini, Tullio, 109

Tassotti, Pietro, 271

Tellera, Giuseppe, 394, 404

Teruzzi, Attilio: criticism of Balbo's attitude toward Ethiopian war, 341; investigates dissident fascists, 121; suggested as triumvir for militia, 96; vice-secretary of Fascist Party, 103

Il Tevere (newspaper): polemic of *Corriere Padano* against, 346–47

Tobruk, Libya: site of Balbo's death, 3–4, 190, 397–400

Torti, Guido: expulsion from Fascist Party, 121, 124; negotiator for Balbo's secretaryship of *fascio*, 42, 43

Treaty of Rapallo, 79

Trenchard, Lord Hugh, 201

Triple Alliance: Italy and, 17

Tripoli, Libya: automobile traffic in, 306; Balbo's improvements of, 305–7; building codes for, 305–6; Grand Prix at, 304–5; Libyans migrate to, 306; Mussolini's visit to, 309–10; public works projects, 306, 307. *See also* Libya

Turati, Augusto: Balbo opposes, 271; *ras* of Brescia, 115

Ulivi, Gaetano: dissident fascist, 120–21; expulsion from Fascist Party, 121, 124

United States: anti-fascist groups in, 204; Balbo's fascination with, 233; Balbo's first visit to, 202–4; Balbo's impressions of, 204; Italian-American communities in, 203–4. *See also* North Atlantic cruise

University of Florence: Balbo's education at, 29–31

Urban fascism, 38

Valle, Giuseppe, 212, 285

Ventimila. See Libya: mass colonization project

Verduzio, Rodolfo, 169, 171

Vere Novo: Balbo founds, with Giuseppe Ravegnani, 15–16

Vicentini, Giuseppe, 44

Victor Emmanuel III, 96, 113, 210, 226, 231, 249, 276, 356

Vittorio Veneto: Italian victory at, 25

La Voce Repubblicana (newspaper): Minzoni affair and, 128, 131; prints memo from Grandi to Balbo, 134

Volpi di Misurata, Giuseppe, 266, 287, 367

Voting: Balbo's attitude toward, 372

Vuillemin, Joseph, 260

Western Mediterranean cruise: map of route, 196; route of, 194–95

Wing Days (Giornata dell'Ala), 181–82

World War I: Balbo's justification of, 21; Italy's neutrality and, 17

World War II: Balbo's opposition to Italian intervention, 376–78; beginning of, 360; Italy's nonbelligerent status, 375–76; Italy's reluctance to join, 375–76; Mussolini's hope for a short war, 381; Rhodes meeting of Balbo, De Bono, and De Vecchi, 377. *See also* Libya: World War II in

Wright, Orville, 16, 203

Young Catholic Scouts, 127

Yugoslavian threat to Fiume, 101

Zanella, Riccardo, 79

Zappata, Filippo, 165

Zirardini, Gaetano, 36, 50

Compositor: Huron Valley Graphics
Printer: Murray Printing
Binder: Murray Printing
Text: 11/13 Caledonia
Display: Caledonia